ASPECTS OF ISLAMIC CIVILIZATION

ASPECTS
OF
ISLAMIC
CIVILIZATION

*As Depicted
in the Original Texts*

BY
A. J. ARBERRY

Ann Arbor Paperbacks
The University of Michigan Press

Third printing 1978
First edition as an Ann Arbor Paperback 1967
Copyright © by George Allen and Unwin Ltd. 1964
All rights reserved
ISBN 0-472-06130-5
Published in the United States of America by
The University of Michigan Press
For sale in the United States and its dependencies only
Manufactured in the United States of America

CONTENTS

INTRODUCTION

What is meant by the term Islamic civilization? What lies at the roots of the present-day movement towards Arab unity, and in what relation does that movement stand *vis-à-vis* the wider aspiration, the millennial dream of reunion between all the Muslim peoples? How stands Islam in the contemporary battle of faiths and ideologies?

The western observer of world politics, perhaps surprised by the vitality of a religion and a culture whose imminent demise was being confidently predicted a bare generation ago, will do well to examine in greater depth, and with a keener historical perspective than hitherto, the long processes and the massive forces which have culminated in the present situation. Held closely together in the common bonds of a shared tradition and way of life, despite passing domestic differences whose significance should not be over-estimated, is a powerful group of nations, for the most part newly liberated from colonial rule and therefore passionately self-assertive, extending from Morocco in the west to Indonesia in the east, from Turkey in the north to Sudan in the south, comprising (together with large minorities in neighbouring lands) a world total of some 400,000,000 Muslims. All take pride in a common inheritance, all aspire to recapture the glories of a civilization which in its golden age dominated the world.

Not a few admirable books are available to those wishing to study the history of Islamic civilization, as reconstructed and analysed by western scholars. The present volume is not intended as a competitor with Brockelmann and Hitti, Gibb and von Grunebaum, Rosenthal and Lewis, Lévi-Provençal and Spuler and Gabrieli—to name but a few of the brilliant historians whose writings have done so much to recover and reinterpret the record. Its scope is at once more modest and, in a certain way, more fundamental. This book is a series of documents illustrating the development of Islamic civilization, texts translated from the languages in which they were originally composed by famous protagonists of that culture. The intention is to present a panorama of Muslim life and thought and achievement as depicted from within. The translations, a considerable part of which has not been published hitherto, are all the work of a single scholar and represent the gleanings of more than thirty years of assiduous reading. They are meant to throw light on the literary, intellectual and religious movements within Islam, as well as illuminating something of the politics and the sociology, ranging from the origins in the sixth century down to the present day. It should of course be confessed that they constitute the merest fragments of literatures preserved in overwhelming abundance, exceeding many times what has survived from ancient Greece and Rome, a repertory of many tens of thousands of volumes, the majority still in manuscript, not a few of immense length. The passages chosen, however, have been taken from the most highly esteemed and authoritative works; and the attempt has been made to construct a balanced and rounded picture.

To the specialist student of Islamic history, the relevance of the selections to the whole record will be obvious. But in order that the general reader may the more easily realize their significance and interconnection, a short sketch is here prefixed setting out the historical background to these writings.

Through the long centuries when Rome ruled the world Arabia, the cradle of Islamic civilization, had remained a backwater remote from the march of great events. By the eve of the rise of Islam, Rome had collapsed into anarchy; Byzantium, the fortress of Eastern Christianity, was locked in a bitter and protracted war, ultimately fatal to both parties, with Sassanian Iran, the homeland of Zoroastrianism. Two Christian kingdoms in the northern reaches of Arabia, Monophysite Ghassān and Nestorian Ḥīra, were encouraged to survive as buffer-states between the rival empires and the inhospitable wastes, being tributary to Byzantium and Iran respectively. Christian and Jewish communities were scattered about the Peninsula, the great majority of whose inhabitants however followed a pagan way of life, 'a form of polydaemonism linked with the paganism of the ancient Semites',[1] realizing itself in the cult of fountains, trees and sacred stones.

Against a background of warring tribes each led by a shaikh, and extending their rivalries into the urban settlements, a remarkably lively tradition of fine poetry had sprung up whose main purpose, it seems, was to extol one side of the quarrel and to pour contumely on the other. These poems, and the legends remembered or fabricated to explain their purport, remain our principal if highly suspect source of information on Arabian affairs in the century of Muhammad's birth. 'In those days poetry was no luxury for the cultured few, but the sole medium of literary expression. Every tribe had its poets, who freely uttered what they felt and thought. Their unwritten words "flew across the desert faster than arrows", and came home to the hearts and bosoms of all who heard them. Thus in the midst of outward strife and disintegration a unifying principle was at

[1] B. Lewis, *The Arabs in History*, p. 30.

work. Poetry gave life and currency to an ideal of Arabian virtue which, though based on tribal community of blood and insisting that only ties of blood were sacred, nevertheless became an invisible bond between diverse clans, and formed, whether consciously or not, the basis of a national community of sentiment.'[1]

The origins of this literature, accepted as a model of excellence by all succeeding generations, are lost in the mists of antiquity. Writing was an exceedingly rare accomplishment amongst the pagan Arabs, and the great wealth of long odes and shorter fragments have escaped oblivion solely because the Arabs rejoiced to carry them in their capacious memories. What we possess of these ancient poems—and it is not small in bulk—suggests a maturity, one might say a classicism, which could only be the product of a long tradition. Though many diverse dialects were spoken by the various tribes, the language of the poems is astonishingly uniform, a prestige literary norm common to the greater part of the Peninsula. The structure of the ode was already fixed, and in danger of becoming fossilized. The complex prosody, a rich repertory of subtle and complicated rhythms, had been completely perfected. A vocabulary of themes, images and figures, extensive but nevertheless circumscribed, was firmly established. By the time that Muhammad began to preach, and to reveal to his astonished townsmen the Word of Allah, literary Arabic had evolved into a marvellously abundant, supple and expressive language understood of the people.

Muhammad was born between 570 and 580 in Mecca, 'a busy and wealthy commercial town, almost monopolizing the entrepôt trade between the Indian Ocean and the Mediterranean'.[2] His ancestors were noble, being the Banū Hāshim of the powerful tribe of Quraish; his circumstances were poor and pitiable, for he was orphaned in his earliest childhood. Yet this man, battling down the bitterest opposition of the rulers of Mecca which constrained him in 622 to migrate with a few faithful followers to Yathrib (Medina), proved to be the chosen vessel for a Message of purest monotheism which was to sweep the world, the Founder of Islam. When he died in 634, Islam was secure as the paramount religion and political system of all Arabia. The believing Arabs were firmly welded together into an Umma (theocratic community) 'obedient to Allah and His Prophet', to be joined in a bewilderingly short time by countless multitudes of non-Arabs accepting or capitulating to the Call. Palestine and Syria were annexed by 640, Mesopotamia (Iraq) by 641, Egypt by 642, Tripolitania by 647, Persia by 650, Afghanistan by 661, in which

[1] R. A. Nicholson, *A Literary History of the Arabs*, p. 72.
[2] H. A. R. Gibb, *Mohammedanism*, p. 24.

year the capital of the new Empire was moved from Medina to Damascus. Tunisia submitted in 693, Algeria and Morocco were mastered by 705, Sind conquered in 712. Within a century of the Hijra Islam ruled in Spain. Where for centuries Greek and Latin, Aramaic and Pahlavi had divided the world, Arabic, the language of Islam, united all. From the Atlantic coasts to the borders of China the Call to Prayer, in the tongue of Mecca, rang out from minarets summoning the faithful to prostrate themselves to the Lord of the Worlds.

The rapidity of the spread of Islam, noticeably through extensive provinces which had long been Christian, is a crucial fact of history which has naturally engaged the speculative attention of many critical investigators. Certainly Christendom was in desperate disarray, torn asunder by dogmatic quarrels, submerged by waves of pagan invaders, fatally weakened by external wars. The military triumph of the martial Arabs, impetuous horsemen with their long spears and sharp swords sure of the justice of their cause, is not so difficult to understand. That they could hold their wide conquests, and govern them efficiently despite dynastic squabbles and a succession of internecine wars, is less easy to explain, except when it is remembered that the converted peoples had been used for centuries to produce and submit to competent and resourceful administrators. When all military, political and economic factors have been exhausted, however, the religious impulse must still be recognized as the most vital and enduring.

The sublime rhetoric of the Koran, 'that inimitable symphony, the very sounds of which move men to tears and ecstasy'[1]—this, and the urgency of the simple message it carried, holds the key to the mystery of one of the greatest cataclysms in the history of religion. The Call was a call to an austere and disciplined life, the life of Covenanters who had made compact with Allah to submit in all things to His Will, and to strive to bring all mankind to acknowledge His unique authority. Reinforced by the liveliest and most graphic threats and promises, of Heaven or Hell to come, perhaps on the very morrow, the creed of two articles, 'There is no god but Allah, and Muhammad is His Messenger', was very apt to command assent.

That was well; but when undreamed-of wealth from the conquered regions began to flow into the treasury, and the rough life of the desert warrior gave way before the luxurious manners of imperial masters, a ferment arose within Islam which led to puritanical revolts, setting up a tension between the 'haves' and 'have-nots' that has triggered off uprisings down to the present day. The Messenger,

[1] M. Pickthall, *The Meaning of the Glorious Koran*, p. vii.

self-declared to be a mortal amongst mortals, died; the legend of his life of wisdom and holiness was reverently cherished and piously added to by the saints down the bewildering centuries. His immediate Companions and Followers were associated in this nostalgic canonization.

The Messenger died, but the Message remained, carried to the ends of the earth by warrior-preachers, transmitted to the next generations by teachers and traditionists. But soon the doctrinal wranglings began, natural enough amongst the conquered peoples who included Greeks and Syrians, men with an inherited taste for theological hairsplitting. Was man free, or were all his actions predestined by God? The Koran could be, and was, interpreted both ways on this vital crux which in Islam, as in Christianity, touched off a succession of schismatic explosions. When the Koran referred to the 'hands' and 'face' of Allah, and to His 'sitting upon the Throne', were these descriptions to be taken literally? Some fundamentalists went so far as to pronounce on the precise shape and size of God; 'it was said that God, when he grows angry, grows heavier and the throne groans under his weight like a camel saddle'.[1] Men who allowed their more recalcitrant intellects freer rein in these rarefied reaches proposed a metaphorical interpretation for all the material images in the Koran, so that they ended by defining God exclusively in terms of negation. The fiercest controversy of all, however, raged over the nature of the Koran itself: the Speech of God—was it co-eternal with God, or was it created in time and space? (If the latter, then it was evidently reinterpretable in time and place.) This issue became the focal point in a long and bloody debate, ending in the defeat of the Mu'tazilites who had urged the 'created' view.

Greek philosophy and science had already begun to infiltrate into Islamic thought before the Omayyads, successors to the four 'rightly-guided caliphs', were replaced in 749 by the Persianizing Abbasids. Then, under the liberal rule in their new capital Baghdad of Hārūn al-Rashīd and his son al-Ma'mūn, Platonic and Aristotelian studies experienced an amazing renaissance. The *corpus* of the Athenian and Hellenistic schools was translated into Arabic, mainly by the hands of Christians. Greek logic, further refined, sharpened the wits of theologians in their sectarian disputes, and their lofty polemics against Christianity and Judaism. The lawyers too, developing the science of Islamic jurisprudence in their various schools, recognized the virtues of induction and deduction. The 'books of the ancients' were eagerly collected not only in Baghdad but in remote Bokhara, where Avicenna grew to greatness. Medicine, the natural sciences,

[1] A. S. Tritton, *Muslim Theology*, p. 48.

mathematics and astronomy entered the curricula of the Islamic colleges. After the translators came the epitomizers and the commentators, from al-Kindī and Rhazes in the east to Avempace and Averroes in the west. But it has often been remarked that the Arabs, who accepted so much so readily from the Greeks, never knew, or never cared to know, the glories of Greek literature. True, Aristotle's *Poetics* was translated along with the rest of the canon; but as may be seen from the summary of that work by the philosopher al-Fārābī, which it was the good fortune of the present writer to rediscover, the terms 'tragedy' and 'comedy' were quite meaningless to the Arabs, and in fact the drama in our western sense remained unknown to the Islamic peoples until comparatively modern times. Though Homer was still being recited in Baghdad into the eighth century, the *Iliad* was first published in an Arabic version in 1904. The explanation seems to be that the Arabs by then already possessed an ample literature, particularly of poetry, in which they took fierce and understandable pride. Literary theories were evolved and refined which established a close link between language and form, so that there was no room to admit, no motive to seek borrowings from abroad. Not until the nineteenth century did Muslim writers turn to western models, to assist their work of literary renaissance.

Meanwhile Iran too yielded up her ancient wisdom to enrich the hospitable culture of Islam. Her principal contributions were in the fields of political expediency and mystical speculation. Even before Plato's *Republic* and *Laws* and Aristotle's *Politics* and *Ethics* became available to Arab readers, Ibn al-Muqaffaʻ, a Persian convert and secretary to the last of the Omayyads and the first of the Abbasids, had translated out of the Pahlavi the royal chronicles and court manuals of Sassanian Iran. Very influential in forming an elegant prose style in his acquired Arabic, he also put into that language the perennially popular *Kalila and Dimna*, animal fables derived ultimately from India, but now given a cunning and sophisticated political slant. The art of a Byzantine statecraft, introduced into Islam when Muʻāwiya supplanted the Prophet's cousin and son-in-law ʻAlī, developed rapidly as intrigue multiplied in the metropolitan and provincial courts. Long Persian experience, practised by Persian viziers and their apt Arab pupils, made its mark in the rapid secularization of a system of government which had started out as an aspiring theocracy.

The Empire continued to increase in wealth, as trade went farther and farther afield; the wealth was concentrated in the hands of the grasping few, who relished an affluence which would have amazed their Bedouin forebears. Gorgeous palaces and lavishly-appointed mansions adorned the capital Baghdad and the provincial centres, Bokhara, Samarkand, Balkh, Shiraz, Damascus, Aleppo, Jerusalem, Cairo, Tripoli, Tunis, Fez, Palermo, Cordova. The *dolce vita* of the gilded aristocracy is brilliantly portrayed, as it was lived in Andalusia on the eve of the Norman Conquest of England, in *The Ring of the Dove*, a highly sophisticated manual of courtly love composed by an eminent theologian, Ibn Ḥazm. Slaveboys and singing girls, amenities unknown to the ancient Arabs, provided Muslim gentlemen with novel pleasures and the poets with a new vocabulary. Wine was forbidden to the Faithful by the unambiguous prohibition of holy writ; but the rulers of Islam indulged to the full, and their minstrels vied with one another to celebrate the praises of the daughter of the grape.

The formal ode still enjoyed its old primacy, but the object of panegyric changed, from the embattled tribe to the monarch and his ministers, whose favours were shamelessly and extravagantly courted. Meanwhile the lyric, traces of which mount back to pre-Islamic times, now blossomed forth in riotous profusion, with love-making and drinking its main themes. Shorter metres were invented to suit the newly popular genre, the readier to match the softer words to sweeter music. As the storehouse of themes and images became exhausted, rhetorical embellishments multiplied to prove, if not so much originality, then the highly prized accomplishments of virtuosity and wit. Over a show of virginal simplicity layer upon layer of arabesque decoration was lovingly superimposed.

For all the manifest corruption, for all the scandal of flaunted riches and abused power, the heart of Islam still beat strongly. The study of philosophy continued to flourish, and presumed to invade the sanctum of theology; then the conflict between revelation and reason grew sharper, as these belated disciples of the Academy promoted their ideal of intellectual union above the promised physical delights of Paradise. Yet from the beginning as it seems, even in the life of the Prophet, another way to truth, the path of direct experience of the Divine, drew simpler souls out to make the spiritual pilgrimage. Ascetic beginnings and ecstatic climaxes led on to theosophical speculation, as the Sufis came under the all-pervading influence of Neoplatonic thought. Abū Yazīd of Bistam, a Persian, claimed to have met and conversed with God, indeed to have been absorbed into God; al-Junaid of Baghdad, an Arab, worked out with Koranic texts and dicta of Muhammad a doctrine of spiritual union. By the tenth century the three currents—theological, philosophical and mystical—made confluence to attempt an all-embracing harmony, an end to dispute. Orthodox Islam, though suspicious of the mystics, ever ready to excommunicate, even to execute the extremists, finally accepted the Sufis as allies against the far more dangerous enemies, the freethinking philosophers; al-Ghazālī, eminent jurist, theologian and practising mystic, routed from the field the followers of Rhazes and Avicenna. Amongst these latter was Omar Khayyám, whose famous quatrains take on a wealth of new meaning when studied in the light of pure reason's banishment in his own lifetime.

Omar composed his shafts of wit and shapes of beauty in his native Persian, which by the tenth century had recovered from the stunning blow dealt it by Arabic. Generations of thinkers, scholars and poets of Persia had been constrained to express themselves—and they did so supremely well—in the conquerors' language. Then provincial autonomy, symptomatic of the break-up of central government, encouraged a new growth of native literature. The mystics—and every Persian has in him something of the mystic—made a massive contribution to Persian poetry and prose. Persian prosody followed closely the patterns invented by the Arabs; the poetic forms of ode and lyric were eagerly adopted, with their full complement of rhetorical embellishments. Additionally, the Persians developed a genre which the Arabs had known but scorned to encourage, the rhyming couplet, so that the epic and the idyll enjoyed unrestrained popularity. The couplet suited admirably the requirements of didactive and narrative, both necessary to mystical instruction. Thus it came about that whereas in Arabic literature only one truly great mystical poet, Ibn al-Fāriḍ, emerged, Persian produced a constant succession—Sanā'ī, 'Attār, Rūmī, Jāmī are the most famous names, the greatest of all being Rūmī.

It was the wide vogue of mysticism, far more than formal theology, that enabled Islam to survive the appalling catastrophe of the Mongol invasions. The practise of fortitude and contemplation, and the hope and realization of experiencing the love of God, sustained men's hearts and souls through the senseless butcheries and insane devastations of the terrible thirteenth century. By then the political device which had contrived, though in decreasing effectiveness, the unity of Islam, the Baghdad caliphate, vanished in the holocaust; it was replaced by a less spectacular but in the end more enduring bond, the worldwide network of the Sufi brotherhoods. When Persia emerged from the anarchic centuries as a strong and independent kingdom, the founders of the Safavid dynasty took pride in their Sufi origin. Even in this twentieth century a kingdom has arisen from the ruins of foreign domination whose ruling house, the Sanussis of Libya, derived their authority from a mystical Order.

The lyrical poems of Ḥāfiẓ, the greatest of Persia's poets, do not become fully comprehensible until it is realized that the references are as much to the preceptor in his circle of mystical disciples as to the prince and his courtiers.

Islam receded in the west already from 732, when Charles Martel hammered back the troops of 'Abd al-Raḥmān between Tours and Poitiers. The withdrawal from Europe (apart from the Balkans) took place gradually. Sicily was surrendered to the Normans in 1091; Granada capitulated in 1492. The flood tide of the Crusades submerged for a while vital Muslim provinces, but the current ebbed back until in the end all was regained. Then the Turks, invaders from eastern Asia turned ardent believers, destroyed Byzantium at last and captured Constantinople in 1453, thereafter advancing westwards until halted before Vienna. The Ottomans, claiming succession to the caliphate (a pretension not abandoned till the fall of the dynasty in 1924), carved out a new and extensive empire which at its height included all the Balkans, Asia Minor, Mesopotamia, parts of Arabia, the Fertile Crescent, and the whole of North Africa excepting Morocco. This powerful empire was more than matched in brilliance by the Mogul rule in India, which added Delhi to the list of famous Muslim capitals and witnessed a new and luxuriant flowering of Islamic culture comparable with Baghdad, Cairo and Cordova in their heyday.

The decline of Islamic civilization threatened utter ruin even before the advance of European imperialism added to debility humiliation. The defeat of the Indian Mutiny brought an end to the Mogul Empire, and from 1857 until 1947 India was 'the brightest jewel in the British Crown'. Egypt, under Turkish rule for three and a half centuries, became a British Protectorate in 1882 and did not attain full independence until 1936. Algeria was conquered by France by 1848, and it was only in 1962 that French annexation ended. French domination of Tunisia lasted from 1883 to 1956, of Morocco from 1912 to 1956, of Lebanon and Syria from 1920 to 1945; Britain 'protected' Iraq from 1920 to 1932, Palestine from 1920 to 1948. During the nineteenth century Russia annexed one after another the Muslim Khanates of Central Asia. Of all the Muslim lands only Arabia, Turkey, Persia and Afghanistan maintained throughout, and that not always without difficulty, the semblance of self-rule.

It is against such a background, of abject degradation after imperial glory, that the passionate struggle for national independence through the world of Islam is to be viewed and understood. The political rebirth was heralded in the nineteenth century and after by a cultural renaissance. The main stimuli which started this movement of revival were external: the French Revolution, and British liberal idealism. The literary and artistic models, the scientific, technical, even the political examples, were to a great extent furnished by Europe and the United States. The very impulse to study Muslim history, and to appraise the cultural achievements of medieval Islam—chief sources of pride and inspiration to the new generations of fervent nationalists—this too had its origins in western orientalism. These facts go a long way to account for the love-hate relationship which characterizes the attitude of many Muslims today towards the West.

It remains for the author to express his hearty thanks to his various publishers for printing what he has written in the first place, and for allowing him to reprint what is here gathered together; to the reading public for the measure of support which they have accorded him over the years, and which he hopes they will not now deny him; to the critics, indulgent and chastening alike, who have done him the honour of noticing his works; and above all to his patient and long-suffering wife, who has sustained his labours through so many years by her love, sympathy and miraculous understanding.

ONE

Arabia Deserta

Muhammad, the Messenger of Allah, was born an Arab of the town—the thriving commercial centre of Mecca—member of a noble but impoverished family belonging to a powerful ʰribe which, though settled locally, had its roots and ramifications in the outspread desert. The language he spoke, and in which he later received his revelations, already prided itself upon a rich literature, largely if not wholly unwritten, consisting for the most part of formal odes.

'The Arabian ode sets forth before us a series of pictures, drawn with confident skill and first-hand knowledge, of the life its maker lived, of the objects among which he moved, of his horse, his camel, the wild creatures of the wilderness, and of the landscape in the midst of which his life and theirs was set; but all, however loosely they seem to be bound together, are subordinate to one dominant idea, which is the poet's unfolding of himself, his admirations and his hates, his prowess and the freedom of his spirit. . . . No poetry better fulfils Mr Matthew Arnold's definition of "a criticism of life"; no race has more completely succeeded in drawing itself for all time, in its grandeur and its limitations, its best and its worst. It is in this sense that the poetry of the Pagan Arabs is most truly their history.'[1]

Of the very considerable volume of poetry transmitted from the desert bards of the sixth century and collected in writing by Arab scholars of the eighth, pride of first place belongs to seven odes, acclaimed the best work of their seven authors and known as the *Muʻallaqāt*. The selections of desert poetry which follows has been drawn from that anthology.[2]

[1] C. J. Lyall, *Ancient Arabian Poetry* (London, 1930), p. xviii. This book by a distinguished member of the old Bengal Civil Service is still the best introduction to the subject.

[2] For a more detailed account see my *The Seven Odes* (Allen & Unwin, 1957), from which these passages have been drawn.

Imr al-Qais 'the Wandering King'

Halt, friends both! Let us weep, recalling a love and a longing
by the rim of the twisted sands between Ed-Dakhool and Haumal,
Toodih and El-Mikrát, whose trace is not yet effaced
for all the spinning of the south winds and the northern blasts;
there, all about its yards, and away in the dry hollows
you may see the dung of antelopes spattered like peppercorns.
Upon the morn of separation, the day they loaded to part,
by the tribe's acacias it was like I was splitting a colocynth;
there my companions halted their beasts awhile over me
saying, 'Don't perish of sorrow; restrain yourself decently!'
Yet the true and only cure of my grief is tears outpoured:
what is there left to lean on where the trace is obliterated?

The poet recalls boastingly his amorous exploits which relieved the
hard life of desert riding.

Oh yes, many a fine day I've dallied with the white ladies,
and especially I call to mind a day at Dára Juljul,
and the day I slaughtered for the virgins my riding-beast
(and oh, how marvellous was the dividing of its loaded saddle),
and the virgins went on tossing its hacked flesh about
and the frilly fat like fringes of twisted silk. . . .
Ha, and a day on the back of the sand-hill she denied me
swearing a solemn oath that she should never, never be broken.
'Gently now, Fátima! A little less disdainful:
even if you intend to break with me, do it kindly.
If it's some habit of mine that's so much vexed you
just draw off my garments from yours, and they'll slip away.
Puffed-up it is it's made you, that my love for you's killing me
and that whatever you order my heart to do, it obeys.
Your eyes only shed those tears so as to strike and pierce
with those two shafts of theirs the fragments of a ruined heart.
Many's the fair veiled lady, whose tent few would think of seeking,
I've enjoyed sporting with, and not in a hurry either,
slipping past packs of watchmen to reach her, with a whole tribe
hankering after my blood, eager every man-jack to slay me,
what time the Pleiades showed themselves broadly in heaven
glittering like the folds of a woman's bejewelled scarf.
I came, and already she'd stripped off her garments for sleep
beside the tent-flap, all but a single flimsy slip;
and she cried, "God's oath, man, you won't get away with this!

The folly's not left you yet; I see you're as feckless as ever."
Out I brought her, and as she stepped she trailed behind us
to cover our footprints the skirt of an embroidered gown.
But when we had crossed the tribe's enclosure, and dark about us
hung a convenient shallow intricately undulant,
I twisted her side-tresses to me, and she leaned over me;
slender-waisted she was, and tenderly plump her ankles,
shapely and taut her belly, white-fleshed, not the least flabby,
polished the lie of her breast-bones, smooth as a burnished
      mirror. . . .
Let the follies of other men forswear fond passion,
my heart forswears not, nor will forget the love I bear you.'

The ode concludes with a description of a storm seen in the desert,
and its aftermath.

Friend, do you see yonder lightning? Look, there goes its glitter
flashing like two hands now in the heaped-up, crowned stormcloud.
Brilliantly it shines—so flames the lamp of an anchorite
as he slops the oil over the twisted wick.
So with my companions I sat watching it between Dárij '
· and El-Odheib, far-ranging my anxious gaze;
over Katan, so we guessed, hovered the right of its deluge,
its left dropping upon Es-Sitár and further Yadhbul.
Then the cloud started loosing its torrent about Kutaifa
turning upon their beards the boles of the tall kanahbals;
over the hills of El-Kanán swept its flying spray
sending the white wild goats hurtling down on all sides.
At Taima it left not one trunk of a date-tree standing,
not a solitary fort, save those buttressed with hard rocks;
and Thabeer—why, when the first onrush of its deluge came
Thabeer was a great chieftain wrapped in a striped jubba.
In the morning the topmost peak of El-Mujaimir
was a spindle's whorl cluttered with all the scum of the torrent;
it had flung over the desert of El-Ghabeet its cargo
like a Yemeni merchant unpacking his laden bags.
In the morning the songbirds all along the broad valley
quaffed the choicest of sweet wines rich with spices;
the wild beasts at evening drowned in the furthest reaches
of the wide watercourse lay like drawn bulbs of wild onion.

Tarafa 'Who Died Young'

The ode of Tarafa, who was executed in his twenties, is chiefly prized
for a fine picture of a racing camel.

Ah, but when grief assails me, straightway I ride it off
mounted on my swift, lean-flanked camel, night and day racing,
sure-footed, like the planks of a litter; I urge her on
down the bright highway, that back of a striped mantle;
she vies with the noble, hot-paced she-camels, shank on shank
nimbly plying, over a path many feet have beaten.
Along the rough slopes with the milkless shes she has pastured
in Spring, cropping the rich meadows green in the gentle
     rains;
to the voice of the caller she returns, and stands on guard
with her bunchy tail, scared of some ruddy, tuft-haired stallion,
as though the wings of a white vulture enfolded the sides
of her tail, pierced even to the bone by a pricking awl;
anon she strikes with it behind the rear-rider, anon
lashes her dry udders, withered like an old water-skin.
Perfectly firm is the flesh of her two thighs—
they are the gates of a lofty, smooth-walled castle—
and tightly knit are her spine-bones, the ribs like bows,
her underneck stuck with the well-strung vertebrae,
fenced about by the twin dens of a wild lote-tree;
you might say bows were bent under a buttressed spine.
Widely spaced are her elbows, as if she strode
carrying the two buckets of a sturdy water-carrier;
like the bridge of the Byzantine, whose builder swore
it should be all encased in bricks to be raised up true.
Reddish the bristles under her chin, very firm her back,
broad the span of her swift legs, smooth her swinging gait;
her legs are twined like rope uptwisted; her forearms
thrust slantwise up to the propped roof of her breast.
Swiftly she rolls, her cranium huge, her shoulder-blades
high-hoisted to frame her lofty, raised superstructure. . . .
Her long neck is very erect when she lifts it up
calling to mind the rudder of a Tigris-bound vessel.
Her skull is most like an anvil, the junction of its two halves
meeting together as it might be on the edge of a file.
Her cheek is smooth as Syrian parchment, her split lip
a tanned hide of Yemen, its slit not bent crooked;
her eyes are a pair of mirrors, sheltering
in the caves of her brow-bones, the rock of a pool's hollow. . . .
Her ears are true, clearly detecting on the night journey
the fearful rustle of a whisper, the high-pitched cry,
sharp-tipped, her nobel pedigree plain in them,
pricked like the ears of a wild-cow of Haumal lone-pasturing.

Ṭarafa boasts of his dissolute youth, and frankly exposes his philosophy of life.

>Unceasingly I tippled the wine and took my joy,
>unceasingly I sold and squandered my hoard and my patrimony
>till all my family deserted me, every one of them,
>and I sat alone like a lonely camel scabby with mange;
>yet I saw the sons of the dust did not deny me
>nor the grand ones who dwell in those fine, wide-spread tents.
>So now then, you who revile me because I attend the wars
>and partake in all pleasures, can you keep me alive forever?
>If you can't avert from me the fate that surely awaits me
>then pray leave me to hasten it on with what money I've got.
>But for three things, that are the joy of a young fellow,
>I assure you I wouldn't care when my deathbed visitors arrive—
>first, to forestall my charming critics with a good swig
>of crimson wine that foams when the water is mingled in;
>second, to wheel at the call of the beleaguered a curved-shanked
>   steed
>streaking like the wolf of the thicket you've startled lapping the
>   water;
>and third, to curtail the day of showers, such an admirable season,
>dallying with a ripe wench under the pole-propped tent,
>her anklets and her bracelets seemingly hung on the boughs
>of a pliant, unriven gum-tree or a castor-shrub.
>So permit me to drench my head while there's still life in it,
>for I tremble at the thought of the scant draught I'll get when
>   I'm dead.

Zuhair 'The Moralist'

Zuhair has sometimes, though without real justification, been called
a Christian poet. He lived to a great age and met the Prophet, but
did not accept conversion to Islam. His ode is notable for a high
moral tone uncommon in pre-Islamic poetry.

>Do not conceal from Allah whatever is in your breasts
>hoping it may be hidden; Allah knows whatever is concealed,
>and either it's postponed, and put in a book, and stored away
>for the Day of Reckoning, or it's hastened, and punished betimes.

The parallel between the foregoing verses and certain passages in the
Koran is startlingly obvious. Not less remarkable is Zuhair's attitude
to war, the endemic sickness of ancient Arabia.

War is nothing else but what you've known and yourselves tasted,
it is not a tale told at random, a vague conjecture;
when you stir it up, it's a hateful thing you've stirred up;
ravenous it is, once you whet its appetite; it bursts aflame,
then it grinds you as a millstone grinds on its cushion;
yearly it conceives, birth upon birth, and with twins for issue—
very ill-omened are the boys it bears you, every one of them
the like of Ahmar of Ad; then it gives suck, and weans them.
Yes, war yields you a harvest very different from the bushels
and pieces of silver those fields in Iraq yield for the villagers.

Yet in the end it is despair, and not faith in a higher order, that
inspired Zuhair's final outburst.

Weary am I of the burdens of life; whoever lives
fourscore years, believe me you, grows very weary.
I have seen the Fates trample like a purblind camel; those they
    strike
they slay, those they miss are left to live on into dotage. . . .
I know what is happening today, and what passed before that
    yesterday,
but as for knowing what tomorrow will bring, there I'm utterly
    blind.

Labīd 'The Centenarian'

Labīd lived to an even greater age than Zuhair, surviving into the
reign of Mu'āwiya the cunning. A rare tenderness characterizes his
descriptions of animals.

Is such my camel? Or shall I liken her to a wild cow, whose calf
the beasts of prey have devoured, lagging, though true herd-
    leader?
Flat-nosed, she has lost her young, and therefore unceasingly
circles about the stony waste, lowing all the while
as she seeks a half-weaned white calf, whose carcase the grey
    robber-wolves
in greed unappeasable have dragged hither and thither;
they encountered her unawares, and seized the little one from her,
and of a truth the arrows of Fate miss not their mark.
All that night she wandered, the raindrops streaming upon her
in continuous flow, watering still the herb-strewn sands;
she crouched under the stem of a high-branched tree, apart
on the fringes of certain sand-hills, whose soft slopes trickled down

while the rain uninterruptedly ran down the line
of her back, on a night the clouds blotted the starlight out,
yet she shone radiantly in the face of the gathered murk
as the pearl of a diver shines when shaken free from its thread;
but when the shadows dispersed, and the dawn surrounded her,
forth she went, her feet slipping upon the dripping earth.
Distraught with sorrow, for seven nights and successive days
ceaselessly she wandered among the pools of Sawá'id
till at last she gave up hope, and her swelling udders shrank
that no suckling and no weaning had ever wrung so dry.
Now she heard the murmur of men's voices, that startled her
coming from the unseen—for man is her sickness of old—
and on both sides, behind and before her, so she deemed,
danger awaited, the awful apprehension of doom.
Then, when the huntsmen, despairing to come to grips, unleashed
their flap-eared hunting-dogs with collars of untanned hide,
they closed on her, and she turned upon them with her horn
pointed and altogether like to a Samhari spear
to repel them, for she was sure that if she repelled them not
Fate inexorable was imminent, and certain death.
So Kasáb came to her doom, a fine hound, horribly smeared
in blood, and Sukhám, another, left on the battlefield.

An important function of the ancient Arab bard was to boast of the
achievements of his tribe, and the courage and wisdom of its leaders.
It was in conformity with this tradition that Labíd composed his
concluding stanzas.

When the assemblies meet together, we never fail
to supply a match for the gravest issue, strong to shoulder it,
a partitioner, bestowing on all the tribe their due,
granting to some their rights, denying the claims of some
for the general good, generous, assisting liberality,
gentlemanly, winning and plundering precious prize,
sprung of a stock whose fathers laid down a code for them,
and every folk has its code of laws and its high ideal.
When alarmed to battle, there they are with their helmets on
and their coats of mail, the rings of them gleaming like stars:
unsullied is their honour, their deeds are not ineffectual,
for their prudent minds incline not after capricious lust.
They have built for us a house whose roof reaches very high
and to it have mounted alike the elders and young of the tribe.
So be satisfied with what the Sovereign has allotted;

He has divided the qualities among us, knowing them well,
and when trustworthiness came to be apportioned among a tribe
the Apportioner bestowed on us an exceeding share.
They are the strivers, whenever the tribe is visited
by distress; they are the tribe's knights and high arbiters;
to those who seek their protection they are as the bounteous
    Spring
as also to widows in their long year of widowhood.
Such a tribe they are, that no envier succeeds to hold back
nor any reviler assists the enemy's reviling tongue.

'Antara 'The Black Knight'

One of the great medieval romances of the Arabs tells of the exploits of the pre-Islamic warrior 'Antar or 'Antara, 'the greatest of the early half-castes of our own era, a lineal giant amongst that virile band of mulattoes whose lives have helped to sustain hope and endeavour through the centuries'.[1] The *Romance of Antar* is almost wholly legendary, but we are on firmer ground when we read the poems preserved in Antara's name from high antiquity. His impetuous spirit is clearly revealed in a long boast of his prowess.

Praise me therefore for the things you know of me; for I
am easy to get on with, provided I'm not wronged;
but if I am wronged, then the wrong I do is harsh indeed,
bitter to the palate as the tang of the colocynth.
It may also be mentioned how often I have drunk good wine,
after the noon's sweltering calm, from a bright figured bowl
in a glittering golden glass scored with lines
partnered to a lustrous filtered flask on its left,
and whenever I have drunk, recklessly I squander
my substance, while my honour is abounding, unimpaired,
and whenever I have sobered up, I diminish not my bounty,
my qualities and my nobility being as you have known them.
And many's the good wife's spouse I have left on the floor
the blood whistling from his ribs like a harelip hissing,
my fists having beaten him to it with a hasty blow
and the spray of a deep thrust, dyed like dragon's blood.
I could advise you, daughter of Malik, to ask the horsemen
if you should happen to be ignorant and uninformed,
for I'm never out of the saddle of a strong swimmer,

[1] Cedric Dover in *Phylon* (1954). Four volumes of *Antar, a Bedoueen Romance*, the translation of Terrick Hamilton, were published by John Murray in 1819–20.

sturdy, assaulted again and again by the warriors, wounded,
now detached for the lance-thrusting, and anon
resorting to the great host with their tight bows.
Those who were present at the engagement will acquaint you
how I plunge into battle, but abstain at the booty-sharing.
Many's the bristling knight the warriors have shunned to take
    on,
one who was not in a hurry to flee or capitulate,
my hands have been right generous to with the hasty thrust
of a well-tempered, strong-jointed, straightened spear
giving him a broad, double-sided gash, the hiss of which
guides in the night-season the prowling, famished wolves;
I split through his accoutrements with my solid lance
(for even the noblest is not sacrosanct to the spear)
and left him carrion for the wild beasts to pounce on,
all of him, from the crown of his head to his limp wrists.

His ode contains a wonderfully graphic description of his horse in
the thick of battle.

When in the midst of the battle-dust I heard the cry
of Murra ascend shrill, and the two sons of Rabí'a,
and all Muhallim were striving beneath their banner
and death stalked beneath the sons of Muhallim's banner,
then I knew for sure that when the issue was joined with them
such a blow would fall as to scare the bird from its snuggling
    chicks.
When I beheld the people advancing in solid mass
urging each other on, I wheeled on them blamelessly;
'Antara!' they were calling, and the lances were like
well-ropes sinking into the breast of my black steed.
Continuously I charged them with his white-blazoned face
and his breast, until his body was caparisoned in blood,
and he twisted round to the spears' impact upon his breast
and complained to me, sobbing and whimpering;
had he known the art of conversation, he would have protested,
and had he been acquainted with speech, he would have spoken
    to me.
The horses frowning terribly plunged into the crumbling soil,
long-bodied mare along with short-haired, long-bodied stallion,
and oh, my soul was cured, and its faint sickness was healed
by the horsemen's cry, 'Ha, Antara, on with you!'

'Amr 'The Regicide'

It fell to the poet 'Amr son of Kulthūm to avenge the murder of
the poet Ṭarafa at the hands of King 'Amr, son of the Christian
princess Hind. He too is said to have lived to a great age, and in the
end to have drunk himself to death. In his poem, full of true Bedouin
boasting, he throws down a withering challenge to his ultimate
victim.

> With what purpose in view, Amr bin Hind,
> do you give heed to our traducers, and despise us?
> With what purpose in view, Amr bin Hind,
> should we be underlings to your chosen princelet?
> Threaten us then, and menace us; but gently!
> When, pray, were we your mother's domestics?
> Be sure, that before your time our lances
> baffled our enemies' efforts to soften them;
> when the spear-vice bit into them, they resisted
> and drove it back like a stubborn, shoving camel,
> a stubborn camel; bend them, and with a creaking
> they strike back at the straightener's neck and forehead.
> Have you been told, regarding Jusham bin Bakr,
> that they ever failed in the ancients' great engagements?
> We are heirs to the glory of Alkama bin Saif:
> he mastered for us the castles of glory.
> I am heir to Muhalhil and his better,
> Zuhair, a fine treasure indeed to treasure,
> heir to Attáb, and Kulthúm, the whole of them,
> by whom we attained the heirdom of the noblest,
> heir to Dhul Bura, of whom you've heard tell,
> our defence, through whom we defend the shelterers,
> and, before him, Kulaib the Striver was one of us:
> so what glory is there we are not possessed of?
> When we tie with a rope our train-camel of battle
> or we break the bond, or the neck of the beast tethered to her.
> We shall be found the firmest men in duty
> and the truest of men to the oath once taken.
> We on the morn the fire in Khazáz was kindled
> gave succour beyond every other succourer;
> we are they who kept to Dhu Urátá
> while the huge, milk-rich camels chawed dry fodder.
> We are the just rulers over obedience,
> we are the just chastisers of rebellion;

we promptly abandon that which disgusts us,
we lay hold eagerly of what pleases us.
We kept the right wing in the great encounter
and on the left wing stood our blood-brothers;
they loosed a fierce assault on their nearest foemen,
we loosed a fierce assault on our nearest foemen;
they returned with much booty and many captives,
we returned leading the kings in fetters.
So beware, you Banu Bakr, beware now:
have you not yet the true knowledge of us?
Do you not know how the squadrons thrusted
and shot their bolts, ours and yours together?
We were caparisoned in helmets, and Yemeni jerkins,
we were accoutred with swords straight and bending,
our bodies were hung with glittering mail-coats
having visible puckers above the sword-belt
that being unbuckled from the warrior
reveals his skin rusted from the long wearing,
mail-coats that ripple like a pool of water
when the furrowing wind strikes its smooth surface.
Short-haired are our steeds on the morn of terror,
known to us, our weanlings, won from the enemy;
them we inherited from the truest of fathers,
them we shall bequeath dying to our sons.

In his concluding sequence the poet's extravagant vaunting seems to merge into a prophetic vision of that Arabia, united by the Prophet's message into an irresistible host of Allah's warriors, which burst its bounds and spread a new order of religious law and martial justice from the waters of the Atlantic to the boundaries of China.

Ours is the world, and all who dwell upon it,
and when we assault, we assault with power.
When kings deal with their peoples unjustly
we refuse to allow injustice among us.
We are called oppressors; we never oppressed yet,
but shortly we shall be starting oppression!
When any boy of ours reaches his weaning
the tyrants fall down before him prostrating.
We have filled the land till it's too strait for us,
and we are filling the sea's back with our vessels.
So let no man act foolishly against us,
or we shall exceed the folly of the foolhardiest.

Al-Ḥārith 'The Leper'

Said to have been a centenarian when he composed the ode which
won him immortality by its inclusion in the *Muʻallaqāt*, al-Ḥārith
stricken with leprosy delivered himself of a furious diatribe in
defence of his tribe.

> Tidings have come to us regarding the Arákim
> and a grave matter that concerns and troubles us,
> namely that our brothers the Arákim are going too
> far against us, using intemperate language,
> confounding those of us who are blameless with the
> guilty, so that innocence advantages not the innocent.
> They asserted that all who have smitten the wild ass
> are clients of ours, and ourselves their protectors;
> they concerted their plans by night, and when morning
> dawned, they filled the morning with a great clamour,
> some calling and some answering, commingled with
> a neighing of horses and a grumbling of camels.
> Say, you big-mouthed embroiderer, you who gabble
> about us to Amr, think you your lies are immortal?
> Don't imagine your smear's going to stick to us;
> this isn't the first time enemies have maligned us,
> but for all their hatred we've still survived,
> uplifted by high birth, and power well-grounded
> that long before today blinded the eyes of the
> people, being compounded of pride and stubbornness.
> Fate, battering us, might be stoning a black
> towering mountain, its summit the clouds unshrouding,
> ruggedly firm against fortune's artillery,
> unweakened by destiny's inexorable hammering.

The poet is confident that the king will accept the justice of his plea,
and cites in evidence past proofs of his tribe's valour.

> Amr has qualities and feelings towards us,
> every one of them undoubtedly a blessing.
> A just monarch he, the most perfect walking;
> the virtues he possesses excel all praise;
> of the stock of Iram, one for champions to boast of
> and even their enemies concede the evidence;
> a king who thrice has had token of our
> good service, and each time the proof was decisive.

Our sign was seen eastwards of Esh-Shakeeka
when they all came, every tribe with its banner,
about Kais, clad in armour, with a Karazi
chieftain to lead them, a white rock of eminence,
and a band of noble-born warriors, checked only
by the fierce thrust that pierces through to the white bone.
Them we smote with such a brow-blow that the gore gushed
like water spurting from a hole in a water-skin,
and we drove them against the boulders of Thahlán,
helter-skelter, their thigh-veins spouting bloodily,
and we dealt with them as Allah alone knows—
their doom being sealed, their blood unavenged streamed.
Then we fought Hujr, I mean Umm Katán's son,
with his Persian squadron in their dark-green armour,
a lion in the encounter, tawny, soft-footed,
but a spring-shower in the hideous drought-year;
we repulsed them with lance-lunges, like buckets
plunged into the watery depths of a stone-cased well.
Thirdly, we loosed Imrul Kais from his fetters
after his long years of dungeon and misery
and constrained the Lord of Ghassán to compensate him
for El-Mundhir, perforce, when the blood was immeasurable,
and we ransomed them with nine high princes
of noble line, their booty being most precious.
And with El-Jaun, Jaun of the House of Bani l-
Aus, was a swerving band, swooping like a crook-billed eagle;
we did not flinch under the dust-cloud, when they turned
their backs, and the fire of battle blazed hottest.

TWO

The Speech of Allah

In the spreading wastes and thronging townships of Arabia at the turn of the sixth–seventh century A D many voices were heard, their common language being Arabic, expressive of many divergent points of view. Jew and Christian were not uncommon, preaching the messages, albeit somewhat garbled, of Moses and Jesus. Echoes of Zoroastrian doctrines clashed with a vague and rather mysterious monotheism attributed to people known as Ḥanīfs. But drowning the chatter of jarring sects and the chaffer of brisk materialist tradesmen still thundered the loud quarrels of tribe against tribe, and the glorification of petty war and of heroism too often degenerating into heroics.

Suddenly to the man Muhammad in middle life, meditating in a mountain cave outside Mecca, a new voice came announcing a new message.

> Recite: In the Name of thy Lord who created,
>   created Man of a blood-clot.
> Recite: And thy Lord is the Most Generous,
>   who taught by the Pen,
>   taught Man that he knew not.   (Kor. 96: 1–5.)

It was Allah calling Muhammad to be His Prophet, calling in the pure Arabic language with a message to the Arabs, but not only to the Arabs—to the whole of mankind. The first word was the word 'Recite'; in token of this the complete volume of revelations is called the Koran, meaning 'Recitation'—the recitation of God's will to men.

The most urgent communication, as likely the most quickly to recall sinful men from their evil and heedless ways, was a warning that the time left for repentance was running out and that the Day of Judgment would all too soon be dawning. That Day would be ushered in by a panorama of sudden and unbelievable terror.

When earth is shaken with a mighty shaking
          and earth brings forth her burdens,
                and Man says, 'What ails her?'
          upon that day she shall tell her tidings
                for that her Lord has inspired her. (Kor. 99: 1–5.)

          The Clatterer! What is the Clatterer?
          And what shall teach thee what is the Clatterer?
     The day that men shall be like scattered moths,
and the mountains shall be like plucked wool-tufts.

Then he whose deeds weigh heavy in the Balance
          shall inherit a pleasing life,
but he whose deeds weigh light in the Balance
          shall plunge in the womb of the Pit.
And what shall teach thee what is the Pit?
          A blazing Fire!   (Kor. 101.)

The messages gradually became longer and more coherent, linking
themselves up with messages spoken by God to former peoples,
who disregarded the Divine warning and were consequently destroyed.

          By the loosed ones successively
                storming tempestuously,
          by the scatterers scattering
          and the severally severing
     and those hurling a reminder
          excusing or warning,
surely that which you are promised is about to fall!

          When the stars shall be extinguished,
                when heaven shall be split,
          when the mountains shall be scattered
     and when the Messengers' time is set,
          to what day shall they be delayed?
          To the Day of Decision.
And what shall teach thee what is the Day of Decision?
     Woe that day unto those who cry it lies!

          Did We not destroy the ancients,
     and then follow them with the later folk?
          So We serve the sinners.
     Woe that day unto those who cry it lies!

Did We not create you of a mean water,
that We laid within a sure lodging
till a known term decreed?
We determined; excellent determiners are We.
Woe that day unto those who cry it lies!

Made We not the earth to be a housing
for the living and for the dead?
Set We not therein soaring mountains?
Sated you with sweetest water?
Woe that day unto those who cry it lies!

Depart to that you cried was lies!
Depart to a triple-massing shadow
unshading against the blazing flame
that shoots sparks like dry faggots,
sparks like to golden herds.
Woe that day unto those who cry it lies!

This is the day they shall not speak
neither be given leave, and excuse themselves.
Woe that day unto those who cry it lies!

(Kor. 77: 1–37.)

The contrasting rewards awaiting the righteous and sinners are set forth in a sonorous anthem whose refrain thunders God's challenge to men.

The All-merciful has taught the Koran.
He created Man
and He has taught him the Explanation.
The sun and the moon to a reckoning,
and the stars and the trees bow themselves;
and heaven—He raised it up, and set
the Balance.
(Transgress not in the Balance,
and weigh with justice, and skimp not in the Balance.)
And earth—He set it down for all beings,
therein fruits, and palm-trees with sheaths,
and grain in the blade, and fragrant herbs.
O which of your Lord's bounties will you and you deny?

He created man of a clay
like the potter's,
and He created the jinn
of a smokeless fire.
O which of your Lord's bounties will you and you deny?

Lord of the Two Easts,
Lord of the Two Wests,
O which of your Lord's bounties will you and you deny?

He let forth the two seas that meet together,
between them a barrier they do not overpass.
O which of your Lord's bounties will you and you deny?
From them come forth the pearl and the coral.
O which of your Lord's bounties will you and you deny?
His too are the ships that run, raised up in the sea like landmarks.
O which of your Lord's bounties will you and you deny?

All that dwells upon the earth is perishing, yet still
abides the Face of thy Lord, majestic, splendid.
O which of your Lord's bounties will you and you deny?
Whatsoever is in the heavens and the earth implore Him;
every day He is upon some labour.
O which of your Lord's bounties will you and you deny?
We shall surely attend to you at leisure,
you weight and you weight!
O which of your Lord's bounties will you and you deny?
O tribe of jinn and of men, if you are able
to pass through the confines of heaven and earth,
pass through them! You shall not pass through
except with an authority.
O which of your Lord's bounties will you and you deny?
Against you shall be loosed
a flame of fire, and molten
brass; and you shall not be helped.
O which of your Lord's bounties will you and you deny?
And when heaven is split asunder
and turns crimson like red leather—
O which of your Lord's bounties will you and you deny?
on that day none shall be questioned
about his sin, neither man nor jinn.
O which of your Lord's bounties will you and you deny?
The sinners shall be known by their mark,
and they shall be seized by their forelocks and their feet.

O which of your Lord's bounties will you and you deny?
    This is Gehenna, that sinners cried lies to;
    they shall go round between it and between
        hot, boiling water.
O which of your Lord's bounties will you and you deny?

    But such as fears the Station of his Lord,
        for them shall be two gardens—
O which of your Lord's bounties will you and you deny?
        abounding in branches—
O which of your Lord's bounties will you and you deny?
    therein two fountains of running water—
O which of your Lord's bounties will you and you deny?
    therein of every fruit two kinds—
O which ot your Lord's bounties will you and you deny?
    reclining upon couches lined with brocade,
    the fruits of the gardens nigh to gather—
O which of your Lord's bounties will you and you deny?
    therein maidens restraining their glances,
    untouched before them by any man or jinn—
O which of your Lord's bounties will you and you deny?
    lovely as rubies, beautiful as coral—
O which of your Lord's bounties will you and you deny?
Shall the recompense of goodness be other than goodness?
O which of your Lord's bounties will you and you deny?

    And besides these shall be two gardens—
O which of your Lord's bounties will you and you deny?
        green, green pastures—
O which of your Lord's bounties will you and you deny?
    therein two fountains of gushing water—
O which of your Lord's bounties will you and you deny?
        therein fruits,
        and palm-trees, and pomegranates—
O which of your Lord's bounties will you and you deny?
    therein maidens good and comely—
O which of your Lord's bounties will you and you deny?
    houris, cloistered in cool pavilions—
O which of your Lord's bounties will you and you deny?
    untouched before them by any man or jinn—
O which of your Lord's bounties will you and you deny?
    reclining upon green cushions and lovely druggets—
O which ot your Lord's bounties will you and you deny?

Blessed be the Name of thy Lord, majestic, splendid.   (Kor. 55.)

Man's first duty, if he would do the will of God, is to glorify God,
the signs of Whose power and beneficence are everywhere to be seen.

>   So glory be to God
>   both in your evening hour
>   and in your morning hour.
>   His is the praise
>   in the heavens and the earth,
>   alike at the setting sun
>   and in your noontide hour.
> He brings forth the living from the dead,
> and brings forth the dead from the living,
> and He revives the earth after it is dead;
>   even so you shall be brought forth.
>
>   And of His signs
>   is that He created you of dust; then lo,
>   you are mortals, all scattered abroad.
>   And of His signs
>   is that He created for you, of yourselves,
>   spouses, that you might repose in them,
>   and He has set between you love and mercy.
> Surely in that are signs for a people who consider.
>   And of His signs
>   is the creation of the heavens and earth
>   and the variety of your tongues and hues.
> Surely in that are signs for all living beings.
>   And of His signs
>   is your slumbering by night and day,
>   and your seeking after His bounty.
> Surely in that are signs for a people who hear.
>   And of His signs
>   He shows you lightning, for fear and hope,
>   and that He sends down out of heaven water
>   and He revives the earth after it is dead.
> Surely in that are signs for a people who understand.
>   And of His signs
>   is that the heaven and earth stand firm
>   by His command; then, when He calls you
>   once and suddenly, out of the earth, lo
>   you shall come forth.   (Kor. 30: 19–24.)

Man's first article of faith must be belief in Allah, the One and Only
God.

Say: 'He is God, One,
God, the Everlasting Refuge,
who has not begotten, and who has not been begotten,
and equal to Him is not any one?   (Kor. 112.)

In this simple formulation of the Divine Unity an obvious reference
is made to the erroneous doctrine of the Christians touching the
Divinity of Jesus, a prophet of Allah indeed and born of a pure
virgin, but mortal like Muhammad himself and all the other prophets.

And mention in the Book Mary
when she withdrew from her people
    to an eastern place,
and she took a veil apart from them;
then We sent unto her Our Spirit
that presented himself to her
    a man without fault.
She said, 'I take refuge in
the All-merciful from thee!
    If thou fearest God . . .'
He said, 'I am but a messenger
come from thy Lord, to give thee
    a boy most pure.'
She said, 'How shall I have a son
whom no mortal has touched, neither
    have I been unchaste?'
He said, 'Even so thy Lord has said:
"Easy is that for Me; and that We
may appoint him a sign unto men
and a mercy from Us; it is
    a thing decreed." '
So she conceived him, and withdrew with him
    to a distant place.
And the birthpangs surprised her by
the trunk of the palm-tree. She said,
'Would I had died ere this, and become
    a thing forgotten!'
But the one that was below her
called to her, 'Nay, do not sorrow;
see, thy Lord has set below thee
    a rivulet.

Shake also to thee the palm-trunk,
and there shall come tumbling upon thee
    dates fresh and ripe.
Eat therefore, and drink, and be
comforted; and if thou shouldst see
    any mortal,
say, "I have vowed to the All-merciful
a fast, and today I will not speak
    to any man." '
Then she brought the child to her folk
carrying him; and they said,
'Mary, thou hast surely committed
    a monstrous thing!
Sister of Aaron, they father was not
a wicked man, nor was thy mother
    a woman unchaste.'
Mary pointed to the child then;
but they said, 'How shall we speak
to one who is still in the cradle,
    a little child?'
He said, 'Lo, I am God's servant;
God has given me the Book, and
    made me a Prophet.
Blessed He has made me, wherever
I may be; and He has enjoined me
to pray, and to give the alms, so
    long as I live,
and likewise to cherish my mother;
He has not made me arrogant,
    unprosperous.
Peace be upon me, the day I was born,
and the day I die, and the day I am
    raised up alive!'
That is Jesus, son of Mary,
in word of truth, concerning which
    they are doubting.
It is not for God to take a son
unto Him. Glory be to Him! When He
decrees a thing, He but says to it
    'Be,' and it is.
Surely God is my Lord and your
Lord; so serve you Him. This is
    a straight path.   (Kor. 19: 16–37.)

The famous and much-loved 'Throne-Verse', revealed in the later years of Muhammad's mission, restates with greater elaboration the simple message of the Unity.

God
there is no god but He, the
Living, the Everlasting.
Slumber seizes Him not, neither sleep;
to Him belongs
all that is in the heavens and the earth.
Who is there that shall intercede with Him
save by His leave?
He knows what lies before them
and what is after them,
and they comprehend not anything of His knowledge
save such as He wills.
His Throne comprises the heavens and earth;
the preserving of them oppresses Him not;
He is the All-high, the All-glorious.   (Kor. 2: 256.)

In a parallel context from the same chapter of revelation Allah defines for man the meaning of true piety.

It is not piety, that you turn your faces
to the East and to the West.
True piety is this:
to believe in God, and the Last Day,
the angels, the Book, and the Prophets,
to give of one's substance, however cherished,
to kinsmen, and orphans,
the needy, the traveller, beggars,
and to ransom the slave,
to perform the prayer, to pay the alms.
And they who fulfil their covenant
when they have engaged in a covenant,
and endure with fortitude
misfortune, hardship and peril,
these are they who are true in their faith,
these are the truly godfearing.   (Kor. 2: 172.)

In the 'Light-Verse' and those immediately following it, Allah revealed to men a vision of Himself which mystics down the centuries have taken as a richly rewarding theme for meditation.

God is the Light of the heavens and the earth;
the likeness of His Light is as a niche
wherein is a lamp
(the lamp in a glass,
the glass as it were a glittering star)
kindled from a Blessed Tree,
an olive that is neither of the East nor of the West
whose oil wellnigh would shine, even if no fire touched it;
Light upon Light;
(God guides to His Light whom He will.)
(And God strikes similitudes for men,
and God has knowledge of everything.)
in temples God has allowed to be raised up,
and His Name to be commemorated therein;
therein glorifying Him, in the mornings and the evenings,
are men whom neither commerce nor trafficking
diverts from the remembrance of God
and to perform the prayer, and to pay the alms,
fearing a day when hearts and eyes shall be turned about,
that God may recompense them for their fairest works
and give them increase of His bounty;
and God provides whomsoever He will, without reckoning.
And as for the unbelievers,
their works are as a mirage in a spacious plain
which the man athirst supposes to be water,
till, when he comes to it, he finds it is nothing;
there indeed he finds God,
and He pays him his account in full (and God is swift
at the reckoning);
or they are as shadows upon a sea obscure
covered by a billow
above which is a billow
above which are clouds,
shadows piled one upon another;
when he puts forth his hand, wellnigh he cannot see it.
And to whomsoever God assigns no light,
no light has he.   (Kor. 24: 35–40.)

Despite the eloquence and unambiguity of the message, the Messenger was rejected for long years by the greater part of those who heard him. This was merely a recurrent pattern in human affairs; the Prophets before Muhammad had suffered a like rejection, and the rejectors lived to rue their stubbornness.

The Hour has drawn nigh: the moon is split.
Yet if they see a sign they turn away, and they say
'A continuous sorcery!'
They have cried lies, and followed their caprices;
but every matter is settled.
And there have come to them such tidings as contain
a deterrent—
a Wisdom far-reaching; yet warnings do not avail.
So turn thou away from them.

Upon the day when the Caller shall call unto a horrible thing,
abasing their eyes, they shall come forth from the tombs as if
they were scattered grasshoppers,
running with outstretched necks to the Caller. The unbelievers
shall say, 'This is a hard day!'

The people of Noah cried lies before them;
they cried lies to Our servant, and said,
'A man possessed!' And he was rejected.
And so he called unto his Lord, saying,
'I am vanquished; do Thou succour me!'
Then We opened the gates of heaven unto
water torrential,
and made the earth to gush with fountains,
and the waters met for a matter decreed.
And We bore him upon a well-planked vessel
well-caulked
running before Our eyes—a recompense for
him denied.
And We left it for a sign.
Is there any that will remember?
How then were My chastisement and My warnings?
Now We have made the Koran easy for Remembrance.
Is there any that will remember?

Ad cried lies.
How then were My chastisement and My warnings?
We loosed against them a wind
clamorous in a day of ill fortune continuous,
plucking up men as if they were stumps of
uprooted palm-trees.
How then were My chastisement and My warnings?
Now We have made the Koran easy for Remembrance.
Is there any that will remember?

Thamood cried lies to the warnings
and said, 'What, shall we follow
a mortal, one out of ourselves?
Then indeed we should be in error
    and insanity!
Has the Reminder been cast upon him
alone among us? Nay, rather he is
    an impudent liar.'
'They shall surely know tomorrow
    who is the impudent liar.
We shall send the She-camel as a
trial for them; so watch thou them
    and keep patience.
And tell them that the water is to
be divided between them, each drink
    for each in turn.'
Then they called their comrade, and
he took her in hand, and hamstrung her.
How then were My chastisement and My warnings?
    We loosed against them one Cry,
    and they were as the wattles of a
        pen-builder.
Now We have made the Koran easy for Remembrance.
    Is there any that will remember?

The people of Lot cried lies to the warnings.
We loosed against them a squall of pebbles
except the folk of Lot; We delivered them
    at the dawn—
a blessing from Us; even so We recompense
    him who is thankful.
He had warned them of Our assault, but
    they disputed the warnings.
Even his guests they had solicited of him;
    so We obliterated their eyes, saying,
'Taste now My chastisement and My warnings!'
    In the morning early there came upon them
    a settled chastisement:
'Taste now My chastisement and My warnings!'
Now We have made the Koran easy for Remembrance.
    Is there any that will remember?

The warnings came also to Pharaoh's folk.
They cried lies to Our signs, all of them,

so We seized them with the seizing of One
        mighty, omnipotent.

What, are your unbelievers better than those?
Or have you an immunity in the Scrolls? Or
do they say, 'We are a congregation that
        shall be succoured'?
Certainly the host shall be routed, and
        turn their backs.

Nay, but the Hour is their tryst,
and the Hour is very calamitous
        and bitter.
Surely the sinners are in error
        and insanity!

The day when they are dragged on their faces into the Fire:
'Taste now the touch of Sakar!'

Surely We have created everything
        in measure.

Our commandment is but one word,
        as the twinkling of an eye.

We have destroyed the likes of you;
        is there any that will remember?

Every thing that they have done
        is in the Scrolls,
and everything, great and small,
        is inscribed.

Surely the godfearing shall dwell amid gardens
        and a river
in a sure abode, in the presence of
        a King Omnipotent.   (Kor. 54.)

It was not only in the course of human history that evidences of
God's power and purpose were to be found—an encouragement to
Muslims in later centuries to trace and record the course of history.
The created world surrounding man on all sides abounded in signs
of God—a powerful stimulus to scientists and philosophers when
their studies revived in Islam.

It is God who splits the grain and the date-stone,
        brings forth the living from the dead; He
        brings forth the dead too from the living.

So that then is God; then how are you perverted?
He splits the sky into dawn,
and has made the night for a repose,
and the sun and moon for a reckoning.
That is the ordaining of the All-mighty, the All-knowing.
It is He who has appointed for you the stars, that
by them you might be guided in
the shadows of land and sea.
We have distinguished the signs for a people who know.
It is He who produced you from one living soul,
and then a lodging-place,
and then a repository.
We have distinguished the signs for a people who understand.
It is He who sent down out of heaven water, and
thereby We have brought forth
the shoot of every plant,
and then We have brought forth the green leaf of it,
bringing forth from it
close-compounded grain,
and out of the palm-tree, from the spathe of it,
dates thick-clustered,
ready to the hand, and
gardens of vines,
olives, pomegranates,
like each to each, and
each unlike to each.
Look upon their fruits when they fructify and ripen!
Surely, in all this are signs for a people who do believe.

(Kor. 6: 95–99.)

The Christians and the Jews of Arabia might have been expected
to be the first to recognize the truth of the new Message. But they
held fast to the perverted forms of the revelation accorded to Moses
and Jesus, and in the end many of them made common cause with
the pagans who denied and persecuted God's Messenger. Verses
were then revealed pregnant with consequences down to the present
day.

Cursed were the unbelievers of the Children
of Israel by the tongue of David, and
Jesus, Mary's son; that, for their rebelling
and their transgression.

They forbade not one another any dishonour
that they committed; surely evil were
        the things they did.
Thou seest many of them making unbelievers
their friends. Evil is that they have forwarded
to their account, that God is angered
against them, and in the chastisement they
        shall dwell forever.
Yet had they believed in God and the Prophet
and what has been sent down to him, they would
not have taken them as friends; but many of them
        are ungodly.
Thou wilt surely find the most hostile
of men to the believers are the Jews
and the idolaters; and thou wilt surely find
the nearest of them in love to the believers
are those who say 'We are Christians'; that
because some of them are priests and monks, and
        they wax not proud,
and when they hear what has been sent down
to the Messenger, thou seest their eyes
overflow with tears because of the truth
they recognize. They say, 'Our Lord,
we believe; so do Thou write us down
        among the witnesses.
Why should we not believe in God and the
truth that has come to us, and be eager
that our Lord should admit us with
        the righteous people?'
And God rewards them for what they say
with gardens underneath which rivers flow,
        therein dwelling forever;
that is the recompense of the good-doers.
But those who disbelieve, and cry lies
to Our signs—they are the inhabitants of
        Hell.   (Kor. 5: 80–88.)

'No compulsion is there in religion' (Kor. 2: 257): this proclamation
led in due course to the acceptance into the life of the Islamic
community of those whose consciences, or stubborn conformity,
kept them faithful to the beliefs and customs of their forefathers.
As for the believers who at last in increasing numbers rallied to
God's cause as preached by His Prophet Muhammad, they were

constituted into one nation serving God, united in the indissoluble bond of Muslim brotherhood.

> O believers, fear God as He should be feared,
> and see you do not die, save in surrender.
> And hold you fast to God's bond, together,
> and do not scatter; remember God's blessing
> upon you when you were enemies, and He brought
> your hearts together, so that by His blessing
> > you became brothers.
> You were upon the brink of a pit of Fire,
> and He delivered you from it; even so God
> makes clear to you His signs; so haply
> > you will be guided.
> Let there be one nation of you, calling to good,
> and bidding to honour, and forbidding dishonour;
> > those are the prosperers.
> Be not as those who scattered and fell into variance
> after the clear signs came to them; those there awaits
> > a mighty chastisement,

the day when some faces are blackened, and some faces whitened. As for those whose faces are blackened—'Did you disbelieve after you had believed? Then taste the chastisement for that you disbelieved!' But as for those whose faces are whitened, they shall be in God's mercy, therein dwelling forever.

> These are the signs of God We recite to thee
> > in truth,
> and God desires not any injustice to
> > living beings.
> To God belongs all that is in the heavens
> and in the earth, and unto Him all matters
> > are returned.

> You are the best nation ever brought forth
> to men, bidding to honour, and forbidding
> dishonour, and believing in God. Had the People
> of the Book believed, it were better for them;
> some of them are believers, but the most of
> > them are ungodly.   (Kor. 3: 97–106.)

God revealed in His Koran the fundamentals governing His religion of Islam, man's submission to His will. Belief in One God, the worship of God, prayers to God at certain set times and in private devotion, fasting one month in every year, the giving of alms, and if possible the pilgrimage to the Holy Places at least once in a life-time—these are the Pillars on which the fabric of Islam rests. A further duty is incumbent upon the believer—if Islam is attacked by the armed might of unbelief, then to take up arms and to fight in defence of the Faith.

> O believers, take your precautions; then
> move forward in companies, or move forward
>   all together.
> Some of you there are that are dilatory;
> then, if an affliction visits you, he says,
> 'God has blessed me, in that I was not
>   a martyr with them.'
> But if a bounty from God visits you, he
> will surely say, as if there had never been
> any affection between you and him,
> 'Would that I had been with them, to obtain
>   a mighty triumph!'
> So let them fight in the way of God who
> sell the present life for the world to come;
> and whosoever fights in the way of God
> and is slain, or conquers, We shall bring him
>   a mighty wage.
> How is it with you, that you do not fight
> in the way of God, and for the men,
> women, and children who, being abased,
> say, 'Our Lord, bring us forth from this city
> whose people are evildoers, and appoint to us
> a protector from Thee, and appoint to us
>   from Thee a helper'?
> The believers fight in the way of God,
> and the unbelievers fight in the idols' way.
> Fight you therefore against the friends
> of Satan; surely the guile of Satan
>   is ever feeble.   (Kor. 4: 73–78.)

Since the time of the Prophet down to the present day, the call to the Jihad when issued by properly constituted authority, and solemnly proclaimed after due deliberation, has never gone un-answered. The discussion of its proper conditions, like that of the proper conditions governing the Pillars of Islam, has for more than thirteen centuries exercised the acute minds and earnest care of successive generations of canon lawyers. They have been equally anxious to formulate and interpret correctly the many other Koranic ordinances governing the life of the Community—marriage, divorce, the punishment of crimes, the practise of trade or profession, commercial transactions, inheritance.

> To the men a share of what parents and kinsmen
> leave, and to the women a share of what
> parents and kinsmen leave, whether it be
> little or much, a share apportioned;
> and when the division is attended by
> kinsmen and orphans and the poor,
> make provision for them out of it,
> and speak to them honourable words.
> And let those fear who, if they left
> behind them weak seed, would be afraid
> on their account, and let them fear
> God, and speak words hitting the mark.
> Those who devour the property of orphans
> unjustly, devour Fire in their bellies,
> and shall assuredly roast in a Blaze.
> God charges you, concerning your children:
> to the male the like of the portion
> of two females, and if they be women
> above two, then for them two-thirds
> of what he leaves, but if she be one
> then to her a half; and to his parents
> to each one of the two the sixth
> of what he leaves, if he has children;
> but if he has no children, and his
> heirs are his parents, a third to his
> mother, or, if he has brothers, to his
> mother a sixth, after any bequest
> he may bequeath, or any debt.
> Your fathers and your sons—you know not
> which out of them is nearer in profit
> to you. So God apportions; surely God is
>   All-knowing, All-wise
> And for you a half of what your wives
> leave, if they have no children; but
> if they have children, then for you of what
> they leave a fourth, after any bequest
> they may bequeath, or any debt.

And for them a fourth of what you leave,
if you have no children; but if you
have children, then for them of what
you leave an eighth, after any bequest
you may bequeath, or any debt.
If a man or a woman have no heir
direct, but have a brother or a sister,
to each of the two a sixth; but if they
are more numerous than that, they share
equally a third, after any bequest
he may bequeath, or any debt not
prejudicial; a charge from God. God is
        All-knowing, All-clement.   (Kor. 4: 8–15.)

It is not surprising that the laws of inheritance should have come
to be regarded as among the most complex and exacting of all the
laws of Islam, or that the specialist in their administration should
have been required to possess high qualifications in mathematics.

For all that Allah reveals himself in His Koran as All-powerful
and All-compelling, swift to reward and swift to punish, infinitely
mighty above the feeble will and puny comprehension of man, yet
He also declares His boundless mercy and compassion, His un-
swerving justice.

God charges no soul save to its capacity;
standing to its account is what it has earned,
and against its account is what it has merited.   (Kor. 2: 286.)

Allah spoke comfortable words to His Prophet in the days when he
might well have despaired of his mission.

By the white forenoon
and the brooding night!
Thy Lord has neither forsaken thee nor hates thee
and the Last shall be better for thee than the First.
They Lord shall give thee, and thou shalt be satisfied.

Did He not find thee an orphan, and shelter thee?
Did He not find thee erring, and guide thee?
Did He not find thee needy, and suffice thee?

As for the orphan, do not oppress him,
and as for the beggar, scold him not;
and as for thy Lord's blessing, declare it.   (Kor. 93.)

Again, Allah consoled and encouraged His Messenger in terms which have cheered millions of the believers in the hour of doubt and despondency.

> Did We not expand thy breast for thee
> and lift from thee thy burden,
> the burden that weighed down thy back?
> Did We not exalt thy fame?

> So truly with hardship comes ease,
> truly with hardship comes ease.
> So, when thou art empty, labour,
> and let thy Lord be thy Quest.   (Kor. 94.)

It is therefore in perfect faith and tranquillity that the believer repeats the words of God.

> Our Lord,
> take us not to task
> if we forget, or make mistake.
> Our Lord,
> charge us not with a load such
> as Thou didst lay upon those before us.
> Our Lord,
> do Thou not burden us
> beyond what we have the strength to bear.
> And pardon us,
> and forgive us,
> and have mercy on us;
> Thou art our Protector.
> And help us against the people
> of the unbelievers.   (Kor. 2: 286.)

(Versions quoted from *The Koran Interpreted*.)

THREE

The Sunna and the Successors

Allah's message, delivered to His Prophet over many years and after his death collected from the scattered fragments and the tenacious memories of the faithful who heard it spoken into the volume of the Koran, made peace (apart from sporadic apostasies) between the warring tribes of Arabia and consolidated them into an ardent army of believers who in an astonishingly short time mastered a mighty empire. Vast wealth in booty and tribute poured into the treasury, and with it came the peril, and the fact, of corruption. Scandalized by luxury and all manner of excesses in high places, the conscience-keepers of Islam began to ask, 'Was it for this that we were called to be Allah's soldiers? What manner of life did the Messenger of Allah live, whose example it should be our high ambition to follow?' So the materials began to be gathered out of which the biography of Muhammad would later be written. These materials, anecdotes of the sayings and acts of the Prophet, covered a great variety of topics, and served many different ends. The student of the Koran turned to them for light to illuminate dark passages. The establisher of law and order sought in them for guidance in determining rules and regulations for the well-being of a society far more complex than that of early Mecca and Medina. The pious reverently combed the records for proofs and examples of Islam in action in the person of its founder, and of his immediate followers.

A saintly-minded man, a cobbler by trade living in Baghdad, the Islamic Babylon, in the ninth century AD, instructed his circle of disciples in the following terms.

The prophets, and the pious men who came after them, being made aware by God that He afflicted them in this world by means of plenty and the bestowing of possessions, put their trust in God, and not in their possessions. They were God's treasurers in respect of what He gave them to possess, spending it in fulfilment of their duties to God, without shortcoming or transgression or faintness.

They assigned no contrary interpretation to God's purpose, and took no pleasure in their possessions; their hearts were not concerned with what they possessed, nor did they exclude other men from its enjoyment.

So it is related of Solomon, son of David, and the possessions and special favours which God allowed him, when God says:

> 'This is Our gift; bestow or withhold
> without reckoning.'   (Kor. 38: 38.)

The commentators explain, 'not being called to account in the world to come, for it was a mean gift, a sign of God's favour to him'. The learned have related that Solomon used to feed his guests on whitened flour, and his children on unsifted corn, while he himself ate barley-meal. They also relate that Abraham never ate save with a guest. Sometimes no guest would come to him for three days together, and he would fast; and sometimes he would walk a parasang, less or more, to search out a guest.

Likewise, whenever the Prophet Job heard any man taking God's name in vain, he would return to his house and make expiation for him. The learned also relate that, although Joseph was over the treasures of the earth, yet he never ate his fill. Being asked concerning this, he said, 'I fear to take my fill, lest I forget what it is to hunger.' It is further related of Solomon, that one day the wind was supporting him, and the birds drew near to him, while Jinns and men were with him. Now he had on him a new shirt, and the garment clung to his body, and he felt pleasure thereat; and at once the wind was stilled, and set him down upon the earth. He said to the wind, 'What ails thee?' The wind replied, 'We were only commanded to obey thee so long as thou wast obedient to God.' So he considered within himself wherein his disobedience had occurred; and he remembered, and repented, and the wind forthwith supported him again. It is reported that the wind used every day to set him down several times for like cause.

These men therefore, whilst yet in the midst of their possessions, were in reality without them. They took delight in the recollection and service of God, and did not content themselves with their possessions, nor losing them found aught amiss. In nothing took they joy, so that they needed no cure or effort to expel such things from them. God said to His Prophet:

> Those are they whom God has guided; so
> follow their guidance.   (Kor. 6: 90.)

Now it was to this same Prophet that Gabriel appeared, at the time when Gabriel was transformed; and behold, an angel came down from heaven, who had never come down before. Gabriel said, 'I feared that it was he who had come down with a command for me'. He came to the Prophet with a greeting from God, and said to him: 'These are the keys of the treasures of the earth, that they may be thine, both gold and silver; in them thou mayest dwell until the Day of Resurrection, and they shall in no wise lessen the portion that is laid up for thee with God.' But this the Prophet did not choose, but said, 'Once I hunger, and once I am filled'; counting this to be an affliction and a trial from God. He did not reckon this to be a matter left by God to his free-will, for if it had been so he would have accepted it. He knew that the love of God consists in quitting this world, and turning from its gaudy splendours, for in this God had schooled him when He said:

> Stretch not thine eyes to that We have given
> pairs of them to enjoy—
> the flower of the present life, that We may try them therein.
> (Kor. 20: 131.)

It is also related that one day he put on a mantle with a badge, and then cast it from him, saying, 'Its badges almost distracted me. Take it, and bring me an Anbijani cloak'. It is likewise related that a gold seal-ring was made for him, wherewith to seal his letters to whatever person God commanded him to admonish; he put it on, and then cast it from his hand, saying to his companions, 'One glance at it, and one glance at you'. It is further related that on one occasion he changed the strap of his shoe, and put a new one in its place; then he said, 'Give me back the first strap'.

So every heart that is pure and undefiled yearns after the next world, and knows that God is watching over him; he therefore fears greatly lest he should secretly repose in the possession of this world, and take delight in aught that is of it. Such stories are common in the tales. The intelligent, quick-witted man needs but a hint to this.

When Muhammad urged his Companions to almsgiving, Abū Bakr brought all his possessions (and he was the most powerful of the people); and the Prophet said to him, 'What hast thou left for thy children?' 'God and His Prophet,' he replied, 'and with God I have an increase.' Note, then, that Abū Bakr reposed in God, not in any material thing; possessions had no value in his sight, for he took more pleasure in what was laid up with God. Seeing where his duty lay, he left nothing at all, saying, 'I have left God and His Prophet'. Then came 'Umar with half his possessions. The Prophet said, 'What hast thou left for thy children?' 'Half of my possessions,' he replied, 'and with me God has an increase.' So he gave one half of his possessions, saying, 'and with me God has an increase'. Lastly came 'Uthmān, ready to equip the 'army of difficulty' entirely, with all it had need of, and to dig the well of Rūma.

Note, then, that these men reckoned the material possession as belonging entirely to God. As for our statement that these men were without their possessions, whilst they were still in their hands, counting them as God's, this is proved by the saying attributed to the Prophet: 'We are the company of the prophets; we do not bequeath, and what we leave behind is for alms.' Note that during their lifetime they grudged God nothing; likewise they bequeathed nothing, but left it all to God, even as it was God's whilst it was in their hands; they neither added to it, nor bestowed it upon any man that came after them. Surely this is eloquent to the man who understands about God, and does what is just.

Such was the case with the Leaders of Guidance after the death of God's Prophet. When Abū Bakr succeeded to the leadership, and the world in its entirety came to him in abasement, he did not lift up his head on that account or make any pretensions. He wore a single garment which he used to pin together, so that he was known as the 'man of the two pins'. 'Umar ibn al-Khaṭṭāb, who also ruled the world in its entirety, lived on bread and olive-oil; his clothes were patched in a dozen places, some of the patches being of leather; and yet there were opened unto him the treasures of Chosroes and Caesar. As for 'Uthmān, he was like one of his slaves in dress and appearance. Of him it is related that he was seen coming out of one of his gardens with a faggot of firewood on his shoulders. When questioned on the matter he said, 'I wanted to see whether my soul would refuse'. Note then, that he was not heedless of his soul, and of taking care of it and training it. When 'Alī succeeded to the rule, he bought a waistband for four dirhams, and a shirt for five dirhams; finding the sleeve of the garment somewhat long, he went to a cobbler, and taking his knife cut off the sleeve level with the tips of his fingers; yet this same man divided the world right and left. When al-Zubair died, he left behind him debts amounting to more than two hundred thousand dinars, all contracted through liberality and extravagant generosity. Ṭalḥa ibn 'Ubaid Allāh gave away all his possessions, even to his family jewels, to beggars.

All this proves that these men were truly as God described them when He said: 'And expend of that unto which He has made you successors' (Kor. 57: 7). Yet not one man of the people of our time is ashamed of this, for all that he possesses doubtful things.

The highest degree of abstinence in this world was attained by those who conformed with God's wishes. These were men who understood of God; they were intelligent and loving, and they listened to God's condemnation of this world, and how He has belittled its worth, and does not approve of it as an abode for His saints. They were ashamed that God should see them inclining towards anything which He has condemned and not approved. This they imposed upon themselves as a duty, for which they sought no recompense from God. They nobly conformed with God's wishes, and God 'wastes not the wage' of those who do good (Kor. 9: 121). For those who conform with God in all their affairs are the most intelligent of His servants, and enjoy the highest price with God. So it is related that Abu 'l-Dardā' said, 'How sweet is the sleep of the intelligent, and how sweet their breakfasting! How they have despoiled the vigils and fastings of fools! An atom's weight of the man of piety and sure faith weighs more with God than mountains' worth of the deeds of those who are deceived.' Surely this is eloquent to the man who understands of God. God is our help.

It is related that 'Umar ibn 'Abd al-'Azīz once saw a youth who was pale, and said to him, 'Whence comes this paleness, boy?' The youth replied, 'From sicknesses and distempers, O Commander of the Faithful.' 'Tell me truly', said 'Umar. 'Sicknesses and distempers', said the youth. 'Umar said, 'Tell me how'. The youth replied, 'O Commander of the Faithful, I have turned away my soul from this world, and its stone and gold are become equal in my sight; and it is as if I behold the people of Paradise in Paradise visiting each other, and the people of Hell in Hell making moan together'. 'Umar said, 'How comes this, boy?' The youth said, 'Fear God, and He will pour forth knowledge copiously upon thee. Verily, when we were foreshortened of the knowledge of what we practised, we gave up practising even that which we knew; but if we had practised in accordance with what knowledge we had, we should have inherited a knowledge which our bodies could not have supported.'

It is related that Abū Bakr al-Ṣiddīq once asked for a drink. He was brought a vessel; but when he had put it to his mouth and tasted it, he thrust it aside and wept. On being asked about this, he said, 'I saw the Prophet of God one day, pushing away with his hands as though something were falling; and yet I saw nothing. So I said to him, "Messenger of God, I see thee pushing away with thy hands, and yet I see nothing." He said, "Yes: this present world appeared before me, in all its gauds; and I said, Get thee from me! But it answered, Thou shalt not escape from me, nor shall any escape from me that comes after thee." So I fear that it has overtaken me.'

Now there was in the vessel from which he drank water and honey; and yet he wept, being afraid of that.

It is related in a Tradition that the Companions of Muhammad neither ate to have pleasure, nor dressed to take delight. Another version says that when Muhammad's Companions grew in worldly power, after his death, and the whole world lay conquered at their feet, they wept because of it and were afraid, saying, 'We fear lest our good deeds have been rewarded in advance'. Wherefore let a man fear God, and be just, and let him cleave to the path of those who have gone before, acknowledging his shortcomings and asking God to support his stumblings.

The souls of the prophets and true believers were under God's mercy and protection, and so is every believer, according to the power of his faith. Now the confirmation of this is to be found in the Book and the Sunna. . . . For consider, when the Prophet stood in thanksgiving until his feet became swollen, he was giving thanks to God, and God commanded him to repose. It is also related that the Prophet used to worship in the mountain of Ḥirā' for a month or more; and so it is told that he used to be carefully on his guard against his enemy, until this verse was revealed: 'God will protect thee from men' (Kor. 5: 71). Then he gave up being on the watch, for he believed God's words when He told him that He would protect him; and he had sure faith, and was quiet. In like manner with all believers, faith comes to them after weakness.

So it was that the Prophet went out to the cave in the mountain called Thaur and hid himself, he and Abū Bakr al-Ṣiddīq, and then they departed to Medina, fleeing secretly; this was only a time of trial by God, for he was in the station of patience and endeavour. Then, after he had come to Medina, the Quraish made a raid against him on the day of the Battle of Uhud, and slew his Companions, and broke his tooth and dabbled his face with blood. Note then, that evil desire and labour clave to him and pursued him, as with all believers. Then after this he went forth, he and his Companions, crying joyfully as they drove the sacrificial beasts before them, intending to come to God's house; but the Quraish prevented him from entering Mecca, so that his men were thrown into confusion, and they halted in the place which is called al-Hudaibiya, and then returned, and did not enter the Sacred Territory. Now contrast this with the time when the period of trial was ended, and victory came; how he entered Mecca, slaying and converting whom he wished, and then he published an amnesty in the city. At that time God revealed:

Surely We have given thee
a manifest victory,
that God may forgive thee thy former and thy latter sins.
(Kor. 48: 1–2.)
(From *The Book of Truthfulness* by al-Kharrāz.)

Getting on for two centuries before the humble cobbler of Baghdad preached poverty and trust in God in face of the scandal of Abbasid luxury, the fiery preacher al-Ḥasan of Basra had been bold enough (and the zealots in Islam were heirs to all the boldness of the old Bedouins of the Desert) to write to the 'good caliph' 'Umar II warning him against the mortal danger of embracing the world, rehearsing the same legend of the Sunna of the prophets and the Prophet.

Beware of this world with all wariness; for it is like to a snake, smooth to the touch, but its venom is deadly. Turn away from whatsoever delights thee in it, for the little companioning thou wilt have of it; put off from thee its cares, for that thou hast seen its sudden chances, and knowest for sure that thou shalt be parted from it; endure firmly its hardships, for the ease that shall presently be thine. The more it pleases thee, the more do thou be wary of it; for the man of this world, whenever he feels secure in any pleasure thereof, the world drives him over into some unpleasantness, and whenever he attains any part of it and squats him down upon it, the world suddenly turns him upside down.

And again, beware of this world, for its hopes are lies, its expectations false; its easefulness is all harshness, muddied its limpidity. And therein thou art in peril: or bliss transient, or sudden calamity, or painful affliction, or doom decisive. Hard is the life of a man if he be prudent, dangerous if comfortable, being wary ever of catastrophe, certain of his ultimate fate.

Even had the Almighty not pronounced upon the world at all, nor coined for it any similitude, nor charged men to abstain from it, yet would the world itself have awakened the slumberer, and roused the heedless; how much the more then, seeing that God has Himself sent us a warning against it, an exhortation regarding it! For this world has neither worth nor weight with God; so slight it is, it weighs not with God so much as a pebble or a single clod of earth; as I am told, God has created nothing more hateful to Him than this world, and from the day He created it He has not looked upon it, so much He hates it. It was offered to our Prophet with all its keys and treasures, and that would not have lessened him in

God's sight by so much as the wing of a gnat, but he refused to accept it; and nothing prevented him from accepting it—for there is naught that can lessen him in God's sight—but that he knew that God hated a thing, and therefore he hated it, and God despised a thing, and he despised it, and God abased a thing, and he abased it. Had he accepted it, his acceptance would have been a proof that he loved it; but he disdained to love what his Creator hated, and to exalt what his Sovereign had debased.

As for Muhammad, he bound a stone upon his belly when he was hungry; and as for Moses, the skin of his belly showed as green as grass because of it. He asked naught of God, the day he took refuge in the shade, save food to eat when he was hungered; and it is said of him in the stories that God revealed to him, 'Moses, when thou seest poverty approaching, say, Welcome to the badge of the righteous! and when thou seest wealth approaching, say, Lo, a sin whose punishment has been put on aforetime!'

If thou shouldst wish, thou mightest name as a third the Lord of the Spirit and the Word (Jesus), for in his affair there is a marvel; he used to say, 'My daily bread is hunger, my badge is fear, my raiment is wool, my mount is my foot, my lantern at night is the moon, my fire by day is the sun, and my fruit and fragrant herbs are such things as the earth brings forth for the wild beasts and cattle. All the night I have nothing, yet there is none richer than I!' And if thou shouldst wish, thou mightest name as a fourth David, who was no less wonderful than these; he ate barley bread in his chamber, and fed his family upon bran meal, but his people on fine corn; and when it was night, he clad himself in sackcloth, and chained his hand to his neck, and wept until the dawn; eating coarse food, and wearing robes of hair.

All these hated what God hates, and despised what God despises; then the righteous thereafter followed in their path and kept close upon their tracks.

From *Sufism*, pp. 33–5.

Returning now to Baghdad of the Abbasids, we encounter in al-Muḥāsibī an eminent man of learning distressed by the divisions and schisms which had rent the body of Islam, and seeking in the true Sunna a better way to secure salvation. His sovereign remedy has been prescribed by successive revivalists down to this twentieth century.

It has come to pass in our days, that this community is divided into seventy and more sects; of these, one only is in the way of salvation, and for the rest, God knows best concerning them. Now I have not ceased, not so much as one moment of my life, to consider well the differences into which the community has fallen, and to search after the clear way and the true path, whereunto I have searched both theory and practice, and looked for guidance on the road to the world to come, to the directing of the theologians. Moreover, I have studied much of the doctrine of Almighty God, with the interpretations of the lawyers, and reflected upon the various conditions of the community, and considered its diverse doctrines and sayings. Of all this I understood as much as was appointed for me to understand; and I saw that their divergence was as it were a deep sea, wherein many had been drowned, and but a small band escaped therefrom; and I saw every party of them asserting that salvation was to be found in following them, and that he would perish who opposed them.

Then I considered the various orders of men. For some there are who are acquainted with the nature of the world to come, and do prefer it; such are hard to find, but they are very precious. And some know nothing of this; to be far from them is a boon. Some make show to be like them that know, but are in love with the present world, and prefer it. Some carry an uncertain knowledge of the other world, but with that knowledge seek after respect and elevation, obtaining through their otherworldliness worldly goods. Some carry a knowledge, but know not the interpretation of that knowledge. Some make a show to be like the godly, and to resemble good folk, only they have no strength in them; their knowledge lacks in penetration, and their judgment cannot be trusted. Some possess intellect and intelligence, but are lacking in piety and goodness. Some secretly conform with their desires, being ambitious for worldly gain, and seeking to be rulers of men. Some are devils in human form; they turn their faces from the world to come, and rush madly after this world, greedy to collect it, avid of enrichment in it; report says they live, but in truth they are dead; with them virtue becomes an abomination, and evil-doing a virtue.

In all these classes of men I sought for my aim, but could not find it. Then I sought out the guidance of them that were right guided, looking for rectitude, truth and guidance; I looked to knowledge for direction, thinking deeply and considering long. Then it was made clear to me, from God's Book and the Prophet's Sunna, and the consensus of believers, that the pursuit of desire blinds to right direction and leads astray from truth, causing one to abide long in blindness. So I began to expel desire from my heart. I paused before the divergences of the community, ardently seeking the party

of salvation, and anxiously avoiding fatal schisms and sects bound
for ruin; for I feared that I might die before finding the light. With
all my soul I sought for the path of salvation; and I found, through
the consensus of believers regarding the revealed Book of God, that
the path of salvation consists in laying hold of the fear of God, and
performing His ordinances, abstaining from what He has made
lawful and unlawful alike and following all that He has prescribed,
sincere obedience to God, and the imitation of His Prophet.

So I sought to inform myself of God's ordinances, and the Prophet's practices, as well as the pious conduct of the saints. I saw
that there was both agreement and contrariety; but I found that
all men were agreed that God's ordinances and the Prophet's
practices were to be found amongst those who, knowing God and
knowing of God, laboured to win His pleasure. I therefore sought
from among the community men such as these, that I might follow
in their footsteps and acquire knowledge from them; and I saw that
they were exceedingly few, and that their knowledge was utterly
swept away. As the Prophet said, 'Islam came a stranger, and shall
return a stranger as it began.'

Great then was my trouble, when I could not find godfearing men
to be my guides; for I feared lest death should suddenly overtake
me while my life was yet confused. I persevered in my quest for
that which I must by all means know, not relaxing my caution nor
falling short in counsel. Then the Merciful God gave me to know a
people in whom I found my godfearing guides, models of piety,
that preferred the world to come above this world. They ever
counselled patience in hardship and adversity, acquiescence in fate,
and gratitude for blessings received; they sought to win men to a
love of God, reminding them of His goodness and kindness and
urging them to repentance unto Him. These men have elaborated
the nature of religious conduct, and have prescribed rules for piety,
which are past my power to follow. I therefore knew that religious
conduct and true piety are a sea wherein the like of me must needs
drown, and which such as I can never explore.

Then God opened unto me a knowledge in which both proof was
clear and decision shone, and I had hopes that whoever should draw
near to this knowledge and adopt it for his own would be saved. I
therefore saw that it was necessary for me to adopt this knowledge
and to practise its ordinances; I believed in it in my heart, and
embraced it in my mind, and made it the foundation of my faith.
Upon this I have built my actions, in it moved in all my doings;
and I ask God to quicken me to gratitude for His blessing me
therewith, and to enable me to keep the ordinances He has thereby

taught me. Yet know I well my shortcoming in this, and that I can never thank my God for all that He has done for me.

From *Sufism*, pp. 47–50.

The 'godfearing guides' to whom al-Muḥāsibī referred were the Sufis, men dedicated to the service of God and the imitation of His Prophet who, in times when the empire of Islam seemed wholly given over to worldly glory and comfort, in their little circles and brotherhoods sought to re-enact the simple and otherworldly lives traditionally credited to the Companions of Muhammad. They discussed amongst themselves the nature of prophecy, and how the Messengers of God stood in relation to the angels and the saints.

The majority of the Sufis refrain from entering into the question whether the Messengers are to be preferred above the Angels, or *vice versa*, saying that superiority belongs to those whom God has preferred, and that it is a matter of neither essence nor act. Some however prefer the messengers, and some the angels. Muḥammad ibn al-Faḍl said, 'The whole body of angels is more excellent than the whole body of believers, but there are certain ones among the believers who are more excellent than the angels'. This is as much as to say that the prophets are more excellent.

They are agreed that certain of the messengers are more excellent than others, citing God's words: 'And We have preferred some Prophets over others' (Kor. 17: 57). They refuse however to specify which of them is preferred, and which not, thereby agreeing with the behest of the Prophet: 'Do not choose between the prophets.' Nevertheless they lay it down as a principle that Muhammad is the most excellent of all the prophets, basing their doctrine on his saying, 'I am the lord of the sons of Adam, without boasting: Adam and all after him are beneath my banner', and other of his sayings; as well as on the words of God, 'You are the best nation ever brought forth to men' (Kor. 3: 106)—and since they were the best of nations, and they were his nation, it follows that their prophet was the best of prophets—this, and the other proofs of his pre-eminence which are to be found in the Koran.

They are all agreed that the prophets are more excellent than men, and that there is no man who can contest with the prophets in excellence, be he true believer, saint, or any other, however great his power and mighty his position. The Prophet said to 'Alī, 'These twain are the lords of the elders of the people of Paradise, both former and latter, save only the prophets and messengers,' referring in these words to Abū Bakr and 'Umar, and implying that they are the best of mankind after the prophets. Abū Yazīd al-Bisṭāmī said, 'The final end of true believers is the first state of the prophets, and the end of the prophets has no attainable goal'. Sahl ibn 'Abd Allāh said, 'The purposes of the gnostics reach as far as the veil, and they there halt with glance cast down. Then leave is given them, and they make greeting; and they are clothed with the robe of divine strength, and are assigned exemption from error. The purposes of the prophets, however, move around the Throne, and are clothed with lights; their values are exalted, and they are joined with the Almighty; and He causes their personal ambitions to pass away, and strips off their quality of desire, and causes them to be concerned only with Him and for Him.' Abū Yazīd said, 'If a single atom of the Prophet manifested itself to creation, naught that is beneath the Throne would endure it'. He also said, 'The gnosis and knowledge of men is, compared with the Prophet's, like the drop of moisture which oozes out of the top of a bound waterskin'.

(From *The Doctrine of the Sufis*, pp. 53–5.)

From this it was but a short step to the establishment of a cult of the Prophet which, though always stopping short of worship (which in Islam belongs to Allah alone), gave a degree of colour to Europe's medieval fantasy that the Muslims adored an idol called Mommet or Mahound. In the mystical odes of the Egyptian poet Ibn al-Fāriḍ, who died in 632/1235, the Spirit of Muhammad is identified with the First Epiphany of the Godhead. Using the language and imagery of the romantic rhapsodists of ancient Arabia, the poet woos his spiritual beloved as passionately and as eloquently as ever Majnūn courted Lailā, or Jamīl his adored Buthaina.

Be proud in thy coquetry, for so 'tis thy right to be;
    and take thou the power and rule, as Beauty hath given thee
        leave.
'Tis thine to command; decree whate'er thou desirest, for lo!
    Loveliness hath herself made thee governor over me.
And if in my ruin alone I may become thy intimate,
    O hasten now my ruin, and let my life be thy ransom;
and as thou wishest, try me in this my passion for thee,
    for whatsoever thy pleasure is, that is my choice;
and whate'er be my case, thou hast better title to me
    than myself, since but for thee I had never been.
Glory enough it is for me, to be humble and lowly
    in loving thee, for truly I am not thy peer;
and if I scarce can presume to union with thee, so lofty
    is that relationship, while thy claim over me is secure,

it sufficeth me to be suspected of loving thee,
    and to be numbered of my kinsmen among thy slain.
There belongeth to thee in the tribe one that is perished, yet liveth
    through thee, one that hath found sweet delight to perish in
    passion's cause,
a slave in bondage, yet never he fawned to be freed; hadst thou
    declared thyself rid of him, he would not have let thee go.
Entranced was he by a beauty which thou hadst veiled in a
    majesty;
    and therein he deemed torture to be all sweetness;
and whene'er the security of hope brought thee nigh him,
    straightway the fear of the reason drove thee far from him,
so, when he cometh toward thee, boldly urged by his eagerness,
    that moment he dreadeth thee with all the shrinking of terror.
My heart is dissolved: O give me leave to desire thee,
    while still a remnant is left to my heart to hope for thee;
or command sleep to visit mine eyelids, that are nigh
    to disobedience, yea, while even in obeying thee,
and it may be that in slumber the fancy will come to me,
    and inspire me to know that secretly thou art journeying by
    night to me.
But if thou quickenest not my dying breath with the sweet relief
    of desire, and thy survival requireth that I should perish,
and if the sacred law of passion prohibits sleep
    to close mine eyelids, and makes it unlawful for me to meet thee,
O leave to me at least an eye, that haply one day,
    before I die, I may see therewith one who hath seen thee.
Yet alas, how far from me is this that I have yearned for!
    And indeed, how should mine eye aspire even with its lid to kiss
    thy dust?

And if any messenger came to me with good tidings of thy
    compassion,
    and my being were still in my grasp, I would cry to him, 'Take it!'
Surely enough is the blood that has flowed from my wounded
    eyelids
    for thee: is this that has come to pass enough for thee?
So protect from thy hatred one sore wearied because of thee,
    that desired only thee, ere ever he knew of passion.
Suppose that the Slanderer in his ignorance hath forbidden thy
    lover
    to come to thee, yet tell me—who hath forbidden thee to unite
    with him?

Beauty hath summoned him to adore thee; who then,
    thinkest thou, hath summoned thee to repulse him?
Who, thinkest thou, hath decreed that thou shouldest shrink from
    me?
And who hath decreed that thou shouldest love another?
Now, by my broken spirit, my humiliation, my abasement,
    by my desperate need, by my poverty, by thy great wealth,
deliver me not to the powers of fortitude, that hath already
    betrayed me; for lo, I am become one of thine own poor weak-
    lings.
Of old, when thou wert cruel to me, I had some endurance:
    now God give thee consolation, for my endurance is dead.
How long thou hast shrunk from me! Perchance thou wilt have
    compassion
    on my complaining, if but by giving ear to my cry 'Perchance'.
False, infamous tales have the rumour-mongers spread that thou
    hast
    broken with me, yea, and put it about that I have forgotten my
    ancient passion.

Not with hearts such as theirs did I love, that I could console me
    a single day for the loss of thee—God forbid! Let them rave as
    they will:
how could I forget thee, seeing mine eye, whenever
    a lightning-flash gleams, turneth eager to meet thee?
If thou smilest behind the flash of thy veil,
    or if thou breathest upon the breeze thy tidings,
then I am glad at heart, for the dawn of thy glittering teeth
    hath shone to mine eyes, and the scent of thy perfume is wafted
    abroad.
All who dwell in thy sanctuary do desire thee,
    but I, even I alone, for all who dwell in thy sanctuary.
Indwelling in thee is a truth that hath adorned thee to my reason's
    eye;
    wherefore my sight is busied with thy adornments.
Thou hast excelled in beauty and goodness all the people
    of loveliness; and they have dire need of thy inner truth.
All lovers at the Last Day shall be raised up under
    my banner, and all the lovely ones shall be raised under thine.
Not wasting sickness hath turned me from thee: how then,
    O lovely coquette, hath it turned thee from me?
Nigh thou art unto me, for all that thou art far from me;
    yea, and I have found in thy cruelty a true compassion.

Yearning hath taught mine eye to be watchful through all the
     night,
   so that it now beholdeth thee, even without slumber.
O sweet the night, wherein I trapped thee nightly journeying,
   spreading out my vigilance to be my nets!
The moon at the full might have deputy been to the phantom of thy
     bright countenance, shining upon my wakeful eye, so close it
     resembled thee;
and so thou showedst thyself in a form not thine, to an eye
   that rejoiced in thee; and naught else but thee I beheld:
So Abraham (ere I was born) turned about his gaze,
   what time he was watching the heavens.
And now the shadows of night are for us through thee full of
     brightness,
   since thou hast given us guidance in thine own radiant light;
and whensoe'er thou to outward sense art absent from my
     beholding,
   I cast my gaze on my inward heart, and there I encounter thee.
The people of Badr were a cavalcade in which thou didst journey
     by night; nay, rather they travelled by day, in the glow of thy
     luminousness.
And if men borrow lights from my outward form, not strange is it,
   since my inward heart is thy lodging-place.
The perfume of musk is wafted abroad whenever my name
   is mentioned, since thou didst summon me to kiss thy mouth;
and the odour of ambergris is redolent in every assembly,
   and it a remembrance giving expression to thy sweet scent.
The beauty of every lovely thing that revealeth itself said
     unto me,
   'Take thy joy in me'; but I declared, 'My purpose lieth beyond
     thee.
I have a beloved, on account of whom I perceive thee too to be
     troubled:
   others—not I—have been deluded; I see thee in him alone to
     have meaning.
If he turneth his back, he doometh the death of all spirits;
   or if he revealeth himself, he enslaveth all godly men.
My guidance is changed to error because of him, and for rectitude
   I receive misguiding, and my decent covering is turned into
     shameless exposure.
My heart hath declared the unity of his love; to glance at thee
   is therefore polytheism, and I am not one who believes in
     plurality.'

O thou who upbraidest because of one, for whose sake Beauty
  herself,
    like me, is distraught by passion (let me have none of thy
      brotherhood!)
hadst thou beheld that loveliness by reason of which he made me
  captive—
    but thou wilt never descry it—surely thou too wouldst have
      been taken captive.
And when at last he appeared to me in his glory, I forgave
  my sleeplessness, saying to mine eye, 'Accept this in return for
    that!'

In another famous ode—and these poems continue to be recited by
heart by the Sufi mystics—Ibn al-Fāriḍ varied his usual erotic and
panegyric imagery and employed instead the bacchanalian convention which had already been established by the pre-Islamic bards,
and was refined into great art by that boon-companion of caliphs,
Abū Nuwās. Before quoting this ode in full, let us analyse its contents and see how the legend of the Spirit of Muhammad, carrier of
the wine-cup of revelation, had been refined into a splendid transcendental allegory after six centuries.

The poet opens by making an unambiguous 'reprobate's confession': he and his companions in the mystical circle have drunk
wine at the mention of the Beloved's name—but it is a Wine with
which they were intoxicated, before ever the Vine was created, this
Vine being the physical universe. What is the Wine then? Surely
the source of holy rapture, the Love of God manifested in His creation, and indwelling in the human soul. The Moon, symbol of the
radiant Spirit of Muhammad, is the cup in which that sun-like Wine
is contained; this cup of esoteric knowledge is passed round the
circle of Muslim mystics by the 'new moon', whose crescent shape is
perhaps intended to suggest the Elder bent by long devotions; the
lights of spiritual illumination, kindled by the fervour of the Wine
mingling with the mystics' souls, twinkle like stars in a darkened
firmament.

Once the Wine was all-pervading, but now its glory is greatly
dimmed; only its fragrance and unimaginable lustre have guided
the poet's footsteps to the inn where it may still be found, the inner
circle of the Sufi mysteries, for all that is left of it in these latter
days is as it were a last gasp, hidden deep in the breasts of the
faithful few. Indeed, it has wholly vanished but for its name; yet
the mention of its name alone suffices to intoxicate the innocent
mystic. The very thought of the Wine brings great joy and drives

away sorrow; the observation of its effect upon the saints is enough to transport the neophyte.

The Wine's powers, had they been put to the test, would have proved truly miraculous, bringing the dead to life, healing the sick, making the paralysed to walk and the dumb to speak, unstopping the stopped-up nostrils, giving light to those in darkness, restoring sight to the blind and hearing to the deaf, rendering harmless the snake's venomous bite, mending the mind deranged, spurring warriors to superhuman valour, endowing all amiable qualities, strengthening the resolve of the irresolute, converting the fool to prudence.

The attributes of this Wine are those of the four elements themselves, but without their gross materiality. It inspires matchless eloquence, and moves the heart to infinite gladness. It existed before Time was, and through it all living things subsisted from the beginning in a unification of spirit with Spirit. The fatherhood of Adam relates only to the carnal soul; the immortal spirit is the child of the Vine, being an epiphany of the Love of God. This spirit informs the body with its own ethereality, while the body extends the spirit's dominion over the material world, the Vine in which the Wine is perpetually renewed; but the Wine itself exists from all eternity, being the seal set before creation upon all succeeding ages.

To drink that Wine is no sin, as some allege; rather is it the unforgivable sin not to taste of it. The Christians, though never having drunk of this Wine, knew of it, and therefore experienced some part of its intoxication; the poet himself, being a Muslim born, has always been and will always be enraptured by it. He charges his hearers to drink it pure; or if mingled, then only watered with the gleaming moisture of the Beloved's mouth, the teachings of the Prophet. It is to be found in the mystic circle, to the accompaniment of music; it drives out all sorrow, and accords the mystic partaking of it a sense of transcending Time even for the brief space of his holy rapture.

Not to drink of this Wine is to miss all the true gladness and wisdom of life; he that refuses to be a mystic may well weep for himself and his wasted sum of days.

> We quaffed upon the remembrance of the Beloved a wine
> wherewith we were drunken, before ever the vine was created.
> The moon at the full its cup was; itself was a sun, that a crescent
> moon
> passeth round; how many a star gleams forth, when that wine is
> mingled!

And but for its fragrance, never had I been guided unto its tavern;
and but for its radiance, never had the mind's imagination pictured
  it.
And Time hath not left aught of it, save a last gasp;
as if its being vanished were a concealment in the breasts of
  human reasons;
though if it be but mentioned among the tribe, the people of the
  tribe
become intoxicated, yet guilty of no disgrace or crime.
From the very bowels of the vats it has mounted up,
and naught remains of it in truth but a name:
yet if on a day it cometh into the thought of a man,
great joy will dwell in him, and all sorrow depart.
And had the boon-companions beheld no more than the impress of
  the seal upon its vessel,
that impress would surely have made them drunken, without the
  wine itself;
and had they sprinkled therewith the dust of a dead man's tomb,
the spirit would surely have returned unto him, and his body been
  quickened.
And had they but cast, in the shade of the wall where groweth its
  vine,
a sick man, and he nigh to death, his sickness would have departed
  from him;
and had they brought nigh to its tavern one paralysed, he would
  have walked;
yea, and the dumb would have spoken upon the mention of its
  flavour;
and had the breaths of its perfume been wafted through the East,
and in the West were one whose nostrils were stopped, the sense of
  smell would have returned to him;
and had the hand of one touching it been stained as with henna
  from the cup of it,
he would not have strayed in the night-time, having in his hand
  such a star;
and had it been secretly unveiled to one that was blind, forthwith
  would he
have been dowered with sight; and the deaf would hear at the
  sound of its filtering;
and had there set forth a cavalcade seeking the soil of its native
  earth,
and there were among the riders one stung by a snake, the poison
  would not have mischiefed him;

and had an enchanter drawn its name on the forehead of one afflicted
with madness, the letters drawn would have cured his sickness;
and had its name been inscribed above the banner of an army,
surely that superscription would have inebriated all beneath the banner.
It amendeth the manners of the boon-companions; and by its aid
he that was irresolute is guided to the path of firm resolve;
and he whose hand never knew munificence becometh suddenly generous;
and he is clement in time of rage in whom no forbearance was.
And the fool of the tribe, had his lips attained to kiss its filter,
that kiss would have endowed him with the very essence of its fine qualities.
They tell me, 'Describe that wine, for thou art well-informed of its description.' Indeed, I have some knowledge of its attributes:
purity (yet 'tis not watered), subtility (yet not as with air),
light (and no fire there burning), spirit (not clothed in body)—
beauties, the which do guide its describers aright to praise it,
so that in prose and verse they tell of it with beauteous words;
and he who knew it not rejoices when its name is mentioned,
as Nuʿm's yearning lover whenever Nuʿm is named.
More ancient than all existing things was the tale of it told
in eternity, when neither was shape nor trace to be seen;
and there did all things subsist through it for a purpose wise,
whereby it was veiled from all that had not an understanding mind.
And my spirit was distraught with love for it, in such manner that the twain
were mingled together in unification, and not as a body is permeated by another:
'tis a soul and no wine there, when Adam is reckoned my father,
but a wine and no soul there, when the vine thereof is reckoned my mother.
Now, the subtility of the vessels is really consequential upon the subtility
of the inward truths, and the inward truths augment by means of the vessels:
and the division truly has taken place, while yet the whole is one:
our spirits being the wine, and our corporeal shapes the vine.
Before it is no 'before', and no 'after' after it;
and as for the priority of all posterities, the Wine has this for a surety:
and ere Time's term was straitened, then was its pressing-time:

after the Wine was our father's age, itself being orphan.

They said then, ''Tis sin that thou hast quaffed.' Nay, but this I drank

was truly, as I view, that the which it were sin to eschew.

Good health to the folk of the monastery! How oft they were drunken with it;

and yet they had never quaffed it, but only aspired thereto.

But I—I was set awhirl with it, before ever I grew to manhood,

and with me that rapture shall abide forever, though my bones may crumble.

I charge thee to take it pure; yet if thou desirest to mingle it,

to turn away from the Beloved's mouth's lustre were wrong indeed.

So look thou for it in the tavern, and seek its unveiling there

to the tuneful notes of melodies, wherewith 'tis a noble prize:

for ne'er did it dwell with sullen care in the selfsame place,

as sorrow has ne'er cohabited with sweet tunefulness,

and be thy intoxication therewith but the life of an hour, yet shalt

thou see Time's self become an obedient slave, and thine the command of it.

No joy is there in this world for him who lives sober;

and he that dies not of drunkenness misses true prudence—

then let him weep for himself, whose life is all wasted

and he not in all his days of the Wine taken part or portion.

                    (From *The Mystical Poems of Ibn al-Fāriḍ*.)

FOUR

Wisdom from the East

The ideal form of Islamic government is a theocracy, the foundation God's Speech in the Koran, the elaboration modelled on the Sunna of His Prophet. This has been the heavenly model which has inspired the labours of Muslim reformers now for nearly fourteen centuries—a model of a City of God extended through the outspread empire of Islam, and believed to have been attained under the rule of the first four 'right-guided' caliphs.

But the rapid diffusion of Islam, and the pressing need to organize the newly-converted peoples and provinces into a monolithic state, brought in quick time a multitude of complex and baffling problems unimagined by the fervent spirits of the early faithful. Counsels were not lacking on how those problems might be solved. Priority in time and esteem was naturally accorded to a purely Islamic solution; and to this end Koran and Sunna were diligently studied, the first resource of the constitutional and civil lawyers, the theologians, the teachers of religion, rite and morals.

Conquered Persia brought into the arena of ideas and speculation the traditions of a sophisticated and, for many centuries, successful statecraft expressing itself in a wealth of popular wisdom. The Persians, clever at manipulating human affairs as much in defeat as in triumph, won their opportunity of reorganizing the Islamic empire when the Umayyads were driven from power. One such attempt, brief and ill-fated but with lasting consequences, was made by the learned and ingenious Persian whose career we shall briefly summarize, and whose writings we shall offer as well illustrating the kind of advice tendered by Persian experts to their rulers from time immemorial, and now to their foreign masters.

The Abbasid caliph al-Manṣūr, founder of Baghdad, having defeated a dangerous conspiracy, desired as an act of royal clemency to pardon his uncle 'Abd Allāh who had aspired to wrest the caliphate from him. To mark the solemnity of the occasion he decided to draw up a deed of amnesty which should be binding on both parties, and sought the advice of 'Abd Allāh's brother 'Īsā. The latter recommended to him his personal secretary, a man of Persian descent experienced in the drafting of documents. Al-Manṣūr accepted 'Īsā's counsel, and Ibn al-Muqaffa' secured the commission.

The Persian expert was in his middle thirties at the time (about AD 757), and already had many years of confidential duties behind him. His father Dadoe had been a tax-collector in a place called Jur or Firuzabad in the province of Fars; accused, not implausibly, of extortion, he was so harshly handled in the torture which preceded his confession that his hand shrivelled and he remained marked for life. His son, whose given name was Rozbeh, came to be better known as Ibn al-Muqaffa', the Son of the Shrivelled Man. Of his education we know nothing, but may reasonably deduce that it included a thorough grounding in Pahlavi, the ancient language of his people, and Arabic, the conquerors' speech. Like many a Persian before and after him, he attained such a mastery of the foreign idiom as to surpass even the best of its native exponents. Amongst his friends was 'Abd al-Ḥamīd ibn Yaḥyā, secretary to the last of the Umayyads, commonly accounted the inventor of *inshā'* or elegant Arabic prose.

In due course the draft prepared by Ibn al-Muqaffa' was brought to al-Manṣūr for his approval. The caliph read it through, and flew into a sovereign rage; for the ingenious Persian had inserted a clause to the effect that 'if at any time the Commander of the Faithful should act perfidiously towards his uncle 'Abd Allāh ibn 'Alī, his wives should be divorced from him, his horses should be confiscated for the service of Allah, his slaves should become free, and the Muslims loosed from their allegiance towards him.' Al-Manṣūr ordered Sufyān ibn Mu'āwiya al-Muhallabī the governor of Basra to put the insolent clerk to death, leaving the method of execution to his imagination.

Sufyān obeyed his master's command with the greater alacrity, since he was smarting from the contempt with which Ibn al-Muqaffa' had persistently favoured him. The governor had an uncommonly large nose and whenever Ibn al-Muqaffa' visited him he would enquire, 'How are the pair of you?' On one occasion Sufyān, trying to be clever, boasted that he 'never had reason to repent of keeping silence'; which drew from Ibn al-Muqaffa' the retort, 'Dumbness becomes you excellently; so why should you repent of it?' Now Sufyān was glad to settle the score once and for all. He directed the furnace to be stoked, then he had the executioner hack off the prisoner's limbs one by one and throw them in the flames, finishing up with his trunk.

An end so premature and so violent was certainly a poor recompense for a man who had done more in his short life than any before him to transform Arabic prose into a polished medium for literature, a task he accomplished largely through translation. From Greek— or perhaps rather from a Pahlavi intermediary—he is stated to have rendered into Arabic Aristotle's *Categories*, *Hermeneutics* and *Analytics*, and Porphyry's *Eisagoge*, thus laying solid foundations for the study of logic in Islam. Out of his native Pahlavi he translated the *Khvadaināmagh*, that ancient 'Book of Kings' which later furnished Firdausī with inspiration and materials for his *Shāh-nāma*, as well as two manuals of statecraft and royal etiquette. All these massive productions have perished, apart from casual citations. But most famous of all, he translated the work known in Arabic as *Kalīla wa-Dimna*, that splendid collection of animal fables which mounts back to the Sanskrit *Pancatantra* and is one of the world's great classics.

As will be seen from the extract from this book which follows (and the version has been based on a compromise between the different recensions), this repertory of animal fables is by no means the simple entertainment it might at first be presumed to be. The stories are a shrewd and sometimes caustic commentary on political life under an absolute monarchy, and it is not far-fetched to suppose that the portraits presented are thinly disguised cartoons of the entourage of the caliph himself. The animals are made to deliver themselves of sententious wisdom matured through centuries of Sassanian rule, and the work itself clearly belongs to the 'Mirror for Princes' tradition. Immensely popular in its Arabic dress and numerous Persian adaptations, calligraphed repeatedly in finely illustrated manuscripts, the *Kalīla wa-Dimna* epitomizes and splendidly exemplifies that worldly 'wisdom from the East' which came to supplement—and, as purists would say, to corrupt—the simpler traditions of Arabia and the holier teachings of Koran and Sunna.

The Lion and the Ox

This chapter tells about two intelligent and clever men. One was cast astray from the straight path by social ambition; moreover his reasoning power had been overcome by the strength of his appetite, and the light of his perception shrouded in the veil of darkness; as a consequence he was ruined both materially and spiritually, and lost his chance in this world and the next. The other man sat upon the throne of contentment irradiated by the light of guidance, and wore upon his brows the crown of true nobility; his powerful intellect enabled him to realize all his designs and desires, and he could therefore hold his head high both sides of the grave. Let the man of perfect understanding look into this story and he will realize that mundane longings and mortal pleasures bear no fruit other than repining, whereas if he clothes himself in the vest and coat of obedience to God's commandments he will enjoy the fruits not only of worldly success but also of eternal felicity.

King Dabshaleem of India spoke thus to Bidpay, Chief of the Brahmins: 'Expound to me the parable of two men who loved one another, but by reason of a cunning slanderer stirring up mischief between them the fabric of their friendship was shattered, and converted into enmity and separation.'

Bidpay replied: 'Whenever two friends are afflicted by the inter-ference of an evil rogue, inevitably they fall apart and break with each other. Among the many examples and instances of that is the story of the Lion and the Ox.'

'What kind of history is that?' the king asked.

'Listen, and I will tell you,' answered Bidpay. And he related as follows.

There was once a wealthy merchant who had several grown-up sons, but they turned away from learning a trade and earning an honest living and instead stretched out their hands to squander their father's fortune. Their father exhorted and chided them much, as he thought fit to do, and these were among the wise words he uttered.

'O my sons, the people of this world seek after three goals, and do not arrive at them except they possess four qualities. The three goals at which men aim are an ample livelihood, high esteem among their fellows, and the heavenly reward. The four conditions that are necessary for achieving these ambitions are the acquisition of wealth by respectable means, the careful preservation of a fortune once it has been won, the prudent expending of one's substance so as to secure a good life and satisfy one's friends and family whilst pro-viding for the journey to eternity, and the guarding of one's soul so far as possible against the various accidents and vicissitudes which may corrupt it. Whoever neglects any one of these four qualities, destiny will assuredly interpose a veil of opposition between him and his desires. For if he turns away from earning a living and plying a craft, he cannot acquire the means to a good livelihood for himself, much less look after others. If he wins a fortune and neglects to nurse and increase it, he soon becomes poor; so collyrium, which women daub upon their eyes, though it is used but a little at a time, in the end is consumed entirely. If he is not energetic to guard and augment his wealth, but spends it recklessly, he will certainly regret his folly and the tongue of censure will be shot out against him; whilst if he stingily declines to use it on right and proper occasions he is no better than a beggar, being deprived of all worldly pleasures. Moreover the decrees of heaven and the accidents of fortune will nevertheless scatter his wealth from his hands in time, like a cistern into which water is continuously pouring, but there is no waste-pipe adequate to carry off as much as is coming in; inevitably the water seeks a way out through the sides and oozes, and oozes until the cistern splits and the water all runs to waste.'

The sons listened attentively to their father's advice and good counsel and recognized fully the wisdom and profit of his remarks. The eldest brother thereupon turned his attention to commerce and elected to go on a far journey, taking with him two oxen, one named Shatraba and the other Bandaba. On the way he came upon a bog, into which Shatraba promptly got stuck. They managed after considerable labour to pull him out, but now the beast could not budge; the merchant therefore hired a man to look after Shatraba and care for him until he should regain his strength, when he was to bring him after him. In a day or two however the hired man wearied of his charge and left Shatraba to his fate, hastening forward to rejoin his master, whom he informed that the beast was done for.

After a little while Shatraba recovered, and wandered off in search of pasture. Presently he came to a broad meadow adorned with all manner of succulent grasses and aromatic herbs, such as the Garden of Eden itself would have bit the finger of envy to behold, and Paradise looked upon with eyes wide open in amazed stupefaction. Shatraba approved of it heartily and stayed there for quite a while, happily chewing the rich cuds that fortune had put in his way. It was not long before he became fat and prosperous, and the insolence of ease and the intoxication of plenty overcame him, so that he lowed with ever greater sprightliness.

Now there lived in those parts a lion, and many wild and savage beasts attendant upon his command, the lion comporting himself amongst them like some arrogant, self-opinionated tyrant. It so happened that he had never seen an ox, nor heard its bellow before; so that when Shatraba's lowing reached his ears he was seized by fear and panic. Not wanting the other beasts to discover that he was afraid, he stood his ground quietly and made no movement in any direction. Amongst his retinue were two jackals, one called Kalila and the other Dimna; both were exceedingly cunning, but Dimna was the more ambitious and had the grander ideas.

One day Dimna said to Kalila, 'What's wrong with the king, do you think? He sits all the time in the same spot, and doesn't stir an inch. He seems to have given up hunting entirely.'

'What business is it of yours?' Kalila answered. 'Why ask questions about what doesn't concern you? We're comfortable enough living here in the court of this king; we get all the food we need. We don't belong to the class that hobnobs with monarchs; we can't aspire to be honoured by being taken into their confidence, or expect them to listen to what we have to say. Stop your foolish chatter; if anyone presumes to meddle in matters he's not fitted for, the same thing will happen to him as happened to the monkey.'

'Why, what happened to the monkey?' Dimna asked.

'Once upon a time,' said Kalila, 'a monkey saw a carpenter sitting on a log of wood and splitting it in two. He used two pegs; each time he hammered one, he took out the other and moved it forward. Whilst he was in the middle of the job he got up to go somewhere. The monkey immediately squatted down on the log and set about trying to split it. He sat with his testicles hanging through the split already made; then he took out the peg that was stuck in the gap before hammering in the other, with the result that the two pieces of wood at once sprang together and his testicles were caught fast in the log. The pain was so terrific that he fainted. When the carpenter came back he belaboured the monkey soundly, until the brute died. That's why they say that carpentry is no job for monkeys.'

'Yes, I quite see that,' Dimna commented. 'But not everyone who aspires to associate with kings does so merely for the sake of a good meal. The belly can be filled anywhere and with anything. The big thing about keeping in with kings is the social advancement it leads to; then you can give pleasure to your friends, and smash your enemies. To be content with a little shows a mean spirit and an ignoble mind. People with no higher object in life than food ought really to be counted among the beasts, not as human beings at all; they are like the dog that is quite happy with a bone and a scrap of bread. Now with a lion, if it's hunting a rabbit and then spots a wild ass in the offing, at once it drops the rabbit and is off after the wild ass. The man who rises to a high position, though his life be as short as the blossoming of a rose, yet the wise will say of him that he lived to a great age, because of the splendid achievements and fine reputation he leaves behind. But the fellow who is satisfied to remain obscure, though his days may last as long as the leaves of the cypress, yet in the eyes of the noble they weigh nothing.'

'I've listened to all you have said,' Kalila replied. 'But now come back to your senses. You must be aware that everyone has his position in life, and should be content to remain in his proper station. We aren't the sort to move in those rarefied heights or give ourselves such fancy airs; we should be glad enough to be as we are, quite snug and safe.'

'But don't you see, the top jobs are open to everyone to compete for, provided they've got the spark of ambition and grandeur in them,' Dimna persisted. 'Anyone that has a noble soul and the proper stuffing can lift himself out of his humble origin and reach the heights. In the same way if a man is stupid and feckless, though he may be born at the top he soon slides down to the bottom. It's tough work climbing up the ladder; it's easy enough to tumble down. It takes a big effort to lift a heavy stone from the ground and load it on to your back; it's no trouble at all to let it drop again. The man who aspires to greatness and finds nobody of high purpose to give him a helping hand may be excused if he fails; the bigger the task, the fewer the volunteers. But we're different; if we keep together we can easily reach the heights. Don't let us be content with our present obscurity; we deserve something better.'

'Well, what's your scheme?' Kalila asked.

'I want to take advantage of the present opportunity,' Dimna answered. 'Here is the lion, obviously in a fix, baffled what to do next. I propose to seek an audience of him; it may be that I can offer him some advice which will get him out of his difficulties. If so, I shall be made; he'll promote me at once, and I'll enjoy a nice high position at court.'

'How do you know the lion is in a fix?' Kalila demanded.

'Oh, I use my wits,' Dimna said. 'I'm something of a clairvoyant, you know. I see all the signs. A clever chap tells at a glance what is going on in another fellow's mind, just by looking at him.'

'That's all very well,' Kalila objected. 'But how are you going to get anywhere near the lion? That's the first thing you've got to manage. Besides, you've never been at court; you don't know the etiquette they use in palaces.'

'When a chap is strong and cunning, it's no trouble at all for him to tackle big jobs and shoulder heavy loads,' Dimna replied. 'The man with clear-sighted resolve soon reaches the heights; it's no handicap to the intelligent fellow to be alone and a stranger.'

'But kings don't scatter their bounties at large for every virtuous and deserving fellow to pick up,' Kalila remarked. 'They only favour the people who are near them, people who have either inherited court appointments or earned the royal regard by the approved means. It's like the vine, that attaches itself not to the best and strongest tree, but to whatever happens to be nearest.'

'You're wrong there,' Dimna interposed. 'The big men and their forebears haven't always occupied those positions. They climbed up gradually, by hard work and tremendous guts. I'm after the same thing, and I mean to get there. The man who waits upon kings must not be afraid of shouldering heavy loads and swallowing bitter medicines. He must learn to extinguish the fires of wrath with the waters of self-control. He must know how to bottle the genie of desire by using the magic spell of reason. He must not allow deluding greed to get the better of his right-guiding intelligence. He must build the fabric of his labours upon the foundations of honesty and prudence. He must meet the accidents of fortune with quiet dignity and unfailing good manners. If he observes all these rules, he will without doubt live to see his desires coming out to meet him, decked up in the finest array.'

'Well then,' said Kalila. 'Let's pretend for a moment that you've actually succeeded in getting near the king. How do you propose to get him to look at you, and by what lucky chance do you expect to be shown to one of the best seats?'

'That's simple,' Dimna answered. 'Once I get near him I shall carefully study his character, and serve him devotedly and with utter sincerity. I shall confine my efforts to following his opinions and wishes, and sedulously abstain from criticizing anything he says or does. If an enterprise begins to go well and shows promise of promoting the interests of his kingdom, I shall make it appear most attractive in his eyes and eloquently extol its benefits and advantages, so that he will be delighted with the soundness of his judgment and very happy to find himself proved so clever. But if any undertaking should threaten to end up disagreeably and to prove mischievous and disadvantageous to his realm, after the most careful reflection and deliberation I shall mention to him the pitfalls and perils in the gentlest and suavest terms, comporting myself with all deference and humility, until I have made him aware of the insalubriousness of the situation, in a manner he has never experienced with other courtiers. A clever man with a glib tongue can show right to be wrong if he so chooses, and similarly he is able to prove what is false to be true. The cunning artist will paint a picture on a wall in such a way as to make it appear that the figures are standing out whilst all the time they are flat, and vice versa. Once the king has seen how brilliant I am, he will be even more eager to patronize me than I to serve him.'

'Well,' said Kalila, 'I see your mind's made up. Since you're determined to go on with this thing, let me give you a bit of advice. You go very carefully; it's a big risk you're taking. You know what the philosophers say. There are three things that none but a fool will venture on—to keep the company of kings, to try what poisons taste like, and to tell a woman a secret. Clever men have compared a king with a high, steep mountain where there are all kinds of rare fruits and precious ores, but lions also and snakes and other noisome things; very difficult to climb, and very dangerous to stay there.'

'True enough,' Dimna agreed. 'But the man who dodges dangers never gets anywhere worth while. You know the other saying. There are three things that can't be ventured on except by people with high ambitions and iron wills: working for kings, trading overseas, and engaging the enemy. The clever also say that the really virtuous man only comes into his own in two situations: when he is successful and honoured in the service of kings, or when he lives content and respected amongst ascetics.'

'I don't agree with you in the least,' Kalila declared. 'All the same I wish you luck, and may God preserve you and prosper your enterprise in every possible way!'

So Dimna went off, and saluted the lion from afar.

'Who is that fellow?' the lion asked his courtiers.

'Oh, he's so-and-so,' they told him. 'His father was called so-and-so.'

'Ah yes, I remember his father,' the lion remarked. He then called to Dimna, asking him where he was.

'Here I am,' Dimna replied. 'I have come to dwell at the court of the king, and have made it the goal of my hopes and the altar of my needs. Here I wait, in case perchance some matter of moment may arise where my intelligence and opinion may be of some slight service. Many such matters occur at royal courts, in which the assistance of humble underlings like myself may be required. In this mighty realm, that is proud and splendid as a peacock, even the fly is not without its usefulness. However insignificant the servitor of your majesty may be, he is surely not entirely incapable of warding off some mischief, or procuring some advantage. Even a dry stick that is flung by the wayside eventually proves to possess some utility; a man may make a toothpick of it, or scratch his ears with it. Why should any animal be turned away and not made use of that can possibly be put to some good purpose, or may alternatively prove mischievous if left unemployed?'

When the lion heard these words he thought that Dimna might perhaps have some good advice to tender, and he marvelled within himself.

'The man of understanding and virtue may be of humble origin, and he may have many enemies,' he commented, turning to his courtiers. 'Nevertheless his intelligence and courage will out sooner or later, and be recognized by all. So it is with a fire; the person kindling it may want to keep it low, yet for all that it blazes up in the end.'

Dimna was made very happy by these remarks, for he realized that his charm had had its effect on the lion's ears.

'It is the duty of all the king's servants and entourage,' he said, coming forward more boldly, 'to offer whatever advice may happen to occur to them, so that the king may know the extent of their knowledge and comprehension. So long as the king is not well informed about his subjects he cannot take full advantage of their capacities to serve him, and so long as he is not cognizant of the degree of judgment and reflection and loyal counsel each possesses he cannot issue an edict for their promotion. Nobody bothers to tend the almond seed that is hidden in the soil; but when the veil of dust is lifted from its face and its emerald beauty adorns the earth, then it is recognized for what it is, and is undoubtedly tended with great care; for men are eager to enjoy the benefit of its fruits. There isn't anyone who doesn't prove of some use, according to how the king looks after him and trains him; everything depends on the royal favour. The king owes it to his subjects to promote them in accordance with their intelligence, virtue, loyalty and counsel; he should not raise them up and abase them simply as his caprice may dictate. Nor should he see fit to prefer the idle and stupid over the energetic and cunning; two things make a king look absurd and ridiculous—to put a necklace on his foot, and to hang an anklet about his neck. To mount pearls and rubies in lead doesn't diminish the value of the jewels; it merely exposes the man who does it to ridicule, and proves what a fool he is. A multitude of short-sighted and incompetent helpers are a great mischief; things get done not by employing a crowd of adjutants and assistants, but by choosing a few men of vision and understanding. The man who has a ruby in his pocket doesn't carry around a great load, yet for all that he is able to achieve all that he intends; the man who humps on his back a sack of stones gets worn out, carrying them around, and on the day of need they are no good to him at all. The wise man doesn't despise the virtuous, although he may be obscure and of humble rank; tendons are taken from carrion, yet they are used in making the saddles on which kings ride, and for stringing bows, and are highly esteemed and honoured for the royal and noble purposes to which they are put. Kings ought not to neglect wise men on account of their lowly origin, and prefer in their favour ignoramuses just because they have inherited high rank. The royal regard should rather be directed towards every man according to his usefulness and qualification to serve the interests and discharge the business of the realm. When ignorant men exploit the services rendered by their ancestors to procure their own comfort, the affairs of the state are gravely prejudiced and the intelligent people are wasted. Nothing is nearer to a man's heart than his own person; if any part of his body falls sick, he will send by far routes and to distant cities for medicine to cure his ills. The mouse lives in the same house as a man and shelters under the same shadow, but when it proves a nuisance he quickly drives it out and does all he can to destroy it; though the falcon is a wild and strange creature, yet because it can be useful it is highly honoured and brought to hand, so that it perches even on the king's finger.'

When Dimna ended this speech the lion marvelled at him more than ever. He answered him very civilly, and showed him many marks of esteem and consideration. Dimna waited for an occasion of being alone with him, and then remarked that it was a long time since the king had stirred and gone out hunting; what, he asked, was the reason for his immobility? The lion desired to conceal from Dimna his state of panic; but all at once Shatraba let out a loud bellow, which so upset the lion that he lost his nerve completely, and let the reins of his self-control slip from his hands.

'There,' he said, turning to Dimna and laying bare his secret to him. 'That's the reason. It's the voice you've just heard. I don't know what direction it's coming from, but I suspect the owner of it must be terribly strong and powerful, like his voice. If that's the case, this is no place for me.'

'Is there nothing but this voice that disquiets your majesty?' Dimna enquired.

'No, nothing,' the lion confessed.

'The king doesn't need to quit his palace simply because of that,' Dimna said soothingly. 'That's no sort of reason for him to flee from his familiar haunts. It has been said that flattery is the bane of a good brain, slander ruins virtue, and a loud voice is the plague of a weak heart. The proverb remarks that one shouldn't pay attention to every loud voice and powerful body. It's like the story of the drum and the fox.'

'What story is that?' the lion asked.

'Once upon a time,' Dimna related, 'a fox ran into a thicket, and there saw a drum thrown down beside a tree. Every time the breeze stirred the branch of the tree swang against the drum, and a frightful noise struck the fox's ears. The fox, observing its huge bulk and hearing its terrible sound, greedily fancied that its skin and flesh must be worthy of its voice, and set to with a will to tear it apart;

but all he got for his pains was skin. He thereupon set a-gallop the steed of regret, remarking that he never realized before that the bigger the bulk and the more horrible the noise, the less the profit.

'I have brought up this parable,' Dimna went on, 'to the end that the king may see the more clearly how unnecessary it is for him to be so distraught. Let him only say the word, and I will go at once and investigate, and report to his majesty the true facts of the case.'

The lion found this speech wholly agreeable, and off Dimna ran at his bidding. But as soon as he was out of sight the lion reflected again, and regretted having despatched him.

'I've managed this business very badly,' he said to himself. 'I see now I was wrong to take his advice. When a man has been treated badly at court for no reason and has suffered hardship and privation for a long time without having done anything wrong, when he has lost all his money and position or been deposed from the office with which he was formerly charged, or if he is known as a mischief-maker anxious to stir up trouble and intent on no good, or if he has belonged to a gang of criminals and his fellow crooks have all been pardoned whilst he has had to pay the bitter penalty, or if he has been punished along with them but in his case the punishment was unduly severe, or if he has rendered good service along with other capable colleagues and they have been more handsomely rewarded than he, or if some enemy of his has outstripped him in the race for promotion, or if he has proved unreliable in his religious views or in respect of his virtue, or sought his own advantage in ways detrimental to the king's interests, or if some enemy of the king has sought refuge with him and found a welcome—on any or all of these counts it behoves a king not to act too hastily, and not to send such a man on a confidential mission to an adversary before proving and testing him thoroughly. This fellow Dimna is very shrewd and cunning; he spent a long time at my court, and never got a step forward for all his pains. If he is still embittered, and is meditating some treachery and intends to stir up trouble, it is possible that he may find the enemy to be more powerful and prosperous than myself and will therefore decide to try his luck with him; in that case he will surely disclose my secret to him.'

With these disquieting thoughts running through his mind the lion could not be still for an instant; he kept jumping up and sitting down, watching the road all the time. Suddenly Dimna appeared in the offing; the lion at once felt a little better, and sat quietly on his throne, for he did not want Dimna to suspect him of being uneasy.

'Well, what have you done?' he asked as soon as Dimna arrived and stood before him.

'I have seen the ox whose bellow troubled the king's ears,' he replied.

'And how strong is he?' the lion demanded.

'I didn't notice any airs or arrogance about him to suggest that he is so powerful,' Dimna answered. 'As soon as I came up to him I addressed him like an equal. He didn't show any signs of expecting me to treat him with greater deference, and I didn't feel any awe of him that should have made me more respectful.'

'Ah, you mustn't put that down to weakness in him,' the lion retorted. 'Don't let yourself be taken in. A violent wind doesn't overthrow a feeble blade of grass, but it plucks up mighty trees and shatters strong buildings and tall palaces. Great and powerful men consider it inappropriate to their dignity to attack their inferiors and underlings; they believe in showing their strength and might only against doughty and valiant foes. They negotiate with everyone according to his circumstances; men of true virtue make it a point of honour to match themselves in all matters with their equals.'

'But truly, the king ought not to attach so much importance to this ox at all,' Dimna insisted. 'Only command me, and I will fetch him here to be your majesty's obedient slave.'

The king was delighted with this suggestion, and directed Dimna to bring the ox. Dimna at once hurried off to Shatraba, and addressed him boldly and without the least hesitation or diffidence.

'The lion has sent me,' he stated. 'He has ordered me to bring you to him. He has decreed that if you hurry up and come quietly I am to grant you complete security from the just consequences of your past shortcomings, in failing so long to present yourself before him and wait upon his pleasure. But if you delay, I am to return at once and report what has happened.'

'Who is this lion?' Shatraba asked innocently.

'The king of the animals. The monarch of the wild beasts,' Dimna answered.

When Shatraba heard the words lion and wild beasts he felt very frightened.

'If you will put me in good heart,' he said to Dimna, 'and promise me that I have no cause to fear his violence, I'll come with you.'

Dimna assured Shatraba solemnly and with the most binding oaths that he would be quite safe; and so the two of them went off to the lion's court. When they arrived, the lion began to question the ox very, very gently.

'When did you come to these parts?' he asked. 'And what brought you here?'

The ox recounted his story, whereupon the lion told him that he was very welcome to stay, and that he would find nothing but kindness and consideration. The ox thanked him warmly, and cheerfully bound up his loins to wait upon the lion's commands. The lion gave him a place quite near his throne and treated him with extreme courtesy and affability; meanwhile he explored his capabilities, and discovered that he possessed a good brain and sound judgment, reinforced by considerable experience. After due reflection and consideration he allotted him a position of trust, and made him intimate with his secrets. The more he tested his character and habits, the greater confidence he felt in his knowledge, his sagacity, his wide comprehension and shrewdness. Every day he promoted him to higher office, and conferred greater and greater favours upon him, until presently he surpassed all his generals and ministers.

When Dimna saw what was happening, and how the lion was taken with the ox and every hour was advancing him in position and authority, the hand of envy smeared his eyes with the collyrium of indignation, and the flame of wrath fanned the fire of jealousy in his mind, until sleep and repose deserted him entirely. In this state he went off to complain to Kalila.

'Dear brother,' he cried, 'see now what a fool and an idiot I have been. I confined my purpose to easing the lion's mind, and neglected my own interests completely. I brought this ox to wait upon him, and now he has become his favourite, and I have been ousted from my position.'

'The same thing has happened to you as happened to the pious man in the story,' Kalila commented drily.

'Why, how did it fall out with him?' asked Dimna. And Kalila related as follows.

A pious man once received a fine garment as a present from a king. But a thief, seeing him arrayed in such splendour, desired to possess himself of the gown. To this end he set forth to visit him.

'I wish to become your companion,' he told the saint, 'so that I may learn from you the discipline of the mystic way.'

He was accordingly admitted into the good man's confidence, and treated his intended victim with the utmost respect and politeness, waiting for the opportunity to come along. It came; and he seized the ascetic's gown and made off with it. The saint realized as soon as he missed the robe that it was his erstwhile disciple who had stolen it, and he at once set out in his pursuit, taking the road to a certain city. On the way he encountered a pair of mountain-goats that were locked in combat, butting each other so briskly that the blood ran out of them both. A fox presently arrived on the scene and began greedily to lap up their gore; whereupon the goats simultaneously set upon him with their horns and poked him to death.

That same night the saint reached the city and sought a place where he might unlace his shoes. After a while he came to the house of a loose woman, and was there given lodging. This woman kept a number of girls engaged upon that business. Now one of the girls, whose beauty would have moved the very houris of paradise to envy, and before whose fair loveliness the sun in heaven fell down in worship, happened to have fallen in love with a most handsome youth, tall, well-spoken, amusing and of fine physique; she therefore absolutely refused to let any other customer get near her. The woman was so furious about the loss of income resulting from the girl's infatuation that she was ready to cast all shame aside and risk everything to mend the situation. She designed to destroy the young man, and her plans were well forward by the night the ascetic lodged with her. Waiting her chance, she plied the fond couple with strong drink until both were tipsy and staggered off dead to the world. When they were fast asleep, the woman poured some poison into a long reed and laying one end by the young man's backside, she placed the other in her mouth intending to blow the poison in. Before she could do so however the sleeping youth broke wind, and all the poison at once spilled into the old woman's mouth, so that she dropped stone dead on the spot. All this the ascetic witnessed.

The next morning, as soon as early dawn illuminated the broad firmament with the light of its beauty, the saint delivered himself from those shades of abomination and wickedness and sought another lodging. A certain shoemaker, eager to win his blessing, carried him off to his home and bade his wife take care of him, charging her to tend him well; meanwhile he himself departed to a friend's revel. Now the shoemaker's wife had a lover; and as soon as her husband was gone she sent a messenger, a barber's wife who did these errands for her, to inform her paramour that her man had been invited out, and to bid him come as arranged between them. The fellow in due course came along that night; but the shoemaker also returned, to find him hanging about by the doorstep. He had already had his suspicions of him before; now he burst into the house in a rage, thrashed his wife soundly and tied her to a pillar, after which he betook himself to bed. When all the world was hushed in slumber, the barber's wife came to the window and called softly.

'Why are you keeping your lover waiting so long?' she whispered. 'If you're going to come, come quickly; otherwise tell him to go away.'

'My dear sister,' the shoemaker's wife cried out, 'if you have any feelings for me, please come and release me, and let me tie you to the pillar in my place. I just want to apologize to my boy friend; I'll be back at once, and I'll be eternally grateful to you.'

The barber's wife agreed to this arrangement, and released her. Just then the shoemaker woke up and called his wife. The barber's wife was afraid to answer, in case he should recognize her voice. He called several times, but she didn't utter a sound. More furious than ever, he picked up his cobbler's knife, rushed upon the woman and slashed off her nose and stuck it in her hand.

'There,' he shouted. 'Give this to your lover with my compliments.'

When the shoemaker's wife returned she found her friend with her nose cut off, and felt very sorry. She begged her pardon more than once, and set her free; then she bound herself to the pillar. The barber's wife for her part went off home with her nose in her hand. All this the ascetic both saw and heard.

The shoemaker's wife rested for a while, then she raised her hands to heaven and began to pray in a loud voice.

'King of Heaven,' she cried, 'if Thou knowest that my husband has falsely suspected me and done me wrong, of Thy grace have pity on me and give me back my nose.'

'You wicked witch!' the shoemaker exclaimed. 'What words are these?'

'You cruel brute!' his wife retorted. 'Get up and see how good God has been to me, to make amends for your savage impetuosity. As soon as my innocence was established God gave me back my nose, and would not suffer me to be seen amongst people maimed and put to shame.'

At this the man jumped out of bed, lighted a lamp and rushed to the pillar. There he saw his wife perfectly whole, her nose right in the middle of her face. He at once begged her pardon, confessing his sin and imploring her to forgive him, saying that he should never have done such a thing without clear proof, and ought never to have listened to vile slander and inflicted such suffering on his good and innocent wife.

Meanwhile the barber's wife arrived home, greatly distraught and casting about in her mind how to explain her predicament to her husband and neighbours. Presently her husband woke up and called to her to bring him his instruments, as he had to go to attend a very respectable gentleman. She delayed some while, then she gave him his razor and nothing else. In a rage the barber flung the razor out into the night, and sent his wife sprawling after it.

'My nose, my nose!' the woman screamed.

The barber was dumbfounded when he saw the state she was in, and all the neighbours ran up and rebuked him considerably. When the world-illuminating dawn like a maid in waiting lifted the night-cap of darkness off and revealed the beauty of radiant day to all the dwellers upon earth, the woman's kinsfolk rallied round and carried off the barber to the magistrate.

'Why,' the magistrate asked severely, 'did you see fit to mutilate this poor woman without a shred of evidence and for no obvious crime?'

The barber was completely at a loss, and could offer no explanation. The magistrate therefore passed judgment against him and sentenced him to condign punishment. At this the pious man, unable to contain himself any longer, stood up in court.

'You should reflect upon this matter, and deliberate well before jumping to conclusions,' he said mildly. 'It wasn't the thief who took my gown. It wasn't the goats that killed the fox. It wasn't the poison that slew the bad woman. It wasn't the barber who cut off his wife's nose. We all brought these calamities upon ourselves.'

Thereupon the magistrate removed his hand from the barber's throat and turned to the ascetic, waiting with interest to hear the full explanation of his deep remark.

'Yes,' the saint continued. 'If I hadn't desired to have many disciples and followers, if I hadn't been taken in by the thief's tarradiddle and let him into my house, he would never have found the chance to steal my cloak. If the fox hadn't been so greedy and had refrained from blood-sucking, the goats would never have butted him. If the bad woman hadn't plotted to poison her fellow creature, she wouldn't have flung her precious life to the wind. If the cobbler's wife had been an honest woman, she wouldn't have got a beating; and if the barber's wife hadn't aided and abetted her in her naughtiness, she would never have had her nose chopped off.'

'I have quoted this instance' Kalila concluded, 'so that you may realize that you have brought this misfortune upon yourself, and that you did so by being stupid enough to overlook the likely consequences of your actions.'

'Indeed that is so,' Dimna admitted. 'I did it all myself. Well now, how do you think I can get out of the mess?'

'You tell me,' Kalila replied. 'Have you any ideas of your own?'

'Well,' Dimna reflected, 'I reckon I had better think it over a bit, and see what sort of cunning dodges and clever tricks I can invent to get round the problem. Whatever way may be possible, I'm determined to work to drive him out. In my opinion no proud and self-respecting man is at liberty to let things slide. If I'm careless now, I can't expect sensible people to feel sorry for me and say I couldn't help myself. One thing I must make clear, I'm not looking for further promotion; I don't intend trying to better my position, otherwise I shall be accused of being greedy and a self-seeker. There are three things the intelligent man is entitled to strive for, and plot and scheme his utmost to attain. First, he should work hard to regain the advantage he once held, and to avoid the damage he has already suffered. Secondly, he should aim to preserve his present advantage, and rescue himself from his immediate troubles. Thirdly, he should have an eye cocked anxiously on the future, to attract to himself all the good he can, and to ward off the bad. If I'm to have reasonable hopes of recovering my former position and repolishing my somewhat tarnished lustre, the thing I must do is to contrive by every means to secure that he bids farewell to this fair world and transfers his lodging to the cold cold earth. My own peace of mind depends on that, not to mention the lion's welfare. There's no doubt that the lion has favoured the ox far too much, so that everyone now thinks him quite idiotic.'

'I don't see how the lion is to be blamed for marking out the ox for promotion,' Kalila interposed. 'What harm has it done him?'

'He's advanced him far beyond his merits,' Dimna replied. 'In doing so he has made light of all his other advisers, and naturally they're dissatisfied and feel hurt. They have lost the advantages of serving him, and he has lost the benefits of their company. There are six things that mischief a king: deprivation, commotion, caprice, scurvy luck, bad temper and stupidity. Deprivation is when he denies himself his well-wishers and despises people of sound judgment and long experience. Commotion results from unforeseen wars and unpremediated actions, when his opponents unexpectedly unsheathe their words against him. Caprice is shown by undue fondness for women, hunting, music, drinking and the like. Scurvy luck consists in such things as famines, floods, fires and so forth. Bad temper is exhibited in unbridled anger, hatred, and undue severity in punishing offenders. Stupidity is proved by acting too kindly when strong measures are called for, and being ruthless when a little gentleness would do the trick.'

'I know all that,' Kalila retorted impatiently. 'But to come back to earth: how are you going to set about destroying the ox? He's stronger than you, and has more friends and allies.'

'That's the wrong way of looking at things,' Dimna sniffed. 'It isn't strength and powerful helpers that count in the long run. Shrewdness and cunning can achieve results where physical force would fail completely. Haven't you heard how the raven destroyed the snake by sheer guile?'

'No, I haven't heard that one,' Kalila replied. 'Do tell me.'

And Dimna proceeded thus.

A raven lived in a tree at the top of a mountain, and close by a snake had his hole, so that every time the raven hatched out an egg the snake gobbled up the chick. One day the raven came up to the snake, determined to reason with him.

'My dear brother,' she began gently, 'haven't you ever read the saying of the old philosophers, that whoso draweth the sword, by the sword he shall perish?'

Of course this admirable advice got her nowhere. Seeing that all her expostulations were in vain, the distracted raven betook herself to her old friend the jackal and told him her troubles.

'But I think I've hit upon a scheme,' she ended. 'I believe I know how to rescue myself from the mischief of this murderous oppressor.'

'And how do you propose to embark upon such a momentous enterprise?' enquired the jackal.

'When the snake is asleep,' the raven explained, 'I propose to pick out his world-ranging eye, so that in the future the apples of my eye and the darlings of my heart will be secure from his malice.'

'I don't think that plan is very wise, dear,' the jackal murmured. 'A sensible person attacks his enemy in a way that doesn't expose his own life to danger. You be careful, or you may find yourself in the same boat as the heron that wanted to do in the crab, and instead threw away his own valuable life.'

'Oh, how did that happen?' the raven asked anxiously.

'I'll tell you,' the jackal replied.

There was once a heron which dwelt on the bank of a lake and caught as many fish as he wanted, so that he lived a life of ease and luxury. But eventually old age began to creep on, and he was no longer able to hunt as before.

'Alas!' he lamented to himself. 'Life has galloped past and is gone, and all the compensation that remains to support and succour my old age is the experience and practice I have had. Today, now that I have no strength left, I must trust to my cunning.'

As he sat by the water, dejected and woebegone, a crab spied him from afar, and came up and spoke to him.

'Why do I see you so downcast?' he asked solicitously.

'How should I not be dispirited?' the heron replied. 'All that I have ever lived on has been the fish or two that I caught every day. I was quite content with that to keep body and soul together, and the fishes didn't grow any fewer. But today two fishermen passed this way, and I heard them remark that in this pool there are lots of fish, and well worth catching. Then one of them said that yonder is a still better place, and that when they have finished there they can move on here. If that's the state of affairs I can say goodbye to living, and must resign myself to cruel starvation and bitter death.'

At that the crab crawled off and told the fishes what the heron had said.

'We have come to consult you,' the fish said, crowding round the heron. 'What do you advise? The intelligent man will take the advice even of his enemy, especially in matters where the enemy too stands to gain. Your survival depends on our continuing to breed. What do you think is best for us to do?'

'It's useless trying to resist the fishermen,' the heron answered. 'I can't suggest anything to you on those lines. But I know a pool not far off where the water gleams brighter than a lover's tears, and winks more slily than the eye of dawn, so that you can count every grain of sand on the bottom, and see the fishes' eggs floating on the surface. If you could manage somehow to move there, you would fall into the very lap of peace and plenty.'

'That's a splendid idea,' the fish all exclaimed together. 'But without your help we can't possibly shift.'

'I don't grudge you my assistance,' the heron assured them. 'But I'm afraid it will take some time; and from one hour to the next the fishermen may come, and the chance will be gone.'

Thereupon they all begged and implored him to help them; and in the end it was arranged that every day he should carry off a few of the fish. This he did; but when he reached the top of a nearby hill he ate them up. Meanwhile the fish rushed and raced with one another to be the first to be taken, while the heron looked on at their witless folly with the eye of meditation.

'Whoever allows himself to be deceived by his enemy's stratagem,' he would say with the tongue of admonition, 'and sees fit to rely upon a vile scoundrel, deserves all that he gets.'

So the days went by, until the time came when the crab also desired to be transferred. The heron took him on to his back and made for the hill that was the fishes' last resting-place. When the crab spotted from far off the great heap of fish-bones he at once realized what had been happening.

'When a man meets his enemy in a dangerous situation,' he thought, 'and sees that he is intent upon his destruction, if he then gives up the struggle he will have conspired against his own life. If he puts up a fight and wins, he acquires a glorious name; if things fall out otherwise, at least his self-respect and courage and honour are safe from the tongue of scorn, and he will attain the reward of eternal bliss to crown his blessed martyrdom.'

Encouraged by these reflections, he hurled himself upon the

heron's throat and throttled him until he dropped senseless, and departed to pay his respects to the Ruler of the world. The crab, very pleased with himself, waddled back triumphantly to the surviving fish; he condoled with them on the loss of their friends, whilst congratulating them on their own escape. When he had told them the whole story they were without exception delighted, reckoning the death of the heron to be a new life for themselves.

'I have told you this parable,' the jackal ended, 'in order that you may appreciate how sometimes people destroy themselves by their own craft and cunning. But I will show you a way of managing this business whereby you can preserve yourself and destroy the snake.'

'Nobody can afford to neglect the advice of friends,' the raven said, 'and it is absurd to go against the opinion of the wise.'

'This is the idea,' the jackal proceeded. 'You fly high up in the sky, and cast your eye over the rooftops and fields. As soon as you sight some bright shawl or anything of that kind spread out in the sun and easy to catch, swoop down and pick it up. Carry it off, but in such a way as never to be out of view. Then, when you reach where the snake is, drop it right on top of him. The men who are chasing you will let you go in order to collect the scarf.'

The raven without delay flew off to the nearest village, and there saw a woman spreading a scarf out on the edge of her roof and washing it. She darted down and snatched it in the manner recommended by the jackal, and threw it down upon the snake. The men who were after her at once stopped to beat the snake's head in, and the raven got clear away.

'I have told you this story,' Dimna concluded, 'so that you may realize that cunning can do things which brute force cannot.'

'But the ox is a different proposition,' Kalila demurred. 'He combines strength and force with brains and intelligence. How do you think you can get the better of him by guile?'

'What you say is perfectly true,' conceded Dimna. 'But you must remember that he is deluded as regards me, and feels quite secure where I am concerned. I can catch him unawares; you know how it is, a treacherous attack launched from an unexpected quarter is always the most successful. That's how the hare destroyed the lion, you remember.'

'No, I can't say I do,' Kalila said. So Dimna told him.

In a certain meadow, which the soft breeze perfumed with the sweet odour of Paradise, and the reflection of its sheen brightened the countenance of Heaven, where a thousand stars glittered on every branch and a thousand spheres stared amazed at every star, many beasts came to graze and water and to enjoy the lush plenty there abounding. But in the neighbourhood there was a lion, which quite spoiled the ease and comfort of the other animals. So one day they came together and decided to speak to the lion.

'Look,' they said. 'Every day after much toil and boundless hardship you succeed in catching and chewing up just one of us. We are always in a frightful flap, and you have all the bother of searching. Now we've thought up a scheme whereby you can be free of trouble and worry, and we can live quietly and at ease. If you agree to stop chasing us, every day without fail we will send one of our number at dinner-time to the king's kitchen.'

The lion consented to this arrangement, and matters so continued for some while. Then one day the lot fell upon the hare.

'My friends,' he addressed his fellow animals, 'if you are willing to be a little indulgent about sending me, I guarantee to rescue you all from this bloodthirsty tyrant.'

'Well, there's no harm in trying,' they agreed.

So he delayed for an hour or so, until the lion's dinner-time was past; then he shuffled off slowly in his direction. He spied the lion looking very upset; the fires of hunger blazed within his belly, fanned by the wind of emptiness. The burning light of rage glared in all his gestures; the water in his mouth had gone completely dry. He was all keyed up for the attack, ready to trample in the dust the covenant into which he had entered with the animals. When he saw the hare coming, he let out a great roar.

'Where are you coming from?' he shouted. 'What's the matter with the animals?'

'They sent another hare along with me,' the hare explained. 'But on the way a lion seized him. I told him over and over again that he was the king's meal, but he took no notice. As a matter of fact he was very rude about you. He said this was his hunting-ground, and anyway the hare belonged to him by right because he was stronger than you. So I hurried on to tell your majesty.'

'Show me where he is!' the lion roared, rising in his wrath.

The hare sprinted ahead and brought the lion in no time to a well of sparkling water, bright and clear as a mirror, so that every face and form was reflected in it in all its details and lineaments.

'He's in this well,' the hare whispered. 'I'm afraid of him. But if the king will take me into his bosom I will show him his enemy.'

The lion picked up the hare, and peeped into the well. Seeing the image of himself and the hare, he at once dropped the hare and flung himself into the well and was drowned. So the hare came back safe and sound to the other animals, who all crowded round and asked him what had happened.

'Oh, I drowned the lion,' the hare said modestly. 'That's all.'

The animals thereupon mounted the steed of gladness and galloped about in the meadow of peace and plenty, innocently exulting in the death of their dreaded foe.

'If you can manage to destroy the ox without hurting the lion, that's fair enough,' Kalila commented. 'It's a perfectly sound and reasonable thing to do. But if you cannot contrive to do so except by injuring the king, then beware; you surely don't want to damage the lion's interests. No sane person will hurt his boss just for his own selfish peace of mind.'

That ended the discussion. For some days after this Dimna abstained from visiting the lion. Then one day, knowing that the lion was alone, he seized his chance and came before him.

'Why, I haven't seen you for days,' the lion exclaimed. 'Is everything all right?'

'Well enough,' Dimna replied coolly, and made to depart.

'What's wrong?' the lion asked, stopping him. 'Has anything happened?'

'As a matter of fact, yes,' Dimna answered.

'Well, come along, tell me,' the lion said.

'I'll wait until you've nothing to do, and aren't expecting any company,' Dimna countered. 'It can wait till then.'

'This is the very time,' the lion urged. 'Quick, tell me now. The sooner the better. Important business brooks no delay. Never put off to tomorrow what you can do today. That's what all the wise men say.'

'If a man wants to tell his friend something by way of advice, and with his friend's best interests at heart,' Dimna began portentously, 'and he knows that what he has to say won't be very agreeable to the other party, he won't have the courage to speak his mind, unless of course he has complete confidence in the other party's good sense and intelligence. Especially is this the case if what he has to say is of advantage only to the listener, and the speaker stands to gain nothing except the sense of having discharged his obligations for favours received, and of having offered the best advice in his power. If as a result of what he says the other party escapes the danger by which he is threatened, that is the end of the matter. He can rest satisfied that he has achieved all that he set out to do; more than that, he is entitled to consider it a real triumph. Now I am encouraged to take this bold step,' he went on, warming to his subject, 'because the king is far superior to all other kings in excellence of judgment, mature deliberation, distinction of mind and thought; therefore he will undoubtedly bring his royal discrimination to bear on what I tell him. Moreover it is no secret to him that my words are inspired by the purest altruism and benevolence, and are entirely innocent of dark designs. The scout never tells a lie, they say. The survival of all the beasts is bound up with the continuing life and welfare of their king. The wise and well-bred man must do his duty and tell the truth. Whoever denies the king the benefit of his good counsel, or hides from the doctor the ailment from which he is suffering, or thinks it unfitting to reveal to his friends his need and poverty, is a traitor to his own self.'

'Of course you are trustworthy, beyond question,' the lion said. 'That's written all over you. You can speak freely. Tell me what has happened. You can be sure that I shall not in the slightest degree suspect your motives, but put it all down to sheer good will and loyal counsel.'

'Shatraba has had secret meetings with army leaders,' Dimna stated. 'He has seduced each one with a different kind of approach, saying that he has tried out the lion and formed an exact estimate of his force, strength, judgment and cunning, and found in all of them some defect and weakness. That's the kind of ungrateful and treacherous wretch the king has been so generous to, treating him as an equal in rank and authority, giving him the last word in the control of affairs, making him a virtual dictator. Now of course the demon of temptation has laid an egg in his heart; the desire to revolt has erected an airy loft on his head. The philosophers have remarked that when a king sees that any of his servants has climbed so high as to reach a level of rivalry and equality with himself in respect of influence, following and wealth, he should at once drop him, otherwise he himself will tumble down. Of course I realize that nobody can reach the same intellectual heights as the king; but I also know that the ox had better be dealt with pretty quickly, before he gets beyond control and the mischief can no longer be repaired.

'There are two classes of people, they say,' Dimna continued. 'Those who are resolute, and those who are incompetent. The resolute are further subdivided into two kinds. The first consists of those who diagnose trouble and danger before they actually occur, and having anticipated accurately at the very beginning what others only come to realize at the end, take effective measures at the start to deal with the conclusions when they arrive. Forewarned is fore-armed. When a thing has already taken place, there is nothing to choose between the clever man and the fool; everyone can recognize trouble when trouble has come. The shrewd man watches the situation all the time, and is able to keep control of affairs the whole way; he can contrive to make port without foundering in the dread whirlpool. The second kind of resolution is seen in the man who faces calamity when it visits him with a stout heart, and doesn't allow himself to get flummoxed and flustered; he never loses sight of the right way to deal with the situation, and so he comes out on top. The incompetent man is always in a flap; he is so scatterbrained that everything gravels him. When the worst happens he loses his head completely, and is so busy bellyaching and cursing his luck that he's entirely incapable of lifting a finger to help himself. These three varieties of people are like the three fishes in the story.'

'What story?' the lion asked.

'Listen,' said Dimna.

In a sequestered pool, far from the traffic of passers-by, three fishes once lived. One was clever, one very clever, and the third was a dunce. Now it happened that one day two fishermen chanced that way, and made a rendezvous to come back with a net and take the three fishes. Thereupon the very clever one (for the fish heard all that the fishermen said) quickly got moving; for he had often observed the tricks of tyrant destiny and the sauciness of treacherous fortune, and therefore stood firm of foot on the carpet of wisdom and experience. Jumping out slippily by the way the water came in, he was soon off and away. At that same moment the fishermen returned, and fastened their net on both sides of the pool. The ordinarily clever fish, that was not wholly destitute of reason but had no previous experience, was still in the lake.

'Ah,' he said to himself, 'I've been a fool. This is what always happens to fools. Now is the time for cunning. Though clever tricks generally fail when left too late, and plans made in haste rarely succeed when the trouble has already started, all the same the intelligent fellow never despairs of being able to make use of his brains, and sees no sense in putting off grappling with the enemy's wiles. This is the hour for resolution and craftiness.'

So saying he made out to be dead, and floated on the surface of the water. The fishermen, thinking him to have really expired, flung him away; and he cunningly threw himself into the neighbouring stream and got safely away.

The dunce, however, being quite incapable of sensible action and proving himself all too obviously a fool, floundered about in a hopeless dither, leaping up and down and wriggling this way and that, until eventually he was caught.

'I have mentioned this instance,' Dimna proceeded, 'so that the king may be convinced that in this matter of Shatraba haste is essential. The successful monarch always takes time by the forelock and concerts his plans well ahead, ere the opportunity is lost and action is no longer possible. With one stroke of his glittering sword he smites the enemy hip and thigh, and flourishing the brand of his world-consuming resolution he sets his foe's bag and baggage blazing to high heaven.'

'I understand perfectly,' the lion retorted. 'But I can't possibly suspect Shatraba of plotting treason, or of requiting his former good treatment with later ingratitude. To this very hour he has met with nothing but goodness and kindness at my hands.'

'That's very true,' Dimna agreed. 'The king has been far too generous to him. That's what has made him so insolent. The scoundrel and rapscallion is always loyal and faithful until he gets where he wants. Then he begins to aspire to greater heights, far beyond his capabilities; and his soaring hopes and grandiose ambitions urge him to every rascality and treachery. The fabric of untrue service and baseless loyalty rests upon the foundations of fear and hope. As soon as he feels secure and independent, he sets about fouling the waters of goodness and raising high the fire of evil. The philosophers have said that the king ought not to deprive his servants of his sympathy and generosity to such an extent that they altogether despair and shy off, turning to his enemies to try their luck with them; neither should he shower his bounties and benefactions upon them in so great profusion as to make them rich, for then they are wide open to the most extravagant and impertinent notions. Rather he should contrive that they pass their days always oscillating between fear and hope; the boldness engendered by despair will then not got hold of them, and the insolence bred of independence will not find a way into their souls.

'The king must understand that straightness can never be produced out of crooked dispositions, and all the care and trouble in the world will not succeed in bringing the depraved and vicious nature to follow decent habits. However tightly you may bind the sting of the scorpion and the tail of a dog and try to make them stand upright, the moment you undo them they revert to their original twist. The man who refuses to listen to the words of a good counsellor, though he speaks bluntly and without havering, will assuredly live to regret his folly. It is like the sick man who makes light of his doctor's advice, and eats and drinks whatever he fancies; every moment his malady gets a firmer hold on him, and in the end he becomes a chronic invalid.

'It is the duty of ministers to discharge their obligation for past favours by offering to the king the benefit of their best counsel; the most loyal of subordinates is he who strives his utmost to advise the ruler wisely, and does not occupy himself with watching his own interests. The best work is that which begins decently and ends praiseworthily. The most heart-warming praise is that uttered by the *élite* and noble. The best wives are those who agree with their husbands. The most congenial of friends is he who abstains from opposition and lends a helping hand in all matters. The most laudable life is that passed in piety and self-denial. The strongest character is that not fettered by greed and covetousness. The most perfect man is he who is unaffected by the insolence of riches and unvanquished by the weariness of affliction; these two attributes are peculiarly characteristic of women, in whom indeed they are innate.

'The man who takes fire for his mattress and a snake for his pillow certainly does not sleep very restfully, and finds small pleasure in his repose. The virtue of an accurate judgment and a powerful intellect is seen when a friend suddenly proves to be an enemy, or a subordinate loses his head and gives himself undue airs; the man so blessed then immediately takes matters into his own hands, and will have nothing further to do with such as they; before they have the chance to eat the fine breakfast of which they are dreaming, he serves them a most unpalatable supper. An enemy grows more powerful by being neglected, and the longer he is left alone the stronger his armament becomes.

'The most incompetent king is the one who overlooks the consequences of his actions, and takes too frivolously the weighty affairs of his kingdom. Whenever any serious situation develops and matters become difficult, such a one fails in resolution and omits to take the necessary precautions; and whenever a golden opportunity is lost and his enemies triumph over him, he blames his intimates and accuses them of every crime in the calendar. It is a primary duty of kingship to repair weaknesses in the defences of the realm before the adversary becomes firmly established and the foe begins to get the upper hand. Then matters can be managed as sound statesmanship requires, and no time need be wasted watching the enemy's tricks and subterfuges. In these circumstances determination, reinforced by maturity of judgment and strengthened by youthful fortune, is easily translated into action. Wealth cannot endure without trading, nor knowledge without discussion, nor kingship without statecraft.'

'You have certainly spoken very bluntly and forcefully,' the lion remarked. 'The words of the good counsellor should not be brusquely rejected, but listened to with due attention. Since Shatraba is now my enemy, it is pretty obvious how much he can do and what mischief is to be reckoned with from his quarter. We must keep our sense of proportion. After all, I can gobble him up in one mouthful;

he ambles about eating grass, whereas my strength is derived from good red meat. Besides, I have promised him security; and by what argument can betrayal be reconciled with virtue? Again, I have praised him publicly on many occasions, and made special mention of his wisdom, godliness, loyalty and sincere counsel; if I now say the opposite I shall lay myself open to the charge of inconsistency and flabby judgment, and my word will hereafter be regarded as worthless.'

'The king should not be deceived by saying that he can gobble up the ox in one mouthful,' Dimna retorted. 'Even though he cannot put up a fight by himself, he may find friends to support him, and handle the business with fraud and jugglery. What I am really afraid of is that the animals will all make common cause with him; he has been inciting them to attack you, and painting the attractions of rebellion in glowing colours. All the same the base ingrate will never be content to leave everything to others; he will certainly cast himself for the main part. You must get rid of him.'

'Well,' exclaimed the lion, for Dimna's words of guile at last had their effect on him. 'Supposing all this is true, what do you recommend?'

'When a tooth becomes rotten, there's no other remedy for the ache but pulling it out,' Dimna remarked sententiously. 'When the stomach can't digest something, and you feel upset and sick, the only cure is to vomit. If the enemy doesn't come to heel when treated gently and kindly, but only becomes more refractory as a result of your friendly overtures, your sole salvation is to drive him away as far as possible.'

'I don't care for Shatraba to live here any more,' the lion said at last. 'I shall send someone to tell him how I feel, and that I give him permission to move on elsewhere.'

Now Dimna was not at all pleased with this; for he realized that should Shatraba be informed of the substance of what he had said he would immediately establish his innocence, and his own lies and roguery would stand patent to the light of day.

'That's not at all a resolute way of acting,' he protested. 'So long as nothing is said about your feelings you still retain complete freedom of action; once you disclose your true sentiments you can't repair the situation any more. Once a word has escaped from the mouth's prison, once an arrow has sped from the haft of the bow, that word cannot be hidden again, nor that arrow brought back to hand. The awe of silence is a precious robe and a priceless ornament to a king. Furthermore it is possible that if he discovers how things really are and sees himself disgraced, he may think to match himself against you and take the field well-armed, or alternatively he may cock a snook at you and take himself off with all flags flying. Prudent kings never punish secretly an open crime, and never punish openly a secret offence.'

'To drive away one's intimate friends on mere suspicion and with no clear proof,' the lion demurred, 'and to exert oneself into the bargain to nullify their supposed schemings, is to keep oneself perpetually in torment and to lay the axe at one's own feet. The king needs to meditate long and carefully upon all he purposes to do, and especially when it comes to applying sanctions and carrying out drastic measures.'

'It is for the king to command,' Dimna murmured. 'But when this perfidious traitor next comes to court, let the king be alert and ready, so that he may not find any opportunity of doing damage. If he is examined attentively, his perfidy will be apparent in his ugly face and uncomely physiognomy. It is too easy to tell friend from foe; nobody with a grain of discernment can possibly be bamboozled into taking one for the other. You will soon recognize the symptoms of his twisted mind; as soon as he enters you will remark the change in his complexion, and how he trembles in all his joints, and looks left and right, and moves his horns forth and back as if making ready to give battle.'

'That's all very interesting,' the lion remarked. 'If I detect any of these signs in him, then all my doubts will be at an end.'

Having now completed the process of provoking the lion, and being satisfied that he had successfully fanned the flame of uneasiness in his mind, Dimna also desired to set a cold wind blowing under the ox's seat. At the same time he wanted to contrive that it should be at the lion's command that he executed the next part of his plan, that of going to the ox and putting him in a draught; in this way he hoped to escape all suspicion in that quarter too.

'What about if I were to go and see Shatraba?' he suggested slily. 'I could sniff out his thoughts, and let you know anything I may discover of his secret intentions.'

The lion gave Dimna the instructions he sought; and he went off to Shatraba, casting down his head as though full of anxiety. Shatraba gave him a great welcome.

'It's days and days since I last saw you,' he cried. 'I trust all's well with you?'

'How can things be well with anyone, when he isn't his own master, but always at someone else's beck and call?' Dimna replied. 'You feel in a flutter the whole time; every minute you're in dread and danger. You can't utter a single word without being afraid how it may be taken.'

'Why, what has put you into the dumps so?' Shatraba enquired. 'Why are you so desperate?'

'Oh, it's my fate,' Dimna answered. 'What's written is written. Who can fight against his destiny? Is there anyone who rises in the world and tastes success and prosperity, without becoming drunk and insolent? Is there anyone who pursues his own desires, without exposing himself to destruction? Is there anyone who keeps the company of women, without being tempted and falling? Is there anyone who turns in his need to the mean and miserly, and isn't received with contempt? Is there anyone who associates with the base and wicked, and doesn't rue the day? Is there anyone who chooses to dance attendance on rulers, and escapes unscathed?'

'Your words seem to suggest that you feel troubled perhaps with regards to the lion,' Shatraba hazarded.

'You're dead right,' said Dimna. 'But not on my own account. Look here. You know well enough the old friendship and affection I have for you. You remember the promises I made the day the lion sent me to fetch you. You are well aware how I have always kept those promises, and striven to do the right thing by you. Now I see no alternative but to tell you exactly what is happening, whether you find it pleasant or unpleasant, familiar or strange.'

'My dear old friend and faithful comrade!' Shatraba exclaimed. 'Come along, tell me everything.'

'I have been informed by a trustworthy source,' Dimna said, 'that the lion has been heard to remark that Shatraba has grown nice and plump, and that he has no further use for him alive; so he will make a royal feast, and entertain his friends the beasts on his flesh. As soon as I heard this, knowing of old his temper and impetuosity I came at once to inform you, and so prove once more how true I am to my covenant; incidentally to do my duty as a religious and strictly virtuous jackal, and to discharge all the obligations of jackalry and honour. Now the best and most appropriate course is for you to think up some plan, and the quicker the better. Apply your mind to inventing some shift; it may still not be too late to find a way out of your troubles.'

Hearing these words, and remembering Dimna's former promises, said Shatraba did not doubt for one moment that everything he had was true, and he had complete faith in the sincerity of his counsel.

'But I don't understand,' he cried. 'It doesn't make sense. Why should the lion betray me so? I've never been guilty of any treachery towards him. People must have poisoned his mind against me with lies and fabrications; that's what's made him angry with me. He's surrounded by a pack of scoundrels, every one of them a past master at treachery and double-dealing. He's grown so used to them that now he believes everything they tell him regarding others, judging everybody by their low standard. Of course, keeping bad company naturally renders a man suspicious of virtuous folk; that sort of experience is bound to lead him astray, so that he makes the same mistake as the duck.

'A duck, seeing the reflection of the moon shining brightly in the pool, thought it was a fish and tried to catch it. Of course he caught nothing. He tried the same thing several times, always with the same result; and so in the end he gave it up. Next day, whenever he sighted a fish in the water he thought it was mere moonshine, and made no attempt to catch it. The fruits of that experience were that he remained hungry all the day.

'If they have whispered something about me to the lion with ulterior motives,' Shatraba went on, 'and if he has believed them, then I am only sharing the same fate as others before me; their lies are being accepted as proof of my guilt. But if this is not the case, and he hates me without any reason, then I am left swinging in the air, with nothing solid to stand on. When a man is angry for some good cause, it is always possible to mollify him by offering a reasonable excuse; whereas when lies and defamation have done their deadly work the damage is irreparable, and disaster inescapable. Defamation and falsehood never lose their venom, and there's no limit to the mischief they can wreak. I am not conscious of having committed any crime in what has passed between the lion and myself. All the same it is impossible to be on one's guard all the time, and to keep a check on one's every action, when two people are fast friends and night and day together, in season and out of season, sharing each other's good luck and bad, happiness and sorrow. Some slip may always occur; nobody's infallible. But so long as such a mistake is not attributable to a deliberate breaking of faith, there's ample room to overlook it and close the eyes. Forgiveness and benevolence never so become the great, as when lesser men are guilty of foul treachery against them.

'If he is set on counting my mistakes against me,' he continued, 'I do not think I have erred save by occasionally opposing his views, and then solely in his interests. Possibly he has attributed this to boldness and disrespect on my part. Yet there has never been any indication that my interventions were not profitable and advantageous; and of course I have never uttered my objections in public. I have always been most careful to show him the greatest deference, and to treat him with the utmost reverence and veneration. How then could I guess that my sincere counsel should so offend him, or my loyal service make him hostile towards me? If a man is pleased to be let down gently when he asks his counsellor for advice, his doctor for treatment, or his priest for guidance, he cannot expect to derive any advantage from the sound judgment of the first, any benefit from the skilful attention of the second, or any lasting help from the ghostly ministration of the third.

'But if it's none of these things, then possibly it is the well-known intoxication of power and fickleness of rulers that have moved him to act thus. It is a familiar foible of kings to be well-disposed towards the treacherous, and only on their loyal advisers to pour out the vials of their wrath. The learned have for this reason observed, that to plunge into a river infested with crocodiles is a risky business, and to suck the lips of a wounded snake is a considerable hazard, but far more dangerous and terrifying than either is it to live in the court of princes.

'Again, it may be my very wisdom that is the cause of his hating me. It is the mettlesome horse that is wearied in the chase because he is known to be powerful; it is the good tree whose branches get broken under the weight of their fruit; the peacock's beauty always renders him liable to be plucked. The clever man is exposed to destruction because of the envy of fools. The eminent have foes in plenty amongst the worthless and despicable, who prevail over them by sheer weight of numbers; for the contemptible and mean always constitute the great majority. The miser cannot bear to look upon the generous; the ignorant cannot stomach sitting with the learned; the fool wearies intolerably of the company of the clever. The stupid go so far in vilifying the wise that they represent their every gesture to be a crime and depict them to the ruler as traitors and male-factors, converting the very wisdom which should have secured them happiness into the instrument of their undoing.

'If this is what the wicked have been aiming at, and if fate should conspire to the same end, then it will be difficult indeed to avert disaster. It is destiny that chains the raging lion, and imprisons in a wicker basket the deadly serpent; it is destiny that turns to be-dazzled stupefaction the far-sighted intelligence of the wise, and renders sprightly and vigilant the leaden-witted fool. Destiny makes the heroic and reckless cautious and timid, the fearful and cowardly brave and impetuous; destiny beggars and bewilders the prosperous and wealthy, and converts the penniless beggar into a triumphant millionaire.'

'You are all wrong,' Dimna said gently. 'These things which you have enumerated as accounting for the king's present attitude towards you—the trouble-making activities of enemies, the fickleness of kings, and so forth—none of these is the actual cause. It is nothing short of downright bad faith and treachery that has induced him to act like this. He is a successful tyrant, a treacherous trickster. At first he is all sweetness; at the last he is rank poison.'

'Well, I have sucked his honey,' Shatraba answered. 'Now I must expect to taste his sting. In truth this is the end; my number is up. Anyway, how should I associate with a lion? I am his natural food, and naturally he wants to eat me. It was fate, and my own overweening ambition and greed, that plunged me into this abyss. Today it is too late to do anything to mend the situation; the shrewdest wit would be powerless to find a way out. The honey-bee settles on the nenuphar, and is entranced by the sweet perfume and fragrancy of the flower; the petals of the nenuphar close over him, and when he would fly away he cannot stir, but is caught fast and perishes. The man who is dissatisfied with a modest mouthful of life, and strains after superfluous riches, is like the fly that was not content to frolic amongst the sweet herbs and delicious blossoms of the meadow, but conceived the notion of settling on the rogue elephant's ear; with one flick of his ear the elephant killed him. The fellow who offers his services and counsel to someone who doesn't recognize their value is in no better case than the man who sows his seed in a salt-marsh hoping for a rich harvest, or consults the advice of a corpse, or whispers his grief and joy into the ear of a deaf mute, or scribbles a riddle on running water, or falls in love with a picture daubed in a public bath.'

'Don't talk in that strain,' Dimna snapped. 'Think how to save yourself.'

'Save myself? How can I save myself?' Shatraba returned. 'I know the lion's character. I'm sure he only wishes me well. But his cronies are out to destroy me. That being so, it's no easy matter. When a bunch of crooks gang up shoulder to shoulder with one object in view, they very soon get what they want, and it's just too bad for their victim. It's the story of the wolf, the raven and the jackal all over again. You remember how they made a dead set on the camel, and came up smiling.'

'No, I can't say I do,' said Dimna. 'I'd love to hear.'

So Shatraba told him.

A raven, a wolf and a jackal once joined the service of a lion, and they all lived together in a thicket near the public highway. One day some merchants passed along the road, and one of their camels dropped out of the caravan to hunt for fodder thereabouts. Coming into the forest and finding himself close to the lion, he saw no other course open to him but to join his service also, as humbly as could be. The lion, taking a fancy to him, decided to find out something about him.

'What is your intention in staying here, and moving on there?' he asked mildly.

'Whatever your majesty pleases,' the camel replied.

'Well, if you like to join my group, I guarantee you'll be safe, and very well provided for,' the lion assured him.

This made the camel very happy, and he stayed on in the forest. So some time passed. Then one day the lion was out hunting when he fell in with a raging elephant, and a terrible battle ensued, both sides throwing in all they had. The lion, gored by the elephant's tusks, came home bleeding and miserable, and for days was quite incapable of hunting. The wolf, the raven and the jackal therefore got no food; the camel went on eating grass. The lion, seeing how thin the three old friends were getting, urged them to make an effort for themselves.

'Why suffer like that?' he said. 'There's plenty of game in these parts. Go out and search, until I can sally forth again and provide for you.'

So the three went off; but instead of hunting they fell into a huddle in a corner.

'There's that camel,' they argued. 'What's he staying here for? He's a foreigner. What use is he to us? We've nothing in common with him, and he's no good to the lion. Let's persuade the lion to finish him off; then our troubles will be at an end. The lion will get a good meal, and there'll be plenty over for us too.'

'But we can't do that,' the jackal objected. 'The lion promised him he would be safe, and has taken him into his service. Anyone who incites the king to break his promise and act treacherously, thereby lands his own friends and pals into the ballista of destruction, and spins the noose of disaster about his own neck.'

'Oh, we can easily get over that difficulty,' the raven croaked. 'It won't be hard to provide the lion with a pretext for going back on his engagement. You wait here till I return.'

So saying, he went straight off to the lion, and stood quietly before him.

'Well,' said the lion, 'have you caught anything?'

'We're all so hungry that we can't see straight,' the raven answered. 'But there's another way out of the difficulty. If the king approves of the plan we've concocted, we can all live in the lap of luxury.'

'What is your plan?' the lion asked.

'There's that camel,' the raven replied. 'He's a foreigner. The king gets no benefit from his presence. He's utterly useless here.'

'What you're hinting at is far removed from nobility and good faith,' the lion roared angrily. 'It's not at all in accordance with the rules of chivalry. What possible justification can there be for me to break faith with the camel?'

'I fully understand your majesty's premises,' the raven retorted. 'But the philosophers say that it is right if needs must to sacrifice one life for the good of the family, and one family for the good of the tribe, and one tribe for the good of the people, and the people for the safety of the king's person. Besides, there's a way out of this promise to be found, so that the king escapes entirely the ugly charge of perfidy, and is immediately rescued from his present hardship and the fear of imminent destruction.'

The lion thereupon hung down his head and said no more; and the raven went back to his friends.

'He was furious at first,' he told them when they asked what had happened. 'He was very stiff and pig-headed for a time. But in the end he became quite tame, and was ready to eat out of my hand. Now this is the plan. We all go to the camel and begin talking about the lion; we describe his present predicament, and how much he is suffering. We say how happy we have been, living under his protection and in the shadow of his imperial majesty. Now that he has fallen on evil days, it would be rank ingratitude on our part if we didn't offer ourselves, souls and bodies, to be his ransom and to save him from his misfortune, and we would deserve to be despised and shunned by all decent people. That's the general idea. Then we all go to the lion, and thank him for all his past favours, and report that there is nothing else we can do, but that we freely offer our lives for the king's deliverance. After that each of us in turn says, "Today the king shall dine on me." The others cry out, "No, no, not you," offering some objection which suffices to prove our deep love for the lion, and at the same time brings us no harm.'

They retailed all this rigmarole to the long-necked, stuck-up camel, who was completely taken in by their persiflage; and it was agreed between them accordingly. So they trooped off together to the lion, and began by singing his praises and expressing their infinite gratitude. When all this was finished, the raven took up the cue.

'May the king live for ever!' he cried. 'The comfort of us all hangs upon the king's well-being. Now that the king is in need, though my body and soul are but poor, weak things, I offer them joyfully to ransom the king's royal person. The king may be able to assuage his pangs for today by eating my flesh; so let him slay me.'

'Why, what good would come of eating you?' the others objected. 'Your skin and bones would make a very poor meal.'

The jackal next started off in the same fashion.

'No, no,' the others shouted. 'Your flesh stinks, and is bad to eat. It's not at all suitable for the king's dinner.'

The wolf followed suit in his turn.

'Never,' the others exclaimed. 'Wolf-meat brings on fits and strangulation. It's no better than poison.'

Finally the camel spoke; and he spoke well and eloquently, expressing his gratitude in well-turned phrases, and extolling the excellence and wholesomeness of his own flesh. Thereupon the wolf, the raven and the jackal all cried out together.

'You're right, you're right,' they exclaimed with one voice. 'Your loyalty and affection are proved beyond question.'

And they fell upon him and tore him to pieces.

'I have mentioned this instance,' Shatraba explained, 'to show you that the guile of ruthless people, especially when they are agreed upon a common purpose, is not without effect.'

'Well,' retorted Dimna, 'what do you think you can do about it?'

'There's nothing left but to resist and fight,' Shatraba replied. 'Though a man should pass his whole life praying and giving alms to the poor, that will not bring him so great a reward in heaven as the single hour of a single day when he fights to guard his property and to protect his own soul. In fighting such a battle it is possible that he may win the martyr's crown, and the sublime forgiveness of God. When the swordthrust pierces to the bone, and the life flows out of his broken body, if his struggle has been truly dedicated to the defence of true religion he will receive as his reward blessings immeasurable, and a happiness that passes all understanding.'

'A wise man does not make haste to war,' Dimna interjected. 'He holds it to be in no way allowable to take the initiative in armed combat; to enter upon great dangers of one's own volition is in his view totally incorrect. Prudent people so far as possible treat with the enemy civilly and politely, thinking it better to counter belligerence with peaceableness. Neither is it proper to despise the enemy because he is weak; if he fails in strength and force, he may stir up trouble by craft and cunning and win the day that way. The lion's boldness, imperiousness and intrepidity are well established facts; it would be superfluous to dilate upon them further. The man who scorns his foe, and neglects to consider what the end of the engagement may be, lives to regret his folly. That was what happened to the clerk of the sea who despised the sandpiper.'

'What happened to him?' Shatraba asked.

'I'll tell you,' said Dimna.

A pair of sandpipers lived on the seashore, and when the mating season came round the hen sandpiper spoke seriously to the cock sandpiper.

'We must look for a place where I can lay my eggs, dear cock,' she said.

'Why, what's wrong with here?' the cock replied. 'It's a nice enough place. This is no time for moving house. Lay here.'

'We must consider things carefully,' the hen objected. 'If the sea gets rough, and the waves break up the shore and carry off our chicks, what shall we be able to do then?'

'Pooh,' said the cock. 'I don't think the clerk of the sea will dare do that. He would never treat me with such disrespect. And if he did, I'd soon have the law on him.'

'It's best to know one's limitations,' the hen retorted. 'What strength and resources have you got, that you should threaten the clerk of the sea with reprisals? Come off it. Give over your high and mighty ideas, and choose a nice safe place for me to lay my eggs. People who won't listen to good advice come to a bad end, like the turtle.'

'Why, what happened to the turtle?' the cock inquired.

'This,' the hen told him.

Two ducks and a turtle once lived in a pond, and being near neighbours they became fast friends. One day without warning the hand of perfidious fortune scratched the cheeks of their happiness, and the mirror-bright sphere of heaven revealed to their surprised gaze the image of separation. For the water in the pool, which had been the mainstay of their existence, suddenly changed character to a shocking degree. As soon as they observed this the ducks came to break the news to the turtle.

'We have come to say goodbye,' they cried. 'Farewell, dear friend and delightful companion.'

The turtle, pained by this parting, lamented and shed bitter tears.

'Old friends,' he groaned, 'this change in the water is a much more serious matter for me than for you. I can't live without water. Surely virtue and generosity demand that you should devise and discover some method of carrying me with you.'

'It hurts us even more to leave you,' they answered. 'Wherever we may go, whatever plenty and prosperity yet come our way, we shall find no pleasure or enjoyment in it without the sight of your dear face. If only you were not so indifferent to the good advice of your well-wishers, and so feckless with regards to what touches your own best interests! If you really want us to carry you, we will gladly do so; but there is one condition. When we lift you up and fly with you in the air, whatever men may say on seeing us you must on no account open your mouth to argue with them.'

'I accept your instructions,' the turtle promised. 'If you do your part, as virtue and generosity require, I on my side agree not to say a single word, though it may break my heart to keep silence.'

The ducks thereupon brought a stick, and the turtle took it firmly between his teeth; the ducks lifted up the stick by both ends, and so carried him off aloft. People were astounded when they saw them high up in the air, and a shout went up on all sides.

'Look at that turtle flying with those ducks!'

The turtle kept quiet for a time, but finally he could contain himself no longer.

'You're blind!' he shouted. 'Can't you see they're carrying me?'

As soon as he opened his mouth, down he fell to the earth.

'You can't say we didn't warn you,' the ducks gabbled as they saw him go.

'It's the black humour of destiny,' the turtle sobbed as he fell. 'When fate turns bilious and attacks a man in a frenzy, it's no use for him to snap his prisoner's chains; all the cunning and craft in the world cannot help him then. No intelligent body attempts to fight against fate.'

'That's all very well,' the cock sandpiper said when the story was ended. 'But never you fear. You just stay where you are.'

So the hen sandpiper laid her eggs on the shore. Now when the clerk of the sea heard of their conversation, he flew into a rage at the cock bird's conceit and arrogance. The sea at once surged up and broke over the sands, sweeping away the chicks. Then the hen made a great commotion.

'There!' she screamed. 'I knew perfectly well that water was no joke; but you knew better, of course. Now you've flung our chicks to the wind, and rained fire on my head. You dusty fool, what do you propose to do next? You'd better think quickly.'

'A little more respect and reasonableness, if you please,' her husband retorted. 'I fully intend to keep my promise. You'll see. I'll get even with the clerk of the sea.'

So saying, he strutted off to the other birds, and collecting the chiefs of each variety together he told them the whole story.

'If you don't stand by me now,' he said among other things, 'and if you don't all pull together to set this business to rights, the clerk of the sea will become more insolent than ever. If this thing becomes a habit with him, you'll every one of you be caught the same way in turn.'

The birds hopped off together to the griffon, and laid the incident before him.

'If you don't exert yourself now to take vengeance,' they told him bluntly, 'you can't be king of the birds any more.'

The griffon flapped his wings and bustled best foot foremost into action. Fortified by his action, the birds took heart and firmly resolved to exact revenge. The clerk of the sea, knowing of old the griffon's strength, and realizing the furious determination of the other birds, found himself obliged to give back the chicks to the sandpipers.

'I have told you this fable,' Dimna said, 'to make you understand that one must never underestimate one's enemies.'

'I certainly don't want to begin a war,' remarked Shatraba. 'But I have to protect myself. That I can't dodge.'

'Bravo!' Dimna exclaimed. 'Now listen. When you approach close to the lion, if you see the signs of mischief in him—if he's standing erect, stretched to his full height, and beating the ground with his tail—then you'll know he's in a rage, and intends no good by you.'

'Yes,' Shatraba agreed. 'If I see him like that I'll not doubt any more. I'll know for sure he means to betray me.'

Dimna was greatly delighted now, and hurried off to tell Kalila.

'Well,' said Kalila, 'how are things going?'

'Famously,' Dimna replied. 'Couldn't be better. Success is in sight. Our troubles will soon be over.'

The two of them hastened to the lion; and it so happened that the ox arrived immediately behind them. As soon as the lion saw Shatraba he stood up roaring, and drummed his tail on the ground; and Shatraba realized that he was after his blood.

'The servant of a sultan is fearful and anxious the whole time, as a man would be who shared a cottage with a lion or a bed with a snake,' he said to himself. 'Though the snake may be asleep and the lion in hiding, in the end the latter will rear his head and the former open his mouth.'

Thinking on these things he made ready for battle, waving his horns this way and that. The lion, observing him to be prepared for action, leaped upon him; and the two beasts began to fight. Soon the blood was flowing out of both of them.

'There, you fool!' Kalila shouted at Dimna when he saw what was happening. 'Now look at the frightful results of your trickery.'

'Frightful results?' Dimna retorted. 'Frightful for whom?'

'First for the lion,' answered Kalila. 'See how he's suffering, in addition to the disgrace of having broken his word. Next for the ox; he's done for, and all his blood is being spilled. Thirdly for the army; they're thrown into confusion, and all the troops are scattered. And fourthly for yourself; the shallowness of your boasts is exposed, claiming as you did that you would manage this affair subtly and without hurt to the lion. Well, you see what you've succeeded in doing. Things are come to a pretty pass. There's no one more stupid than the man who needlessly involves his master in hostilities. Wise men abstain from warfare even when they are strong and powerful and on top of the world; they most carefully avoid stirring up trouble and exposing themselves voluntarily to danger. When a minister incites his royal master to fight over an issue which could readily be settled by peaceful methods, he thereby proves himself a fool and an idiot, and provides conclusive evidence of his stupidity and perfidy. It is no secret that prudence ranks higher than courage; affairs of the sword can be managed equally well by prudence, whereas in matters where prudence succeeds the two-fisted sword often fails completely. Again, where prudence is lacking the stoutest courage may prove of no avail. Similarly in a discussion the man of feeble intelligence and flabby reasoning will often be struck dumb, and all his glossy eloquence will not help him.

'I have always known you to be conceited and puffed up about your cleverness. I have always known you to be mesmerized by the thought of worldly success, which is a sheer delusion, as deceptive as the ghoul of the waste or the shimmering mirage of the desert. But I have been watching and waiting, all the time you were showing off, to see whether you would come to your senses and awake out of your idle dreams. But things have now gone too far. The time has come for me to offer a few remarks about your utter stupidity and ignorance, your folly and shamelessness. The time has come for me to enumerate a few of your errors of judgment and monstrous misdeeds; though what I shall say will only be a drop in the ocean, a speck of dust out of the mountain.

'It has been said that there is no greater danger to a king than a minister whose words are bigger than his deeds, and whose speech is more spectacular than his actions. That's you all over. Your talk far outballasts your skill; and the lion has been completely bamboozled by your chatter. There isn't much virtue, they say, in words without deeds, appearances without substance, means without sense, love without fidelity, knowledge without righteousness, charity without a good heart, and life without peace and health.

Though a king may be naturally just and mild, when he has a wicked minister the benefits of his justice and clemency are cut off from his subjects. In the same way though a river may flow with the purest and sweetest water, if a crocodile inhabits it no thirsty swimmer, however great his need, will dare stretch forth his hand or dip his foot into it.

'Well-trained servants and capable assistants are the ornament of kings. Yet you would not allow any other person to have the chance of serving the king, desiring to be alone favoured by his intimacy and trust. It is the last word in stupidity to seek one's own advantage by injuring others, to expect to have loyal friends without being sincere and energetic oneself, to look for the heavenly reward whilst being a hypocrite in one's religion, to court the love of women by being rude-mannered, and to imagine that one can acquire learning easily and without serious effort. But I realize that my words are quite useless, since they will not make any impression on you. I am like the man who told the bird it was not worth taking pains to treat a trouble that was incurable.'

'Oh, when was that?' Dimna asked curiously.

'Once upon a time,' Kalila began.

A colony of monkeys lived on a mountain. Now once, when the king of the stars moved majestically towards the western horizon, mantling his world-adorning beauty in the veil of darkness, when the Ethiop army of night, he vanishing, triumphed over the Turk warriors of day, like the sinner's deeds on the day of resurrection, the north wind, loosening his rein and spurring his steed, charged furiously upon the monkeys; who, shivering in the bitter cold, sought high and low for shelter. Suddenly they saw a glow-worm and, supposing it to be a fire, gleefully swooped upon it; they then collected a pile of brushwood, set the glow-worm on top, and blew.

'It's only a worm,' called a bird to them out of a nearby tree. 'It has wings, and looks at night like a lamp; it isn't a fire at all.'

Of course the monkeys took no notice of what the bird said. Just then a man came along, and addressed the bird.

'Don't give yourself needless trouble,' he cried. 'They won't desist because of what you say, and you'll only bother yourself for nothing. To try to put sense into such people is like testing the edge of a sword on a stone, or hiding a lump of sugar under a cup of water.'

The bird disregarded the man's well-intentioned remarks, and flew down out of the tree and hopped up to the monkeys to explain to them about the glow-worm in more detail. The monkeys seized the bird and cut off its head.

'What you've been doing is exactly like that,' Kalila went on. 'You never accept advice. You won't listen to the warnings of your well-wishers. You remain as headstrong and opinionated as ever. One day, when it's too late, you'll repent all your fraud and roguery. It won't be any use then to bite your hand and beat your breast. You'll be in the same case as the clever man with the idiot partner.'

'Tell me more,' Dimna invited. And Kalila did.

There were two partners, one clever and the other a fool, and they went on a business trip together. On the way they found a purse of gold.

'There are plenty of people in the world who don't make a penny profit,' they said. 'Let's be satisfied with this.'

So they turned back homewards. When they came near the city they wanted to divide the treasure trove; but then the clever one had an idea.

'Why divide it?' he asked. 'Let's take as much as we need now, and carefully hide the rest. Then whenever we want more we can come and help ourselves.'

They agreed accordingly, and taking a few pounds each they buried the rest in the bag under a tree, and entered the city. The next day the clever one came out and took the remainder of the gold. Some days later the foolish one, needing some cash, went up to his partner and told him.

'Come, let's take some of our buried treasure,' he said. 'I need some money.'

So off they went together; and of course when they came to the tree they found nothing.

'You've taken the gold,' shouted the clever one, seizing the fool by the collar. 'You've grabbed the lot behind my back.'

The fool swore mighty oaths that he had done nothing of the sort, but all in vain. The clever one haled him before the governor and demanded his share.

'Have you witnesses and proofs?' the judge asked when he had heard the story.

'The tree under which we buried the gold will give evidence,' the clever one replied. 'The tree will bear witness that this scoundrel has taken the lot and robbed me of my share.'

The judge was much astonished at these words; but after a long dispute a time was fixed when he would come out and sit beneath the tree, and give judgment according to the tree's evidence. The cunning partner then went off home, and told his father everything.

'I'm relying on you to stand by me,' he said. 'I counted on your help when I said I would call the tree as a witness. If you agree to support me I'll bring the gold and we'll divide it equally between us.'

'What do you want me to do?' the father asked doubtfully.

'The tree is hollow,' his son explained. 'Anyone can hide in there and not be spotted. Tonight you must go and sit inside the tree, and tomorrow when the judge comes, you give evidence in the usual manner.'

'My son,' the old man remarked, 'many a rogue has been ruined by his own roguery. God forbid that your trickery should turn out the same way as the frog's.'

'Why, how was that?' the son enquired.

'This way,' the father answered.

A frog once lived near a snake, and whenever the frog had little ones the snake ate them up. Now the frog was friends with a crab, and so she went to him to discuss the situation.

'My dear brother,' the frog implored, 'do help me, and think up some way out of my troubles. A powerful enemy and formidable foe has taken the field against me; I cannot resist him, neither can I move house, because this is such a nice spot. The dell is so pleasant and spacious—a lawn studded with emeralds and lapis lazuli, and crowned with coral and amber.'

'You can't get the better of a stronger enemy except by craft,' the crab observed. 'Now yonder lives a weasel. Catch a few fishes' and strew them on the ground from the weasel's hole to where the snake is hiding. The weasel will eat them one by one until he comes to the snake; and then that will be the end of your troubles.'

In this manner the frog destroyed the snake. Some days elapsed. Then the weasel came out to hunt for fish that way, as had become his wont. Not finding any fish, he ate the frog with all her little ones.

'I have told you this fable,' the old man concluded, 'to make you realize that many a time cunning and trickery have been the ruination of people.'

'My dear father,' the clever fellow retorted, 'do stop talking. Don't be so long-winded. This business means a very little trouble for plenty of profit.'

The old man was so carried away by his greed for money and his love for his son that he threw all religious scruples and honesty to the winds, and agreed to commit this offence against law and morality. The next day the judge came out of the city, attended by a large crowd of spectators. Going up to the tree, he asked about the gold which the two merchants had buried there.

'The fool took it,' came a voice from the tree.

The judge in great amazement walked round about the tree, and realized that someone must be inside it; for roguery can never outwit the noble mind. He therefore ordered firewood to be brought and laid about the tree, and then set fire to it. The old man endured the flames for a while, but presently, finding himself at death's door, he begged for quarter. The judge directed him to be brought out, and spoke encouraging words to the old man, so that he virtuously repented. The innocence and good faith of the fool thus stood revealed, whilst his partner's roguery became fully established. Meanwhile the old man departed this fleeting world into the kingdom of eternity, where he reaped the reward appropriate to martyrdom and divine forgiveness. His son, after being soundly disciplined and severely thrashed, went off home with his dead father on his back. The fool, as a recompense for his honesty and good faith, took the gold and departed.

'I have related this instance to you,' Kalila resumed, 'to teach you that trickery comes to an undistinguished end, and that the conclusion of treachery is far from amiable. As for you, Dimna, you have sunk so low in rascality, greed and improvidence that the tongue is as powerless to describe as the mind is beggared to picture your present situation. The profit your cunning and roguery have brought your master is as you now see; the final disastrous consequences will fall on your own head. You are like a two-faced rose; whoever aspires to be possessed of you is wounded by the thorns, and discovers no consoling constancy in the bloom. You are double-tongued like a snake; but how far superior the snake is to you, seeing that not one but both your tongues drip poison. It has been well said that the water of a conduit or a river is so sweet because it has not run into the sea. A household is wholesome and righteous so long as no devil in human guise has penetrated into it; brothers continue loving, and friends remain true, so long as no double-faced intriguer or double-tongued slanderer has had the chance of coming between them.

'I have always felt fearful of having you for a neighbour. The learned have observed that one should beware of the unrighteous and sinful man, even though he be a dear friend or a near kin. To associate with the sinner is like nurturing a snake; however much pains the snake-trainer may take to look after his pet, in the end it will show him its teeth, and convert the day of fidelity and sympathy into the dark night of treachery and malice. Rather should one attach oneself to the society of the intelligent, even if certain aspects of his character may outwardly seem undesirable; one must profit of the virtues of his intelligence and understanding, and be on one's guard against those features which are less pleasant and less meriting approbation. Of the company of the ignorant one should altogether beware; it is impossible that his ways should ever become other than reprehensible, and no good can come of mixing with him; rather will his ignorance lead one more and more astray.

'You are the kind of person from whose evil propensities and crooked nature one ought to flee a thousand leagues. How can one hope for faithfulness and nobility in you? For you have seen fit to behave in this manner towards a king who was so gracious and generous to you, making you honoured and respected amongst your fellows; in the shadow of his rule you stretched forth your hand to grasp the girdle of Saturn, and kicked your feet high over the roof of heaven. Not all the just claims of his benevolence and benefaction availed to hold you back from your knavishness. You treat your friends like the merchant who said, that in a land where a mouse could eat five hundredweights of iron it was not so strange if a hawk could carry off a four-stone child.'

'What on earth do you refer to?' Dimna asked.

'The well-known story,' Kalila replied.

There was once a merchant who had very little substance, and he wanted to go on a journey. Now he owned five hundredweights of iron, which he deposited in the house of a friend and so departed. During his absence the good and trusty fellow sold the deposit and spent the proceeds. When the merchant returned he presently came to his friend's house and asked for the iron back.

'I put your iron in the basement,' the man replied. 'I took the greatest care of it. But there was a mousehole there, and before I realized what was happening the entire consignment was nibbled up.'

'Of course, you're quite right,' the merchant commented. 'I can well believe it. Mice love iron, and their teeth are so sharp that they soon chew it up.'

The worthy friend was delighted with this reception, for he supposed that the merchant was entirely mollified and had given up all concern for the gold.

'Come and be my guest today,' he said hospitably.

'Thanks,' the merchant replied. 'I'll come tomorrow.'

So saying he went off; but when he reached the end of the street he saw one of his friend's children playing there. He picked up the boy, and carried him off and hid him. Soon there was a hue and cry for the child all through the town.

'Oh,' the merchant said, 'I saw a hawk carrying the child off.'

'Stuff and nonsense!' his friend shouted. 'How can you tell such lies? How could a hawk carry off a child?'

'Nothing easier,' the merchant answered laughing. 'In a town where a mouse can eat five hundredweights of iron, a hawk can certainly make off with a four-stone child.'

At this the friend realized the true situation.

'The mouse didn't eat the iron,' he confessed. 'Give me back my child, and take your iron.'

'I have recited this instance to you,' Kalila finished, 'so that you may realize that since you have done this to the king, nobody will ever rely on you or set any store on your fidelity again. Nothing is more worthless than the friendship of a man who shuffles on his flat feet into the jousting-yard of generosity, and hangs his head sheepishly in the vaunting-field of faithfulness. These things are impermissible: to do good to a man who believes in not requiting kindnesses and being ungrateful for favours, to tell a secret to someone whose stock-in-trade and mission in life is slander, and to give advice to those whose ears are too deaf and hearts too hardened to receive it.

'It is as clear to me as daylight now that I should have been wary of your midnight mischief and perfidy. The company of the wicked is the root of corruption and misery; the society of the virtuous is the alchemy of happiness. It is like the morning breeze; if it blows over sweet basil it brings the perfume of its odour to the nostrils, but if it passes by a cesspool it carries along its stench wherever it may go. It is easy to see that my words fall heavy upon your ears; truth is bitter, and uncongenial to the hearing of the wilful and stupid.'

By the time their exchanges had reached this point the lion was through with the fray. Seeing the ox cast down before him drenched in gore, and the turbulence of his fury being by now somewhat assuaged, he began to reflect upon the spectacle and to ruminate sadly.

'Alas!' he said to himself. 'Poor Shatraba, so clever, so wise, so prudent! I do not know whether I acted rightly in this affair, or whether I made a mistake. I do not know whether what they reported concerning him was truly and loyally said, or the invention of treachery and wickedness. Whatever the case may be, I have certainly procured misfortune for myself, and all my self-pity and regrets will be unprofitable.'

Seeing the lion so evidently and indubitably sorry over what had passed, Dimna cut short Kalila's eloquence and addressed himself to his royal master.

'Why so pensive, majesty?' he asked tenderly. 'What season could be happier, what day be counted luckier than this? The king exultantly striding the scene of victory and triumph, his enemy sprawling upon the pallet of discomfort and humiliation. . . .'

'Whenever I recall Shatraba's companionship, his loyal service and his wisdom,' the lion replied, 'I am overcome by feelings of tender compassion, and surrender to sorrow and uneasiness. In very truth he was the backbone of my army, the strong right arm of my retinue; he was a thorn in the eye of my enemies, a mole upon the cheek of my friends.'

'The king needs not to pity that ungrateful traitor,' Dimna returned. 'Let him instead rejoice in the victory and triumph that have been granted him, and be glad and make merry the more. Let him count this amongst the great benefits of fortune, the boasts and memorable exploits of his reign, that the journal of prosperity should be so brilliantly illustrated, and the chronicle of felicity so splendidly embroidered. It is contrary to reason to have compassion on such a one, from whose malice the king's soul could never feel secure. For the king's enemies there is no prison like the grave, no whip like the sword. Wise kings promote to their intimacy many a one with whom they are but triflingly acquainted because of their skill and devotion, and drive far from them friends in plenty owing to their ignorance and perfidy. So it is that a man will swallow unpalatable medicines on account of their beneficial properties, and not out of any desire or appetite for them. Similarly the finger, that is the ornament of the hand and the instrument of graspng and releasing, if it is bitten by a snake will be cut off, so that the rest of the body may be saved, and the hardship of parting with it is reckoned the acme of relief.'

These words quietened the lion a little. But destiny was yet to avenge the ox, and bring Dimna to disgrace. His hypocrisy and falsehood, his mendacity and fabrication became known in due season to the lion, who slew him most miserably in reprisal for Shatraba.

The stem of a man's deeds and the seed of his words, like as the former is nurtured and the latter sown, so do they thrive thereafter and bear fruit accordingly. Whosoever planteth thorns shall assuredly not gather in grapes. This I say, that you may know that the consequences of craft and treachery are never laudable, neither is the issue of malice and guile blessed; whoever thrusts forth his foot to the one, or reaches out his hand to the other, in the end himself suffers of it, and his back is outstretched in the dust.

(*Kalīla wa-Dimna.*)

FIVE

Science from the West

The establishment of the Abbasid empire with its teeming capital in Baghdad and its great provincial cities, from Kairouan to Bukhara (for the furthest west disowned the claim of the Umaiyads' supplanters to rule all Islam), created a situation of relative stability and ushered in the birth of an affluent society. Byzantium was contained but could not for some centuries be mastered, and only then under very different auspices. Europe of the Dark Ages was hardly worth troubling about. India constituted no menace, and the Far East would not erupt for nearly half a millennium.

Iran was yielding up her secrets of statecraft and gracious living. Now ancient Greece, mediated through the Hellenistic world and the Christians within the frontiers, began to reveal treasures of philosophy and science which could greatly enrich the material and intellectual life of Islam. Avid to gather in this inherited capital, caliphs and their ministers encouraged the handful of scholars learned in the Greek and Syriac to put into Arabic the writings of Plato and Aristotle, of Euclid and Ptolemy, of Hippocrates and Galen. To the 'religious sciences'—Koran and its exegesis, Traditions, Canon Law, theology—now came to be added medicine, mathematics, astronomy, botany, zoology, mineralogy, logic, metaphysics, ethics, politics, in all of which the Greeks and their commentators had made fundamental contributions to human knowledge. In the space of a hundred years all these writings, far exceeding what has survived until today, had been translated into the language of the Koran, and Muslims who knew no Greek, having mastered the ancient canon, began to adventure beyond the Greeks in exploring the mysteries of mind and matter.

In this chapter fragments are offered of the writings of three Muslim scholars who assimilated the Greek learning, and in their different ways sought to accommodate it to the faith and the tradition to which they held unwaveringly. What they thought and wrote set up conflicts within Islam, episodes in the war between Revelation and Reason, a war which will continue to be waged for as long as Islam survives.

First of the three is Abū Bakr al-Rāzī, the Rhazes of medieval writers. Born at Raiy near Teheran in AD 864 and dying there in AD 925, he devoted himself in particular to the study and practice of medicine which he pursued mainly in Baghdad. His greatest work, the encyclopaedia of medicine called in Arabic *al-Ḥāwī* and translated into Latin by Farragut under the title *Continens*, in its Latin dress was published five times between 1488 and 1542 but the original text has had to wait until the 1960s to be printed for the first time. His adventures into philosophy earned him the obloquy of orthodox theologians, who deplored his awarding the primacy to human reason as the surest guide to truth. Here we present the apologia which he wrote in his later years when, already threatened by blindness and disabled by partial paralysis, he defended his reputation against the attacks already being levelled against it.

Second of our trio of Muslim intellectuals is Abū Naṣr al-Fārābī, born of Turkish stock in Transoxiana, who died in Damascus near eighty years of age in AD 950. A pupil in Baghdad of Christian scholars who had themselves played a prominent part in the first renaissance of Greek learning, he directed his interest to logic and politics as parts of philosophy; his most famous and influential book is the *Ideal State*, in which he attempted to Islamize Plato's model *Republic*. The text here chosen to illustrate his writings is a treatise on poetics, based upon Aristotle but with some inevitable misunderstandings, the original of which it was our own good fortune to discover.

Third stands Abū 'Alī Ibn Sīnā, Avicenna, truly a giant among men of science and learning, the story of whose life and writings is told in graphic detail in the autobiographical fragment, continued by his pupil, reproduced in these pages.

Apologia Pro Vita Sua

Certain men there be, speculative and discriminating and of undoubted attainments, who observing that we maintain relations with our fellows and engage in various manners of earning a livelihood, have therefore criticized and found fault with us, asserting that we have swerved away from the philosophic life and in particular that of our leader Socrates. For of him it is recorded that he frequented not the company of kings, and treated them with scant respect if ever they sought his; that he ate no tasty food, wore no fine raiment, raised no edifice, acquired not wealth, begat no issue; that he con-

sumed no meat, drank no wine, and attended no amusements, but
contented himself with eating herbs, wrapping himself in threadbare
garments, and sheltering in a barrel in the waste. It is further
reported that he practised dissimulation neither before the common
people nor in the presence of authority, but confronted all with the
truth as he conceived it, and that in the frankest and bluntest
language.

We on the other hand are, they say, the opposite of all that; and
yet they go on to condemn the life which our leader Socrates lived,
on the grounds that it was contrary to the course of nature and the
maintenance of tilth and issue, and that it tended to the desolation
of the world and the ruin and destruction of mankind. These are
the several charges which we now propose to answer to the best of
our ability, God willing.

As for what they have related concerning Socrates, there they
describe truly the sort of life he led. But they have at the same time
ignored certain other equally relevant matters; they have in fact
deliberately failed to mention them, no doubt in order to strengthen
their argument against us. To be explicit, their detailed account of
Socrates' behaviour is perfectly true as regards his early career and
for a considerable stretch of his life; but he subsequently changed
many of his habits, so that for instance he died leaving daughters;
he fought against the enemy; he attended entertainments; he ate
good food (though he always abstained from flesh); and he took
intoxicants in moderation. All this is well known and familiar to
those who have troubled to investigate the records of the man.

The manner of his early life is fully explained by the intensity of
his admiration and love for philosophy; he was eager to devote to
it the time he would otherwise have spent upon his normal passions
and pleasure. Moreover his natural temperament disposed him in
any case to this sort of conduct. He scorned and despised those who
did not look upon philosophy with the respect it merited, preferring
baser occupations. It is inevitable that at the beginning of much
desired and beloved enterprises, the inclination will be excessive
and the love and attachment for them exaggerated; whilst those
who have a contrary disposition will be correspondingly detested.
But when one has made a deep penetration of the object, and
matters have become more or less settled, the exaggeration drops
away and balance once more returns. As the proverb has it, 'Novelty
has its charm.'

This was Socrates' state of mind during that period of his life.
The record of those matters is of course ampler and more famous,
because they are more curious, amusing and eccentric. Men are over

fond of publishing news that is curious and unusual, and of overlooking the familiar and the habitual. Now we are by no means at
variance with the more laudable part of Socrates' life, even though
we ourselves fall far short of him in that respect and readily confess
our failure to practise the just life perfectly, to suppress passion,
and to be in love with and eager for knowledge. Where we differ
from Socrates is not regarding the quality but rather the quantity
of that life. And if we confess ourselves his inferior, we do not
thereby demean ourselves; for that is the plain truth, and it is always
nobler and more honourable to acknowledge the truth. So much for
that subject.

Now as for the criticism that is levelled against the first manner
of Socrates' life, we repeat that here the fault, such as it is, is again
a question of quantity, not quality. It is obvious that the reckless
indulgence of the passions is not the better and nobler way; this we
have clearly stated in our book *The Spiritual Physick*. True virtue
consists in taking of every need so much as is indispensable, or so
much as will not involve pain exceeding the pleasure thereby procured. In fact Socrates gave up the more extreme position which he
had formerly adopted—and it was that that was truly at fault,
tending as it did towards the desolation of the world and the ruin
of mankind—when he took to procreating children, fought the
enemy, and attended amusements. When a man acts thus, he has
ceased to labour for the desolation of the world and the ruin of
mankind; but it is not necessary for him to be otherwise, in order
to plunge into a career of gratifying his passions. As for ourselves,
if we do not deserve the name of philosopher in comparison with
Socrates, yet we certainly have some claim to the title when compared with those who do not attempt to practise philosophy.

Since this has now all been sufficiently dealt with, let us proceed
to discourse upon the philosophic life, for the benefit of the true
lovers of knowledge.

We need to build our affairs, in respect of the object we have in
view in our present treatise, upon certain fundamental principles
which we have already expounded in other books, to which recourse
must be had in order to lighten the content of this essay. Amongst
these are our books *On Theology, The Spiritual Physick, In Reproof
of So-called Philosophers Who Occupy Themselves with Geometrical
Superfluities*, and *The Noble Science of Chemistry*; especially important
is the second, which is quite indispensable to fulfil completely our
purpose in the present treatise. Now the principles upon which we
are building are in effect the several branches of the philosophic life;
these we will accordingly now take and summarize.

After death we shall find ourselves in a state that is either admirable or reprehensible according to the life we have lived whilst our souls were associated with our bodies.

The supreme end for which we were created and towards which we have been led is not the gratification of physical pleasures, but the acquisition of knowledge and the practice of justice. These two occupations are our sole deliverance out of the present world into the world wherein is neither death nor pain.

Nature and passion prompt us to prefer present pleasure; but reason frequently urges us to eschew present pleasures for the sake of other objects which it prefers.

Our Ruler, for Whose reward we hope (whilst fearing His punishment), is watching over us with compassion, and does not desire that we should suffer pain. It is hateful to Him that we should be unjust and ignorant; He loves us to have knowledge and to be just. This same Ruler will punish those of us who inflict pain, and those who deserve to be pained, each according to his deserts.

We must not suffer pain alongside any pleasure, when that pain exceeds the pleasure both in quantity and in quality.

The Almighty Creator has entrusted to us all the particular things that we need, such as husbandry, spinning and the like, upon which the world itself and our own livelihood alike depend.

The foregoing are the principles which we ask to be taken for granted, in order that we may build upon them.

Since the pleasures and pains of this world come to an end with the end of life itself, whilst the pleasures of the world where no death is are everlasting, unending and infinite, surely that man is demented who would purchase a pleasure which perishes and comes to an end at the price of an everlasting, enduring, unending and infinite pleasure. This being so, it likewise follows necessarily that we ought not to seek any pleasure, the attainment of which would inevitably involve us in the commission of an act barring our deliverance into the world of Spirit, or that would oblige us in this present world to suffer pain exceeding both quantitively and qualitively the pleasure we have chosen. All other pleasures are of course free for us to take; except that the philosopher may sometimes eschew many of these lawful pleasures in order thus to train and habituate his soul, so that it may be easier and simpler for him so to do when the occasion requires. This we have dealt with in our *Spiritual Physick*. For habit, as was said of old, is a second nature, making easy for us what was difficult, and rendering the unfamiliar task congenial, whether it be a spiritual or a physical matter that confronts us. Thus, we may observe that couriers are hardier upon the march, and armies bolder in the war; all this is no secret, and it is obvious that habit facilitates the performance of labours which were hard and difficult before one grew accustomed to them.

Although this statement is brief and concise—I mean the account we have given of the amount of circumscribed pleasure—there are underlying it many matters of detail, as we have explained in our *Spiritual Physick*. For if the principle which we have laid down is sound and true in itself, or is logically postulated, namely that the intelligent man ought not to indulge a pleasure when he fears that its accompanying pain may outweigh the pain he would suffer in striving to eschew that pleasure and to suppress that appetite—if all this is true, it necessarily follows that if we were in a position to master the entire earth for the whole of our lives through the commission of certain acts unpleasing to God, whereby we were prevented from attaining eternal good and everlasting bliss, it would not be right for us to do or choose that. Similarly, if we were certain, or if it were overwhelmingly likely that by eating for instance a plate of fresh dates we would suffer from ophthalmia for ten days, we ought not to choose to eat them. The argument holds equally in all cases lying between the two examples we have quoted, even though the first is a large matter and the second relatively small; it applies to every individual instance, for each is small in relation to one that is greater, and great in relation to one that is smaller. However, it is not possible to discuss every example, for there are so many isolated and individual instances underlying this broad generalization.

As the principle which we have laid down is that our Lord and Ruler is merciful, and that He watches over us compassionately, it follows from this also that it is not His pleasure that any pain should befall us; also, that whatever pain befalls us not of our own earning and choice but in accordance with nature is a matter of necessity, whose occurrence is inevitable. Accordingly it is incumbent upon us not to cause pain to any sentient being whatsoever except it deserve so to be pained, or in order that we may avert from it a yet severer pain.

This generalization likewise comprehends a wide range of detail, and embraces every manner of wrongful act, alike the pleasure kings take in hunting animals and the excessive labour men impose on their domestic beasts. All this ought to be done in moderation and according to a certain code and method, a just and reasonable manner which must not be exceeded or transgressed. Pain may however be inflicted when it is hoped thereby to ward off a greater pain, such as lancing a wound or cauterizing a festering limb, or taking bitter and disagreeable medicine, or refraining from delicious food for fear of serious and painful maladies. Beasts may also be put to hard labour in moderation, provided they are not used harshly; except in circumstances where necessity dictates harsh treatment and reason and justice alike require it. Thus one may drive one's horse hard when seeking to escape from the enemy; for then justice demands that the animal be urged on, and even destroyed, if the rider's safety is thereby hoped for, especially if he be a man of learning and benevolence, or if he be greatly endowed in some manner beneficial to the whole of mankind. For the endowment and survival of such a man in this world clearly advantage its inhabitants more than the survival of the horse. In the same way if two men chance to be in a waterless plain, and one of them has water just sufficient to save his life but not his companion's, in such a case it is right that the water should go to the one who is of greater benefit to his fellows. This is the logical criterion to adopt in such and similar instances.

As for hunting, stalking, killing and exterminating, this should only be done with animals which are purely carnivorous, such as lions, tigers, wolves and the like; and those which cause great mischief and are neither desired for their useful properties nor needed for any use whatsoever, such as snakes, scorpions and so forth. There are two reasons for destroying these animals: first, if they are not destroyed they will destroy many other animals (this is a special category applying to carnivorous beasts), and secondly, the souls of animals cannot escape from their bodies but only those of men, which being the case, to liberate such souls from their bodies is tantamount to rescuing them and effecting their release. Since both these arguments apply simultaneously to purely carnivorous animals, it is obligatory to exterminate them to the utmost possible extent, for this will diminish the pain suffered by other creatures and will allow the hope that their souls may lodge in more salutary bodies. Snakes, scorpions, hornets and the like are both hurtful to other creatures and unsuitable for human use in the way domestic animals are used; it is therefore permissible to destroy and exterminate them.

On the other hand it is not right to exterminate and destroy domestic and herbivorous animals; on the contrary, domestic animals are to be handled gently as we have described, and taken as little as possible for food, neither should they be bred in such quantities as to necessitate excessive slaughtering, but rather in moderation and as need arises. If it were not for the fact that there is no hope for a soul to escape save from the human body, the judgment of reason would not have permitted their slaughter at all. Philosophers indeed have held different opinions on this subject, some taking the view that men should not feed on flesh, whilst others have not so taught. Socrates was amongst those not allowing it.

Since the arbitrament of both reason and justice is against a man inflicting hurt upon another, it follows from this that he may not hurt himself either. Under this general rule come many matters which the reason rejects, such as the Indian custom of seeking to propitiate God by setting fire to their bodies and casting them down on sharp spikes, or the Manichæean habit of castrating themselves when they cannot overcome their sexual impulses, exhausting themselves by fasting and not drinking, and making themselves filthy by avoiding the use of water and employing urine in its stead. Under this same heading, though at a much lower level, come the Christian practice of monasticism and seclusion in cloisters; and the habit many Muslims have of passing their whole time in mosques, giving up gainful employment, and restricting themselves to a minimum of coarse food and rough, uncomfortable clothing. In all this they do themselves wrong, and inflict pain upon themselves without thereby warding off any correspondingly greater pain. Socrates followed a similar course in the early part of his life, but afterwards gave it up as we have mentioned before.

People are by no means alike in this respect, and in fact there is a very great difference between them; we must therefore make an approximate statement on the subject, to serve as an example. As we have said, men vary very greatly in their circumstances. Some have been brought up luxuriously, some wretchedly; some are much more strongly beset by certain passions than others, such as a predilection for women, wine, love of authority and the like, and they find it correspondingly more painful than do their fellows to suppress these passions. The offspring of kings, being reared in royal luxury, find it intolerable to their skins to wear rough clothes, whilst their stomachs cannot abide the wretched sort of food which satisfies those born of the common people, and indeed they suffer acute discomfort when they try to do so. In the same way men accustomed to enjoy any sort of pleasure are pained when denied its gratification, and their suffering is many times greater and more severe than with those who have never been accustomed to that particular pleasure. It is therefore not possible for all men to be charged with an equal burden, but this must differ according to their different circumstances. The philosopher-prince cannot be required to confine himself to the same food and drink and other means of sustenance as the offspring of the masses, unless indeed he is gradually brought to it if necessity dictates.

There is however a certain limit which cannot be transgressed. All men must refrain from such pleasures as may not be gratified without perpetrating such injustice or committing murder—in short, all such acts as may anger God and are condemned by reason and justice. Short of this, all things are lawful to be enjoyed. This then is the upper limit, that is to say in regard to the luxury that may be properly indulged. As for the lower limit, the degree of abstinence and self-denial that may be practised, the rule here is that a man should eat such things as will not harm him or cause him sickness, while not exceeding this so as to seek the gratification of extreme pleasure, having as his aim not the mere satisfaction of hunger but the indulgence of pleasure and appetite. He should wear such clothes as his skin can tolerate without hurt, but not hanker after splendid and ornate raiment; he should live where he may find shelter from excessive heat and cold, but not go beyond this so as to dwell in magnificent, splendid mansions with fancy decorations and ornaments; unless indeed he is possessed of such ample wealth that he can easily afford to live in such circumstances without injustice or aggression or undue exertion to acquire the wherewithal. Children of poor parents who have been brought up in shabby circumstances obviously have the advantage in this respect, since it is easier for them and their like to deny themselves and live hard. It was easier for Socrates to be abstinent and self-denying than for Plato.

Whatever lies between these two extremes is permissible, and whoever takes advantage of this broad category of allowed gratification does not thereby forfeit the name of philosopher, but rather may well be so called; though the advantage lies with those who lean towards the lower rather than the upper limit. Noble spirits, though they may be associated with bodies used to luxurious food, have ever brought their bodies down gradually to accept the lower limit. But to surpass the lower limit is to quit philosophy and to fall into those Indian and Manichæan and monkish and ascetic practices which we have mentioned; it is to abandon the just life, and to anger God Himself, by paining the spirit to no purpose. Such conduct truly merits expulsion from the name of philosophy. This is of course equally true when the upper limit is transgressed. And we ask God, the giver of reason and deliverer from grief and sorrow, to assist, direct and aid us to that life which is higher and more pleasing unto Him.

In short, since the Almighty Creator has the attributes of knowledge wherein is no ignorance, and justice that is innocent of wrong, whereas He is Himself absolute knowledge, justice and mercy, and whereas He is our Creator and Ruler and we are His slaves and bondservants, and those servants are most beloved of their masters who most faithfully adopt their masters' way of life and most carefully follow their code of conduct—that man is therefore the nighest of God's servants unto his Master who is the most knowing, just, merciful and compassionate. All this statement means in fact what every philosopher has asserted, namely that 'philosophy is the imitation of Almighty God so far as lies within man's power.' Such is the sum of the philosophic life; as for its details, these are set forth in our *Spiritual Physick*, in which we have described how evil characteristics may be rooted out of the soul, and to what extent the philosopher may devote his attention to gainful employment, the acquisition and expending of wealth, and the quest of high office.

As we have now explained what we had in mind to expound in this context, we will go back again and set out our case as against our critics; asserting that we have done nothing in our life so far (God helping and succouring) that would merit our being excluded from the name of philosopher.

That man truly deserves to be erased from the roll of philosophy who has fallen short of fulfilling the two separate parts of philosophy together—I mean theory and practice—through ignorance of what it behoves the philosopher to know, or living not as it is fitting for the philosopher to live.

First as to theory. We may claim that if we had possessed no greater qualification in this respect than the capacity to compose such a book as the present, that in itself would have prevented our being expunged from the roll of philosophy. That is quite apart from our other works, such as the *Demonstration*, the *Theology*, the *Spiritual Physick*, the *Introduction to Physical Science* (or *Natural Acoustics*), our dissertations *On Time, Space, Extension, Duration and Void, On the Shape of the World, Why the Earth is Fixed in the Middle of the Sky, Why the Heavens Revolve, On Composition*, and *That the Body has its own Motion and that Motion is Determinable*, our books *On Psychology* and *On Matter*, and our medical works such as the *Mansuri, Every Man His Own Doctor, On Drugs, The Royal Medicine*, and the *Compendium* (which last is without precedent or successor so far in this country), not to mention our treatises *On the Practice of Wisdom* (popularly called Alchemy). In short, we have produced about two hundred books, treatises and essays up to the actual date of this present discourse, ranging over the various branches of philosophy, both natural and divine. As for mathematics, I confess that I have only studied this subject to the extent that was absolutely indispensable, not wasting my time upon tricks and refinements; this I have done deliberately, and not out of incapacity for the study. If anyone desires to have my excuse, I make it boldly on the grounds that what I have done is in fact the right course, rather than the way chosen by those so-called philosophers who devote their whole lives to indulging in geometrical superfluities. If after all this I have not attained that degree of theory which will qualify me to be called a philosopher, I should very much like to know who has, of those now living.

Then as to practice. With God's help and succour I have not transgressed in any way, in my manner of life, the two limits which I have defined; neither has any act of mine ever been apparent that justified the statement that my life was not the philosophic life. I have not kept the sovereign's company in the way of bearing arms or acting as an official on his behalf; my association with him has only been as a physician and a courtier whose functions were precisely twofold—when he was sick, to minister to him and restore his body to health, and when he was physically well, to be sociable with him and to advise him (God be my witness) with the sole object of securing his welfare and that of his subjects. I have never been observed to be greedy to amass wealth, to be extravagant in spending it, to dispute and quarrel with my fellows or to do them wrong; on the contrary it is well known that I have always been the very reverse, even to the point of surrendering many of my own rights.

As for my habits of eating, drinking and amusement, those who have frequently observed me so engaged may be aware that I have never erred on the side of excessive indulgence; similarly with all my other habits, connected with clothes, riding, servants and maids. And as for my love of learning, and my desire and passionate endeavour to possess it, it is well known amongst my friends and those who have observed me at it that I have never ceased since my youth up to this present time to be intent upon learning; so much so, that whenever I have chanced upon a book which I have not read, or a man whom I have not hitherto met, I have not heeded any other occupation—even though it has been to my great loss—until I have mastered the book and found out all that the man knew. So vast indeed have been my patience and endeavour that I have written, in a minute script like that in which amulets are inscribed, more than 20,000 sheets within a single year. I was engaged continuously upon the great *Compendium* for fifteen years, working night and day, until my sight grew dim and I was affected by a paralysis in the muscles of my hand, so that at the present time I am disabled from reading and writing. Yet I still continue these two occupations to the utmost of my power, and always engage the assistance of someone to read and write for me.

If all that I have practised in these respects still appears to these people to disqualify me from attaining the rank of philosopher, and if their conception of the object in following the philosophic life is other than what we have described, then let them state their case, either orally or in writing, so that we may be in the position to accept what they say if it be informed by superior knowledge, or to rebut them if we establish any point of error or deficiency in their argument. And suppose I spare them the trouble, and readily confess my shortcomings on the practical side—yet what can they have to say as regards theory? If they consider me deficient in this respect too, let them say what they have to say against me, so that we may examine their case and thereafter concede where they are in the right, or rebut their errors. If however they do not hold me wanting on the theoretical side, they will do better to profit by my theory and not give heed to my conduct. As the poet says:

> Practise what I have preached; for if it be
> That in my practice lies deficiency,
> Still thou canst profit of my theory
> And where I failed, no harm will come to thee.

This is all that we desired to include in the present discourse. Infinite thanks be ascribed to the Giver of Reason, as He merits and is worthy; and may God's blessing rest upon His chosen servants and virtuous handmaidens.

(*The Asiatic Review*, Vol. XLV, pp. 703–12.)

The Canons of Poetry

Our intention in the present disquisition is, to set forth statements and mention ideas which will assist those who are acquainted therewith to understand what the Philosopher[1] laid down on the Art of Poetry. We do not however propose to describe in detail and due order all that is requisite to the practice of the said art; for the Philosopher himself did not even complete his discourse on the Art of Sophistry,[2] much less that on the Art of Poetry. Now the reason for this was, as he himself declares at the end of his disquisitions on

[1] Sc. Aristotle.

[2] The reference is to Aristotle, *De Sophisticis Elenchis*. The author offers an almost literal translation of the concluding paragraph of that work.

the Art of Sophistry, that he found nothing written by his predecessors which he could use as foundations and canons, to put in order and build upon and assess a true evaluation. It would therefore hardly be proper for us to attempt to complete what the Philosopher, for all his skill and genius, did not venture to bring to a conclusion; rather we should limit ourselves to indicating such canons, examples and sayings, profitable to the study of this Art, as may occur to us at the present time.

Words, broadly speaking, are either significant or lack significance. Of the former, some are simple, some compound. Compounded words may either be statements, or not statements. Of statements, some are categorical, others not; of the categorical, some are true, others false. Of false statements, some register in the mind of the hearer the object referred to, taking the place of a direct statement, whilst others register in his mind an imitation of the object; these last are poetical statements. Of such imitations some are more perfect, some more imperfect; to investigate fully the nature of such perfection or imperfection comes within the province of poets, or students of poetry, in the various languages and dialects, and they have indeed written on this subject.

Now let no man suppose that the terms 'sophistry' and 'imitation' are identical; on the contrary, they differ in several respects. To begin with, their purposes are different. The sophist deludes his hearer into supposing that he is listening to a contrary proposition, so that he imagines that what is is not, and what is not is; the imitator, however, causes his hearer to imagine, not a contrary, but a like proposition. A parallel to this is provided by sensation. A person at rest is sometimes in a state which causes him to imagine that he is moving, as when he is on board a ship travelling, and looks at persons on the bank; or when he is standing on the ground in springtime, and looks at the moon and the stars behind fast-travelling clouds. These are circumstances which actually deceive the senes. When however a man looks into a mirror, or any reflecting body, that circumstance makes him fancy that he is seeing a likeness of the object.

Statements may also be divided in another way as follows. A statement must be either categorical, or the reverse. If a statement is categorical, it must either be an analogy, or not. If it is an analogy, it must either be potential, or actual; if potential, it may be either a deduction or an imitation. Imitation is mostly used in the Art of Poetry; it is therefore clear that a poetical statement is an imitation.

Analogies, and in fact statements generally, may be divided in yet another manner. Statements are either absolutely true, or absolutely false, or mainly true but partly false, or the reverse of this, or true and false in equal proportions. The absolutely true statement is called demonstrative; that which is mainly true, disputative; that which is equally true and false, rhetorical; that which is mainly false, sophistical; that which is wholly false, poetical. This analysis proves that the poetical statement is one which is neither demonstrative, nor argumentative, nor rhetorical, nor sophistical; yet for all that it belongs to a kind of syllogism, or rather post-syllogism. (By 'post-syllogism' I mean a deduction, image, intuition or the like, something which has the same force as an analogy.)

Having proceeded thus far, it is now proper for us to describe the different varieties of poetical statements.

Poetical statements may be classified according either to their metres, or to their contents. Classification according to metres is an investigation belonging properly to the musician or the prosodist, according to the language in which the statements are composed, and the class of music to which they belong. Scientific classification according to contents comes within the province of the expert in allusions, the interpreter of poetry, the investigator of poetical meanings, the student of the poetry of different nations and different schools. We have such experts now living, who have made a study of Arabic and Persian poetry and have written books on the subject; they divide poetry into satire, paean, competitive verse, enigmatic, comic, ghazal, descriptive, and so on. In this fashion they enumerate the various classes in their books, which are not hard to come by, so that we need not to mention them at any great length. Let us turn therefore to another subject.

The majority of the poets of past and present nations of whom we have any information make no distinction between metre and subject-matter, and do not prescribe a special metre for each variety of poetical theme. The only exception to this rule is the case of the ancient Greeks. They reserved a particular metre for each variety of poetical theme. With them the metre of paean was not the same as the metre of satire, neither was the metre of satire the same as that of comic verse, and so on. Other nations and tribes, however, compose paeans in a variety of metre identical with those in which satire is written, using either all or the majority of such metres in common, and not dividing each class off so scrupulously as did the Greeks.

We will now enumerate the varieties of Greek poetry, following the classification used by the Philosopher in his discourses on the Art of Poetry,[1] and referring to each class in turn.

[1] The section following does not occur in Aristotle's *Poetics*, and I have been unable to trace its source.

Greek poetry was confined to the following classes, which I here enumerate: Tragedy, Dithyramb, Comedy, Iambus, Drama, Ainos,[1] Diagramma,[2] Satyric, Poemata, Epic, Rhetoric, Amphi Geneseōs, and Acoustic.

Tragedy is a kind of poetry having a particular metre, affording pleasure to all who hear or recite it. In tragedy good things are mentioned, praiseworthy matters which are an example for others to emulate; governors of cities are also praised in it. Musicians used to sing tragedy before kings, and whenever a king died they would insert in the tragedy certain additional melodies lamenting the dead king.

Dithyramb is a kind of poetry having a metre double that of Tragedy. In dithyramb good things are mentioned, universal praiseworthy characteristics, and virtues common to all humanity, without the intention of praising any particular king or person, but only universal good works are mentioned.

Comedy is a kind of poetry having a particular metre. In comedy evil things are mentioned, personal satires, blameworthy characteristics and reprehensible habits. Sometimes additional melodies are inserted in which are mentioned blameworthy characteristics which are common to men and beasts, as well as ugly physical features likewise common to them.

Iambus is a kind of poetry having a particular metre. In iambus are mentioned well-known sayings, whether they be of good or evil works, only provided they are well known, such as proverbs. This kind of poetry was used in disputes and wars, during the moods of anger or disquiet.

Drama is exactly the same variety as the last, except that in it are mentioned proverbs and well-known sayings relating to particular men and particular persons.

Ainos is a kind of poetry in which are mentioned sayings which give pleasure because of their exceeding excellence, or because they are remarkable and striking.

Diagramma is a kind of poetry which was used by lawmakers; in it they described the terrors which await the souls of men when they are not disciplined or educated.

Epic and Rhetoric are a kind of poetry in which are described early forms of law and government. In this kind are also mentioned the characters and exploits of kings, their battles and adventures.

Satyric is a kind of poetry with a metre invented by the musicians; using this metre, they contrived with their chanting to cause

[1] Perhaps Êthē (suggestion by Professor D. S. Margoliouth).
[2] Perhaps Dikaia (Margoliouth).

wild beasts, and in general all animals, to make certain movements of an astonishing kind, quite different from any natural movements.

Poemata is a kind of poetry in which is described poetry excellent and atrocious, regular and irregular; each kind of poetry representing the matters beautiful and excellent, ugly and depraved, which it resembles.

Amphi Geneseōs is a kind of poetry invented by scientists, in which they described the natural sciences. Of all varieties of poetry this is the farthest removed from the Art of Poetry.

Acoustic is a kind of poetry intended for the instruction of students of the Art of Music; to this use it is confined, and it has no utility in any other direction.

These are the varieties and several meanings of Greek poetry, so far as we have been informed by those familiar with their poetry, and so far as we have read in the discourses attributed to the philosopher Aristotle on the Art of Poetry, to Themistius, and other ancient writers, as well as the Commentators on their books. We have also found in certain of their discourses additional statements appended to their catalogue of these varieties; these we will now mention in the exact form in which we found them.

Poets may be divided into three classes. The first are possessed of a natural gift and faculty for composing and reciting poetry; these have an excellent bent for inventing similes and images, either in the majority of the varieties of poetry, or in some particular variety. These poets are not acquainted with the Art of Poetry itself in any way, but are confined to their excellent dispositions and bent for achieving what they set out to do. They are not 'syllogizing' poets in the true sense of the word, for their vision[1] is not quite perfect, and they are not firmly grounded in the Art. Such a poet is only called 'syllogizing' by virtue of the activity he displays as a poet.

The second class of poet is fully familiar with the Art of Poetry; none of its idioms or canons is foreign to him, in whatever field he may enter. By reason of his Art he excels in similes and images. Such a poet fully deserves the name of 'syllogizing' poet.

The third class consists of those who imitate the poets of the first two classes and their works, perpetuating their activities and following their lead in similes and images, without themselves having any poetical disposition, or any understanding of the canons of the Art. It is amongst poets of this class that slips and errors are most frequent.

The products of each one of these three classes of poets must

---

[1] Perhaps 'composition'.

necessarily proceed either by natural gift or by compulsory invention. By this I mean, that it may happen with a man who is naturally gifted in the composition of panegyric, that circumstances may require him to compose satire, and so with the other varieties of poetry. Similarly with the man who has studied the Art, and familiarized himself with a particular kind of poetry which he has chosen above all others: it may happen, owing to a special circumstance, that he is obliged to undertake some form which he has not mastered, and so writes verse under compulsion, whether from within or without. The finest poetry, however, is that produced spontaneously.

Moreover, poets differ in their composition of verse in degree of perfection or imperfection, this phenomenon being due either to the poet's own ideas or to the subject-matter of his poem. With regard to the former, it may happen that his ideas are more helpful at certain times than at others, because the necessary psychological conditions are now overwhelming, now fail. It is however not proper to the present discourse to go into detail about this, and in any case it is clearly explained in the books on ethics and psychological conditions and their individual effects. As for the subject-matter of the poem, sometimes the resemblance between the two objects compared is far-fetched, whilst at other times it is close and manifest to all; the criterion of the poet's perfection or imperfection is in this case the question whether his subjects resemble each other closely or not.

It may sometimes happen that the occasional practitioner of the Art of Poetry produces exceptionally brilliant verses, which the expert artist would find difficulty in rivalling. This is due however to pure chance and coincidence, and such a poet cannot really be called 'syllogizing'.

Similes also differ in degree of excellence. This is due either to the subject-matter itself, and whether the comparison is close and suitable; or to the skill of the poet in his craft, so that he is able to present two objects which differ from one another as though they resemble one another, by the adroit use of additional phrases, in a manner obvious to every poet. For example, a poet will compare A with B and B with C, because there is a close and suitable and familiar resemblance between A and B, and similarly between B and C; so he makes his narrative flow on in such a way at to impress the mind of the hearer or reciter with the idea that there is a resemblance between A and C, although in actual fact that resemblance is distant. There is great virtuosity in this Art in making such impressions. A similar instance is provided by the practice of contemporary poets; when they wish to place a certain word at the end of a line, to rhyme, they mention at the beginning of the line an apposite feature connected with that word, and this produces an extraordinarily graceful effect.

Now we say that there is a certain relationship between the practitioners of this Art and painters; one might almost say that the materials of their crafts differ, but their forms, their activities, their intentions are the same, or at least that they are similar. The art of poetry operates with words, the art of painting with colours, and therein they differ; but in practice both produce likenesses, and both aim at impressing men's imaginations and senses with imitations.

These then are universal canons which may usefully be studied in acquiring a knowledge of the Art of Poetry. Many of these canons might be elaborated in detail; but such elaboration in an art of this kind leads a man to specialize in one particular variety or aspect of the art, and to neglect the other varieties and aspects, and for this reason the present discourse has not attempted anything of that kind.

(*Rivista degli Studi Orientali*, Vol. XVII, pp. 273–78.)

Life of a Philosopher

My father was a man of Balkh, and he moved from there to Bukhara during the days of Nuḥ ibn Manṣūr; in his reign he was employed in the administration, being governor of a village-centre in the outlying district of Bukhara called Kharmaithan. Near by is a village named Afshana, and there my father married my mother and took up his residence; I was also born there, and after me my brother. Later we moved to Bukhara, where I was put under teachers of the Koran and of letters. By the time I was ten I had mastered the Koran and a great deal of literature, so that I was marvelled at for my aptitude.

Now my father was one of those who had responded to the Egyptian propagandist (who was an Ismaili); he, and my brother too, had listened to what they had to say about the Spirit and the Intellect, after the fashion in which they preach and understand the matter. They would therefore discuss these things together, whilst I listened and comprehended all that they said; but my spirit would not assent to their argument. Presently they began to invite me to join the movement, rolling on their tongues talk about philosophy, geometry, Indian arithmetic; and my father sent me to a certain vegetable-seller who used the Indian arithmetic, so that I might learn it from him. Then there came to Bukhara a man called Abū 'Abd Allāh al-Nātilī who claimed to be a philosopher; my father invited him to stay in our house, hoping that I would learn from him also. Before his advent I had already occupied myself with Muslim jurisprudence, attending Ismā'īl the Ascetic; so I was an excellent enquirer, having become familiar with the methods of postulation and the techniques of rebuttal according to the usages of the canon lawyers. I now commenced reading the *Isagoge* with al-Nātilī. When he mentioned to me the definition of *genus* as a term applied to a number of things of different species in answer to the question 'What is it?' I set about verifying this definition in a manner such as he had never heard. He marvelled at me exceedingly, and warned my father that I should not engage in any other occupation but learning. Whatever problem he stated to me, I showed a better mental conception of it than he. So I continued until I had read all the straightforward parts of Logic with him; as for the subtler points, he had no acquaintance with them.

From then onwards I took to reading texts by myself; I studied the commentaries, until I had completely mastered the science of Logic. Similarly with Euclid I read the first five or six figures with him, and thereafter undertook on my own account to solve the entire remainder of the book. Next I moved on to the *Almagest*; when I had finished the prolegomena and reached the geometrical figures, al-Nātilī told me to go on reading and to solve the problems by myself; I should merely revise what I read with him, so that he might indicate to me what was right and what was wrong. The truth is that he did not really teach this book; I began to solve the work, and many were the complicated figures of which he had no knowledge until I presented them to him, and made him understand them. Then al-Nātilī took leave of me, setting out for Gurganj.

I now occupied myself with mastering the various texts and commentaries on natural science and metaphysics, until all the gates of knowledge were open to me. Next I desired to study medicine, and proceeded to read all the books that have been written on this subject. Medicine is not a difficult science, and naturally I excelled in it in a very short time, so that qualified physicians began to read medicine with me. I also undertook to treat the sick, and methods of treatment derived from practical experience revealed themselves to me such as baffle description. At the same time I continued between whiles to study and dispute on law, being now sixteen years of age.

The next eighteen months I devoted entirely to reading; I studied Logic once again, and all the parts of philosophy. During all this time I did not sleep one night through, nor devoted my attention to any other matter by day. I prepared a set of files; with each proof I examined, I set down the syllogistic premises and put them in order in the files, then I examined what deductions might be drawn from them. I observed methodically the conditions of the premises, and proceeded until the truth of each particular problem was confirmed for me. Whenever I found myself perplexed by a problem, or could not find the middle term in any syllogism, I would repair to the mosque and pray, adoring the All-Creator, until my puzzle was resolved and my difficulty made easy. At night I would return home, set the lamp before me, and busy myself with reading and writing; whenever sleep overcame me or I was conscious of some weakness, I turned aside to drink a glass of wine until my strength returned to me; then I went back to my reading. If ever the least slumber overtook me, I would dream of the precise problem which I was considering as I fell asleep; in that way many problems revealed themselves to me whilst sleeping. So I continued until I had made myself master of all the sciences; I now comprehended them to the limits of human possibility. All that I learned during that time is exactly as I know it now; I have added nothing more to my knowledge to this day.

I was now a master of Logic, natural sciences and mathematics. I therefore returned to metaphysics; I read Aristotle's *Metaphysica*, but did not understand its contents and was baffled by the author's intention; I read it over forty times until I had the text by heart. Even then I did not understand it or what the author meant, and I despaired within myself, saying, 'This is a book which there is no way of understanding.' But one day at noon I chanced to be in the booksellers' quarter, and a broker was there with a volume in his hand which he was calling for sale. He offered it to me, but I returned it to him impatiently, believing that there was no use in this particular science. However, he said to me: 'Buy this book from me; it is cheap, and I will sell it to you for four dirhams. The owner is in need of the money.' So I bought it, and found that it was a book by Abū Naṣr al-Fārābī *On the Objects of the Metaphysica*. I returned home and hastened to read it; and at once the objects of that book became clear to me, for I had it all by heart. I rejoiced at this, and upon the next day distributed much in alms to the poor in gratitude to Almighty God.

Now the Sultan of Bukhara at that time was Nūḥ ibn Manṣūr, and it happened that he fell sick of a malady which baffled all the physicians. My name was famous among them because of the breadth of my reading; they therefore mentioned me in his presence, and begged him to summon me. I attended the sick-room, and collaborated with them in treating the royal patient. So I came to be enrolled in his service. One day I asked his leave to enter their library, to examine the contents and read the books on medicine; he granted my request, and I entered a mansion with many chambers, each chamber having chests of books piled one upon another. In one apartment were books on language and poetry, in another law, and so on; each apartment was set aside for books on a single science. I glanced through the catalogue of the works of the ancient Greeks, and asked for those which I required; and I saw books whose very names are as yet unknown to many—works which I had never seen before and have not seen since. I read these books, taking notes of their contents; I came to realize the place each man occupied in his particular science.

So by the time I reached my eighteenth year I had exhausted all these sciences. My memory for learning was at that period of my life better than it is now, but today I am more mature; apart from this my knowledge is exactly the same, nothing further having been added to my store since then.

There lived near me in those days a man called Abu 'l-Ḥasan the Prosodist; he requested me to compose a comprehensive work on this science, and I wrote for him the *Compendium* which I named after him, including in it all the branches of knowledge except mathematics. At that time I was twenty-one. Another man lived in my neighbourhood called Abū Bakr al-Barqī, a Khwarizmian by birth; he was a lawyer at heart, his interests being focused on jurisprudence, exegesis and asceticism, to which subjects he was extremely inclined. He asked me to comment on his books, and I wrote *The Import and the Substance* in about twenty volumes, as well as a work on ethics called *Good Works and Sin*; these two books are only to be found in his library, and are unknown to anyone else, so that they have never been copied.

Then my father died, and my circumstances changed. I accepted a post in the Sultan's employment, and was obliged to move from Bukhara to Gurganj, where Abu 'l-Ḥusain al-Sahlī was a minister, being a man devoted to these sciences. I was introduced to the Amir, 'Alī ibn al-Ma'mūn, being at that time dressed in the garb of lawyers, with scarf and chin-wrap; they fixed a handsome salary for me, amply sufficient for the like of me. Then I was constrained to move to Nasa, and from there to Baward, and thence successively to Tus, Shaqqan, Samanqan, Jajarm the frontier-post of Khurasan, and Jurjan. My entire purpose was to come to the Amir Qābūs; but it happened meanwhile that Qābūs was taken and imprisoned in a fortress, where he died.

After this I went to Dihistan, where I fell very ill. I returned to Jurjan, and there made friends with Abū 'Ubaid al-Jūzjānī.

(Here the Autobiography ends. The story of Avicenna's remaining years is told by al-Jūzjānī.)

From this point I mention those episodes of the Master's life of which I was myself a witness during my association with him, up to the time of his death.

There was at Jurjan a man called Abū Muḥammad al-Shīrāzī, who loved these sciences; he had bought for the Master a house near where he lived, and lodged him there. I used to visit him every day, reading the *Almagest* and listening to him lecturing on Logic; he dictated to me *The Middle Summary* on that subject. For Abū Muḥammad al-Shīrāzī he composed *The Origin and the Return* and *The General Observations.* He wrote many books there, such as the first part of the *Canon,* the *Summary of Almagest* and many essays. Then he composed in the Jebel country the rest of his books.

After this the Master removed to Raiy, where he joined the service of al-Saiyida and her son Majd al-Daula; they knew of him because of the many letters he brought with him containing appreciations of his worth. At that time Majd al-Daula was overcome by melancholy, and the Master applied himself to treating him. At Raiy he composed the *Book of the Return,* staying there until Shams al-Daula attacked the city following the slaying of Hilāl ibn Badr ibn Ḥasanawaih and the rout of the Baghdad army. Thereafter circumstances conspired to oblige him to leave Raiy for Qazwin, and from Qazwin he proceeded to Hamadhan, where he entered the service of Kadhbānūya in order to investigate her finances. Shams al-Daula then became acquainted with him, and summoned him to his court because of an attack of colic which had afflicted him; he treated him, until God cured him of the sickness, and he departed from his palace loaded with many costly robes. So he returned home, having passed forty days and nights at the palace and become one of the Amir's intimates.

Now it came to pass that the Amir went up to Qarmisin, to make war on 'Anāz, the Master accompanying him; but he was routed, and returned to Hamadhan. They then asked him to take the office of vizier, and he accepted; but the army conspired against him, fearing for themselves on his account. They surrounded his house, haled him off to prison, pillaged his belongings, and took all that he possessed. They even demanded of the Amir that he should put him to death, but this he refused, though he was agreeable to banishing him from the State, being anxious to conciliate them. The Master concealed himself for forty days in the house of Abū Sa'd ibn

Dakhdūk, at the end of which time Shams al-Daula was again attacked by colic, and sent for him. He came to court, and the Amir apologized to him profoundly; so the Master applied himself to treating him. As a result he continued in honour and high consideration at court, and was appointed vizier a second time.

Then it was that I asked him to write a commentary on the works of Aristotle; but he remarked that he had not the leisure at that time, adding, 'If you will be satisfied for me to compose a book setting forth the parts of those sciences which I believe to be sound, not disputing therein with any opponents nor troubling to reply to their arguments, I will gladly do so.' This offer I accepted, and he began work on the physical sections of the *Shifa*. He had already composed the first book of the *Canon*; and every night students gathered in his house, and by turns I would read the *Shifa* and another the *Canon*. When we had finished the allotted portion the various musicians would enter; vessels were brought out for a drinking party; and so we occupied ourselves. The studying was done by night because during the day his attendance upon the Amir left him no spare time.

We continued after this fashion for some while. Then the Amir set out for Tarm, to fight the prince of that place. Upon this expedition the colic again visited the Amir near Tarm; the attack was severe, and was aggravated by complications brought on by his irregular habits and his disinclination to follow the Master's advice. The army feared he would die, and at once returned towards Hamadhan carrying him in a cradle, but he died on the way. Shams al-Daula's son was thereupon sworn in as Amir, and the army now requested that the Master should be appointed vizier, but this he declined; he corresponded in secret with 'Alā' al-Daula, seeking to come to his court and join his service. Meanwhile he remained in hiding in the house of Abū Ghālib the Druggist. I requested him to complete the *Shifa*, and he summoned Abū Ghālib and asked for paper and ink; these being brought, the Master wrote in about twenty parts (each having eight folios) in his own hand the main topics to be discussed; in two days he had drafted all the topics, without having any book at hand or source to consult, accomplishing the work entirely from memory. Then he placed these parts before him, took paper, and began to examine each topic and write his comments on it. Each day he wrote fifty leaves, until he had completed the natural sciences and metaphysics, save for the books of zoology and botany. He commenced work on the logic, and wrote one part of this; but then Tāj al-Mulk suspected him of corresponding with 'Alā' al-Daula, and disapproving of this instituted a search for him. The

Master's whereabouts were betrayed by an enemy, and he was committed to a fortress called Fardjan, where he remained for four months.

Then 'Alā' al-Daula attacked and captured Hamadhan; Tāj al-Mulk was routed, and passed into the very same fortress. Presently 'Alā' al-Daula withdrew from Hamadhan; Tāj al-Mulk and the son of Shams al-Daula returned, carrying with them the Master, who took up his lodging in the house of al-'Alawī and busied himself with composing the logic of the *Shifa*. Whilst imprisoned in the fortress he had written the *Book of Guidance*, the allegory of *Living the Son of Wakeful*, and the *Book of Colic*; as for the *Cardiac Remedies*, this he composed when he first came to Hamadhan.

So some time elapsed, and Tāj al-Mulk was all the while encouraging him with handsome promises. Then it seemed good to the Master to betake himself to Isfahan; he went forth in disguise, accompanied by myself, his brother and two slaves, in the habit of Sufis, and so we reached Tabaran at the gate of Isfahan, having suffered great hardships on the way. Friends of the Master and courtiers of 'Alā' al-Daula came out to welcome him; robes were brought, and fine equipages, and he was lodged in a quarter called Gun-Gunbadh at the house of 'Abd Allāh ibn Bābā; his apartment was furnished and carpeted in the most ample manner. At court he was received with the respect and consideration which he so richly merited; and 'Alā' al-Daula appointed every Friday night a meeting for learned discussion before him, to be attended by all the scholars according to their various degrees, the Master Abū 'Alī amongst them. In these gatherings he proved himself quite supreme and unrivalled in every branch of learning.

At Isfahan he set about completing the *Shifa*; he finished the logic and the *Almagest*, and had already epitomized Euclid, the arithmetic and the music. In each book of the mathematical section he introduced supplementary materials as he thought to be necessary; in the *Almagest* he brought up ten new figures on various points of speculation, and in the astronomical section at the end of that work he added things which had never been discovered before. In the same way he introduced some new examples into Euclid, enlarged the arithmetic with a number of excellent refinements, and discussed problems on music which the ancient Greeks had wholly neglected. So he finished the *Shifa*, all but the botany and zoology which he composed in the year when 'Alā' al-Daula marched to Sabur-Khwast; these parts he wrote *en route*, as well as the *Book of Deliverance*.

The Master had now become one of the intimate courtiers of 'Alā' al-Daula. When the latter determined to attack Hamadhan, the Master accompanied him; and one night a discussion took place in the Amir's presence concerning the imperfections that occur in the astronomical tables according to the observations of the ancients. The Amir commanded the Master to undertake observations of the stars, supplying him with all the funds he might require; he thus began this new work, deputing me to select the instruments and engage the skilled assistants needed. So many old problems were elucidated, it being found that the imperfections in the former observations were due to their being conducted in the course of many journeys, with all the impediments resulting therefrom.

At Isfahan the Master also wrote the *'Ala'i*. Now one of the remarkable things about the Master was, that during the twenty-five years I accompanied and served him I never saw him take a new book and read it right through; he looked always for the difficult passages and complicated problems and examined what the author had said on these, so as to discover what his degree of learning and level of understanding might be.

One day the Master was seated before the Amir, and Abū Manṣūr al-Jabbān was also present. A philological problem came up for discussion; the Master gave his views as they occurred to him, whereupon Abū Manṣūr turned to him and remarked, 'You are a philosopher and a wise man; but you have never studied philology to such an extent that we should be pleased to hear you discourse on the subject.' The Master was stung by this rebuke, and devoted the next three years to studying books on philology; he even sent for the *Refinement of Language* of Abū Manṣūr al-Azharī from Khurasan. So he achieved a knowledge of philology but rarely attained. He composed three odes full of rare expressions, as well as three letters—one in the style of Ibn al-'Amīd, one after the fashion of al-Ṣāḥib, and the third imitating al-Ṣābī; then he ordered these to be bound, and the binding to be rubbed. So he suggested to the Amir that he should show this volume to Abū Manṣūr al-Jabbān, remarking that 'we found this volume in the desert whilst hunting, and you must look through it and tell us what it contains.' Abū Manṣūr examined the book, and was baffled by many passages occurring in it. The Master suggested to him that 'all you are ignorant of in this book you can find mentioned in such-and-such a context in the works on philology,' naming books well known in that science; for he had memorized these phrases from them. Abū Manṣūr merely conjectured as to the words which the Master introduced, without any real certainty as to their meaning; then he realized that the letters had in fact been composed by the Master, and that he had been induced to do so by the affront he had offered him that day; he therefore extracted himself from the situation by apologizing to the Master. The latter then composed a work on philology which he entitled *The Arabic Language*, the like of which was never composed; he did not transcribe it into a fair copy, so that at his death it was still in the rough draft and no man could discover a way to put it in order.

The Master had many remarkable experiences in the course of the various treatments he undertook, and he resolved to record them in the *Canon*; he had actually annotated these on some quires, but they were lost before the *Canon* was completed. At Jurjan he had composed the *Smaller Epitome* on Logic, and it is this that he afterwards placed at the beginning of the *Deliverance*. A copy of this came to Shiraz, where it was examined by a group of scholars; they took objection to a number of points, and wrote their observations upon a separate quire. The Cadi of Shiraz was one of their persuasion, and he forwarded the quire to Abu 'l-Qāsim al-Kirmānī the friend of Ibrāhīm ibn Bābā al-Dailamī, who had much to do with esoteric matters; the Cadi enclosed a letter of his own to Abu 'l-Qāsim, and delivered the two documents into the hands of a post-messenger, with the request that he should present the quire to the Master and elicit from him his answers. Abu 'l-Qāsim came to the Master when the sun was yellowing upon a summer's day; he showed him the letter and the quire. The Master read the former and returned it to Abu 'l-Qāsim, whilst the latter he kept before him, examining it while a general conversation was in progress. Then Abu 'l-Qāsim went out; and the Master commanded me to bring fair parchment and cut some quires. I sewed up five quires for him, each of ten folios of a generous format. We prayed the evening prayer; candles were brought, and the Master ordered drinks to be laid out. He made me and his brother sit with him and drink, whilst he commenced to answer the questions that had been propounded to him. So he continued writing and drinking until half the night was gone, when I and his brother were overcome by sleep; he therefore bade us depart. In the morning a knock came at the door, and there was the Master's messenger summoning me. I found him at his prayers, and before him the five quires completed. 'Take them,' he said, 'and go with them to Abu 'l-Qāsim al-Kirmānī; tell him I made haste to reply, so that the post-messenger might not be delayed.' When I brought the communication to him he was most astonished; he dispatched the messenger, and informed his friends of the circumstances of the matter. The story became quite an historic occasion.

While engaged upon his astronomical observations the Master

invented instruments the like of which had never been seen before; he also composed a treatise on the subject. I remained eight years engaged upon this work, my object being to verify the observations which Ptolemy reported on his own account, and in fact some part of these were confirmed for me. The Master also composed the *Book of Rectification*, but on the day when Sultan Mas'ūd came to Isfahan his army plundered the Master's luggage; this book was part of it, and was never seen again.

The Master was powerful in all his faculties, and he was especially strong sexually; this indeed was a prevailing passion with him, and he indulged it to such an extent that his constitution was affected; yet he relied upon his powerful constitution to pull him through. At last in the year when 'Alā al-Daula fought Tāsh Farrāsh at the gates of al-Karkh, the Master was attacked by the colic. Because of his eagerness to cure himself—being afraid the Amir might suffer defeat, in which case his sickness would not allow him to travel back—he injected himself eight times in a single day, so that his intestines were ulcerated and the abrasion showed on him. Yet he must needs accompany 'Alā' al-Daula; so they made haste towards Idhaj where the epilepsy which sometimes follows colic manifested itself. Despite this he continued to treat himself, taking injections for the abrasion and the rest of the colic. One day he ordered the mixing of two *dangs* of celery-seed in the injection, desiring to break the wind of the colic; one of the physicians attending him put in five *dirhams* of celery-seed—I know not whether purposely or in error, for I was not with him—and the sharpness of the celery aggravated the abrasion. He also took *mithradatum* for the epilepsy; but one of his slaves went and threw in a great quantity of opium, and he consumed the mixture; this being because they had robbed him of much money from his treasury, and they desired to do away with him so that they might escape the penalty of their actions.

In this state the Master was brought to Isfahan, where he continued to look after himself, though he was now so weak that he could no longer stand; nevertheless he went on treating himself, until he was able to walk. He once more attended the court of 'Alā' al-Daula; however, he was incautious and indulged his sexual appetite too far, so that he was never wholly cured, suffering repeated relapses. Then 'Alā' al-Daula marched towards Hamadhan, and the Master went with him; the same malady revisited him upon the way, and when he finally reached Hamadhan he knew that his strength was exhausted and no longer adequate to repel the disease. He therefore gave up treating himself, and took to saying, 'The manager who used to manage me is incapable of managing me any more; so it is no use trying to cure my sickness.'

So he continued some days, and was then transported to the Presence of his Lord. He was buried at Hamadhan, being 58 years old; his death occurred in the year 428 (1037).

(From *Avicenna on Theology*, pp. 9–24.)

The After-Life

The after-life is a notion received from religious teaching; there is no way of establishing its truth save through religious dogma and the acceptance of the prophets' reports as true. These refer to what will befall the body at the resurrection, and those corporeal delights or torments which are too well known to require restating here. The true religion brought into this world by our Prophet Muhammad has described in detail the state of happiness or misery awaiting us hereafter so far as the body is concerned. Some further support for the idea of a hereafter is attainable through reason and logical demonstration—and this is confirmed by prophetic teaching— namely that happiness or misery posited by spiritual appraisement; though it is true that our conjecture falls short of realizing a full picture of them now, for reasons which we shall explain. Metaphysicians have a greater desire to achieve this spiritual happiness than the happiness which is purely physical; indeed they scarcely heed the latter, and were they granted it would not consider it of great moment in comparison with the former kind, which is proximity to the First Truth, in a manner to be described presently. Let us therefore consider this state of happiness, and of contrasting misery: the physical sort is fully dealt with in the teachings of religion.

Every faculty of the soul has its own particular pleasure and good, its own especial pain and evil. For example, pleasure and good as appertaining to the appetite consists in the realization of a congenial sensual state through the senses. Pleasure in relation to choler is the achievement of mastery; pleasure in terms of the imagination is the sensation of hope; the pleasure of memory is the reminiscence of agreeable circumstances that happened in the past. Pain in each case is the opposite of the corresponding pleasure. All of these have one feature in common, that consciousness of agreeable and congenial circumstances which constitutes the good and pleasure of each. What is essentially and really agreeable to each is the realization of a sense of fulfilment which is relatively speaking the achievement in actuality of its potential perfection.

While the various faculties have these features in common, in reality they differ amongst themselves in degree: one kind of perfection is completer and more excellent, another is quantitatively greater, another is more enduring, another is more readily attainable. The sort which is in actuality more perfect and excellent, and is in itself more intense in realization, of course involves a more exquisite and satisfying pleasure.

Moreover it may happen in the actualization of some sorts of perfection that the perfection is known to exist and to be pleasurable, but that its state cannot be pictured in the mind, nor the pleasure connected with it sensed until the state itself is realized; and that which cannot be sensed consciously is not desired or yearned after. Thus, whilst an impotent man may be quite convinced that intercourse is pleasurable, yet he does not desire and long for it in the manner peculiar to that sensation but with quite another appetite—like that of a man who is experimenting to discover how a certain sensation may be achieved, even if it be in fact painful: in short, he cannot imagine it at all. Similar is the state of the blind man in relation to beautiful forms, or of the deaf in regard to melodious tunes.

Hence it behoves not the intelligent man to suppose that every pleasure is connected with the belly and the sexual instinct, as is the case with asses; that the First Principles, which dwell in close proximity to the Lord of All, are wholly without pleasure and exultation; or that Almighty God in His sublime splendour and infinite power does not enjoy a state of noble pre-eminence and well-being which we reverently refrain from calling pleasure. Asses and wild beasts have it is true their own sort of well-being and pleasure; but what relation is there between these mean delights, and the sensation enjoyed by the Lofty Principles? Their beatitude we may only imagine and contemplate; we cannot know it in our conscient minds, but solely by analogy; our state being that of the deaf man who never in all his life heard or could imagine the joy of music, yet he was sure that it was truly excellent.

It can further happen that perfection and absolute congeniality may be within the reach of the apprehending faculty, but there is some impediment or preoccupation in the soul which causes it to hate that perfection and to prefer its opposite. Thus, a sick man will sometimes hate wholesome food and desire only the unwholesome, which is essentially detestable. Or one may not actually hate a certain perfection, but merely lack all sense of pleasure in it; as when a man much afraid secures a triumph or a pleasure of some sort but is not aware of the fact, and feels no pleasure in it.

Again, the apprehending faculty may be atrophied by that which is the opposite of its perfection and so not sense or recoil from its state until, when the obstacle is removed, it is pained by the realization of its situation and so reverts to its normal condition. A bilious person may not be aware of the acidity in him until his temperament is restored and his members healed; only then will he recoil from the condition which has befallen him. Similarly an animal may have no appetite for food at all and may positively dislike it, though it is the most suitable thing it can have, and continue so for a long time; but when the obstacle is removed it will return to its natural course of feeling violently hungry, and have so great an appetite for food that it cannot endure to be without it, and will perish if it cannot find any. One can be exposed to conditions causing great pain, such as burning or freezing, yet because the senses are impaired the body may not feel any discomfort until the injury is repaired; then it will feel the severe pain.

Having established the foregoing principles, we may now return to our immediate object.

Now the peculiar perfection towards which the rational soul strives is that it should become as it were an intellectual microcosm, impressed by the form of the All, the order intelligible in the All, and the good pervading the All: first the Principles of the All, then proceeding to the Noble Substances and Absolute Spirituality, then Spirituality connected in some fashion with corporeal things, then the Celestial Bodies with their various dispositions and powers, and so continuing until it realizes completely within itself the shape of all Being, and thus converts itself into an intelligible cosmos of its own in correspondence with the whole existing Cosmos, contemplating perfect comeliness, absolute good and true beauty, and united therewith. So it will have become graven after its idea and pattern, and strung upon its thread as a pearl is strung upon a necklace, being refashioned into the selfsame substance thereof.

When this state is compared with those other perfections so ardently beloved of the other faculties, it will be found to be of an order so exalted as to make it seem monstrous to describe it as more complete or more excellent than they; indeed, there is no relationship between it and them whatsoever, whether it be of excellence, completeness, abundance or any other of the respects wherein delight in sensual attainment is consummated. For if it be a question of durability, how shall eternal continuance be compared with changefulness and corruptibility? Or if it be a matter of the degree of accomplishment, how can the accomplishment of surface contact be measured against that of penetration into the very substance of the recipient, so that it is as if the twain are one without any division whatsoever? For intelligence, intelligible and intelligent are one thing, or nearly so. That the object so apprehended is more perfect in itself is manifest at once; that the realization too is more intense is likewise immediately obvious, if the foregoing argument is kept at all in mind.

The rational soul has far more numerous objects to apprehend, and is far more strenuous in seeking out its object and isolating it from those accretions which affect not its real meaning save accidentally; it is able to penetrate the object of its apprehension both internally and externally. How indeed can the two sorts of apprehension be at all compared, or this spiritual pleasure be measured against the other sensual, bestial, choleric pleasure? But we within our world and body, plunged as we are into all kinds of abomination, do not sense that other pleasure even when any of the means of attaining it are within our power; so we have already indicated above. Consequently we do not seek or yearn after that at all, save indeed if we have torn from our necks the yoke of appetite, anger and their sister passions, and so catch a glimpse of that higher pleasure. Even so, the image we perceive is but faint and feeble, and then only at a time when all our entanglements are loosened and our eyes are strained towards the precious objects of our quest. Our delight before and after may then be thought to stand in the same relation to each other as the sensual delight in inhaling the odours of delicious foods compared with the delight of tasting them; indeed the contrast is infinitely greater.

You yourself know how, when you are meditating some abstruse matter that engages you, and then some sensual appetite supervenes, and you are constrained to choose between the two competing interests, you pay no heed to that appetite, if you be a man of noble spirit. Even common spirits too will deny chance lusts and prefer terrible pains and frightful sufferings, because they are ashamed of being exposed to disgrace or opprobrium, or because they are eager for some signal triumph. All these are intellectual states; some of them are preferred above natural influences, and for their sake natural discomforts will be endured. From this it is realized that intellectual ends are more ennobling to the soul than other worthless things; how far exceeding then those pure and lofty objects of the spirit! But mean souls sense only the good and evil that are attached to worthless things, and perceive not the circumstances attending noble objects, because of the impediments already stated.

When the time comes for us to be separated from the body, and our soul has become aware whilst still in the body of that perfection which is the object of its love, yet has not attained it though naturally still yearning after it—for it has in fact realized that it exists, though its preoccupation with the body has caused it to forget its own essence and its true beloved (and so sickness will cause us to forget the need of replacing the parts that are dissolved within us, or even the pleasure of sweet things and the appetite for them; and unnatural desire will make a sick man incline after revolting things)—then at that time our soul is truly affected by pain at the loss of our cherished object, equal to the supervening pleasure whose existence we have proved and whose lofty rank we have indicated. This then is a misery and a torment far exceeding the bodily pain and physical anguish of burning and freezing. At that moment we are like to a man who has been drugged, or so affected by fire or cold that the material clothing his senses prevents him from feeling anything, so that he senses no discomfort for the while; but then the intervening obstacle is removed, and he is conscious of great suffering. If however the intellectual faculty has achieved such a degree of perfection within the soul that the latter is able, on leaving the body, to realize that full perfection which lies within its power to attain, the soul will then resemble a man drugged who is given to taste some most delicious food, or confronting him a most ravishing situation, without his being conscious of the fact; when the drug passes off, he discovers great pleasure all at once. But the pleasure enjoyed by the soul at that moment is not at all of the order of sensual or animal delight; rather does it resemble that delectable state which belongs to pure vital substances, mightier and nobler than all other pleasure. This then is the happiness, and that the misery which await every soul at death.

Now that misery does not come upon every man who is in any way wanting; rather is it the portion of those who have invested their intellectual faculty with the yearning to achieve perfection. This happens when it has become conclusive to them that it is the business of the soul to apprehend the very essence of perfection, by attaining through knowledge the unknown and striving to actualize its potential perfection. This is no natural and inborn property of the soul, nor indeed of any of the faculties; on the contrary, most of the faculties become conscious of their respective perfections only as a result of certain causes.

Simple, unsophisticated souls and faculties are as it were mere objectified matter, and never acquire this yearning. For this yearning only occurs, and is graven upon the substance of the soul, when it is conclusively proved to the spiritual faculties that there are certain matters, the knowledge of which they can acquire in the processes of logic. Otherwise there is no yearning the soul for these far heights; yearning follows upon opinion, and opinion such as this belongs not *a priori* to the soul but is acquired. So when these men acquire this opinion, this yearning necessarily attaches to their souls. If their souls depart out of the body not having as yet acquired that state which will bring them after separation from the flesh to completion, they fall into this sort of everlasting wretchedness; for the elements of the faculty of knowledge were only to be acquired through the body, and now the body has passed away. Such men are either incapable of the effort required to achieve human perfection, or else they are obstinate, unbelieving, fanatically attached to wrong opinions contrary to the true; and the unbelieving are in the worst case of all, having acquired dispositions diametrically opposed to perfection.

As for the question how far the human soul needs to be capable of conceiving intelligible abstractions, so that it may pass beyond the point where this misery is bound to befall, and in transgressing which that happiness may be justly hoped for, this is a matter upon which I can only pronounce approximately. I suppose this position is reached when a man achieves a true mental picture of the incorporeal principles, and believes in them implicitly because he is aware of their existence through logical demonstration. He is acquainted with the final causes of events happening in universal (not partial), infinite movements; he has a firm grasp of the disposition of the All, the mutual proportions of its parts, and the order pervading the Cosmos from the First Principle down to the remotest beings, all duly arranged. He can apprehend Providence in action, and realizes what kind of being belongs exclusively to the Essence preceding all, what sort of unity that Essence possesses, how that Essence achieves cognition without any consequent multiplicity or change of any kind, in what manner other beings are related in due order to that Essence. The clearer the inward vision of the speculative becomes, the more fully qualified he is to attain supreme happiness.

A man will hardly free himself from this world and its entanglements, except he be more firmly attached to the other world, so that his yearning to be gone thither and his love for what awaits him there block him from turning back to gaze at what lies behind him.

I would add, that this true happiness cannot be consummated save by amending the practical part of the soul. Character, as I have remarked elsewhere, is a 'habit' whereby certain actions issue out of the soul easily and without prior deliberation. Aristotle in his *Ethics* lays it down that we should observe the mean between two opposing characteristics, and not that we should strive to make our individual actions conform with the mean: we must acquire the habit of the mean. Now this habit of the mean appears to belong to both the rational and the animal faculties; to the latter, through acquiring the disposition to submit and be passive, and to the former, through acquiring the disposition to dominate. Similarly the habits of excess and shortcoming belong equally to the rational and the animal faculties, but in an inverse relationship. It is well known that excess and shortcoming are necessary features of the animal faculties; when the animal faculty is strong, and it acquires the habit of domination, the rational soul finds itself disposed to submit; once passivity becomes ingrained in the rational soul, it strengthens its attachment and confirms its subservience to the body. The habit of the mean aims to liberate the rational soul from all disposition to yield, to maintain it in its natural state, and to endow it moreover with the disposition to dominate and to defy— an attitude which is by no means contrary to its true substance, or apt to incline it towards the body, but rather away from it. Always the mean plucks the rational soul from the two extremes.

As for the true substance of the soul, it is the body which over-whelms it and diverts it, causing it to forget its proper yearning and its quest for perfection; it kills within it all sense of pleasure in that perfection should it ever achieve it, or of the pain of imperfection when falling short of its goal. It is not the case that the soul is as it were ingrained and submerged in the body. The bond which unites body and soul—that natural yearning of the soul to control the body and its preoccupation with the body's exploits, the crises that it brings upon itself, and the habits which become fixed in it— this bond has its origin in the body.

When a man departs this life having within him the habits resulting from his union with the body, he is in a state closely similar to that which was his whilst still in the body. As that state diminishes, he becomes correspondingly less heedless of the motion of yearning after perfection; to the degree that it remains with him, he continues veiled from absolute union with the place wherein his happiness resides, so that he is affected by confused motions which prove exceedingly painful.

Such a bodily disposition is contrary to the very substance of the soul, and is injurious to its substance; the body, and the soul's complete immersion therein, diverts the soul from all consciousness of itself. When the soul leaves the body it senses that mighty opposition and is greatly pained by it; yet that pain, that anguish is not due to any necessary circumstance but is the result of an accidental contingency, and as such is not permanent and ever-lasting. It passes away and is nullified with the abandonment of those actions whose repetition strengthened that disposition; so that it follows that the torment resulting from this circumstance is not eternal, but passes away and is obliterated little by little until the soul is purified and attains its proper happiness.

As for those foolish souls which have never acquired the yearning for perfection, yet leave the body without having acquired any vicious bodily disposition, these pass to the wide mercy of God and attain a kind of ease. If however they have acquired some vicious bodily disposition and have no other condition but that, nothing within them to oppose or strive with it, then they continue inevi-tably to be bemused by their yearning after what is for them an absolute necessity, and are exquisitely tortured by the loss of the body and all the body's requirements without being able to attain the object of their desire. For the instrument of their desire has been destroyed, whilst the habit of attachment to the body still survives.

It may also be true, as some theologians state, that when souls, supposing they are pure, leave the body, having firmly fixed within them some such beliefs regarding the future life as are appropriate to them, being the sort of picture which can properly be presented to the ordinary man—when such men as these leave the body, lacking both the force to draw them upwards to complete perfection (so that they achieve that supreme happiness) and likewise the yearning after such perfection (so that they experience that supreme misery), but all their spiritual dispositions are turned towards the lower world and drawn to the corporeal; since there is nothing to prevent celestial matter from being operable to the action of any soul upon it, these souls may well imagine all those after-life circumstances in which they believed as actually taking place before them, the instrument reinforcing their imagination being some kind of celestial body.

In this way these pure souls will really be spectators of the events of the grave and the resurrection about which they were told in this world, and all the good things of the after-life; whilst the wicked souls will similarly behold, and suffer, the punishment which was portrayed to them here below. Certainly the imaginative picture is no weaker than the sensual image; rather is it the stronger and clearer of the two. This may be observed in dreams: the vision seen in sleep is often of greater moment in its kind than the impression of the senses. The image contemplated in the after-life is however more stable than that seen in dreams, because there are fewer obstacles in the way of its realization; the soul being isolated from the body, the receiving instrument is therefore absolutely clear. As you know, the image seen in dreams and that sensed in waking are alike simply impressed upon the soul; they differ only in this, that the former kind originates from within and descends into the soul, whilst the latter sort originates from without and mounts up into the soul. It is when the image has already been impressed upon the soul that the act of contemplation is consummated. It is this impression, then, that in reality pleases or pains the soul, not any external object; whatever is impressed upon the soul does its work, even if there be no external cause. The essential cause is the impression itself; the external object is the accidental cause, or the cause of the cause.

These then are the baser sorts of celestial happiness and misery, which are apposite to base souls. As for the souls of the blessed, they are far removed from such circumstances; being perfect, they are united to the Essence, and are wholly plunged in true pleasure; they are forever free of gazing after what lies behind them, and the kingdom that once was theirs. If there had remained within them any trace of those things, whether by reason of dogmatic belief or through acceptance of a physical theory, they would be so injured thereby as to fall short of scaling the topmost peak of heaven, until that thing be finally obliterated from their souls.

(From *Avicenna on Theology*, pp. 64–76.)

SIX

La Dolce Vita

For the privileged few, the aristocrats of birth, wealth or wit, medieval Islam offered a way of life, if they elected to take it, very different indeed from the austere model which has been described in our earlier pages. It is true that great power and great comfort were enjoyed under the constant threat of catastrophe—conspiracy ending in assassination for the ruler, intrigue followed by disgrace and often enough by execution for his intimates. But if the shadow cast by events all too likely to come could be forgotten, one might happily bask in the sunshine of prosperity and varied pleasures secured by the dogged labours of the enslaved millions of tillers and toilers.

The splendours and sensual gratifications competing to gratify the appetites of caliphs in their palaces are familiar to all who have passed their time in perusing the pages of the *Arabian Nights*. The picture drawn by sober historians, though lacking much of the element of magic and mythical hyperbole so greatly enjoyed in those popular entertainments, yet in broad outline confirms the impression of a society given over to worldly pursuits, a ready target for the barbed shafts of the outraged moralists. In this chapter we shall draw on documents more reliable than the *Nights* to highlight a few features of the glittering panorama.

Our first extract, a symposium at the court of an Abbasid caliph in which the theme was the art of cooking as described by poets, is drawn from the *Murūj al-dhahab* ('Meadows of Gold') of the esteemed historian al-Mas'ūdī—'professedly a universal history beginning with the Creation and ending at the Caliphate of Muṭī', in 947 AD, but no description can cover the immense range of topics which are discussed and the innumerable digressions with which the author delights or irritates his readers, as the case may be.'[1]

---

[1] R. A. Nicholson, *Literary History of the Arabs*, p. 353.

A Symposium on Cooking

One day the caliph al-Mustakfī[1] said: 'It is my desire that we should assemble on such-and-such a day, and converse together about the different varieties of food, and the poetry which has been composed on this subject.'

Those present agreed; and on the day prescribed al-Mustakfī joined the party and bade every man produce what he had prepared. Thereupon one member of the circle spoke up.

'Commander of the Faithful, I have some verses by Ibn al-Mu'tazz[2] in which the poet describes a tray containing bowls of *kāmakh*.'[3]

Being invited by the caliph to repeat them, he proceeded:

> Accept, I beg, this tray of wicker made
> With serried cups symmetrically laid;
> Whate'er yon red and yellow bowls contain
> The man of taste will surely not disdain.
> Here *kāmakh* is of flowering tarragon,
> Here capers grace a sauce vermilion
> Whose fragrant odours to the soul are blown
> Like powdered musk in druggist's fingers strewn.
> Here, too, sweet marjoram's delicious scent
> With breath of choicest cloves is richly blent;
> Whilst cinnamon, of condiments the king,
> Unblemished hue, unrivalled seasoning,
> Like musk in subtle odour rises there
> Tempting the palate, sweetening the air.
> Here crowns the bowl fresh-gathered savory,
> Rival to musk and pitch in fragrancy;
> Here pungent garlic greets the eager sight
> And whets with savour sharp the appetite,
> While olives turn to shadowed night the day,
> And salted fish in slices rims the tray.
> Behold thereon the onion's argent frame,
> A silver body filled with inward flame;
> There circles of horse-radish garnished are
> With meat, and blend their tang with vinegar—
> Meat that, in slices white and scarlet laid,
> Like gold and silver coin is arrayed.

---

[1] Unfortunate caliph of Baghdad (333–4/944–6), he was blinded and deposed by the Buyid Aḥmad ibn Abī Shujāʿ and died in 338/949.

[2] Prince and poet, he ruled for one day only and was put to death in 296/908.

[3] A kind of relish.

From every corner, gloriously bright,
A star doth gleam with dawn's refulgent light:
So might a garden flower in turn be kissed
By sun and moon, by radiance and mist.

Al-Mustakfī commanded that the bowls should be prepared exactly as prescribed, adding, 'We will eat nothing today except what you portray.'

Then another of the company exclaimed, 'Commander of the Faithful, Maḥmūd ibn al-Ḥusain Kushājim[1] has described a dish of rarities as follows'—and he recited:

When to banquet we are eager
    Well the table floweth o'er,
And the ready cook doth fill it
    With the choicest foods in store:
Forth it comes with goodly burden,
    Garnished by his precious lore.

First a roasted kid, a yearling,
    With its inwards firmly strung,
And upon it, well to season,
    Tarragon and mint are hung.

Next a chicken, full and tender,
    Fattened many moons agone,
And a partridge, with a fledgling,
    Roast with care, and nicely done.

After pastry of *tardīna*
    Follows *sanbūsaj*, well-fried:
Eggs vermilioned after boiling
    Lie with olives side by side.

Strips of tender meat in slices,
    Dipped in oil of finest make,
Tempt anew the flagging palate
    And the appetite awake;

Lemons, too, with *nadd* besprinkled,
    Scented well with ambergris,
And, for garnishing the slices,
    Shreds of appetizing cheese.

[1] Poet, astrologer and culinary expert in the service of the Hamdanid ruler Saif al-Daula, died in 350/961 or 360/971.

Vinegar that smarts the nostrils
    Till they snuffle and they run;
Little dates like pearls, that glisten
    On a necklace one by one.

Sauce of *būrān* served with egg-plant
    That will tempt thy very heart,
And asparagus—enchanted
    With asparagus thou art!

Lastly, lozenge, soaked in butter,
    Buried deep in sugar sweet.
And a saki's cloven dimples
    Promise joy when lovers meet:

There is passion in his glances,
    There is softness in his word;
And a ringdove, cooing softly,
    Sings new measures never heard:

'Pity for the mournful lover
    Far from home, where she doth mourn:
No excuse, if thou supposest
    He was not for passion born.'

'Well said!' al-Mustakfī cried. 'The poet described the scene excellently.' Then he commanded that everything which had been mentioned in the verses should be brought in, so far as was possible.

'Has any other here any verses on the same theme?' the caliph demanded.

Another then stood up, and recited a poem of Ibn al-Rūmī[1] describing *wasṭ*:

If thou wouldst know the world's supreme delight,
Then listen to this tale that I recite:
Well is my story woven, free of blot—
A finer panegyrist there is not.
So come, *feinschmecker*, do as I repeat.
Take first a pair of loaves, of finest wheat,
The like of which on earth was never seen;
Then cut the crusts around, and lift them clean.
When naught remaineth but the supple dough,
Cover one round with fresh-cut slices, so!

[1] Famous poet murdered by al-Muʿtaḍid's vizier, probably in 283/896.

Of flesh of chicken, and of flesh of cock,
And, blowing, baste about with syrup stock.
Thereon impose a regimented line
Of almonds and of walnuts, flavoured fine;
With cheese and olives prick the points thereon,
And add the vowels of mint and tarragon.
Let flowing cream the layers twain between
Like *Washy* cloth of Yemen intervene.
Next boil the eggs, and smear them all in red—
With gold and silver let the *wast* be spread!
Now dust the lines with salt, yet not in haste
But in appropriate measure, well to taste.
With watchful eye examine it anon,
And let thy gaze with pleasure feast thereon;
But when full satisfied hath grown thy sight,
Replace the loaf, and eat with appetite;
With gusto chew, and let thy teeth be filled:
Destroy in haste the structure thou didst build.

Another then spoke up. 'Commander of the Faithful, Isḥāq ibn
Ibrāhīm of Mosul[1] described *sanbūsaj* as follows'—and he declaimed:

If thou wouldst know what food gives most delight,
Best let me tell, for none hath subtler sight.
Take first the finest meat, red, soft to touch,
And mince it with the fat, not overmuch;
Then add an onion, cut in circles clean,
A cabbage, very fresh, exceeding green,
And season well with cinnamon and rue;
Of coriander add a handful, too,
And after that of cloves the very least,
Of finest ginger, and of pepper best,
A pinch of cummin, murri just to taste,
Two handfuls of Palmyra salt; but haste,
Good master, haste to grind them small and strong.
Then lay and light a blazing fire along;
Put all into the pot, and water pour
Upon it from above, and cover o'er.
But when the water vanished is from sight
And when the burning flames have dried it quite,
Then, as thou wilt, in pastry wrap it round,
And fasten well the edges, firm and sound;

---

[1] Famous musician and author, died in 236/851.

Or, if it please thee better, take some dough,
Conveniently soft, and rubbed just so,
Then with the rolling-pin let it be spread
And with the nails its edges docketed.
Pour in the frying-pan the choicest oil
And in that liquor let it finely broil.
Last, ladle out into a thin tureen
Where appetizing mustard smeared hath been
And eat with pleasure, mustarded about,
This tastiest food for hurried diner-out.

Another added, 'Commander of the Faithful, Maḥmūd ibn al-Ḥusain ibn al-Sindī Kushājim the Scribe has described asparagus'—and he said:

Lances we have, the tips whereof are curled,
Their bodies like a hawser turned and twirled,
Yet fair to view, with ne'er a knot to boot.
Their heads bolt upright from the shoulders shoot,
And, by the grace of Him Who made us all,
Firm in the soil they stand, like pillars tall,
Clothed in soft robes like silk on mantle spread
That deep hath drunk a blazing flame of red,
As if they brushed against a scarlet cheek
Whereon an angry palm its wrath doth wreak,
And as a coat-of-mail is interlaced
With links of gold so twine they, waist to waist;
Like silken *miṭraf*[1] that the hands display—
Ah, could it last for ever and a day!—
They might be bezels set in rings of pearl.
Thereon a most delicious sauce doth swirl
Flowing and ebbing like a swelling sea;
Oil decks them out in cream embroidery
Which, as it floods and flecks them, fold on fold,
Twists latchets as of silver or of gold.
Should pious anchorite see such repast,
In sheer devotion he would break his fast.

When the recital ended al-Mustakfī observed, 'At such a season, in such a land, a vegetable of this kind cannot well be found. Let us write then to the Ikhshid Muḥammad ibn Ṭughj[2] and request him

---

[1] A kind of square-shaped wrap with ornamental borders.
[2] Founder of the Ikhshidid ruling house of Egypt, died in 334/946, made himself master of Damascus when he drove out Saif al-Daula.

to send us such asparagus from Damascus. Meanwhile, rehearse what can be obtained now.'

Another then recited the following lines descriptive of *aruzza*[1] written by Muḥammad ibn al-Wazir, known as the Ḥāfiẓ of Damascus:[2]

> O glorious *aruzza*! What a boon,
> Thou cook as lovely as high heaven's moon!
> Purer than snow that hath been furrowed twice
> By handiwork of wind and frosted ice;
> Set out in ordered strips upon the dish,
> White as the whitest milk that heart could wish,
> Its brilliance dazzles the beholding eye
> As if the moon ere evening shone in sky;
> Whilst sugar sprinkled upon every side
> Flashes and gleams, like light personified.

Yet another now spoke up, 'Commander of the Faithful, I will quote the verses of a modern poet on the subject of *harīsa*'—and he recited:

> Of all the foods of man the tastiest,
> When host has been oblivious of his guest
> And kid or lamb is tardy on the grill,
> Give me *harīsa*, made by woman's skill—
> For women's hands are resolute and pure,
> They have a lightness and a vigour sure.
> Within one saucepan let each other greet
> Kidney and fat of tail, butter and meat;
> Then goose well-fattened, with the whitest cheese
> Deposit, following with little peas,
> Almonds and nuts, the very choicest kind,
> Which first the millstone thoroughly must grind;
> And, lastly, sprinkle salt, and galingale
> From knotting which the aching fingers fail.
> When with so fine a dish the lads regale
> The diners, every other dish grows pale.
> Behold it on the table, served at need
> Surmounted by a vault of bamboo reed,
> While walls support the balustraded roof
> That from auxiliar pillars rides aloof!

[1] A dish of rice and sugar.
[2] Ḥāfiz is a title given to a man who knows the Koran by heart.

The lads bring forth these dainties to the board,
Preferred by starving, as by filled adored:
All, hosts and guests, are eager to attain
This food for which the Sultan's self is fain;
For by its magic mind and brain both shine,
And all the body's humours fall in line.
The Sasan in his day invented this,
King Nushirwan essayed it to his bliss.[1]
When hungry, ravenous men behold this dish,
They cannot wait to gratify their wish.

Another then said, 'Commander of the Faithful, another modern poet has written on *maḍīra*'—and he read:

Maḍīra on the festive tray
Is like the moon in full array;
Upon the board it gleams in light
Like sunshine banishing the night,
Or as the crescent moon, whose beams
Transfix the clouds that shroud men's dreams.
Upon a platter it is brought
Of onyx, in Tehama wrought.
Abū Huraira[2] gladdened were
Had he been served a dish so rare,
And in his zeal for this repast
Might have forgot the will to fast,
Yet had been cautious not to try
This food beneath the abbot's eye.
Maḍīra cannot rivalled be
To heal the sick man's malady:
No wonder this our meal we make
Since, eating it, no law we break.
'Tis as delicious as 'tis good—
A very miracle of food.

'Commander of the Faithful,' another then broke in, 'Maḥmūd ibn al-Ḥusain[3] has pictured *jūdhāba* thus'—and he declaimed:

Jūdhāba made of choicest rice
As shining as a lover's eyes—

---

[1] Anūshirwān the Great, of the Sasanian dynasty of Persia (531–78).
[2] Famous Companion of the Prophet, reputed for his strict abstemiousness, died about 57/676.
[3] Sc. Kushājim.

How marvellous in hue it stands
Beneath the cook's accomplished hands!
As pure as gold without alloy,
Rose-tinted, its creator's joy;
With sugar of Ahwaz complete,
In taste 'tis sweeter than the sweet.
Its trembling mass in butter drowned
With scent the eater wraps around;
As smooth and soft as clotted cream,
Its breath like ambergris doth seem;
And when within the bowl 'tis seen
A star in darkness shines serene,
Or as cornelian's gold is strung
Upon the throat of virgin young;
It is more sweet than sudden peace
That brings the quaking heart release.

Another next spoke. 'Commander of the Faithful, a certain modern poet has described another *jūdhāba*'[1]—and he sang:

Jūdhāba so bright, no cornelian so fine,
In flavour, meseems, worthy rival to wine,
With sugar composed of the purest degree
And saffron well-brayed, for its tinting to be;
In fat of ripe chicken anointed and drowned—
With such an immersion no finer were found!
Delightful to taste when to palate presented,
Like choicest *khaluq*[2] it is coloured and scented.
The bowl, passed around, spreads its odorous mist,
Its sweetness is sweeter than soul can resist.

Another said, 'Commander of the Faithful, Maḥmūd ibn al-Husain Kushājim has depicted *qaṭā'if*[3] also'—and he read:

When in my friends the pang of hunger grows
I have *qaṭā'if*, like soft folios;
As flow of lambent honey brimming white
So amidst other dainties it is bright,
And, having drunk of almond-essence deep,
With oil it glitters, wherein it doth seep.

[1] A confection of meat, rice and sugar.
[2] A kind of scent, viscid in consistency, yellow or red in colour.
[3] An esteemed pastry-cake.

Rose-water floats thereon, like flooding sea,
Bubble on bubble swimming fragrantly;
A foliated book laid fold on fold—
Afflicted hearts rejoice when they behold;
But when divided, like the spoils of war,
All have their heart's desire, and sated are.

The narrator concluded, 'Never have I seen al-Mustakfī so over-joyed, since the day of his accession. To all present, revellers, singers and musicians, he gave moneys, causing all the silver and gold with which he stood possessed to be brought out of the Treasury, in spite of his straitened circumstances. Never a day like this did I behold, until the day when Aḥmad ibn Buwaih the Dailamite seized him and put out his eyes.'

(*Islamic Culture*, Vol. XIII, pp. 21–30.)

If Baghdad was a splendid and pleasure-thronged city, at least for the powerful and the wealthy, the opportunities for enjoying *la dolce vita* were no less abundant in Cordova under Arab rule. The lucky chance of the survival of a solitary manuscript provides charming and poignant descriptions of life in the Andalusian capital as lived by *la jeunesse dorée* in the early years of our eleventh century. The author of this book is as surprising as the book itself: he was Ibn Ḥazm, a very learned Muslim theologian and canon lawyer, famous for his treatises on jurisprudence and for an un-usually well documented study of religions and sects, certainly one of the greatest scholars produced in Arab Spain. It is thus all the more astonishing that he should also have composed *The Ring of the Dove*, a tender and humorous dissertation on the art of courtship and the joys and sorrows of love, enlivening his discourse with many personal anecdotes and liberal extracts from his own romantic poetry.

Abū Muḥammad 'Alī ibn Muḥammad ibn Sa'īd ibn Ḥazm, to give our author his full name, belonged to a notable family con-verted from Christianity several generations before. His father was a high official in the service of al-Manṣūr, regent of Hishām II, and of his son al-Muẓaffar; al-Manṣūr and al-Muẓaffar were members of the Banū Ā'mir who had succeeded in arrogating to themselves all the power and privileges of the Caliphate but its name. Being the son of such a man, to whom he always refers as 'the late vizier', Ibn Ḥazm enjoyed a happy though secluded childhood, and the advantages of an excellent education; he tells us that most of his early teachers were women.

'I have myself observed women, and got to know their secrets to an extent almost unparalleled; for I was reared in their bosoms, and brought up among them, not knowing any other society. I never sat with men until I was already a youth, and my beard had begun to sprout. Women taught me the Koran, they recited to me much poetry, they trained me in calligraphy; my only care and mental exercise, since first I began to understand anything, even from the days of earliest childhood, has been to study the affairs of females, to investigate their histories, and to acquire all the knowledge I could about them. I forget nothing of what I have seen them do. This all springs from a profound jealousy innate in me, and a deep instinctive suspicion of women's ways I have thus discovered not a little of their habits and motives. All this,' Ibn Ḥazm adds, 'shall be set forth at length in the appropriate chapters, God willing.'

The fall of the Banū 'Āmir led soon after to the dismissal and house-arrest of their faithful minister, who died four years later on June 22, 1012. The Umaiyads were now near their end in Spain, where they had outlived their kinsmen in the East by getting on for three centuries. Andalusia was in a state of anarchy; in 1013 the Berber insurgents seized and sacked Cordova, and on July 13th of that year Ibn Ḥazm fled from the city of his birth and set out upon extensive wanderings.

'A visitor from Cordova informed me,' he wrote in exile, 'when I asked him for news of that city, that he had seen our mansion in Balat Mughith, on the western side of the metropolis; its traces were wellnigh obliterated, its waymarks effaced; vanished were its spacious patios. All had been changed by decay; the joyous pleasauncies were converted to barren deserts and howling wilder-nesses; its beauty lay in shattered ruins. Where peace once reigned, fearful chasms yawned; wolves resorted there, ghosts frolicked, demons sported. Wild beasts now lurked where men like lions, abounding in wealth and every luxury, once paid court to statuesque maidens; who were all now scattered and dispersed to the four corners of the earth. Those gracious halls, those richly ornamented boudoirs, that once shone like the sun, the loveliness of their pano-rama lifting all cares from the mind, being now entirely overwhelmed by desolation and utter destruction seemed rather like the gaping mouths of savage beasts, proclaiming the end that awaits this mortal world, and revealing visibly the final destiny of those who dwell therein, the ultimate fate of those you now see abiding here below; so that you would be moved, after so long reluctance to abandon the world, henceforth eagerly to renounce it.

'Then I remembered the days that I had passed in that fair mansion, the joys I had known there, the months of my ardent youth spent in the company of blooming virgins, very apt to awaken desire in the heart of the most sedate young man. I pictured those maidens now lying beneath the dust, or dispersed to distant parts and far regions, scattered by the hand of exile, torn to pieces by the fingers of expatriation. I saw in my mind's eye the ruin of that noble house, which I had once known so beautiful and thriving, and in the shadow of whose well-ordered establishment I had passed my childhood; empty were those courts once so densely thronged. I seemed to hear the voices of owls hooting and screeching over those passages, astir of old with the busy concourse of people in whose midst I grew to manly estate. Then night followed day with the selfsame bustle, the selfsame coming and going of countless feet; but now day followed night there, and all was forever hushed and desolate. These sad reflections filled my eyes with tears and my heart with anguish; my soul was shattered as if by a jagged rock, and the misery in my mind waxed ever greater. So I took refuge in poetry, and uttered the following stanza.

> If now our throats are parched and dry,
>   Yet long its waters slaked our thirst;
>   If evil now has done its worst,
> Our happiness was slow to die.

Separation engenders deep regrets, profound emotions, and melancholy recollections, as I have remarked in these verses.

> Ah, would the raven but restore
>   To me that inauspicious day,
> And, as it drove my friends before,
>   Now drive my loneliness away!
>
> I speak; and over all extend
>   Night's shadows, like a mighty veil;
> Night swore that she would never end,
>   And in her promise does not fail.
>
> Yon star, bewildered, hangs on high
>   Immovable in heaven's heart;
> Lost in the desert of the sky,
>   It knows not whither to depart.

It calls to mind a man astray,
  His spirit fearful and afraid,
Or under threat, and in dismay,
  Some lover lovesick for his maid.'

In 1016 'Alī ibn Ḥammūd proclaimed himself caliph, but did not long survive his usurpation of power. The next fourteen years were chaotic in the extreme, as Umaiyad and Hammudid pretenders struggled for possession of the precarious throne. In 1030 the citizens of Cordova, weary of so much disorder, declared the Caliphate to be at an end and set up in its place a sort of republic; but the authority of Cordova had meanwhile dwindled away, and Andalusia was split between numerous independent principalities.

Ibn Ḥazm's first refuge after his flight from Cordova was Almeria, where he lived quietly and in comparative security for a time. But in 1016 Khairān, the governor of that city, made common cause with 'Alī ibn Ḥammūd against the Umaiyad Sulaimān, accused Ibn Ḥazm of harbouring Umaiyad sympathies, and after imprisoning him for some months banished him from his province. Our author made a brief stay at Aznalcazar, and then betook himself to Valencia, where 'Abd al-Raḥmān IV al-Murtaḍā the Umaiyad had just announced his succession to the Caliphate. He served al-Murtaḍā as vizier and marched with his army to Granada; but the cause he supported was not successful, and he was captured and thrown into prison. However his release was not long delayed; and in February 1019 he returned to Cordova after an absence of six years, to find al-Qāsim ibn Ḥammūd in power. In December 1023 the Umaiyads again seized the Caliphate, and Ibn Ḥazm became vizier to 'Abd al-Raḥmān V al-Mustaẓhir. He had only seven weeks' enjoyment of this turn of fortune, for al-Mustaẓhir was assassinated and he himself was once again in jail. History does not record how long his new incarceration lasted; we only know that in 1027 he was in Jativa, where he composed *The Ring of the Dove*. He appears to have kept clear of politics for the rest of his days, which ended on August 15, 1064; but he by no means kept clear of trouble, for his religious views were in conflict with the prevalent orthodoxy and his writings were publicly burned in Seville during his lifetime.

The circumstances attending the writing of *The Ring of the Dove* were that a friend invited Ibn Ḥazm to compose 'an essay describing Love, wherein I should set forth its various meanings, its causes and accidents, and what happens in it and to it, after the way of truth, neither adding anything nor embroidering anything, but only setting down exactly what I have to tell according to the manner of its occurrence, and mentioning all to the full extent of my recollection and the limit of my capacity. I have accordingly hastened to fulfil your desire; though but for the wish to comply with your commission I would never have undertaken it at all, being too poverty-stricken to attempt so great a task. Indeed it behoves us rather, considering the brief duration of our lives, not to expend them save upon those enterprises which we may hope will secure for us a spacious destination and a fair homecoming upon the morrow. Yet it is true that the Cadi Humām ibn Aḥmad has informed me on the authority of Yaḥyā ibn Mālik, who had it from 'Ā'idh upon a chain of authority mounting to Abu 'l-Dardā', that the latter said, "Recreate your souls with a little vanity, that it may the better aid them to hold fast to the truth." A righteous and well-approved father of the faith declared, "The man who has never known how to comport himself as a cavalier will never know how to be truly godfearing." The Prophet is reported to have said, "Rest your souls from time to time: they are apt to rust, in the same way that steel rusts." '

True to the scholastic tradition in which he was brought up, Ibn Ḥazm 'divided this treatise into thirty chapters. Of these, ten are concerned with the root-principles of Love, the first being the immediately following chapter on the Signs of Love. After this comes a chapter on Those who have fallen in Love while Asleep; then a chapter on Those who have fallen in Love through a Description; next a chapter on Those who have fallen in Love at First Sight; a chapter on Those whose Love has only become True after Long Association; a chapter on Allusion by Words; a chapter on Hinting with the Eyes; a chapter on Correspondence; and lastly (of these first ten) a chapter on the Messenger.

The second section of the book comprises twelve chapters on the accidents of Love, and its praiseworthy and blameworthy attributes. . . . This section is made up first of a chapter on the Helping Friend, then a chapter on Union, then a chapter on Concealing the Secret, and after that chapters on Revealing and Divulging the Secret, on Compliance, and on Opposition; a chapter on Those who have fallen in Love with a certain Quality and thereafter have not loved any other different to it; and chapters on Fidelity, on Betrayal, on Wasting Away, and on Death.

In the third part of the essay there are six chapters on the misfortunes which enter into Love. These chapters deal respectively with the Reproacher, the Spy, the Slanderer, Breaking Off, Separation, and Forgetting. . . . Finally come two chapters to terminate the discourse: a chapter discussing the Vileness of Sinning, and a chapter on the Virtue of Continence. I have planned the matter thus so that the conclusion of our exposition and the end of our discussion may be an exhortation to obedience to Almighty God, and a recommendation to do good and to eschew evil; which last commandment is indeed a duty imposed upon all believers.'

The selections which follow illustrate in their various ways life in high society as Ibn Ḥazm knew it, in Muslim Spain during the first years of the eleventh century—indeed, on the eve of our Norman Conquest.

Every love-affair must necessarily have some original cause. I shall now begin with the most unlikely of all causes of love, so that the discourse may proceed in due order, starting as ever with the simplest and easiest example. Love indeed is sometimes caused by things so strange, that but for having myself observed them I would not have mentioned them at all.

Now here is an instance from my own experience. One day I visited our friend Abu 'l-Sarī 'Ammār ibn Ziyād, the freedman of al-Mu'aiyad, and found him deep in thought and much preoccupied. I asked him what was amiss; for a while he refused to explain, but then he said, 'An extraordinary thing has happened to me, the like of which I have never heard.'

'What is that?' I enquired.

'Last night,' he answered, 'I saw in a dream a young maiden, and on awaking I found that I had completely lost my heart to her, and that I was madly in love with her. Now I am in the most difficult straits possible, with this passion I have conceived for her.'

He continued cast down and afflicted for more than a month; nothing would cheer him up, so profound was his emotion. At last I scolded him, saying, 'It is a vast mistake to occupy your soul with something unreal, and to attach your fantasy to a non-existent being. Do you know who she is?'

'No, by Allah!' he replied.

'Really,' I went on, 'you have very little judgment, and your discretion must be affected, if you are actually in love with a person whom you have never seen, someone moreover who was never created and does not exist in the world at all. If you had fallen for one of those pictures they paint on the walls of the public baths, I would have found it easier to excuse you.'

So I continued, until at last by making a great effort he forgot his trouble.

The poet Yūsuf ibn Hārūn, better known as al-Ramādī, was one day passing the Gate of the Perfumers at Cordova, a place where ladies were wont to congregate, when he espied a young girl who, as he said, 'entirely captured my heart, so that all my limbs were penetrated by the love of her'. He therefore turned aside from going to the mosque and set himself instead to following her, while she for her part set off towards the bridge, which she then crossed and came to the place known as al-Rabad. When she reached the mausolea of the Banū Marwān, God have mercy on their souls, that are erected over their graves in the cemetery of al-Rabad, beyond the river, she observed him to have gone apart from the rest of the people and to be preoccupied solely with her.

She accordingly went up to him and said 'Why are you walking behind me?'

He told her how sorely smitten he was with her, and she replied, 'Have done with that! Do not seek to expose me to shame; you have no prospect of achieving your purpose, and there is no way to gratifying your desire.'

'I am satisfied merely to look at you,' he countered.

'That is permitted to you,' she replied.

Then he asked her, 'My lady, are you a freewoman, or are you a slave?'

'I am a slave,' she answered.

'And what is your name?' he enquired.

'Khalwa,' she told him.

'And to whom do you belong?' he asked next.

To this she retorted, 'By Allah, you are likelier to know what inhabits the seventh heaven than the answer to that question. Seek not the impossible!'

'My lady,' he begged, 'where may I see you again?'

'Where you saw me today,' she replied. 'At the same hour, every Friday.' Then she added, 'Will you go off now, or shall I?'

'Do you go off, in Allah's protection!' he replied.

So she went off in the direction of the bridge; and he could not follow her, because she kept looking round to see if he was accompanying her or not. When she had passed the gate of the bridge he came after her, but could find no trace of her whatsoever.

'And by Allah,' said Abū 'Umar (that is to say, Yūsuf ibn Hārūn), recounting the story of his adventure, 'I have frequented the Perfumers' Gate and al-Rabad the whole time from then till now, but I have never come upon any further news of her. I know not whether the heavens have devoured her, or whether the earth has swallowed her up; and the feeling I have in my heart on her account is hotter than burning coals.'

This is the Khalwa whose name he celebrates in his love lyrics.

Thereafter he had news of her after he journeyed to Saragossa for her sake, but that is a long story.

A young fellow I know, the son of a clerk, was one day observed by a lady of noble birth, high position and strict seclusion; she saw him passing by, while peeping out from a place of vantage in her home, and conceived an attachment for him which he reciprocated. They exchanged epistles for a time, by ways more delicate than the edge of a fine-ground sword; and were it not that I purpose not in this essay to uncover such ruses and make mention of such subterfuges, I could have set down here such things as I am certain would have confounded the shrewdest and astonished the most intelligent of men. I pray that God in His great bounty will draw over us and all good Muslims the curtain of His mercy. He is indeed sufficient for our needs.

I indeed marvel profoundly at all those who pretend to fall in love at first sight; I cannot easily prevail upon myself to believe their claim, and prefer to consider such love as merely a kind of lust. As for thinking that that sort of attachment can really possess the inmost heart, and penetrate the veil of the soul's recess, that I cannot under any circumstances credit. Love has never truly gripped my bowels, save after a long lapse of time, and constant companionship with the person concerned, sharing with him all that while my every occupation, be it earnest or frivolous.

So I am alike in consolation and in passion; I have never in my life forgotten any romance, and my nostalgia for every former attachment is such that I wellnigh choke when I drink and suffocate when I eat. The man who is not so constituted quickly finds complete relief and is at rest again; I have never wearied of anything once I have known it, and neither have I hastened to feel at home with it on first acquaintance. Similarly I have never longed for a change for change's sake, in any of the things that I have possessed; I am speaking here not only of friends and comrades, but also of all the other things a man uses—clothes, riding-beast, food, and so on. Life holds no joy for me, and I do nothing but hang my head and feel utterly cast down, ever since I first tasted the bitterness of being separated from those I love. It is an anguish that constantly revisits me, an agony of grief that ceases not for a moment to assail me. My remembrance of past happiness has abated for me every joy that I may look for in the future. I am a dead man, though counted among the living, slain by sorrow and buried by sadness, entombed while yet a dweller on the face of this mortal earth. Allah be praised, whatever be the circumstances that befall us; there is indeed no other God but He!

I have meditated upon this theme in verse as follows.

True love is not a flower
That springeth in an hour;
Its flint will not strike fire
At casual desire.

Love is an infant rare
Begotten, slow to bear;
Its lime must mingle long
Before its base is strong.

And then not soon will it
Be undermined, and split;
Firm will its structure stand,
Its fabric still expand.

This truth is readily
Confirmed, because we see
That things too quickly grown
Are swiftly overthrown.

Mine is a stubborn soil
To plough with arduous toil,
Intractable indeed
To tiller and to seed.

But once the roots begin
To strike and thrive therein,
Come bounteous rain, come drought,
The lusty stem will sprout.

The first device employed by those who seek union, being lovers, in order to disclose their feelings to the object of their passion, is allusion by means of words. Either they will quote a verse of poetry, or despatch an allegory, or rhyme a riddle, or propose an enigma, or use heightened language. Men vary in their methods according to the degree of their perspicacity, or the amount of aversion or sympathy, wit or dullness which they remark in their loved ones. I know a man who commenced his declaration of love by quoting to his lady some verses of my own composition. This and the like are the shifts resorted to in the first stages of the love-quest. If the lover detects some sign of sympathy and encouragement, he then proceeds further. . . .

I know of a youth and a girl who were very much in love with each other. In the course of one of his interviews with her, the young man made a slightly improper suggestion. At this the girl exclaimed, 'By Allah, I shall make a public complaint against you, and I shall put you to shame privately.' Some days later the girl found herself in a company of great princes and the leading statesmen of the realm; present also were a great number of women and of servants, against whom it would be well to be on one's guard. The youth in question was in the concourse too, for he was in the entourage of the master of ceremonies. Other singing girls besides her were in attendance. When it came to her turn to sing, she tuned her lute and began to chant the words of an ancient song.

> Sweet fawn adorable,
> Fair as the moon at full,
> Or like the sun, that through
> Dark clouds shines out to view:
>
> With that so languid glance
> He did my heart entrance,
> With that lithe stature, he
> As slender as a tree.
>
> I yielded to his whim,
> I humbled me to him,
> As lovesick suitor still
> Obeys his darling's will.
>
> Let me thy ransom be!
> Embrace me lawfully:
> I would not give my charms
> Into licentious arms.

Lovers for the most part employ as their messengers to the beloved either a humble and insignificant fellow to whom nobody will pay much attention, because of his youthfulness or his scruffy look or untidy appearance; or a very respectable person to whom no sort of suspicion will attach on account of his show of piety, or because he is of advanced years. Women too are frequently used, especially those who hobble along on sticks, and carry rosaries, and are wrapped up in a pair of red cloaks. I remember how at Cordova young women had been put on their guard against such types, whenever they might happen to see them. Women plying a trade or profession,

which gives them ready access to people, are popular with lovers—
the lady doctor for instance, or the blood-letter, the peddler, the
broker, the coiffeuse, the professional mourner, the singer, the
soothsayer, the schoolmistress, the errand-girl, the spinner, the
weaver, and the like. It is also found convenient to employ a person
who is closely related to the beloved, and who will therefore not be
grudged admittance.

How many an inaccessible maiden has proved approachable by
using messengers like these! How often have apparently insur-
mountable difficulties been easily overcome, and the one who
seemed so far off proved close at hand, the one most refractory
been readily tamed! How many disagreeable surprises have befallen
well-protected veils, thick curtains, close-guarded boudoirs and
stoutly-fashioned doors at the hands of suchlike persons! But for
my desire to call attention to them, I would never have mentioned
these types at all; but I felt bound to do so, in order that others
may have their eyes open and not readily trust in any of their sort.
Happy is the man who takes warning by another's experience, even
if he be his enemy! I pray that Allah may cover us and all good
Muslims with the veil of His protection, and never suffer the shadow
of His preservation to pass away from any one of us.

I know of a pair of lovers whose messenger was a well-trained
dove; the letter would be fastened to its wing. On this topic I have
the following verses.

> Old Noah chose a dove to be
> His faithful messenger, and he
> Was not confounded so to choose:
> She brought him back the best of news.

> So I am trusting to this dove
> My messages to thee, my love,
> And so I send her forth, to bring
> My letters safely in her wing.

I was once acquainted with a man of Cordova, the son of one of
the principal clerks in the civil service—his name was Aḥmad ibn
Fatḥ—and I had always known him as most circumspect, a keen
student of science and letters; in reserve he excelled all his companions, in quiet dignity he was supreme. He was never to be seen
anywhere but in the most virtuous circles, and the parties he
attended were always most praiseworthy, his conduct beyond
reproach; he went his own way, and kept himself to himself.

Then the fates decreed that we should be far sundered. The first

news that came to me, after I had taken up residence in Jativa, was
that he had cast off all restraint on falling in love with a certain
goldsmith's son called Ibrāhīm ibn Aḥmad. I knew this young man,
well enough to be aware that his qualities did not merit his being
loved by a person of a good family, in a prominent position, and
possessed of broad estates and an ample patrimony. Then I had it
confirmed that my friend had uncovered his head, shown his face
abroad, cast off his head-rope, bared his countenance, rolled up his
sleeves—in a word, that he had given himself over to the lusts of
the flesh. He had become the talk of the town; all tongues wagged
of his adventure; his name was banded through the countryside,
and the scandalmongers ran everywhere with tales of his amazing
escapade. All that he had achieved was that the veil of his private
feelings had been stripped off, his secret had been divulged, his
name besmirched, his reputation blackened; the object of his passion
had run away from him altogether, and forbidden him ever to see
him again.

Yet he might well have spared himself these troubles; he could
easily have escaped, and kept far away from it all. If indeed he had
only concealed his deep secret and hidden his heart's afflictions, he
might have continued to wear the robe of well-being, and the
garment of his respectability would never have become threadbare;
he could still have nourished his hopes, and found ample consolation
in meeting and conversing and sitting with the one for whom he
was so badly smitten. But alas, the cord of his excuses was snapped;
the evidence against him was overwhelming, and the only argument
that might be urged in his favour was that his judgment was
deranged, his reason affected by his shattering experience. That
would certainly have been a valid excuse. But if only a fraction of
his understanding remained intact, if the merest fragment of his
mind was still unimpaired, then he was gravely at fault in acting
in a manner which he was well aware would grievously affront and
distress his well-beloved. That is not how true lovers behave.

One of the wonderful things that occur in Love is the way the lover
submits to the beloved, and adjusts his own character by main
force to that of his loved one. Often and often you will see a man
stubborn by disposition, intractable, jibbing at all control, determined, arrogant, always ready to take umbrage; yet no sooner let
him sniff the soft air of love, plunge into its waves, and swim in its
sea, than his stubbornness will have suddenly changed to docility,
his intractability to gentleness, his determination to easy-going,
his arrogance to submission.

Sa'īd ibn Mundhir ibn Sa'īd, who used to lead the prayers in the cathedral mosque of Cordova during the days of al-Ḥakam al-Mustanṣir Bi'llāh, God be merciful to his soul, had a slave-girl with whom he was deeply in love. He offered to manumit and marry her, to which she scornfully replied—and I should mention that he had a fine long beard—'I think your beard is dreadfully long; trim it up, and then you shall have your wish.' He thereupon laid a pair of scissors to his beard, until it looked somewhat more gallant; then he summoned witnesses, and invited them to testify that he had set the girl free. But when in due course he proposed to her, she would not accept him.

Among those present was his brother Ḥakam ibn Mundhir, who promptly said to the assembled company, 'Now I am going to propose marriage to her.' He did so, and she consented; and he married her then and there. Sa'īd acquiesced in this frightful insult, for all that he was a man known for his abstinence, piety and religious zeal. I myself met this same Sa'īd; he was slain by the Berbers, on the day when they stormed and sacked Cordova.

When I was living in the old city at Cordova I one day met Abū 'Abd Allāh Muḥammad ibn Kulaib of Kairouan, a man with an exceedingly long tongue, well-sharpened to enquire on every manner of subject. The topic of Love and its various aspects was under discussion, and he put the following question to me: 'If a person with whom I am in love is averse to meeting me, and avoids me whenever I try to make an approach, what should I do?'

'My opinion,' I replied, 'is that you should endeavour to bring relief to your own soul by meeting the beloved, even if the beloved is averse to meeting you.'

'I do not agree,' he retorted. 'I prefer that the beloved should have his will and desire, rather than I mine. I would endure and endure, even if it meant death for me.'

'I would only have fallen in love,' I countered, 'for my personal satisfaction and aesthetic pleasure. I should therefore follow my own analogy, guide myself by my personal principles, and pursue my habitual path, seeking quite deliberately my own enjoyment.'

'That is a cruel logic,' he exclaimed. 'Far worse than death is that for the sake of which you desire death, and far dearer than life is that for the sake of which you would gladly lay down your life.'

'But,' I said, 'you would be laying down your life not by choice but under compulsion. If it were possible for you not to lay down your life, you would not have done so. To give up meeting the beloved voluntarily would certainly be most reprehensible, since you would thereby do violence to yourself and bring your own soul to its doom.'

Thereupon he cried out, 'You are a born dialectician, and dialectics have no particular relevance to Love.'

'In that case,' I said, 'the lover will certainly be unfortunate.'

'And what misfortune is there,' he ended, 'that is greater than Love?'

I have never seen anything to equal the helpfulness of women. They are far more forward than men in keeping love's secret, in counselling each other to be discreet, and in co-operating to conceal it whenever they happen to know of any such affair. I have never in my life known a woman to reveal the secret of a loving couple, without that she was hated, loathed and unanimously condemned by all her sisters. Old women excel young girls in this particular; the latter do sometimes disclose what they know out of jealousy (though that happens indeed rarely), whereas the former have despaired of further romances, and are therefore now anxious solely for the welfare of others.

I know of a wealthy woman who possessed many slave-girls and servants. It was rumoured that one of her maids was in love with a young gentleman of the family, and that he reciprocated her sentiments; it was further reported that they were behaving disgracefully. A friend remarked to the mistress, 'Your maid so-and-so knows all about the affair, and is intimate with every detail.' The mistress thereupon laid hold of the maid—and she was very cruel in punishing her servants—and let her sample such a variety of blows and pommelings as even the toughest man could not have endured, hoping that the girl would disclose to her something of the matter that had been mentioned to her; but she betrayed nothing whatsoever.

I also know of a great lady, able to recite the Koran from end to end, pious, and devoted to good works. She happened to obtain possession of a letter written by a boy to his lady-love; the boy was the property of a different household. The grand lady let the young man know that she was aware of the romance; he sought to deny everything, but that was impossible. She then said to him, 'What ails you? Who has ever been immune from love? Don't worry about this; by Allah, I will never apprise anyone of your secret. If I could only buy her for you out of my property, even if it took all that I possess, I would gladly place her at your disposal, somewhere that you could come to her without anyone being the wiser.'

You will sometimes see a virtuous, elderly lady, having given up all hope of men, whose fondest occupation (and she has the greatest confidence that this will prove acceptable to God) is to contrive to marry off an orphan girl; she will lend her clothes and her jewels to an impoverished bride.

As for the reason why this instinct is so deeply rooted in women, I see no other explanation than that they have nothing else to fill their minds, except loving union and what brings it about, flirting and how it is done, intimacy and the various ways of achieving it. That is their sole occupation, and they were created for nothing else. Men on the other hand are divided in their interests; some seek to amass a fortune, some aspire to the company of kings, some pursue knowledge, some look after their families, some venture on arduous journeys, some hunt, some ply diverse crafts, some go forth to the wars, some confront armed rebellions, some brave fearful perils, some cultivate the soil. All these different occupations diminish leisure, and divert men from the paths of idleness.

I have read in the biographies of the kings of the negroes, that those monarchs assign their womenfolk to the care of a trusty henchman, who allots to each her task of wool-spinning, so that their whole time is fully employed. For they say that when a woman remains without any occupation, she hankers after men and yearns for the marriage-bed.

One of the significant aspects of Love is Union. This is a lofty fortune, an exalted rank, a sublime degree, a lucky star; nay more, it is life renewed, pleasure supreme, joy everlasting, and a grand mercy from Allah.

Were it not that this world below is a transitory abode of trial and trouble, and Paradise a home where virtue receives its reward, secure from all annoyances, I would have said that union with the beloved is that pure happiness which is without alloy, and gladness unsullied by sorrow, the perfect realization of hopes and the complete fulfilment of one's dreams.

I have tested all manner of pleasures, and known every variety of joy; and I have found that neither intimacy with princes, nor wealth acquired, nor finding after lacking, nor returning after long absence, nor security after fear and repose in a safe refuge—none of these things so powerfully affects the soul as union with the beloved, especially if it come after long denial and continual banishment. For then the flame of passion waxes exceeding hot, and the furnace of yearning blazes up, and the fire of eager hope rages ever more fiercely. The fresh springing of herbs after the rains, the glitter of flowers when the night clouds have rolled away in the hushed hour between dawn and sunrise, the plashing of waters as they run through the stalks of golden blossoms, the exquisite beauty of white castles encompassed by verdant meadows—not lovelier is any of these than union with the well-beloved, whose character is virtuous, and laudable her disposition, whose attributes are evenly matched in perfect beauty. Truly that is a miracle of wonder suspassing the tongues of the eloquent, and far beyond the range of the most cunning speech to describe; the mind reels before it, and the intellect stands abashed.

I have tried to express this in a poem.

> Men sometimes come and question me
> How many years my age may be,
> Seeing my temples silver now
> And flecks of snow upon my brow.
>
> This is the answer that I give:
> 'When I count up the life I live
> Applying all my reason's power,
> I make the total just one hour.'
>
> 'And how,' my questioner replies
> In accents of amazed surprise,
> 'Mak'st thou this sum, which seems to me
> Beyond all credibility?'
>
> 'One day,' I answer, 'she I love
> All other earthly things above
> Lay in my arms, and like a thought
> Her lips with mine I swiftly sought.
>
> And though the years before I die
> Stretch out interminably, I
> Shall only count my life in truth
> As that brief hour of happy youth.'

I know of a young slave-girl who was ardently passionate for a certain youth, the son of a noble household, but he was ignorant of her sentiments. Great was her sorrow, and long her despair, so that she pined and wasted away for the love of him. He in all the pride of youthful indifference was quite unconscious of her suffering, which she was prevented from revealing to him by maidenly modesty; for she was a virgin unspotted, and moreover respected him too highly to surprise him with a declaration which for all she knew he might not find to his liking. As time went on, however, and the girl felt more and more certain of the state of her heart, she at last complained of her plight to a sagacious woman who enjoyed her confidence, for she was her old nurse.

'Hint at your feelings to him in verse,' the latter said to her.

The girl did as she was advised, and that time after time; but the youth paid no attention whatsoever. It was not that he lacked intelligence and wit; quite the contrary; but he had no suspicion of her intention, that his imagination should be alert to look for hidden meanings in her words.

Finally the girl's endurance was at an end; her emotions were insupportable. One night she was seated with him *tête-à-tête*; and God knows that he was most chaste and self-disciplined, very far indeed from committing any impropriety. Finding that she could no longer control her feelings, when she stood up to leave him she suddenly turned and kissed him on the mouth, then, without uttering a single word, coquettishly swaying she withdrew. I have tried to picture the scene in a poem.

> As she withdrew, the lissom maid,
> This way and that she gently swayed
> As a narcissus 'neath the trees
> Swings on its stem before the breeze.
>
> Deep in his heart the lover hears
> The pendants hanging from her ears
> Ring out a tender melody:
> 'I love thee dearly: lov'st thou me?'
>
> I pictured in her poise and grace
> A dove that goes with perfect pace;
> Not over slow he seems to move,
> Nor undue hasty, to reprove.

The young man was stupefied, confused, quite overcome; his heart was deeply stirred, his spirit was overwhelmed by conflicting emotions. Hardly was she out of his sight when he found himself caught in the toils of destruction; his breast was all afire; he sighed and sighed. A multitude of fears assailed him; he was a prey to every apprehension; sleep deserted him, and all through the night he tossed and turned unable to close his eyes. Such was the beginning of a love between them which continued many moons, until the cruel hand of separation broke the cords of their perfect union. There you may say was a very Devil's trick, an incitement to passion no man could have withstood, unless he were under the protection of Allah the All-Powerful.

To grow tired of a thing is an inborn human characteristic: a man afflicted by this failing deserves all the more not to receive the sincere and undiluted affection of any friend, and that none should engage himself to him in true brotherhood. For he is not constant in any covenant; he perseveres in no association; the succour he may render to the lover is of but brief duration; neither his love nor his hatred is to be trusted. The best way with such a man is not to attach him to oneself, and rather to flee from his company and his society, for one will never derive any advantage from his friendship. It is for this reason that we have excluded this quality from our analysis of lovers, and put it in the category of the beloved's attributes; for the latter are in general apt to level false accusations, to entertain dark suspicions, to address themselves to rupturing relations. The person who decks himself out with the name of love, and is easily wearied, is no true lover at all; it is right that the very taste of him should be shunned, and that he be banished from the roll of lovers, and never admitted into their society.

I never saw any man so completely dominated by this quality as Abū 'Āmir Muḥammad ibn 'Āmir, God have mercy upon him. If anyone had described to me a fraction of what I knew of him, I would never have believed him. People of such a temperament are the quickest of beings to fall in love, and the least patient with those they love, as also with those they detest vice versa. They change as rapidly from adoration as they gallop into it. So never put your trust in anyone who is given to weariness, neither occupy your thoughts with him; entertain no false hopes that he will be faithful to you, and if you are constrained by necessity to love him know him for what he is, a creature of passing fancies, and adapt yourself to suit his varying moods as you observe him to change from moment to moment, conforming in general with all his fickle whims.

Abū 'Āmir, whose name I have just mentioned, whenever he clapped his eyes on a slave-girl could scarcely restrain his impatience; he was so overcome by anxiety and trepidation that he wellnigh expired, until at last he possessed her, even if a veritable forest of tragacanth bushes stood between him and his object. Yet as soon as he was certain that she was his for the having, love turned to revulsion, intimacy to aversion, agitation to be with her into agitation to be without her, longing to have her into longing to be rid of her. So he would sell her at the most ridiculous price. Such was his wont, so that he squandered in this way many tens of thousands of gold dinars. Yet for all that, God bless him, he was a man of culture, intelligent, sagacious, noble and sweet in his ways;

he had a penetrating wit, and was withal a great aristocrat, of highly exalted rank, and enjoyed a position of vast prestige. His handsome features and perfect physique were beyond all definition; the imagination boggles to describe even the least part of his manly beauty, and none could adequately accomplish the task of picturing him as he was.

The boulevards of the city were all deserted of promenaders, the whole population being intent to pass the door of his house, which stood in the street running up from the little river, by the gate of my own residence on the eastern side of Cordova, and leading to the avenue adjoining the palace of al-Zāhira; his house was in this avenue, quite close to mine. All, as I have said, thronged his door, for no other reason than simply to catch a glimpse of him. Many a slave-girl died of a broken heart on his account; infatuated by his charm, they would deck themselves out in all their finery to attract his fancy; but he betrayed their hopes, so that they became the victims of wasting passion, and were slain by solitude. I knew one of these girls whose name was 'Afrā'; she did not trouble to conceal her love for him, in whatever company she found herself, and the tears never dried from her cheeks. She passed from his household to Abu 'l-Barakāt al-Khayālī, the prefect of the royal buildings.

Abū 'Āmir told me much about himself, including the fact that he was weary among other things of his own name! As for his friends, he changed them frequently during his brief lifetime. Like the finch, he never remained constant to the same fashion long; sometimes he would dress himself in the robes of a king, sometimes he got himself up like an assassin.

Because betrayal is so common a characteristic of the beloved, fidelity on her part has come to be regarded as extraordinary; therefore its rare occurrence in persons loved is thought to counter-balance its frequency among lovers. I have a little poem on this subject.

> Small faithfulness in the beloved
> Is most exceedingly approved,
> While lovers' great fidelity
> Is taken unremarkably.
>
> So cowards, rarely brave in war,
> Are more applauded when they are
> Than heroes, who sustain all day
> The heat and fury of the fray.

A particularly base type of betrayal is when the lover sends an emissary to the beloved, entrusting all his secrets to his keeping, and then the messenger strives and contrives to convert the beloved's interest to himself, and captures her affection to the exclusion of his principal. I put this situation in rhyme as follows.

> I sent an envoy unto thee,
>   Intending so my hopes to gain;
> I trusted him too foolishly;
>   Now he has come between us twain.
>
> He loosed the cords of my true love,
>   Then neatly tied his own instead;
> He drove me out of all whereof
>   I might have well been tenanted.
>
> I, who had called him to the stand,
>   Am now a witness to his case:
> I fed him at my table, and
>   Now hang myself upon his grace.

Finally there is the separation which is caused by death, that final parting from which there is no hope of a return. This is indeed a shattering and back-breaking blow, a fateful catastrophe; it is a lamentable woe, overshadowing the blackness of night itself; it cuts off every hope, erases all ambition, and causes the most sanguine to despair of further meeting. Here all tongues are baffled; the cord of every remedy is severed; no other course remains open but patient fortitude, willing or perforce. It is the greatest affliction that can assail true lovers; and he who is struck down by it has nothing left but to lament and weep, until either he perishes himself or wearies of his lamentations. It is the wound which cannot heal, the anguish which never passes, the sorrow which is constantly renewed, as ever his poor body crumbles that thou hast committed to the dust. On this matter I have the following to say.

> What things soe'er
> May come to pass,
> Cry not alas
> While hope is there.
>
> Haste not thy heart
> To gloom to yield:
> All is not sealed
> Till life depart.

> But when the veil
> Of death descends
> Then all hope ends,
> All comforts fail.

I have seen this happen to many people, and can relate to you a personal experience of the same order; for I am also one who has been afflicted by this calamity and surprised by this misfortune. I was deeply in love with, and passionately enamoured of, a certain slave-girl once in my possession, whose name was Nu'm. She was a dream of desire, a paragon of physical and moral beauty, and we were in perfect harmony. She had known no other man before me, and our love for each other was mutual and perfectly satisfying. Then the fates ravished her from me, and the nights and passing days carried her away; she became one with the dust and stones. At the time of her death I was not yet twenty, and she younger than I. For seven months thereafter I never once put off my garments; my tears ceased not to flow, though I am a man not given to weeping, nor discovering relief in lamentation. And by Allah, I have not found consolation for her loss even to this day. If ransoms could have been of avail, I would have ransomed her with everything of which I stand possessed, my inheritance and all my earnings, aye, and with the most precious limb of my body, swiftly and willingly. Since her death life has never seemed sweet to me; I have never forgotten her memory, nor been intimate with any other woman. My love for her blotted out all that went before, and made anathema to me all that came after it.

I can tell you with regard to myself, that in my youth I enjoyed the loving friendship of a certain slave-girl who grew up in our house, and who at the time of my story was sixteen years old. She had an extremely pretty face, and was moreover intelligent, chaste, pure, shy, and of the sweetest disposition. She was not given to jesting, and was most sparing of her favours; she had a wonderful complexion, which she always kept closely veiled. Innocent of every vice, and of very few words, she kept her eyes modestly cast down. Moreover she was extremely cautious, and guiltless of all faults, ever maintaining a serious mien; charming in her withdrawal, she was naturally reserved, and most graceful in repelling unwelcome advances. She seated herself with becoming dignity, and was most sedate in her behaviour; the way she fled from masculine attentions like a startled bird was delightful to behold. No hopes of easy conquest were to be entertained so far as she was concerned; none

could look to succeed in his ambitions if these were aimed in her
direction; eager expectation found no resting-place in her. Her lovely
face attracted all hearts, but her manner kept at arm's length all
who came seeking her; she was far more glamorous in her refusals
and rejections than those other girls, who rely upon easy compliance
and the ready lavishing of their favours to make them interesting
to men. In short, she was dedicated to earnestness in all matters,
and had no desire for amusement of any kind; for all that she played
the lute most beautifully. I found myself irresistibly drawn towards
her, and loved her with all the violent passion of my youthful heart.
For two years or thereabouts I laboured to the utmost of my powers
to win one syllable of response from her, to hear from her lips a
single word, other than the usual kind of banalities that may be
heard by everyone; but all my efforts proved in vain.

Now I remember a party that was held in our residence, on one
of those occasions that are commonly made the excuse for such
festivities in the houses of persons of rank. The ladies of our household and of my brother's also, God have mercy on his soul, were
assembled together, as well as the womenfolk of our retainers and
faithful servants, all thoroughly nice and jolly folk. The ladies
remained in the house for the earlier part of the day, and then
betook themselves to a belvedere that was attached to our mansion,
overlooking the garden and giving a magnificent view of the whole
of Cordova; the bays were constructed with large open windows.
They passed their time enjoying the panorama through the lattice
openings, myself being among them.

I recall that I was endeavouring to reach the bay where she was
standing, to enjoy her proximity and to sidle up close to her. But
no sooner did she observe me in the offing than she left that bay and
sought another, moving with consummate grace. I endeavoured to
come to the bay to which she had departed, and she repeated her
performance and passed on to another. She was well aware of my
infatuation, while the other ladies were entirely unconscious of what
was passing between us; for there was a large company of them,
and they were all the time moving from one alcove to another to
enjoy the variety of prospects, each bay affording a different view
from the rest.

You must realize, my friend, that women have keener eyes to
detect admiration in a man's heart, than any benighted traveller
has to discover a track in the desert. Well, at last the ladies went
down into the garden; and the dowagers and duchesses among them
entreated the mistress of the girl to let them hear her sing. She
commanded her to do so; and she thereupon took up her lute and

tuned it with a pretty shyness and modesty, the like of which I had never seen; though it is true of course that things are doubly beautiful in the eyes of their admirers. Then she began to sing those famous verses of al-'Abbās ibn al-Aḥnaf.

> My heart leapt up, when I espied
> A sun sink slowly in the west,
> Its beauty in that bower to hide
> Where lovely ladies lie at rest:
>
> A sun embodied in the guise
> Of a sweet maiden of delight,
> The ripple of her rounded thighs
> A scroll of parchment, soft and white.
>
> No creature she of human kind,
> Though human fair and beautiful,
> And neither sprite, although designed
> In faery grace ineffable.
>
> Her body was a jasmine rare,
> Her perfume sweet as amber scent,
> Her face a pearl beyond compare,
> Her all, pure light's embodiment.
>
> All shrouded in her pettigown
> I watched her delicately pass,
> Stepping as light as thistledown
> That dances on a crystal glass.

And by my life, it was as though her plectrum was plucking at the strings of my heart. I have never forgotten that day, nor shall forget it until the time comes for me to leave this transient world. That was the most I was ever given to see her, or to hear her voice.

Then my father, the vizier, God rest his soul, moved from our new mansion in Rabad al-Zāhira on the eastern side of Cordova to our old residence on the western side, in the quarter of Balat Mughith; this was on the third day of the accession of Muḥammad al-Mahdī to the Caliphate. I followed him in February 1009; but the girl did not come with us, for reasons that obliged her to remain behind. Thereafter, when Hishām al-Mu'aiyad succeeded to the throne, we were sufficiently preoccupied with the misfortunes which came upon us, thanks to the hostility of his ministers; we were sorely tried by imprisonment, surveillance and crushing fines, and were finally obliged to go into hiding. Civil war raged far and wide; all classes suffered from its dire effects, and ourselves in particular. At last my father the vizier died, God have mercy on his soul, our situation being still as I have described, on the afternoon of Saturday, June 22, 1012.

Things remained unchanged with us thereafter, until presently the day came when we again had a funeral in the house, one of our relatives having deceased. I saw her standing there amid the clamour of mourning, all among the weeping and wailing women. She revived that passion long buried in my heart, and stirred my now still ardour, reminding me of an ancient troth, an old love, an epoch gone by, a vanished time, departed months, faded memories, periods perished, days forever past, obliterated traces. She renewed my griefs and reawakened my sorrows; and though upon that day I was afflicted and cast down for many reasons, yet I had indeed not forgotten her; only my anguish was intensified, the fire smouldering in my heart blazed into flame, my unhappiness was exacerbated, my despair was multiplied. Passion drew forth from my breast all that lay hidden within it; my soul answered the call, and I broke out into plaintive rhyme.

> They weep for one now dead,
> High honoured in his tomb;
> Those tears were better shed
> For him who lives in gloom.
>
> O wonder, that they sigh
> For him who is at rest
> Yet mourn not me, who die
> Most cruelly oppressed.

Then destiny struck its heaviest blows, and we were banished from our loved abodes; the armies of the Berbers triumphed over us. I set forth from Cordova on July 13, 1013, and after that one glimpse of her she vanished from my sight for six long years and more. Then I came again into Cordova in February 1019, and lodged with one of our womenfolk; and there I saw her. I could scarcely recognize her, until someone said to me, 'This is So-and-so'; her charms were so greatly changed. Gone was her radiant beauty, vanished her wondrous loveliness; faded now was that lustrous complexion which once gleamed like a polished sword or an Indian mirror; withered was the bloom on which the eye once gazed transfixed seeking avidly to feast upon its dazzling splendour only to turn away bewildered. Only a fragment of the whole remained, to tell the tale and testify to what the complete picture had been. All this had come to pass because she took too little care of herself, and had lacked the guardian hand which had nourished her during the days of our prosperity, when our shadow was long in the land; as also because she had been obliged to besmirch herself in those inevitable excursions to which her circumstances had driven her, and from which she had formerly been sheltered and exempted.

For women are as aromatic herbs, which if not well tended soon lose their fragrance; they are as edifices which, if not constantly cared for, quickly fall into ruin. Therefore it has been said that manly beauty is the truer, the more solidly established, and of higher excellence, since it can endure, and that without shelter, onslaughts the merest fraction of which would transform the loveliness of a woman's face beyond recognition: such enemies as the burning heat of the noonday, the scorching wind of the desert, every air of heaven, and all the changing moods of the seasons.

If I had enjoyed the least degree of intimacy with her, if she had been only a little kind to me, I would have been beside myself with happiness; I verily believe that I would have died for joy. But it was her unremitting aloofness which schooled me in patience, and taught me to find consolation. This then was one of those cases in which both parties may excusably forget, and not be blamed for doing so: there has been no firm engagement that should require their loyalty, no covenant has been entered into obliging them to keep faith, no ancient compact exists, no solemn plighting of troths, the breaking and forgetting of which should expose them to justified reproach.

Here is a story which I have often heard told concerning a certain Berber king. An Andalusian gentleman, finding himself in financial difficulties, had sold a female slave whom he loved passionately; she was bought by a man of the Berber country. The poor fellow who sold her never imagined that his heart would follow her in the way it did. When she reached her purchaser's home, her former owner almost expired. So he searched out the man to whom he had sold her and offered him all his possessions, and himself to boot, if he would restore her to him; but the Berber refused.

The Andalusian then besought the inhabitants of the town to prevail upon him; but not one of them came to his assistance. Almost out of his mind, he bethought himself of appealing to the king; he therefore stood without the palace, and uttered a loud cry. The king, who was seated in a lofty chamber overlooking the courtyard, heard his shout and ordered him to be admitted. The Andalusian entered the royal presence, and standing before his Berber majesty he told his story, and implored and supplicated him to have compassion.

The king, much touched by his plight, commanded that the man who had bought the girl should be summoned to court. He duly came; and the king said, 'This poor fellow is a stranger; you can see what a state he is in. I intercede with you personally on his behalf.' But the purchaser refused, saying, 'I am more deeply in love with her than he is, and I fear that if you return her to him I myself shall be standing here tomorrow imploring your aid, and in an even worse case.' The king and all his courtiers offered him of their own riches to let her go; but he persisted in his refusal, pleading as his excuse the affection he bore her.

The audience having by now dragged on a long time, and there being no sign whatsoever that the purchaser would give way and consent, the king said to the Andalusian, 'My good sir, I can do nothing more for you than this. I have striven to the utmost of my powers on your behalf; and you see how he excuses himself on the grounds that he loves her more than you do, and fears he may come to even greater evil than yourself. You had best endure patiently what Allah has decreed for you.'

The Andalusian thereupon exclaimed, 'Have you no means at all then of helping me?'

'Can I do anything more for you than entreat him, and offer him money?' the king answered.

The Andalusian, being in despair, bent himself double, and with his hands clutching his feet he threw himself down from the topmost height of the audience-chamber to the earth. The king cried out in alarm, and his slaves below ran to where the man was lying. It was his fate not to be greatly injured by the fall, and he was brought up to the king again.

'What did you intend by doing that?' the king said to him.

'O king,' the man replied, 'I cannot live any longer, now that I have lost her.'

Then he would have thrown himself down a second time, but he was prevented.

'Allah is great!' the king thereupon exclaimed. 'I have hit upon the just arbitrament of this problem.' Turning to the purchaser he said, 'Good sir, do you claim that your love for the girl is greater than his, and do you state that you fear to come to the same pass as he is in?'

'Yes,' replied the Berber.

'Very well,' went on the king. 'Your friend here has given us a clear indication of his love; he hurled himself down, and would have died, but that Almighty God preserved him. Now do you stand up and prove your love is true; cast yourself down from the topmost point of this pavilion, as your friend did. If you die, it will mean that your appointed time has come; if you live, you will have the better right to the girl, seeing that she is at present your property; and your companion in distress shall then go away. But if you refuse to jump, I will take the girl from you, whether you like it or not, and will hand her over to him.'

At first the Berber held back, but then he said, 'I will cast myself down.' But when he came near the opening, and looked into the yawning void below him, he drew himself back again.

'By Allah,' cried the king, 'it shall be as I have said.'

The man tried again, but shrunk away once more.

When he would not take the plunge, the king shouted to him, 'Do not make sport of us! Ho, slaves, seize his hands and pitch him to the ground!'

The Berber, seeing the king thus resolved, exclaimed, 'O king, I am content: let him have the girl.'

The king replied, 'Allah give thee a good recompense!'

So saying, he bought the girl from him and gave her over to her former owner; and the two departed.

SEVEN

Religious Counsels

'Bidding to honour and forbidding dishonour' was a duty imposed upon the believers in many Koranic contexts. We have seen that the purveying of proverbial wisdom was as popular in ancient Arabia as in ancient Persia. The latter stream has been exemplified by the artful fables of Kalila and Dimna; the former tributary is well instanced in the strophes of Zuhair.

> Whoever refuses to yield to the ends of the spears' iron heels
> shall surely bow to the sharp tips mounted on their upper shafts.
> Whoever keeps his word goes unblamed; he whose heart is set
> on the sure path of piety needs not to fear or falter.
> Whoever is in terror of the ways Death may come, Death shall
>   yet slay him
> though he aspire to mount to heaven on the rungs of a ladder . . .

It occasions no surprise therefore, that Ibn Ḥazm, whose delightful and sophisticated essay on the gentle art of courtly love we have just been reviewing, should see fit to end his discourse with a sermon; or that, being the man he was, schooled in the polite traditions of his people, he should preach his sermon in verse.

> This mortal world, whose gifts to men
> Are loans demanded back again,
> A life of ease has lent to thee
> Whose green fades all too suddenly;
> And shall the prudent man aspire
> To such brief comfort, or desire
> A life so quickly out of breath,
> So surely visited by death?
> How can the contemplative eye,
> Long tutored to take warning by
> The passing show, one hour delight

To sleep, and shut it out of sight?
How can the soul be pleased so well
In this so transient world to dwell,
When it is sure and satisfied
It shall not ever here abide?
Can it a moment's thought bestow
Upon this fleeting earth below,
Not knowing, when it comes to die,
In what last lodging it shall lie?
What, is it not sufficient care
To labour for salvation there,
And to be anxiously intent
To flee eternal chastisement?
For many spirits, led astray
By a brief hour of trifling play,
Having stumbled in that furnace dire
Of unextinguishable fire:
The cameleer with urgent song
Sped them enticingly along
To bring them home, at journey's end,
Whither they never thought to wend.
There is a purpose for the soul,
But it pursues another goal,
A journey to a blest abode,
But it prefers a different road.
What, hastens it along a way
That on the resurrection day
Shall bring it ruin, though it knows
Its target is eternal woes?
It spurns the feast to it assigned,
Content its wretched scrap to find,
Condemned to misery immense
By pride and disobedience.
It is complacent to remain
In what shall prove its direst pain,
And flees in horror from the thing
That would its sweetest triumph bring;
Turning its back upon the Lord,
Who calls to virtue and reward,
It takes this world to be its friend,
To be deserted in the end.
Then, O deluded one, relent
Thy folly! With all speed repent:

God has prepared a place of ire
Whose awful flames shall ne'er expire.
Choose not the joy that mortal is
In lieu of everlasting bliss:
The choice of pleasures men elect
Proves well their power of intellect.
Knowest thou, truth is found the best
In what thou most abandonest,
And that the path that is thy aim
Abounds in base and secret shame?
Leaving the white and shining way
As if resolved to go astray,
Thou stridest on that path of gloom
Where stumbling brings to certain doom.
On foolish sports thy heart is set
That have no issue but regret,
Amusements over soon, for sure,
Whose consequences aye endure.
For pleasures all are quickly done,
Joys ended almost ere begun,
But folly's wages, sin's disgrace
Outreach the bounds of time and space.
But thou, poor silly dupe, art thou
In truth awake? Already now
The secrets of those dire events
Stand forth revealed, God's evidence.
Rise up betimes, and hasten to
The pleasure of thy Lord: eschew
The things He has forbidden thee,
Whose warning lights shine brilliantly.
Thou art a counter in Time's play
That flings thee carelessly away;
The world allures thee with her guile,
But there is malice in her smile.
How many peoples, long ere we
Were born to trouble, Destiny
Deceived, for us in turn to stare
Upon their dwellings empty, bare!
Remember them, and ponder o'er
The things that were, and are no more;
For pondering, as thou wilt find,
Is a fine sharpener of the mind.
Adventurer and tyrant vied

To scale those summits fortified
Possessing which, as men suppose,
Secures a monarch from his foes;
But now their heights are overthrown,
Their battlements in ruin strewn,
And that they had on loan at last
Again to its true owner passed.
Many have slumbered all their days
Unwary of the fate that slays,
Unheeding Destiny, loin-girt
And ready to their instant hurt.
And many, terrible and strong,
Have lifted up their hands to wrong,
Too arrogant to be aware
God would avenge their victims' prayer.
I see thee eager to pursue
The world, that thou aspirest to
Although thou seest clear as day
How far its guidance runs astray;
Too languid to obey His will
Who would forgive thee all thy ill,
Too dilatory to produce
An even passable excuse;
I see thee anxious and afraid
Of sorrows that shall swiftly fade,
Oblivious to that great care
It is thy duty to beware.
Methinks I see thee, in the hour
The fates in their majestic power
Strike, as they must, thy heart imbued
With impotent disquietude,
When men lament, 'Ah, who will give
Me back again those years to live,
Those precious moments to dispose
As once, precisely as I chose?'
Bethink thee of that day of fear
Whose shadow draws already near,
That dreadful day thy soul shall be
Assailed by its last agony;
Deserted and disowned by those
Whose friendship was thy heart's repose,
Thou watchest all thy edifice
Of hopes crash down to the abyss;

Thy bones shall be deposited
In the dark quarters of the dead,
A narrow and a dusty room
To those who see thee to thy tomb.
Then thou shalt hear a voice proclaim
But wilt not know who calls thy name,
And see in that deserted place
The veil is lifted from life's face;
Thou shalt be summoned to a day
Of awful terror and dismay,
That famous hour of mustering
When all shall rise to meet their King.
Then every beast from den and lair
Shall spring, to be assembled there;
And all the pages of our sin
About our heads shall whirl and spin;
And Paradise shall be displayed
In fair and intimate parade,
The raging fires of Hell below
Be stoked to an intenser glow.
The sun, that fills the noon with light,
Shall darken as if wrapped in night;
The stars, so radiant on high,
Shall swiftly scatter from the sky,
And as by heavenly command
Arrayed in order due they stand,
So at the word celestial
In wide dispersion they shall fall.
And then shall every mountain-range
Be shaken, and earth's contours change;
The dromedaries great with child
Shall roam deserted through the wild.
Then every man shall be endued
With infinite beatitude,
Or to imprisonment assigned
Whose chains are never to unbind.
Before a mighty, gracious Lord
Just in reprisal and reward
The trespasses of men shall all
Be reckoned up, both great and small;
And those who were of small offence
Shall save themselves by penitence,
And those whose sins were great shall be

Condemned to all eternity.
What joy their bodies shall obtain
Whose souls are brought to life again,
When secret thought, put to the test,
Proves one with action manifest!
Encompassed in that dreadful place
By God's forgiveness and His grace
They shall be made at last to dwell
Where wine is lawful, and all well;
Which happiness licentious men
Shall win in equal measure, when
The donkey and the noble horse
Are judged joint winners in the course.
The worldlings all shall flee away
With their loved world in dire dismay,
Whose transient pleasures seemed so true,
Reserved to the so favoured few.
The world's a mother whom her son
Best honours, strictliest to shun,
And whom, to save from mortal hurt,
Is most devoutly to desert;
None wins abiding pleasure there
Except that he despises her,
And they who cultivate her charms
Go down to ruin in her arms.
Suitor to suitor doth succeed
Pursuing her with breathless greed,
Though to the wise, experiment
Has proved long since her ill intent.
Live tranquil, and untroubled be
By fortune's fluctuating sea;
Plunge not into the tumbling wave
That waits to suck thee to thy grave.
Be not deceived or led astray
By luck's illusory display;
The touchstone of unclouded wit
Reveals the falsity of it.
I have observed how worldly kings
Desired the pomp that power brings,
Those pleasures of the appetite
Whose tasting is such sweet delight;
They wandered far from rectitude
To grasp the glitter they pursued,

As with her trail of lambs the ewe
Will quest for pastures ever new;
Yet all their struggle and their strife
Was to attain a span of life
Which those who for salvation make
Do find most easy to forsake.
For what is glory, but to keep
The honour from ambition's steep,
And what is honour, but the will
To stifle every thought of ill?
And who shall final profit find
Except the man with heart resigned,
Rich in contentment of the soul,
Majestic in his self-control?
But those promoted to great power
In fear and trepidation cower,
Unequal to support the cares
That by high privilege are theirs.
All this we plainly see; and yet
Are by such drunkenness beset
That, with the fumes of folly blind,
We cannot grasp the truth to mind.
Reflect on Him Who o'er the earth
Raised up yon roof of massive girth,
Within Whose knowledge are embraced
The fertile field, the arid waste;
Who holds the stars in His wide hand,
And earth, obeying His command,
Without foundations keeps her place
In the vast firmament of space.
He did determine and devise
According to His purpose wise
This ordered world, where ever new
Night follows day in sequence due.
He loosed the flooding waters, so
That over all the land they flow,
Providing nourishment to root
Of swelling grain and shining fruit.
He fashioned all the hues revealed
By all the lilies of the field,
The gold that in the tulip glows,
The crimson glory of the rose,
The ferns so delicately green

That hold enchantment in their sheen,
The jacorandas that amaze
The vision with their fiery blaze.
He channelled out with outmost ease
The rivers running to the seas,
So that the fountains' sudden shock
Split through the hard and granite rock.
Who gave the sun its ball of light
That in the morning shineth white,
But when the day is nigh to close
In golden emanation glows?
Who made the spinning spheres to run
On their far orbits, every one
So firmly on its axis set
That all rotate serenely yet?
And when calamities do vex
And try the wisest intellects,
What living thing but He is there
To whom the needy may repair?
Each creature, as thou canst discern,
To its Creator doth return,
Whose sovereign, eternal sway
All things submissively obey.
And through His prophets He has shown
His wondrous signs, which they have known
Who formerly were powerless,
To master in new blessedness.
He opened mouths, that they might preach
The wisdom He would have them teach,
In toothless infancy as sage
As uninhibited by age.
Out of the stony rock hewed He
A camel, shaped so cunningly
That with no instant of delay
Its bellow echoed far away,
That many through that miracle
Might win to faith; some, infidel,
Led by the sin Qudar there wrought,
Were unto dire perdition brought.
He likewise clove the mighty seas
For Moses with amazing ease,
So that the waves before his rod
Rolled back, to prove the power of God.

And Abraham, whom He called friend,
He rescued from the fiery end
That Nimrod plotted, and the flame
Was impotent his flesh to maim.
And He delivered from the Flood
His servant Noah, of whose blood
A righteous progeny was spared
The ruin all those sinners shared.
And David, and his son beside,
With mighty gifts He fortified,
According them, as did Him please,
In all their difficulties ease;
The mighty tyrant of the land
Bowed to King Solomon's command,
And he was taught the airy speech
Of birds, and how each calls to each.
But on Muhammad's people He
Bestowed, His greatest grace to be,
The Holy Book, and power to ride
Through all the countries far and wide;
He clove for him the shining moon
In heaven, and for special boon
Revealed to him those verses true
Whose strength no shaking can undo;
Its sacred truth delivered us
When unbelief most ruinous
Possessed our minds, and every man
Upon the pole of ruin span.
Alas for us! Then why do we
Forsake not our stupidity,
To save our souls from that dread fire
Whose leaping sparks draw ever nigher?

In an earlier chapter we have quoted from the moralizing letter written by al-Ḥasan al-Baṣrī to the caliph 'Umar II. Our texts furnish us with numerous instances of poor men preaching repentance to the high and the mighty, often enough at great personal risk. These passionate devotees, who came to be called Sufis because they wore cloaks of common wool as a protest against the fine linens and silks and brocades flaunted by the wealthy and the worldly, contracting out of the furious competition for mundane advancement formed their little circles and brotherhoods and counselled one another, by word of mouth and in writing, to prefer the quest after spiritual perfection.

One such letter that has escaped the destruction of a thousand years is that which follows, written by one mystic of Baghdad to another in days when the open profession of mysticism exposed a man to persecution, arrest and even, as in the famous instance of al-Ḥallāj, to cruel execution.

A Mystic's Letter

In the Name of God the Merciful, the Compassionate.

May God keep you in His keeping, wherein He keeps those His friends who are pure; and may He establish us and you upon the path of His good pleasure. May He make you to enter the courts of His intimacy, and give you pasture in the meadows of His manifold blessings. May He watch over you in all your circumstances, even as He watches over the child whilst it is yet in the womb of its mother, and the baby as it lies in its cradle. May God make perpetual for you the life that is withdrawn from the subsistence of life, in the perpetuity of eternity; and may He set you apart from that which is yours through Him, and that which is His through you, so that there may be His Singleness in its eternal continuance, not you, nor your state, nor the knowledge of Him, and so that there may be God alone.

By my father I adjure you, this that I say comes from the continuance of calamity and the consequence of misery, from a heart that is stirred from its foundations and tormented with its ceaseless conflagrations, by itself within itself. For thus it is, being without perception, without speech, without feeling, without joy, without repose, without effort: not in the sense of passing away, but because it is constant in the calamity of its ceaseless torment, a torment without meaning, past indication, beyond limit, irresistible in its fierce onslaughts. If it speaks, speech is an affliction; and if it is silent, silence is an affliction. Unto God is the complaint without complaining; and there comes no answering reply, no easing. So it continues, wholly swallowed up: in loneliness hidden, yet it appears, and is hidden, and appears, and is hidden. I know not what I say, nor what he says whose reins have fallen from him, whose straps have been severed; who wanders in most perilous wildernesses, and thereof has no share in the conditions of blessedness, but driving sings:

> What way to win His pleasure,
>   Whose wrath no treason
> So kindled past all measure,
>   Nor any reason?

Or haply he says:

> No more will I resist my fate:
>   Though grief me slay,
> Whate'er Thy whim, inobdurate
>   I will obey.

It was my wish, my dear friend, that I should not write to you words of raving or evil thoughts, or the talk of one diseased in mind or soul. But as I know you, so I know that you know that fate has more power over a man than his own resolve. So may God take you into His friendship, and choose you for Himself, and make you familiar with the knowledge which is hidden from His creatures, but which manifests from Him to His elect; for these He has changed from state to state, and transported through all the grades. First He raised them up, by confirming the condition of their actions; then He raised them up, through the realities of reaching unto Him. He veiled from them the eyes of the hearts; for these are not worth any definition or description, save as He appoints them in their separate life through His Oneness, being alone Himself with them in the realities of the Unseen. What marvel then is more marvellous than that certainty without doubt in which they dwell, and that doubt without certainty? And God is God alone. My brother, may God crown you with the crown of blessing on the bank of resurrection, and may the Prophets glory in you, and the wise men, and all God's servants. He is our aspiration and hope, and to Him praise belongs, both first and last. May God bless Muhammad the Prophet, and grant him peace evermore.

You have written, may God cherish you, under the protection and preservation of God; and I petition God that He may make in us and you a gratitude whereby we may attain increase in His bounty and favour. Your letter, God keep and bless you, has reached me, and he has come who was united with you; and I have learned how lofty are your purposes in your prayers. I pray that God of His mercy may answer our pious prayers, yours for us and ours for you. Thereafter I learned of the niceness of your words in counselling, and I do not cease through you to enjoy an increase of God's blessings, though ever despairing of being near to you, yet in

your absence taking comfort in those who are your friends; and to
God I commend you. In counsel excelling, in exhortation striving,
with your food satisfying, with your blows stinging—in all you have
followed the manners of the Prophets in gentleness of speech. Before
God I pictured, as I read your writings, Moses and Aaron, God's
blessings be upon them, when they were commanded to speak
gently;[1] and it was a terrible thing to me, that my place should be
the place of the Pharaohs, in your striving to be kindly with me;
for cajoling is only used with one who is insolent and ignorant, or
with a child. But what means have I, seeing that my station with
you is the station of one who must needs be treated with gentleness,
that he may accept the truth, and of one who lags behind in seeking
the right path? And then I recall to myself the words of the poet:

> Not out of weakness we obey,
> But as God destined unto us
> Before time was, fate draws our way:
> We follow thus.

And also I say:

> Know now, my spirit, thy Creator's might,
> Who turns men's destinies to His delight:
> Though your bonds forge my heart's captivity
> I thank you still, abroad and secretly.

I pray that He may bless us with that whereunto He has commanded us, and that He may preserve us from that whereof He has
forbidden us. I heard Aḥmad ibn Abi 'l-Ḥawārī[2] say, I heard Abū
Sulaimān[3] say, 'The deeds of men are not such as to please Him or
to anger Him; but with some people He is pleased, and He employs
them in the deeds of good pleasure, and with others He is angry,
and He employs them in the deeds of anger.' He therefore who flees
from that which is, is only at the beginning of his quests. With God
is the consolation, for from Him is the affliction: may God preserve
us and you from His wrath, and bless us with His greatest good
pleasure, in well-being and safety.

Now you know, may God cherish you, that the Prophets did
indeed possess apostlehood, but that they did not possess the power
of guidance. God says, blessed and exalted is He: 'Deliver that
which has been sent down to thee from thy Lord' (Kor. 5: 71); then
He said: 'Thou guidest not whom thou desirest' (Kor. 28: 56). I

---

[1] See Koran 20:46.
[2] Died in 230/845 or 246/860.
[3] Died in 205/820 or 215/830.

pray God, Who gave you speech wherewith to counsel me and tasked you with the task of writing to me, that He may not make void to me your prayer, in such a place as this in which we do hope for His blessing, O my brother and delight of my heart. Accepted from you is all that you brandish and indicate to the eye. To God I pray for help in this, and that He may reward you for us. If every hair upon my body were a tongue, yet would you be worthy of this from me. May God undertake to thank you, and to reward you for us as you deserve.

I remember, my beloved, that urgent need in you which so hastened unto me, that need concerning which you put hope in me, namely that I should avoid all intercourse save with those who are my true fellows; and I remember, may God guard you, speech whose purport this was. So gentle you were, so tender; and I ask God's help in this, and with Him take refuge, that I may make my pleading a cover for my sins, and that I may fully repay right with right. You know that it is a grievous thing to set a bound to the truth; and I ask God for sincerity in acknowledging the truth.

Moreover, and God is my protection, there is a day when I imagine that I have confirmed the people of my age, both common and elect, in some small particular other than the mere expression of the tongue. I do not know whether this shall be reckoned for me or against me; and as for the path of merit in the assigning of judgment, may God protect us and you from the vision of that. I am satisfied that there should rest for me, in the highest grade of the learned in the law, the burden of His Unity, and in the highest grade of the religious, the eschewing of the greater sins. Perchance with this verse I have made parable:

> O Thou Whose power has kindled in my soul
> > This raging fire,
> Were it Thy will, my heart should be made whole,
> > Its blaze expire.
> It were no shame—so Thou hast dealt with me—
> > Of grief and fear
> If I should die, a victim unto Thee:
> > No shame it were.

And haply I have made parable with this verse:

> > Shall any part
> Of penitence into my soul be brought,
> > Since that my heart
> With all my wretchedness is still distraught?

I have heard that a certain wise man wrote to another: 'May God not cause you to taste of the food of your carnal soul; for if you taste of its food, you will not thereafter taste any good.'[1] I therefore hope that you may preserve your limitations. I heard Dhu 'l-Nūn say, 'He who is ignorant of his own worth is stripped of his veil.'[2] I ask God that He may grant sincerity in confession, and with God I take refuge against making a display of censuring the soul, or of eschewing display. And of you I ask, that you should continue towards me in brotherhood and friendly counsel, recompensing me and favouring me and praying for me, and that you should ever have me in your mind; for you have adorned me with your writing, and wakened me with your counsel—if haply you should find in me a wakeful zeal. And 'Thou only warnest him who follows the Remembrance and who fears the All-merciful in the Unseen' (Kor. 36: 10); and God says, 'That he may warn whosoever is living' (Kor. 36: 70).

> If in the heart there be no goad
>   To prick the heart
> It will not stir, whoe'er its load,
>   Whate'er its smart.

My friend, with your own tongue I have addressed you,[3] and with that wherewith God has profited me both aforetimes and in these latter days I have answered you. If, God cherish you, there be in this writing any error or confusion or any slip of the tongue, you are the most worthy to pardon it; and if there be in it aught that pleases you, it is of you and through you. For you are laudable in all events; you are the Shaikh of all the pious men now living, nay, you are the lord of the wise men and the gnostics of your time; and God's is the praise for this.

Now I do not complain, God cherish you, that certain of those who serve you on our behalf, pious men who are inclined to satisfy themselves with little, have asked assistance of us; for by my life I am as it were a keeper of sustenance. If any man had shown me his goblet I would have found for him one who should fill it, and men would have been satisfied with a satisfaction that has no bound. By my life, if a man amends his inner life God will amend for him his outer circumstance; and if a man makes his peace with God,

---

[1] These words are elsewhere ascribed to Yūsuf ibn al-Ḥusain al-Rāzī in a letter to al-Junaid.

[2] Quoted elsewhere as said by Dhu 'l-Nūn to Yūsuf ibn al-Ḥusain.

[3] Presumably in quoting sayings of his correspondent as noted above.

God will make peace between him and all men; and if a man labours for his portion in the world to come, God will suffice him in the affairs of this world. I pray God to amend our affairs with His mercy.

Now upon you be peace, and God's mercy and blessings, so long as this world and the world to come abide. And upon those who are with you, who desire that which is with God, blessed and exalted is He, and yearn for your intimacy and your friendship, God's greatest and most excellent peace. If you see fit, may God perpetuate your glory, to favour me with your writing, thereby to acquaint me that you are well and that God's protection is with you, together with any need which may be calling and which we can meet, you will thereby rejoice me. And God bless Muhammad the Prophet, and his people, and grant them peace evermore.

(*Journal of the Royal Asiatic Society*, 1935, pp. 499–507.)

A contemporary of the writer of the foregoing letter, a Persian named Abū 'Abd Allāh al-Tirmidhī and nicknamed al-Ḥakīm ('the Wise') who was driven out of his native town because of his preaching, left behind him a large collection of religious writings remarkable for the richness of their poetic imagination; the greater part of them still await publication. The extract which follows shows al-Tirmidhī preaching to his little flock.

A Sufi Sermon

Have you seen a kindler striking his fire-stick, and producing a flame from which he lights a fire in a barren wilderness wherein is no companionable being, because of the destroying cold? That flame lay hidden in a fragment of stone, and in wood from a tree. It was a light burden for you to carry, and you could carry it with you in your journeys easily, without hardship; and then, when you were smitten by the dire need of hunger and cold, that was almost bringing you to destruction, and the desolation of loneliness overcame you, so that you were filled with trepidation at the desolation, you brought forth the flame that was concealed in that fire-stick, and straightway your dire needs ceased, and the cloud of desolation was lifted, because of the consolations which that flame brought you. Then, when you attained to this, that fire-stick became precious in your sight, and its worth was great to your breast, so that you made a girdle about your waist, and with that girdle bound it to you, that it might never be parted from you, since so mightily in the time of need it succoured you.

This thing you have verily witnessed; and are you blind to that light of Divine Unity which is hidden in your heart? Light for you to bear are the burdens of its weight, and well can you carry it; and whensoever you kindle your heart with the kindling of the intellect, you produce a light in your breast which shall bring you to stand before God, making prayer and obeisance and prostrating yourself; and it shall cause you to yield up your very soul and wealth to God, to act as He commands and prohibits, whatsoever His commands and prohibitions may be.

So, when you are brought forth from your grave into the wildernesses of the resurrection, that light will run with you to stand in the place of judgment and review before the King of kings, the Monarch of the heavens. Gathered together will be the lights of your acts of obedience that kindled, by your intellect, that hidden fire-stick of yours, the light of God; and God's light will bring you nigh unto His mercy. And in that place of waiting it will give you to eat of God's tables, and to drink of the cisterns of God's Messengers, yea, it will bring you in nearness to take your proper place in the ranks of God's favoured friends, who took God to be their friend during their days in this world, and gave Him help.

You have indeed bound to your heart a fragment of stone, wherein lay hidden a spark of fire, to which you looked for help and comfort in the wildernesses of this world, so that it went ever with you, not leaving you journeying or at rest; and yet you have forgotten that light which God hid in your heart, the light of spiritual knowledge, and that tinder-stone which He set within your brain, the intellect. Evil lust came and parted them and stood between them; and whensoever the intellect desired to strike fire, the evil lust arose, and you lost the light in your breast, and perished of hunger and thirst for want of obedience, and your heart withered up for lack of recollection and grew insolent and hard, and shrank from remembering 'the meeting with Me: whensoever you remembered death, and the meeting with Me, your heart fled and shrank backwards. Surely this is a strange thing!'

Have you seen a green tree, quivering with freshness and vigour and suppleness, whose root is firm, its fibres strong, and its branches reach high to heaven? It brings forth leaf, and gives shade to a people; it yields fruit, and satisfies a people. The winds toss it about, but not a leaf falls, because of its freshness; not a twig is broken, because of its suppleness; not a fibre stirs, because of its firmness. You wonder at its growth, and watch over it to water it and tend it, taking joy therein. You shelter beneath its shade when the heat is strong, and attain it; you gather its fruits, to be a food sustaining to your heart in time of your summer or your winter, and nourishing your body.

Amongst all the trees, it is upon this tree that your eye is fixed. And when you see amongst them a thin tree, shaggy and full of dust, whose fibres are not strong, nor its twigs well-spread, that gives no shade to shelter any man, and yields no fruit to satisfy, you turn from it and avert your regard, despising it; you avert from it the water-channel unto this quivering, fruitful tree which you admire; you will not care to tend it at all. And the lord of the garden, his eye is upon this tree, and his favour; but from that other tree he turns, the shaggy one, which trails the ground so dry and lean it is. And when it is decreed to cut it down it is cut down, and the lord of the garden grieves not thereat, nor any of his slaves and servants. But when it is decreed that that fruitful tree shall be cut down, then shows he grief at its cutting and weeps about it, grieving after it.

So we learn that David, God bless him and grant him peace, says in his Psalms: 'Not so do I hesitate over anything that I do, as I hesitate to take the soul of My servant who believeth: he hateth death, and I shrink from distressing him, but there is no escape for him from it.' Ibrāhīm ibn al-Mustamirr of Hudhail told me this, and he had it of Abū 'Āṣim al-'Uqadī, who was told it by 'Abd al-Wāḥid ibn Maimūn the client of 'Urwa ibn al-Zubair, who heard 'Ā'isha, God be well pleased with her, relate that the Prophet said: 'God, blessed and exalted is He, says, Not so do I hesitate over anything that I do, as I hesitate to take the soul of my servant who believeth: he hateth death, and I shrink from distressing him, but there is no escape for him from it.' Such a man is only distressed by death because it breaks off his acts of obedience and recollection, and leaves him in the intermediate state. We are informed by Rawād ibn Ḥammād, who had it of Anas ibn Mālik *via* 'Umar ibn Sa'īd al-Dimashqī, Ṣadaqa ibn 'Abd Allāh, and 'Abd al-Karīm al-Jazarī, that the Prophet, God bless him and grant him peace, related the same saying as from God, blessed is His Name.

Have you seen a bird, whose urge it is to fly in the skies, and to perch upon the branches of trees, whose refuge at night is the folds of its nest, and who will yet give up its nest and turn aside from its urge to fly, cleaving to him who holds it to his bosom and makes his hand its perch? He may be one of the kings of the earth, and it a falcon, and it will hunt for him; or it may be a camel that pastures afar, and he would milk it calling it from far away; or it may be a pigeon that mounts into the sky, and then descends in a distant province, bearing his messages and letters as did the hoopoe for the

Prophet of God Solomon, God bless him and give him peace; or as ravening dogs when schooled, and cheetahs cleave to their masters. These creatures cleave to their masters, having grown familiar with them through contact and training. They are used to dwelling with them, and he who trains them is their king; the bird cleaves to him, and is confident, being familiar with him, and stays upon his hand; and whenever the king flights him against aught that appears to him, it goes flying to take it prey for him, and then returns flying to its companion, not turning aside; and whenever he calls it, it knows his whistle and obeys.

Behoves it not therefore the believer, that he should be moved with emulation at this, and overcome with shame? Does it not come to this, that a bird will cleave to its companion, and become familiar with his training, and that it will give up the urge to fly in the skies, with the small birds that fly there, and takes pleasure in the society of its master, who holds it on his hand, and on his stick, until it forgets the pleasure of freedom to fly whithersoever it wishes? Will he not suffer himself to be straitened in the possession of God, and in slavery and ownership?

Or if you say, 'The bird cleaves to him because he has trained it with dainty morsels of food, so that it has found pleasure in the training and grown accustomed to it,' dainty morsels of food lie to hand in the broad plains and pastures of the earth. As for the dainty morsels of the great and bountiful God, for whom are they if not for you? The adornment and bright array of this world, for whom has He prepared them if not for you? How then have you not grown familiar with this that He has given you? Is His regard for you less than that king's for his bird? How then have you not grown accustomed to His regard and cleaved to Him, forgetting all else besides Him and taking your place with Him for a home?

Have you seen a river flowing between partners, and each of them taking his portion of its water? But when your turn is come, you are overwhelmed with drowsiness and slumber, whilst the water overflows in a part of its course and runs into the waste, and your sown and sifted land remains dry and thirsty so that it falls into disorder, and becomes like powder; whilst you have only your regrets, on losing the wealth wherewith you were provided in that water; until the pains of regret awaken you, and slumber is banished from you, because of what has come to pass with you.

Is the water which you were given, then, for the harvest of this world of greater moment than the knowledge which you were given for the harvest of the world to come? You were given knowledge, to perform works for the future world; but the course of your knowledge has overflowed, so that your knowledge has been used up in hunting for this world's goods, and with treacheries seizing them, compassing, of the knowledge which you were given, to take and possess those goods, until the harvest of the world to come is parched in your members; and yet you regret not the loss of the water, and the overflowing of its course.

What will you do, if the Lord of the river, and He who provided you with your nurture, requites you, showering upon you superabundance of water for the harvest of this world, as He has done with His enemies and with unbelievers, but turns away from you the water-course of the next world's harvest, so that you remain bewildered, wandering blindly in error and exceeding disobedience?

(*Rivista degli Studi Orientali*, Vol. XVIII, pp. 323–7.)

Our next extract comes from the unpublished *Heights of Ambition* of an obscure mystic known simply as Abu 'l-Qāsim the Gnostic, who wrote his little manual of spiritual guidance probably in the eleventh century.

The Mystic's Devotion to God

Know, my lordly ones, that God has servants who have given up all desire for their own portion, both in this world and in the next, for the Master's sake, so that they even give no thought to having given it up; no portion remains to them in either world, and they are satisfied with their Friend Who is their associate and delight, and never turn from Him to any other thing. Know too, that the root of clearing the heart of occupation with the two worlds is the giving up of desire for a portion in either world, and that the root of being satisfied with the Master is the giving up of preoccupation with this world and the next. If a man attaches himself to this world, he loses the world to come, and if he attaches himself to the world to come, he loses the Master; but if he attaches himself to the Master, he finds the Master, and His nearest service, as well as the world to come and all that is therein. God says:

> Whoso desires the tillage of the world
> to come, We shall give him increase
> in his tillage; and whoso desires the
> tillage of this world, We shall give him
> of it, but in the world to come he
> will have no share. (Kor. 42: 19.)

It is related in the stories that when God created mankind He presented to them the world and all that is in it; and out of every thousand men nine hundred and ninety-nine attached themselves thereto, and only one remained. Then He created Paradise and presented it to those who remained; and out of every thousand nine hundred and ninety-nine attached themselves to it, and only one remained. Then of those who remained it was asked, 'What desire you, seeing that you did not attach yourselves to this world or the world to come?' 'Lord and Master,' they all replied, 'Thou knowest what we desire.' Then they were told, 'If you desire Me, I shall pour upon you a torrent of affliction such as neither the heavens nor the earth can bear, to try you; and if you are patient with Me, and satisfied with Me instead of with what is with Me, I will bring you unto Me and cause you to taste of the pleasures of My intimacy, and I will raise the veils for you, that you may behold My great glory.' 'O Thou our Delight,' they all replied, 'do with us whatsoever Thou wilt, for Thou art Master over us.'

It is said that 'Alī ibn Abī Ṭālib[1] said one day to Abū Bakr the Faithful,[2] 'By what thing have you attained this pre-eminence over us?' Abū Bakr replied, 'By five things. First, when I entered into Islam I found that men were of two kinds, some seeking this world and the others seeking the world to come; but I was seeking the Master. Secondly, when I entered into Islam I found no pleasure in this world save the pleasure of recollecting God, and the delight of serving Him, and the joy of knowing Him; and these things kept me from seeking all the pleasures of this world. Thirdly, when I entered into Islam I did not eat my fill of the food of this world, nor drank my fill of its liquor, for I feared that I might lose my knowledge, and was anxious lest I should be parted from God. Fourthly, whenever two matters confronted me, of which one was in accordance with God's good pleasure and the other was after my soul's approval and delight, I chose God's approval above my soul's approval, and above the approval of all else but God. Fifthly, I enjoyed the most beautiful companionship of the Prophet; and he guarded his sanctity until he departed from this world, God bless him and grant him peace!' Thereupon 'Alī wept, saying, 'God bless you, Abū Bakr.'

It is also related that 'Alī ibn Abī Ṭālib one day entered the Prophet's mosque and saw a Bedouin in the corner of the mosque, praying and abasing himself before God and saying, 'O God, give me a piece of roast meat! I desire nothing else of Thee, and I will be

---

[1] Cousin, son-in-law and fourth caliph of the Prophet.
[2] The first caliph.

satisfied with this. Thou art too mighty to cheat the hopes of one who comes hungry to Thee, or to send a beggar from Thy door.' Then he saw Abū Bakr in another corner of the mosque, praying and abasing himself before God and saying, 'O God, I desire Thee, wherefore guide me. I am satisfied with Thee above both worlds, wherefore receive me. Cut not off my expectation of Thee, O my Lord and Master.' And 'Alī ibn Abī Ṭālib wept exceedingly and said, 'How diverse are these two men in their desires! The one craves after roast meat, the other after God.'

The Shaikh of Shaikhs[1] said, 'Once when I was in the mosque at Mecca there came a youth wearing a ragged skirt, and I saw on him the marks of hunger and privation. I felt compassion for him, and taking a bag in which there were a hundred dinars I brought it to him, saying, "Make use of this." He did not heed me, so I pressed him vehemently. Then he turned to me and said, 'Sir, these are spiritual conditions which I would not sell for Paradise and all that is in it. These are the abode of glory, the mine of grace and security, the haven of continuance; how then shall I sell them for a poor price and a base, worthless recompense?" '

The poet says:

> When I was in affliction dire
> I made no plaint of my distress;
> Thou only, Lord, wert my desire,
> Not grace, nor hand of tenderness.
>
> Now, if Thou giv'st this world to me,
> Or Paradise, for my reward,
> I pray that all my wealth may be
> Naught but the vision of my Lord.

Know, my lordly ones, that God watches over the secrets of His lovers and the thoughts of those who know Him. When He loves one of His servants and chooses him for Himself and His companionship, He is jealous for him according to the degree of his love for Him and his nearness to Him, with a jealousy stronger than that which you have for your loved ones. If ever looking upon him He sees in his heart a place for other than Himself, or if he turns to any other, He reproaches him, and turns that other thing into an affliction for him.

It therefore behoves every man who sets his foot on the carpet of God's nearness to guard carefully his reverence for God, lest he slip from that carpet. God said to His chosen messenger Muhammad:

[1] Sc. al-Junaid.

> Stretch not thine eyes to that We have given
> pairs of them to enjoy.   (Kor. 15: 88.)

Then God accorded him His protection, so that he should not look upon them, for He said:

> And had We not confirmed thee, surely
> thou wert near to inclining unto them
> a very little.   (Kor. 17: 76.)

That is, he was almost yearning for them. Then God praises him for not heeding other than Himself, and because he was guarded in his manners when on the mat of nearness to Him, saying:

> His eye swerved not, nor swept astray. (Kor. 53: 17.)

And when he turned not from Him towards any other thing, God said, 'O Muhammad, come hither and I will raise the veils between Me and thee, that thou mayest look upon Me without any intermediary.' God says:

> His heart lies not of what he saw. . . .
> Indeed, he saw Him another time.' (Kor. 53: 11, 13.)

It is related that Muhammad said, 'Gabriel came to me with the keys of the treasuries of this world, but I did not heed them nor take them from him, for I kept my reverence for God.'

'Alī ibn Abī Ṭālib one day had set al-Ḥasan on one of his knees and al-Ḥusain on the other, and was looking upon them and kissing them. Al-Ḥasan said to him, 'Father, I see that you love us.' 'Yes, my son,' his father replied. 'Are you not ashamed,' al-Ḥasan said, 'that God may look into your heart and see in it a love for another?' 'Alī wept much at his saying. Then he said, 'What shall I do, my son?' Al-Ḥasan answered, 'Father, love belongs to God, and to us compassion. Whosoever loves God with a pure love, associates none with Him.'

Fatḥ al-Mauṣilī is related to have said, 'I had a son, and love for him entered my heart. One night I omitted my prayers. Thereafter I found no joy in my recitation and no pleasure in my supplications such as I was wont to find. I sat down and asked God to forgive me; but I did not know whence this spiritual languor had come. Then sleep overcame me, and I slept; and behold, a voice from heaven saying, "O Fatḥ, thus We deal with him who makes pretence to love Us, but inclines towards another and has in his heart a place for another." I said, "O my Beloved and Delight, I did but wish that he might succeed me, and that he might obey Thee when I am gone. If what I tell is true, take him unto Thee this hour." Then I awoke, and heard his mother weeping; for the boy had risen up and gone forth from his bed in the night, and fallen into the well.'

It is said that a certain prophet came upon a company of worshippers. He demanded, 'For what thing do you worship God?' They replied, 'We have heard that God has created Paradise and Hell; and for this we are in sore trouble and great labour and long weariness. We join night with day and day with night, hoping for Paradise and fearing Hell.' He said to them, 'Company of worshippers, you are engaged in a matter other than that in which we are engaged. You work in hope of Paradise and in fear of Hell; but we work for the love of God, and in yearning for Him.'

It is also related in the stories that Jesus passed by a number of men whose bodies were wasted, and their hue changed, and he said to them, 'What has come to pass with you, that wrought this in you?' They said, 'The fear of Hell.' Jesus said, 'It is right that God should give the fearful security.' Then he came upon other men; and lo, their bodies were even more wasted, and their hue more greatly changed; and he said, 'What has come to pass with you, that wrought this in you?' They said, 'Yearning for Paradise.' Jesus said, 'It is right that God should grant you hope.' Then he came upon yet other men; and lo, their bodies were still more wasted, and their hue more greatly changed, but in their faces was a trace of light; and he said to them, 'What has come to pass with you, that wrought this in you?' They said, 'Love and yearning for God.' Jesus said to them, 'You are near to God, you are near to God.'

It is said that Dhu 'l-Nūn al-Miṣrī was preaching to the people, and describing to them Paradise and Hell, and all that is in them; and they were weeping bitterly. But amongst them he saw a youth laughing, as the gnostics laugh. Dhu 'l-Nūn said to the youth, 'I see you are laughing, young man, whilst these men are weeping.' The youth began to recite:

> You worship God in fear of Hell
> And reckon your salvation well;
> For your supremest hopes suffice
> The flowered founts of Paradise.
> I seek not timeless bliss above;
> I ask no substitute for love.

(Islamic Culture, Vol. XI, pp. 97–107.)

We round off this small selection of religious counsels with a poem attributed to one of the greatest mystical theologians of Islam and indeed of all mankind, Abū Ḥāmid al-Ghazālī (who died in 505/ 1111), Algazel as he was known to medieval Europe, fierce critic of Avicenna, to whose condemnation of philosophy Averroes afterwards replied. Here we see him in a mood of equally trenchant self-criticism.

A Poem of the Soul

What ails my soul, that maketh long complaint
To men, but for the fear of God is faint?
Its very plaint forbiddeth its release,
Augments its terror, and destroys its peace.
Would it but come with humble love sincere
Unto its Master, He would draw it near;
But since it chooseth those His creatures are
Above their Fashioner, He keeps it far
And makes its need yet more. Let it but flee
To Him, He'll grant it full satiety.
Unto His creatures it complains, as though
They have the power to work it weal or woe;
But would it lay all matters at His feet
In true sincerity and trust complete,
He would not leave it in its long despairs
But give it gladness in return for cares.
It angers God, that it seeks man to please:
A curse upon its self-sought miseries!
If it would dare man's anger to attain,
Pleasing its Lord, it would His pleasure gain.

I have a soul whose nature I would tell,
That we may know it and its habits well.
Hear then my tale thereon, and tell in turn,
That men of wit its mysteries may learn.
It labours after folly as its goal;
Alas, the foolish labour of my soul!
I chide it, but it never will obey,
As if I will not well in what I say,
But idly looking at another's sin
Forgets the faults it cherishes within.
Its evil manners have corrupted me
And leave me neither rank nor piety.
At concert with vain talk it fills the air,

Has small remembrance of its God at prayer,
Receives His favours with scant gratitude
And, suffering, with less patience is endued;
Is slow of foot its remedy to obtain
But swift to seek the things that are its bane;
Finds endless cause its promises to break,
Is false in every claim that it doth make;
Keen-sighted after evil vanities,
But blind to where its own salvation lies;
Grasping at pleasures with alacrity,
At time of meditation sluggardly;
With leaden eye forgets its God to greet
Who fashioned it in symmetry complete;
When all is well in confidence arrayed,
But in distress most mightily afraid;
In pride and in hypocrisy well-versed,
Yea, and by pride corrupted and accursed;
Unstinted in approval and appraise
Of him who seeks its dignity to raise,
But lavish of opprobrium and blame
When any dares its shortcomings to name;
In eating and in drinking takes delight,
And to repose is eager for the night;
Accounts to others where their faults begin,
Forgetful of its own account of sin.

How other far that man, who guards his soul
In cleanliness, godfearing, sweet and whole,
Teaches it righteousness, keeping it keen,
Nurturing it with lawful food and clean.
All night he holds it instant and awake,
Washed with the tears that from his eyelids break.
When lusting after passion, with the fear
Of God he visits it, and brings it cheer;
With fasting trains it, till it is subdued,
Despite its waywardness and turpitude.
So it remembers God with thankfulness
And love sincere doth secretly confess.
How well by God assisted is that soul
Which, seeking refuge, gains in God its goal!
Rank and renown it winneth from its King,
And at the founts of faith finds watering.
It soars to God in loveliness of thought,

By God with love and kindness it is sought,
And if in need unto the Lord it cries
He hears its prayer, and speedily supplies.
He gives it patience in calamity,
And to its call His hand is ever free.

Not so my soul: wildly rebellious,
To orders and restraints impervious,
God's holy ordinance it never heeds.
Alas, my soul! Alas, its sinful deeds!
How shall it ever to its Lord repent,
That serves the Devil, and his blandishment?
Whene'er I say, 'My soul, attend my word,
Be heedful of the orders of thy Lord,'
The truth it will not heed, though hearing all,
As though it were another that I call.
Knew it the purpose of its fashioning,
That knowledge grief and bitter tears would bring;
Were it made ware of God in verity,
Truly sincere would its godfearing be;
But God hath made it ignorant of Him,
Neglect hath made the light of guidance dim.
And ah, my soul! Alas for it, and woe,
If God abandons it, and lets it go!
Beguiled by this world's pleasure, it knows not
What after death shall be its dreadful lot.

Much I have strained to make my soul obey,
But for whose sin I had not gone astray;
When I would be obedient, it was faint
And showed a strange distaste and unrestraint.
I wrestled with my soul as with a foe,
It bidding me to err, I saying no;
We were as ancient enemies at large.
I put on patience, to withstand its charge;
With troops of tempting it came forth to fight—
What patience could withstand such reckless might?—
Which gave it courage when its courage quailed,
And reinforcement when its forces failed.
Now I succeed, now it, in the affray;
Yet, when we meet, it ever wins the day.
I love it well, but it opposes me
As if I held it not in amity;

It is an enemy I cannot hate,
A memory I can ne'er obliterate.
Blindly it swims upon its sinful sea,
Clutching the hems of its iniquity;
I greatly fear, if it doth still rebel,
Its ruin in this life and, after, Hell!
Wherefore, O Lord, bring its repentance near
And wash away its sins in founts of fear.
If Thou, my God, its chastener shouldst be,
O whither shall it look for clemency?
Be gracious then, and all its sins forgive;
Thou art its Lord, for through Thee it doth live.

(The Moslem World, April 1940.)

EIGHT

Mystical Moments

The Sufi, obeying the commands of the Koran and the examples of the Sunna to abandon the material world and to devote his days to the pursuit of eternal happiness, from time to time found solace and comfort in his strict austerities in experience which seemed to him to be direct and unmediated encounters with God. The greatest of the 'sober' Sufis, al-Junaid of Baghdad (d. 298/910), expressed such an experience in a poem.

> Now I have known, O Lord,
> What lies within my heart;
> In secret, from the world apart,
> My tongue hath talked with my Adored.

> So in a manner we
> United are, and One;
> Yet otherwise disunion
> Is our estate eternally.

> Though from my gaze profound
> Deep awe hath hid Thy face,
> In wondrous and ecstatic grace
> I feel Thee touch my inmost ground.

Some of the most striking descriptions of the encounter with the Divine are credited to the founder of the 'intoxicated' school of Sufism, the Persian Abū Yazīd al-Bisṭāmī (d. 261/875), whose ecstatic utterances, a great scandal to the orthodox believers, al-Junaid went to great pains to interpret in more acceptable terms.

Encounters with God

Abū Yazīd al-Bisṭāmī related as follows.

The first time I travelled to His uniqueness I became a bird whose body was of oneness, and its wings of everlastingness. I continued to fly in the air of howness ten years, until I had travelled to the like air a hundred thousand thousand times. I went on flying, until I reached the arena of pre-eternity and there beheld the tree of oneness.

He then described its soil, its trunk, branch, twigs and fruit. Then he said:

I gazed at it, and realized that all this is a deception.

Abū Yazīd also related the following.

I vanished into almightiness, and forded the seas of dominion and the veils of godhead, until I came to the Throne; and behold, it was empty. So I cast myself upon it, saying, 'Master, where shall I seek Thee?'

Then He unveiled, and I saw that I was I, and I was I, turning back into what I sought, and I myself, not other than I, was where I was going.

Abū Yazīd also related the following.

Once He raised me up and stationed me before Him and said to me. 'Abū Yazīd, My creatures desire to see thee.'

I said, 'Adorn me in Thy uniqueness, and clothe me in Thy self-hood, and raise me up to Thy oneness, so that when Thy creatures see me they may say, "We have seen thee"; and Thou wilt be That, and I shall not be here.'

Abū Yazīd also related the following.

When He brought me to the brink of the Divine Unity I divorced myself and betook myself to my Lord, calling upon Him to succour me.

'Master,' I cried, 'I beseech Thee as one to whom nothing else remains.'

When He recognized the sincerity of my prayer, and how I had despaired of myself, the first token that came to me proving that He had answered this prayer was that He caused me to forget myself utterly, and to forget all creatures and all dominions. So I was stripped of all cares, and remained without any care.

Then I went on traversing one kingdom after another; whenever I came to them I said to them, 'Stand, and let me pass.' So I would make them stand, and I would pass until I reached them all. So He drew me near, appointing for me a way to Him nearer than soul to body.

Then He said, 'Abū Yazīd, all of them are My creatures except thee.'

I replied, 'So I am Thou, and Thou art I, and I am Thou.'

Abū Yazīd also reported the following.

I gazed upon my Lord with the eye of certainty, after He had turned me away from other than Him and had illumined me with His light; and He showed me marvellous things of His secret. He also showed me His Selfhood, and I gazed upon my identity with His Selfhood; and there passed away my light in His Light, my glory in His Glory, my power in His Power. I saw my identity with His Selfhood, my honour with His Honour, my exaltation with His Exaltation.

Then I gazed upon Him with the eye of truth, and said to Him, 'Who is this?'

He said, 'This is neither I nor other than I. There is no god but I.'

Then He changed me out of my identity into His Selfhood, and caused me to pass away from my selfhood through His Selfhood, showing me His Selfhood uniquely; and I gazed upon Him with His Selfhood. So, when I gazed upon the Truth through the Truth, I saw the Truth through the Truth; and I continued in the Truth through the Truth for a time, having neither breath, nor tongue, nor ear, nor any knowledge; until God created for me a knowledge out of His Knowledge, and a tongue out of His Grace, and an eye out of His Light.

Then I gazed upon Him with His Light, and knew Him through His Knowledge, and communed with Him with the tongue of His Grace, saying, 'How fares it with me with Thee?'

He said, 'I am thine through thee; there is no god but thou.'

I said, 'Delude me not through me; I choose not me instead of Thee apart from Thee, that I should choose Thee instead of Thee apart from me.'

Then He bestowed upon me Him instead of me, and I communed with Him through Him instead of me; and I said, 'What have I from Thy hand as coming from Thee, O my Desire?'

He said, 'Take My commandment and My forbidding.'

I said, 'And what have I of Thy commandment and Thy forbidding?'

He said, 'My praising thee in respect of My commandment and My forbidding. I thank thee for what thou hast done of My commandment, and I love thee for what thou hast eschewed of My forbidding.'

I said, 'If Thou art thankful, bestow the thanks for it upon Thyself; but if Thou blamest, Thou art not the proper object of blame, O Thou my Desire, and my Hope in my suffering, and my Cure in my misery. Thou art the One commanding, and Thou art the One commanded; there is no god but Thou.'

Then He was silent towards me, and I knew that His silence was a sign of His good pleasure. Then He said, 'Who made thee to know?'

I said, 'He that asks knows better than he who is asked. Thou art the Answerer, and Thou art the Answered. Thou art the Asker, and Thou art the Asked. There is no god but Thou.'

God's proof to me through Him thus ended, and I was well pleased with Him through Him, and He was well pleased with me through Him; for I existed through Him, and He was He, and there was no god but He.

Then He lit me with the light of the Essence, and I gazed upon Him with the eye of Divine Bounty; and He said, 'Ask what thou wilt of My Bounty, and I will give it thee.'

I said, 'Thou art more bountiful than Thy Bounty; Thou art more generous than Thy Generosity. I am content with Thee in Thee, and I have come in the end to Thee. Offer not to me other than Thee, and repel me not from Thee with aught instead of Thee. Delude me not with Thy Grace, Thy Generosity or Thy Bounty. For Bounty is of Thee evermore, and unto Thee it returns. Thou art the Returner, and Thou art the Returned; Thou art the Seeker, and Thou art the Sought. Desire is cut off from Thee, and asking is cut off from Thee through Thee.'

Then He did not answer me for a time; but presently He answered me, saying, 'Truth it is that thou hast spoken, truth thou hast heard, truth thou hast seen, truth thou hast confirmed.'

I said, 'Yes indeed; Thou art the Truth, and through the Truth the Truth is seen. Thou art the Truth, and through the Truth the Truth is confirmed. Thou art the Truth, and through the Truth the Truth is heard. Thou art the Hearer, and the One who gives to hear. Thou art the Truth, and the One who makes true. There is no god except Thee.'

He said, 'Thou art naught but the Truth, and the truth thou hast spoken.'

I said, 'Rather, Thou art the Truth, and Thy words are true, and the Truth through Thee is true. Thou art Thou; there is no god except Thee.'

Then He said to me, 'What art thou?'

I said to Him, 'What art Thou?'

He said, 'I am the Truth.'

I said, 'I am through Thee.'

He said, 'If thou art through Me, then I am thou and thou art I.'

I said, 'Delude me not with Thee instead of Thee. No indeed; Thou art Thou; there is no god except Thee.'

So when I had reached unto the Truth, and stood with the Truth through the Truth, He created for me the wing of glory and majesty; and I flew with my wing, yet I did not attain to the extremity of His Glory and Majesty. So I called upon Him, beseeching Him to succour me against Him, for I had no power against Him save in Him.

Then He gazed upon me with the eye of munificence, and strengthened me with His Strength; and He adorned me, and crowned me with the crown of His Generosity upon my head. He made me unique in His Uniqueness, and one in His Oneness; and He attributed me with His Attributes, the which none shares with Him.

Then He said, 'Become single in My Singularity, and unique in My Uniqueness. Lift up thy head with the crown of My Generosity, and be glorious in My Glory, and majestic in My Majesty. Go forth with My Attributes unto My creatures, that I may see My Selfhood in thy selfhood. Whosoever sees thee, will see Me; and whosoever seeks thee, will seek Me, O thou My light in My earth, and My ornament in My heaven.'

But I said, 'Thou art my seeing in mine eye, and my knowledge in my ignorance. Be Thou Thy Light, that Thou mayest be seen through Thee. There is no god but Thou.'

Then He answered me with the tongue of good pleasure, saying, 'How well thou knowest, O My servant!'

I said, 'Thou art the Knower, and Thou art the Known; Thou art the Singler, and Thou art the Single. Be single in Thy Singularity, and unique in Thy Uniqueness; and do not preoccupy me with Thee, to the exclusion of Thee.'

God's proof to me in His Singularity thus ended, and through His Uniqueness in His Uniqueness; and I abode with Him in His Singularity, without my being singled, so that I abode with Him through Him. My attributes passed away through His Attributes, my name failed in His Name, my primality failed in His Primality, and my ultimity failed in His Ultimity.

Then I gazed at Him through His Essence, that the qualifiers see not, the knowers attain not, and the labourers understand not; whilst He gazed at me with the eye of His Essence, after there had failed my name, my qualities, my first, my last, and my description. Then He called me by His Name, and addressed me by His Selfhood, and communed with me by His Oneness, saying, 'O I!'

I said, 'O Thou!'

Then He said to me, 'O thou!'

God's proof to me by Himself thus ended; not a Name of His

Names did He name me by, without I named Him by the same, and not a Quality of His Qualities did He qualify me by, without I qualified Him by the same. So everything was cut off from me through Him; and I continued for an age without spirit or body, as one dead.

Then He revived me with my life, after that He had mortified me, saying, 'Whose is the Kingdom today?'

I said, when He revived me, 'God's, the One, the Omnipotent.'

He said, 'Whose is the Name?'

I said, 'God's, the One, the Omnipotent.'

He said, 'Whose is the Rule today?'

I said, 'God's, the One, the Omnipotent.'

He said, 'Whose is the Choice?'

I said, 'The Lord's, the All-compeller.'

He said, 'I have revived thee with My Life, and made thee king over My Kingdom, and named thee by My Name, and given thee to rule with My Rule, and made thee to understand My Choice, and matched thee with the Names of Lordship and the Qualities Everlasting.'

I said, 'I know not what Thou desirest. I belonged to myself, yet Thou approvedst not; and I belonged to Thee through Thee, yet Thou approvedst not.'

He said, 'Belong not either to thyself or to Me. I was thine when thou wert not, so be thou Mine when thou art not; and be thine when thou art, and be Mine when thou art.'

I said, 'How can I do that, except through Thee?'

Then He gazed upon me with the eye of Power, and naughted me through His Being, and manifested in me through His Essence; and I existed through Him. The communing thus ended, and the word became one, and the All became one through the All.

Then He said to me, 'O thou!'

And I said through Him, 'O I!'

Then He said to me, 'Thou art the single.'

I said, 'I am the single.'

He said to me, 'Thou art thou.'

I said, 'I am I. If I had been I in respect of I, I would not have said I; so since I was never I, be Thou Thou!'

He said, 'I am I.'

My speaking of His Identity was like in Unity to my speaking of His Selfhood. So my qualities became the Qualities of Lordship, and my tongue the Tongue of Unity, and my qualities were 'He is He, there is no god but He.' Whatever was, it was through His Being that it was, and whatever would be, through His Being it would be.

My qualities were the Qualities of Lordship, my references the References of Everlastingness, my tongue the Tongue of Unity.

(From *Revelation and Reason in Islam*, pp. 95–103.)

About a century after al-Bisṭāmī had encountered God in Khurasan, an obscure and untaught visionary named al-Niffarī was having converse with his Creator in the deserts of Iraq. He recorded in a series of notebooks the things he saw and heard on these preternatural occasions, and his jottings were collected together by a disciple, perhaps his son, and published as *al-Mawāqif* ('Stayings'). Here follow a few extracts from this remarkable book.

Mauqif of the Sea

He stayed me in the Sea, and I saw the ships sinking and the planks floating; then the planks sank also. And He said to me:

Whoso sails is not saved.

He runs a risk who flings himself in and does not sail.

He perishes who sails and does not risk.

In running a risk is a portion of delivery.

And the wave came, and raised up what was beneath it, and ran along the shore. And He said to me:

The surface of the sea is an unreachable lustre, and its depths an unfathomable darkness, and between the two are fishes which may not be trusted.

Do not sail the sea, that I should veil thee by means of the instrument: and do not fling thyself into it, that I should veil thee by means of it.

In the sea are limits: which of them shall support thee?

When thou givest thyself to the sea, and art drowned in it, thou art like one of its beasts.

I deceive thee, if I guide thee to any save Me.

If thou perishest in other than Me, thou belongest to that in which thou hast perished.

This world belongs to him whom I have turned from it, and from whom I have turned it: the next world belongs to him towards whom I have turned it, and whom I have turned towards Me.

Mauqif of Death

He stayed me in Death: and I saw the acts, every one of them, to be evil. And I saw fear holding sway over hope; and I saw riches turned to fire and cleaving to the fire; and I saw poverty an adversary adducing proofs; and I saw every thing, that it had no power over any other thing; and I saw this world to be a delusion, and I saw the heavens to be a deception. And I cried out, 'O knowledge!'; and it answered me not. Then I cried out, 'O gnosis!'; and it answered me not. And I saw every thing, that it had deserted me, and I saw every created thing, that it had fled from me: and I remained alone. And the act came to me, and I saw in it secret imagination, and the secret part was that which persisted: and naught availed me, save the mercy of my Lord.

And He said to me: Where is thy knowledge?

And I saw the Fire.

And He said to me: Where is thy act?

And I saw the Fire.

And He said to me: Where is thy gnosis?

And I saw the Fire. And He unveiled for me His gnoses of uniqueness, and the Fire died down.

And He said to me: I am thy friend.

And I was stablished.

And He said to me: I am thy gnosis.

And I spoke.

And He said to me: I am thy seeker.

And I went forth.

Mauqif of His Reality

He stayed me in His Reality, and said to me: If I made it a sea, thou wouldst be connected with the vessel; and if thou wentest forth from that by my expelling, thou wouldst be connected with the journey; and if thou didst rise above the travelling, thou wouldst be connected with the shores; and if thou didst banish the shores, thou wouldst be connected with the naming, 'reality' and 'sea': and each of these two names invites, and the hearing is lost in two expressions; and thou wilt neither reach Me, nor journey upon the sea.

And I saw the sparklings as darknesses, and the waters as a stony rock.

And He said to me: He who sees this not, is not bound by My reality; but whoso sees this, has been bound by My reality. Whoso is bound by My reality, and addresses other than Me, is an infidel. All limitation is a veil from behind which I do not appear; and there is nothing in the vision of My reality save the vision of it.

And I saw that which never changes: and He gave me a mutable condition, and I saw every thing that was ever created.

And He said to me: Make no exception; that which is created does not persist.

And the vision was divided into two parts, ocular and mental; and lo, the whole of it, neither moving nor making utterance.

And He said to me: How didst thou see it before the vision of My reality?

And I said: Moving and making utterance.

And He said to me: Know the difference, that thou mayest not be lost.

And He made me to turn away from His reality, and I saw nothing.

And He said to me: Thou seest every thing, and every thing obeys thee, and thy vision of every thing is a trial, and the obedience of every thing to thee is a trial.

And He made me to turn away from all that.

And He said to me: All of it I regard not, for it is not fit for Me.

Mauqif of the Learning and the Turning of the Eye

He stayed me, and said to me: Thou art neither near nor far, neither absent nor present, neither alive nor dead. So listen to My testament: when I name thee, do not name thyself; and when I adorn thee, do not adorn thyself. And do not recollect Me: for if thou recollectest Me, I shall cause thee to forget My recollection.

And He unveiled to me the face of every living thing, and I saw it attaching itself to His face: then He unveiled to me the back of every thing, and I saw it attaching itself to His command and prohibition.

And He said to me: Look upon My face.

And I looked. And He said: There is naught beside Me.

And I said: There is naught beside Thee.

And He said to me: Look upon thy face.

And I looked. And He said: There is naught beside thee.

And I said: There is naught beside me.

And He said: Depart, for thou art the learned.

And I departed, and ran about in the learning: and I attained to the turning of the eye, and I turned it with learning, and brought it unto Him.

And He said: I do not look upon any thing that is made.

Mauqif of 'Who art Thou and Who am I?'

He stayed me, and said to me: Who art thou, and who am I?

And I saw the sun and the moon, the stars, and all the lights.

And He said to me: There remains no light in the current of My sea which thou hast not seen.

And every thing came to me, until there remained naught: and each thing kissed me between the eyes, and greeted me, and stayed in the shadow.

And He said to me: Thou knowest Me, but I do not know thee.

And I saw the whole of Him connected with my vesture, and not connected with me.

And He said: This is My service.

And my vesture inclined, but I did not incline. And when my vesture inclined, He said to me: Who am I?

And the sun and the moon were darkened, and the stars fell from the sky, and the lights grew pale, and darkness covered everything save Him. And every thing spoke, and said: God is most great. And every thing came to me, bearing in its hand a lance.

And He said to me: Flee.

And I said: Whither shall I flee?

And He said: Fall into the darkness.

And I fell into the darkness, and beheld myself.

And He said: Thou shalt never more behold other than thyself, and thou shalt not go forth from the darkness henceforth forever: but when I expel thee from it, I shall show thee Myself, and thou shalt see Me; and when thou seest Me, yet shalt thou be further from Me than all that are far.

(From *Mawáqif and Mukhátabát of Niffari*.)

Bahā al-Dīn Walad of Balkh, famous father of a still more famous son, was born about 1148 of a father who was a noted scholar and divine, of stock long esteemed in Khurasan as experts in theology and canon law, claiming direct descent from Abū Bakr the first caliph of Islam. Brought up in the traditional atmosphere of Sunni orthodoxy, he acquired such a reputation as a teacher and preacher that he had conferred on him the title Sultan of the Ulema. He was additionally a Sufi mystic, tracing his spiritual descent from Aḥmad al-Ghazālī, brother of the illustrious Abū Ḥāmid.

A not unexpected *odium theologicum* brought Bahā' al-Dīn into collision with his contemporary Fakhr al-Dīn al-Rāzī, a philosopher and theologian of immense learning and productivity, who is said to have been the cause of the Khwarizmshah's turning against the Sufis, so that he drowned Majd al-Dīn Baghdādī, a prominent member of the circle to which Bahā' al-Dīn himself belonged, in the river Oxus. It was however the imminent threat of the Mongol invasion that drove Bahā' al-Dīn to flee with his family from Balkh, taking along with him into precipitate exile his son Jalāl al-Dīn Rūmī. The refugees after many adventures ultimately found safety and a measure of renewed prosperity in the capital Konia of the western Saljuqs. There he took up honourable appointment as preacher and teacher, in which office he died in 1230.

Bahā' al-Dīn Walad enjoyed many remarkable mystical experiences, as he performed the ritual of prayer or meditated upon the inner meanings of the sacred text of the Koran. He noted down these visions, described in remarkably fine and eloquent Persian, in a journal which he carried about with him. By good chance this journal survived his vicissitudes and journeyings, and was treasured by his son and those who gathered to form a Sufi circle about him; it has now recently been published by the eminent Persian scholar Badī' al-Zamān Furūzānfarr under the title *Ma' ārif* (Gnoses). The pages which follow contain the first portion of this precious record to be translated.

I

Guide us on the straight path (Koran 1: 6). I said, 'O God, of Thy favour convey every part of me to the city of joy and ease, and open to every part of me a thousand portals of joy.' The straight path is that which conveys a man to the city of joy, and the crooked path is that which conveys not a man to the city of joy.

Even so I saw that God had given me and all my parts to taste the savour of all lovely ones, so that it was as if every part of me was commingled with every part of them; and milk came flowing out of every part of me. Every conceivable form of beauty and perfection and savour and love and joy—all of these become as it were visible out of God's essence in the six directions of me. Just as when a man possesses an azure robe, and on that robe are figures of every kind, and every manner of shapes and hues, even so God manifests in me out of Himself a hundred thousand forms of sense and perception; and I behold the forms of all beauteous and lovely ones and their loves, and harmonies, and the forms of all intelligible things, maidens of Paradise and palaces and running water and other marvels beyond all reckoning. I contemplate these forms, that so much beauty appears arrayed within me; God shows me every form that I desire, and I see that those all become visible out of the parts of me.

And I saw that God had made to appear a hundred thousand fragrant herbs, rose and rose-garden, jasmine yellow and white, and had converted the parts of me into a rose-bower. Then God squeezed all those and made them into rose-water; out of its sweet perfume

He created maidens of Paradise, and mingled all the parts of me with them. So I saw in truth that all lovely forms are the form of the fruit of God, and all these delights come to me from God even in this present world.

If they say, 'Do you see God, or do you not see?' I answer, 'Of myself I do not see, for *Thou shalt not see me* (Koran VII: 143). But when He shows Himself, what can I do not to see?'

2

I prayed, and gazed awhile towards God. Just as it is said of the heavenly maiden that she is one half of camphor and one half of saffron, her tresses being of musk, or as it is said of a man that he has a 'head' of modesty and a 'foot' of truthfulness and so forth; even so I was seeing God, that He was all compassion and majesty and grandeur and generosity and omnipotence and wisdom and eternity and life and the imparting of savours. Now I am gazing upon God and the infinite attributes of God, so that I am contemplating the savours of species by species in Him, and I desire that He may give all these to me; and I see that He is indeed giving them.

Now my vision of God is according to the measure of my sight; God shows Himself to me to the same extent as He gives me sight, alike physical and non-physical. My vision of God is the vision of these parts of me, wherein God has opened up so many springs, and as it were laid before me a full table. Now here before me, that is, here in the air before me, I am seeing all God and I am seeing all His attributes; that is to say, no place is without His omnipotence and handiwork and nobility. In all my parts I am seeing God; and all my attributes—perception, knowledge, power, love, affection, beauty, deliberation, prudence, sight, hearing, touch, taste, intellect, reason, nature—all these are eyes from God and from the attributes of God, through which I am gazing upon God and seeing Him, and seeing His infinite compassion and power and grandeur and beauty.

After all, yonder seven revolving stars are the source of worldly pleasures; so if these attributes of God which are sensed by me, and are always connected with my own attributes, should be the source of all that I possess in this world and the world beyond, what is there so strange in that?

Thereupon I lost consciousness. I said, 'It is God who has implanted this quest in me. O God, since Thou hast converted me into a seeker after Thee, make me ever more a seeker after Thee!' Come, to what end do I seek after God? For the sake of all that my heart desires; for all desires derive from God. So I fix my gaze upon the sum total of all desires; I gaze upon every single desire, and see in what manner God gives it life and succours it and brings it into being. Meanwhile I am contemplating God, and the essence of the savours of God, and the beauty of God; and I see, after God, my whole desire is God. Again I gaze into the spring of the perception of the savour of all joys, and see in what manner the savour comes into those joys from God, who is the creator of savours. So it is proved that savour subsists through the act of God, and the act subsists through God; therefore the savour itself subsists through God. In this aspect God is infinite; so, as much as I seek savour from God and gaze upon God, I discover savours infinite. Again I behold the attribute of God, how that both within me and within the parts of me these savours of the attributes of God supervene in such wise that I become heavy, and am the very essence of savour.

3

I rose up in the night saying, 'I will gaze upon God.' I said, 'I will gaze upon myself, what God is bringing to life in me after that I was dead; and I will ask of God, that He may augment that life in me, inasmuch as there are no bounds to God's power to give life. I will praise God and laud Him, and whilst conversing with Him I will gaze upon Him, that He may give me another manner of life; for this favour supervenes from Him only, and no other.'

Now I am beholding what a marvellous vision God has uncovered in me, after that marvellous vision resided not in me at all. I speak God's name, and laud Him, that He may increase infinitely in me that marvellous vision. I see that God has caused to bubble up out of me and within me such marvellous springs, and made such marvellous grasses to grow in me out of those springs. The more I gaze upon God, I see how these springs ever increase in me through Him.

When I become bruised in gazing so long, God gives me sleep and augments for me the waters of refreshment. Then again I gaze upon God, and see how that God augments for me this refreshment every moment.

Now, whilst I was gazing on God, I saw all compassionateness and lordship, and I saw knowledge and wisdom, and omnipotence and grandeur—that is to say, I saw the Essence compounded of these; as when men say, 'I found So-and-so spirit incarnate,' that is to say, 'I found no grossness in him.'

It is true of every man possessed of accomplishment or beauty, that of all the compliments you bestow on him none gives him greater pleasure than that you should say, 'There was never anyone like you in all the world. How could there be anyone like you? Never! And never could there be any beauty like your beauty.'

Now I behold that there is no particle, no prospect, no accomplishment, no beauty save of God and I see all things to be from Him, and I speak words with Him. I said, 'Praise belongs to God'—that is, for all the delights and cherishings that I experience from God, I praise God and laud Him, and perceive that that is pleasing to Him, and that He delights and cherishes me all the more. If it were not pleasing to God to be so served and praised, and if He were not displeased at neglect and ingratitude, He would not have desired such praise, neither would He have inflicted such punishment for neglect and ingratitude. In that case it would have been all the same to God, whether He was praised and served or no; and this would be absurd.

4

I recited *I take refuge* (Sura CXIV) and *Praise belongs to God* (Sura I). Just as when any man is seated before his master, and pronounces a hundred thousand praises and blessings upon him, and lauds him, and weeps and wails, and offers all his heart's love to him; even so you might say that these words which I recite, and these affectionate gazings of mine, are like the songs and the lute and rebeck and drum and flute with which a man woos his beloved. I wander about every where, like a man who plays the rebeck and goes all through the city; and I see that God every hour fills the goblet of my gaze with wine, the which I quaff to His noble countenance. In the midst of this skin and flesh, and on every lovely creature as I gaze, God fills the parts of me with that savour, so that all my parts break into blossom. Such a gaze is the means of bodily health; attention to anything else leads both to a weariness of the spirit and a bodily decline. So now I will wash out this impurity, and will drink other draughts.

Again, I gazed upon the corner of the skirt of the arena of God's wrath. I saw a hundred thousand heads severed from their trunks, and joint sundered from joint. On the other side I beheld a hundred thousand rivers, and robes, and songs, and verses, and lyrics; and in another corner a hundred thousand dancing servitors standing in ecstasy, offering up in their bodily hands the nosegays of the spirit culled from the garden of intimacy. And I saw that all spirits were no more than atoms, that all had taken wing and were alighting upon God and soaring up from God, even as motes restless in the radiant light of God. And I saw that the bodies were as a flower-garden to which God vouchsafes water and air, and hue and scent; or like beggars with wide-open eyes, eager to see whence God may send them the tokens of ease.

5

Sleep had carried me away a little while. The first thing I did on waking was to take an omen: whatever words and whatever magnificat came into my heart, that I would know to be the rising of a sign portending the return of my spirit to my body.

In that time the words *In the Name of God, the Merciful, the Compassionate* came into my mind. That meant, 'By God's name my spirit is scattered through the parts of me, and by God's name my parts are becoming alive.' In the moment of saying *In the Name of God* and *Merciful* and *Compassionate* I contemplate God, how He is seeking these particles of earth. Why, consider how God produces tears in the eyes and burning in the heart of a mother when her child dies, so that she weeps and wails over his dust: all that is the quest of God, and that compassion in the mother derives from God. It is He who brings those parts to life again; but He has made the tears in the mother's eyes, and the burning in her breast, to be a witness to His compassion.

I said: Lord, what ardent love God has for these particles of earth and air and wind and the four elements! Now in nurturing them He gives them life, now in passionate love He slays them and consumes their life. Again I said: Why, do you not see how a cat under the influence of God's love picks up her kitten with her teeth, and how through that same love she eats the kitten up? Now be sure that, being so ardent a seeker and so compassionate as God is, He will not suffer any man to remain dead.

I looked again, and saw that God has a likeness and informing in all His works, only man has not the boldness to declare God's form and likeness. *Like Him there is naught: He is the All-hearing, the All-seeing* (Koran XLII: 11). Now it is impossible for any act to befall without an agent, any work without a worker, anything made without a making: *and He is with you* (Koran LVII: 4) comes very true.

As for 'nearness' and 'farness', 'absence' and 'presence', these are attributes which God creates. The creature has an attribute which is called 'absence' and 'heedlessness' and 'unbelief' and 'estrangement' and 'Hell' and 'agony', as also an attribute called 'nearness' and 'love' and 'belief' and 'Paradise' and 'tokens of ease'. That God creates. God creates you unaware of Him, whilst having free choice in your affairs: that men call 'heedlessness' and 'estrangement' and 'unbelief' and 'chastisement'. Then, when God opens your eye to be aware of Him, they name that 'nearness'. The more He increases the state of knowing Him, men call that 'greater nearness'; till, when this state becomes perfect, it is called 'vision'.

Now every moment I am scattering myself with all my parts, like a rose-tree; so that I see that in every part of me God is producing the bud of new knowledge and new awareness. The greater the extent to which God's action infolds me, the more the Agent and Maker dwells with me, until I reach the point where I drive away all material circumstance like scum and refuse from the surface of being, all imperfections and unworthiness from the face of the beauty of being: that is called 'perfect nearness' and 'vision'. Then that ease and repose which is of the world to come is completely mine: *in a sure abode, in the presence of a King Omnipotent* (Koran LIV: 55). Now whatever desire there may be, I attain it from God, and all my repose is from Him.

I said, 'O God, do not sever me from Thee, for every pain there is springs from severence.' I looked again, and saw two things: reverence of God together with love, which is sought and approved of God, and is life; and reverence without love, which is not sought and not approved of God. So whenever God gives me light and joy and life in my remembrance and gazing and reverence, I take that as proof that that gazing and that remembrance and that reverence are approved of God; whenever I see in my remembrance and gazing and performing and reverence that the light and joy and life diminish, I know that that is not approved of God. So I have recourse to God, and seek what is approved of Him.

I became weary of remembrance and gazing. I said, 'Let me cease gazing, and let me see where my gaze goes and whither God transports it.' I saw that God was every moment giving form to various things, and heaping up the pains of gazing, so that it was as if my eyes would start out of their sockets, my brain would burst forth from my head, my blood would gush from my veins. Then, when the cloud cleared and the ice melted, I discovered a marvellous infinite world. On one side I saw phantasy appearing like a thorn, and then vanishing again. Perchance it is not-being, this marvellous expansive world unbounded; perchance Paradise and Hell are annihilation, and the inhabitants of Paradise and Hell are annihilated. Perchance the phantasy of joys is Paradise, and the phantasy of pains in the world of not-being is Hell, whilst to be unaware of both states, and to go into not-being, that is Purgatory. Now I did not see my own self to belong to any of these three parties.

Again my senses and consciousness became turned from God, and departed to another place. I said, 'O God, since Thou art the consciousness of my consciousness, whither is this gaze of mine departing from Thee? O God, since Thou art the sight of my sight, whither is this sight of mine departing from Thee? O God, since Thou art the gaze of my gaze, whither is this gaze of mine departing from Thee? O God, since Thou art the heart of my heart, whither is this heart of mine departing from Thee? Lastly, since Thou art the pivot of the pivot of all these, whither art Thou consigning them?'

I said, *'Guide us on the straight path'* (Koran I: 6). The straight path is this, that God displays the manner of His wisdom and worship to my spirit, and inclines my spirit to follow the way of the prophets, on whom be peace; and in whatever manner God is sticking me to show the way to other men, He knows the wisdom of that, and has appointed that to be the means of our felicity.

6

I was saying, 'God.' Following this thought, I was saying, 'O God, Thou art all; whither shall I go, and upon what and upon whom shall I gaze? For Thou art the witness, and Thyself makest the power to witness; this gaze of mine goes unto Thee and Thy bounty, and follows after Thee.'

I quickly efface that thought, and return to the Thouness of God; similarly, whatever of the attributes of God come into my mind, I quickly efface and return to the Thouness of God. I say, 'If God's Thouness were not, my entity would not be and I would be effaced. Since my entity and my qualities and my state of being and my breath of being all exist in Thee, and in Thee again are effaced, therefore Thou, God, art my first and my last; Thou art my Paradise and my Hell; Thou art my visible and my invisible. Whither shall I gaze, and wherewithal shall I busy myself, save with Thy Thouness?'

Therefore the clue to saying 'God' is to forget I-ness and to remember the Thouness of God. So I say 'God': that is, 'Thou, God, art my hearing and my sight, my reason and my spirit, my heart and my perception. Why should I think upon the imperfection or perfection of these things?' The conclusion is, that it is necessary to become estranged from all these things, and to belong exclusively to the Thouness of God, living or dead, in sickness or in health. Now we cannot go upon this road save by the light of the heart and intuitive perception; the minds of all the most intelligent men in the world have never caught the scent of this road, and of this world of ours.

I repaired at dawn to the mosque. The imam began to chant the Koran. I gazed, and found that all created things in Hell and Heaven, and the attributes of God, the prophets, the saints, the angels, unbelievers, the pious, earth and heaven, mineral and vegetable, not-being and being—all these were attributes of my own perception. Now I gaze again, to see into what attribute God converts the effect of my perception: He turns it into heaven, into earth, into angels, into prophets, into saints, into unbeliever, into believer. He conveys the fragments of my perception to the East and to the West. He conveys them even to Smarkand, so that so many many men and beasts in the moment of my gazing come into the fragment of my perception; numerous as the threads of the hair, God reveals in my perception realities and distinctions.

Now I gaze again constantly at my perception, to see how God converts it. I said, 'O God, keep firm in my perception the rules of worship and sincere service, of standing and bowing and prostrating, and of trembling in awe, and keep my perception concentrated.' Then suddenly I become distraught of God, and depart from place to no-place, from contingencies to the non-contingent, from creature to the Creator, from self to selflessness; and I see that all the kingdoms belong to the sum of my perceptions.

I was seated. I said, 'Wherewithal shall I busy myself?' God inspired me, saying, 'I gave thouness to thee for this purpose, that when thou becomest distraught in Me, and thy heart is weary of My nearness, thou mayest gaze upon thyself and become busy with thyself.' I said, 'Then there are two existents: one God, and one myself. If I gaze upon God, I become distraught; and if I gaze upon myself, I become confused. Perchance I should offer up myself.'

I gaze upon God, saying, 'O God, Thou hast set before me this broth of being, with all its filth and sourness, a nauseating morsel. It is this that troubles me. Take this away from me, that Thy comfort, O God, may emerge out of the veil. With such a morsel how can I find happiness? Let me gaze only upon this self of mine: God has given me this in order that I may offer it up.' And I weep, and I consider its state, what it will do in the moment of giving up the ghost and how it will die.

I saw that little by little my meditation diminished, and sleep began to overcome me. I said, 'Perchance this is because I am not

making an effort.' So I return to meditating, until I fall asleep.
When I am asleep, it is as though I resemble a tree in that I am in
the earth. If when sleeping I am unaware, it is as though I am in
not-being. When I awake, it is as though I lift my head up from the
earth. When I gaze a little upon myself, it is as though I grow tall.
When I gaze with my eyes and move with my body, it is as though
branches are sprouting from me. When I make a greater effort with
all my heart to meditate, it is as though I am producing clusters of
flowers. When I utter on my tongue the remembrance of God, it is
as though I am bearing fruit. So veil on veil is removed; the more
effort I make, the more marvellous are the things that seem to emerge
out of me; as though all these things are in the mouth of not-being,
and not-being has placed its mouth on my mouth.

7

'O 'Alī, there are three signs of the happy man: lawful food in his
own land'—that means, lawful food is the provision for the road to
the world to come; unlawful is that you should stay behind and not
travel that road. The second sign is 'sitting with learned men'—and
the learned are those who know the roads and travel on those roads;
you must sit with them, and travel with those travellers who know
the roads. The third sign is 'five prayers with the imam'—and the
imam is he who is the lord and governor of that city and that fair
province unto which we are travelling. From them it is necessary to
seek a passport, and a convoy of angels, and lodging-places in that
province, and instructions to the great ones of that province.

Or else the meaning of that saying is, 'O 'Alī, whosoever eats
unlawful food, his heart dies, and his religion becomes threadbare,
and his faith grows weak, and his worship faints, and his prayer is
denied.' A morsel of food is like a seed; your eating is the sowing of
that seed in the soil of your body. Consider well then what its income
and its profit may be, and what its fruit. If these be what we have
described, know that you have eaten unlawful food; if you perceive
the opposite of this, then know that you have eaten lawful food.

8

'Glory be to Thee,' I cried. I gazed on the vision of God, and on the
traces of the wonders and purities of God. Having seen God with all
His purities and wonders in the act of saying 'Glory be to Thee,' I
then cried, 'Praise belongs to Thee'—that is, 'I desire to see the
laudable qualities of God, and His beauties and graces, and I desire

to gaze on all things lovely and good, that I may see God in the attribute of loveliness and goodness.'

And I saw that this beauty and this goodness of God were infinite; only I am seeing according to the measure of the trace—the greater the measure of the trace, the better I see. Even so I see God seated in all His attributes. I gaze again on the loci of the traces of each attribute of these realities, and see God in those traces, only I cannot tell the mode thereof. In prayer I cry 'God is greater'—that is, it is certified that He only is God, and upon whatsoever I gaze only Him I see. Why, *Say, He is God, One* (Koran CXII: 1) is a reference to Him; that is to say, 'O seeker, God is present, but thou art absent. Return out of that absence into His presence, for He is One, and there is none other than He, none omniscient and omnipotent and all-wise but He.'

Now I say 'God'—that is, 'O my God, and O Agent of every part of me'; so that every part of me becomes aware of God as Agent, and collides with the act of God. Again it comes into my mind to reverence God; that is, 'This Agent of all things must needs be reverenced.' I saw again that both God's attribute as Agent, and His attribute as Reverend, smote upon all my parts; and every part of me became like to a bride reverencing her king in the privacy of the bridal chamber. I said, 'O God, how blissful a state is love commingled with the reverence of Thee; very bliss it is.'

9

In the moment of remembering God and saying, 'Glory be to Thee' it behoves me not to be mindful of my own body. For God's attributes of compassion, power, knowledge, beauty, purity, will and the like do not resemble the attributes of things created in time; if they resembled those, then this compassion and power and will of the creature would not be manifested out of the attributes of God, just as they are not manifested out of the attributes of things created in time. For as much as these attributes of things created in time are not naughted, remembrance is not manifested of the attributes of God. Therefore in the moment of saying 'Glory be to Thee' I must think only upon the Face of God, that I may see God and be busy with the contemplation of God. This is the meaning of *put off thy shoes* (Koran XX: 12). For the more I think upon this filthy body, the more agony I see.

Again, when I see God I see the whole world turning before God from state to state; and I see every part of me perforce doing reverence to God, which is the meaning of good-doing. For good-doing means this, that 'you should worship God as if you see Him;

for if you see Him not, yet of a surety He sees you.' It is therefore through prayer and remembrance and invocation that the mystics have become busied with the contemplation of God. Now whenever I remember God, I pour out my head and feet, my veins and sinews, my reason and discrimination, and ask God to bestow on me another kind of existence and another life *ad infinitum*.

I see also that the water of life comes out of the ocean of the unseen, and likewise returns to the ocean of the unseen; even as those essentials of mine come out of not-being into being, and go out of being into not-being. I see that from being to not-being is but a single step, no more; but when I reached the essential I became secure—that is, when I reached the essential I reached God, and discovered my whole meaning.

> O strange and wondrous rose
> That bloomed before my eyes!
> No hue can it disclose,
> Nor ever scent disguise.

The poet means, that the hue of God is invisible, and the scent of His love is undisguisable.

I said to God, 'My heart!' He said, 'It must become roast.' I said, 'My eye!' He said, 'It must become a cloud of rain.' I said, 'My body!' He said, 'It must become a waste.' I said again to God, 'My heart is no more.' He said, 'Abandon the roast!' I said, 'My eye is no more.' He said, 'Abandon the cloud of rain!' I said, 'My body is no more.' He said, 'Abandon the waste!' I said, 'Never, O God, until I see Thee with Thy attributes, will I become concentrated on myself or on any matter whatsoever; for in duality separation inevitably occurs.'

Thereafter at dawn I gazed, to see how any man might behold the oneness of God. I saw that some have seen God with the eye of poverty and naughting, some with the eye of form, some with the eye of direction, some with the eye of matter and temperament and the stars; and God is not without all these. I said, 'O God, sometimes I see Thee with the eye of one who likens; sometimes I see Thee with the eye of poverty and annihilation; sometimes with the eye of compulsion, sometimes with the eye of the passionate, sometimes with the eye of lovers. O God, to whomsoever Thou hast given an eye to see Thee, with whatever manner of constitution and temperament he has been endowed, inevitably his actions and motions have proceeded accordingly. If he sees God as variable, his spiritual state also becomes variable.'

I gazed again, and saw that every form and every phantasy rises out of the Formless and That which is without phantasy; every form is a servant of the Formless, coming at Its bidding, and not coming if the Formless bids not. Again I gazed upon myself, to see what my state might be every moment and what wonders God might show me, greater than the wonders of this material world and far transcending them. I saw myself to be as a vessel; upon my nostrils traces of the mystic knowledge of God alighted one upon another, and other wonders ineffable. I touch it with my hand, and all those many-splendoured things come into motion, as when water puts on chain-mail in the time of the wind. All those things I behold and see in myself.

10

I said, 'God is greater!' I saw that all corrupt thoughts, and every thought but the thought of God, all were put to rout. The idea occurred to me that until a certain form enters the mind, sincerity of worship does not appear; until the word 'God' is uttered, there is no turning from corruption to well-being; until I conceive the image of God's attributes, and gaze upon the attributes of the creature, ecstasy and tenderness and true adoration do not manifest. Then you might say that the Adored is imaged in form; and that God has so created the utterance 'God' and the names of His attributes, that when these are sensibly expressed men at once enter into worship. God, it seems, has made the declaration of His unity to be the means of the cutting off of all hesitations, whereas He has made the ascription of partners to Him to be the cause of bewilderment. He has likewise made all words and thoughts to be as it were pivots.

Beholding this I said, 'Come, let me efface from my gaze all that is perishing and vincible, that when I look I may be able to see only the Victor, the Eternal. I desire that, as much as I efface, my gaze may become fixed on God's attributes as Victor and Eternal, and the true perfection of God.' As much as I effaced, I found myself to be the prisoner of things vincible, things created in time. It was as if God was turning about the things created in time; and in the midst of this I saw that I was upon God's shoulder. I looked again, and saw that not only I, but heaven too, and the skies, earth and the empyrean, all were upon God's shoulder: whither would He cast us?

We cried aloud as passionate lovers cry, 'O God, we are clutching to Thee and clinging to Thy back; we cannot let Thee go, because we are Thy miserable lovers. Now, O God, when for a single instant we cast on Thee our eyes and gaze and behold Thy grandeur and beauty, we find rest and breathe happily. The next moment we are wailing like lovers. In the time of sleep we are in the same case too.'

So when I saw that we were all upon God's back, and that God moves us about, and pours into our throats divers draughts of joy, and that we become drunken with the joys thereof and cry aloud; when I saw how God keeps steady our perceptions, and sets in motion visibly within us other revolutions and other wonders; seeing all this, I became overwhelmed in the savour of it, and it was as though God turns about the spirit of every creature in a separate world, and displays to them His kingdom. By this you may know that God's kingdom is infinite.

II

I said, 'It is not so strange that the actions of the Community are all exposed to the Prophet, peace be upon him. For when I go a little straight towards God and draw nearer to Him, the deeds of my disciples and associates are all exposed to me, my friends and enemies, so that I know all their secrets and the affections of their inmost breasts, penetrating like a phantom into their hearts. If God should separate from my body and bones and flesh the focus of my purity, what would be so strange in that?'

So I said, 'Let me gaze upon the place of my heart's searching, and let me join that up with God, that I may see how God gives form to every thing and brings it forth, then takes that thing forward by ear and draws it along. So I may behold God's drawing, and cast myself idly aside. Whatsoever God draws along, I will focus my eyes upon His drawing and will not accept any form from myself at all; I will gaze steadily on God's hand, how He draws me out of the well of my perception and the like, and I will all the while gaze upon God's drawing, and will not gaze on anything else whatsoever.'

It occurred to me to say 'God' in the following sense: 'O Thou who givest being to all things, Thou makest all to be again and again. Now, O God, I will not gaze upon the things of form that have been made to be, let me gaze only on Him who makes things to be. Where He who makes to be is, why should anyone gaze upon that which has been made to be, and what shall he do?' And I gaze upon all things that have been made to be, and see them all standing powerless before God. I see that He who makes them to be is making them to be either with compassion or chastisement, is making either Paradise and repose or Hell and agony. And I say, 'O God, since my perception was made to be by Thee, where should it be save before Thee, who makest all things to be? O God, one may dispense with things that have been made to be, but with Him who makes things to be one cannot dispense.'

That is to say, God has made every one to be a true and obedient slave and servant to Him who makes all things to be. But sometimes I see one who becomes heedless of Him who makes to be, becoming all form and phantom, his body and brain growing feeble. That is, when his body and brain, which are the locus of the remembrance of Him who makes to be, become preoccupied with some other thing, I see that God sends upon him anguish, as if to say, 'O body, you chose a substitute for Us. Whosoever withdraws from the subtlety of the remembrance of Us is inevitably afflicted with the anguish of the grossness of other than Ourself.'

12

I went to mosque. My head was aching. I said 'I must speak the remembrance of God in such a manner that God may give me deliverance from headache and all other pains and anxieties.' I said, 'When I remember God, by whatever way gaiety and joy come to me, that way I must take and in that way remember God; I must reject all other ways of remembrance which do not bring gaiety and not think of them any more—that is to say, Paradise maidens, palaces, trembling before God out of the fear of His Hell, in the time when I remember God I will not think of these at all.'

I saw that God's control had taken charge of me, so that *Guide us on the right path* (Koran I: 6) came into my mind as I remembered God, after the way of colloquy with God; that is, 'I see God, and groan before Him, so that I think not at all about His modality and location and the conception of Him. Gazing at God has proved the straight path, because suffering is changed to ease.' I become so intoxicated, plunging into the marvels which God reveals during recollection. Now, whether I plunge down or rise up, or whether I am broken into pieces, whither shall I go? Whether into the sea, that is the purse of God; or into the sky, that is the coffer of God; or into the earth, that is the treasury of God.

When again I begin my recollection, I first of all do so on the basis of being absent from God; then after that I perform my remembrance after the way of colloquy—I had been absent, then I come to God and speak the remembrance of God in colloquy, saying, 'O God and Lord, this flesh and body of mine are the threshold of Thy door, whereon I have slept and squatted. I am before Thee, and I will not go from Thy presence to any other place. This body of mine, O God, is Thy workshop, and my senses are engraved by Thee. I have placed them before Thee; whatever Thou wilt, do Thou engrave upon them. O God, I have come before Thee for Thou art my Lord; whom have I but Thee? If I depart hence, God, whither shall I go, and what place have I where I may alight and dwell? For Thou art my Lord; I know no other to be my Lord but Thee.'

13

I was seated in the mosque at morning. Every one was saluting and bowing. I said, 'God is presenting my spirit to them; He is adorning my spirit, and showing it to them adorned. So they are seeing those traces of God's handiwork, and are bowing to me out of love for God. Even though that be out of hypocrisy and deceit and fraud, all the same that too is God's adornment.'

When I see the people bowing to my spirit, I offer God all the more thanks. And I see that God sometimes knots my spirit with other men's spirits, and sometimes unbinds them and brings each one into its separate place. I saw that all this was by the decree of the Living, the Eternal One; and I brought the Living, Eternal God before my heart, and gazed upon the life and craftsmanship of God, and my heart became alive. Again I gazed at the attribute of my own perception, and saw that God has detained a certain folk in the chastisement of cold and bitter chill, while others He has detained in heat and fire.

I gazed next at the world, and saw that the world was duly ordered. I gazed again at the world, and saw all influences and causes. I gazed again, and saw an infinite smooth ocean, and I saw not-being surging incessantly, and valleys outstretched. Once more I gazed upon the world, and I saw neither particles nor aught outstretched. I gazed again upon the world, and discovered Him only who has no associate. Then I gazed upon the infinite and unlimited attributes, and saw that there no ocean manifests and is naughted again.

Again I gazed, and saw some folk plunged in joy and ecstasy and gladness. I said, 'These are the people of Paradise.' Others I saw wailing in agony; I said, 'These are the people of Hell.' I gazed again, and saw envy and hatred and enmity in some men. I said, 'Let me at least gaze behind these, that I may see who it is that has set these things in the air and is showing them to me.' I saw how that God had taken them in His hand and was holding them before me, that I might see; He was drawing these pictures before me, to draw me too and to adorn me.

In that very moment I saw that that thorn-tree of envy and enmity and hatred had become all jasmine before me, and blossoms and flowers, spilling before me. Again, if sorrow and grief visit me, I see that that sorrow and grief are the musky tresses of God which He has scattered over my face. I see again how He lifts them up from me. It is as though God has made these things which I see to be a guide, pointing to my venerableness. For I am the bounty of God; and God's bounty is surely to be venerated.

14

I said to Ḥusain, 'You have delved to this point, that the earth which was dead, and other than yourself, has come back to life. If you were to delve to bring yourself also back to life, that would be a better course. So much joy comes to you because something else, namely the earth, returns to life; what joys would be yours if you yourself came back to life! The task performed is according to the measure of a man's power and knowledge; since there are no bounds to God's power and knowledge, His performance likewise passes all bounds. God has given you this much life; if you labour, He will grant you a life such that this present life is as death in comparison with it. This life which you now possess is as a parcel of earth, the produce whereof is joy or misery; the power and knowledge and choice are yours.'

I went on, 'This orchard and cucumber-bed and cotton-field which you are cultivating—when you depart from them a little way off, you will be sundered and deprived alike of that orchard and of its benefits. Why do you not cultivate an orchard such that, wherever you may go, that orchard and that garden will still be with you? If you do not see the invisible orchard and garden, at least gaze upon this orchard and garden which is manifesting in you from God. For ever savour that you discover in yourself, every beauty that you behold, every garden form that you see, all these are traces of God's handiwork in you. Sometimes they diminish, sometimes they increase; sometimes branches of another kind shoot out of you.

'This world's happiness is a trifling thing; it is like a dream, whereof nothing remains in the root of the teeth; but as for this world's sorrows, the bitterness of them remains in the root of the teeth. The dream therefore is a sweeter thing than this world's joys. So why must one sweat and strain for the sake of a happiness than which a dream is sweeter? Therefore seek less after this world, and address yourself to the quest for the joys of the world to come.

'Now every man says, "I firmly believe in the next world; I am in quest of the next world; but that quest and that belief of mine sometimes grow greater, sometimes less." There is no doubt that these words of his are no more than a picture which he has painted on the door of his bath-house, that has no soul and no life. Though you paint the picture of a tree on the door of your house, you will only gain the benefit of it when you attain the savour of its fruit. Whenever you see in yourself sincere devotion and yearning and belief and questing to encounter God, the true token of this is that you discover "a shrinking away from the abode of delusion, and a turning back to the abode of eternal life". Know then that your tree is living; you will taste its savour. But as for him who tastes no savour, know that he has only the form of a horse on his bath-house; he cannot leap.

'When you stuff your ears with cotton and lead, you can only hear so much, you cannot discriminate between letters and words. Likewise when you have stuffed your mind with the delusion of this world, you know the form of speech but you do not comprehend its meaning. Until you sprinkle over it many times the pure water of penitence and tears, that blackness will not depart. If living faith could exist amidst the luxury and riches and elegance of that painting, the holy Companions would not have exchanged palaces for a humble hut; they would have squatted in castles. But the prophets and the saints, peace be upon them, lived in happiness and perfect enjoyment, so that worldly prosperity and good fortune in the world to come both accrued to them. All temptations derive from wealth and power; what temptation assails the indigent man?'

15

I was saying: I will become distraught in God, and will cut myself off from all affairs; for distraction is not fully realized with the exercise of precaution. God is Self-sufficient; He desires only that all men should become His adorers and lovers. All the forms of religious laws and rules of conduct, settlement of quarrels, sanctions and prohibitions, are to secure that piece by piece I may become a lover of God, and such a lover that I am wholly unaware of happiness and unhappiness. At the time when I recite 'Greetings' I desire to utter all praises to God, and like lovers in the presence of their beloved I speak a hundred thousand verses. When I say 'Glory be to Thee,' I see that 'Glory be to Thee' means becoming distraught at God's beauty, so that I do not care to attend to any man's dues, having no other thought but God. So how should I not realize that observation of the 'pillars' is incompatible with passionate adoration and love of God?

I saw that the attendant circumstances of my entity—such essential and accidental things as remembering the non-existent and the forms, heedlessness and unawareness and sleep and the like—I saw that all those are a veil over the vision of God. I saw likewise that these are all the act of God, and I saw that God is in His unity; therefore God is veiled by His own act. It is therefore necessary that every part of me should be outwardly humble and inwardly lowly; but I do not know whether the pivot of reverence and worship is outward humility or inward lowliness, which ranks with intention. Only I saw that passionate adoration is a spontaneous thing, whereas worship is a prudent reverence; and the two are mutually exclusive. Adoration is like a scent wafted from God; and I take every care and keep it stoppered in a phial, lest that scent should come to all and sundry; for many remedies for the suffering are tied up in that scent.

Now since God is Self-sufficient, I see that He has no homogeneity with any existing thing. I see also that existing things are right fearful of God, because God has made Himself known by the expression 'Self-sufficient'. Again, in order that they may overcome their fear He has said, 'the Merciful, the Compassionate.'

I see, with regard to every existing thing upon which I gaze, that its existence, continuance, passing-away and final issue are all in God's hands, and God knows what will become of it; whatever He wills, even so it comes to pass with it. And I see that every act which I wish to perform comes into being entirely in God's name, not in my name; so that you may say that whatever I do, and whatever act issues out of me, all is the act of God and is wrought by God. I am like a draught-camel; if at the time of my standing God lifts the load from me I stand, and if at the time of prostrating God makes me sleep I slumber, and so likewise at the time of kneeling. What does any man know, in these loads of tasks which I perform, what things there are, what marvels, and of what great price?

I see moreover that God every moment is plunging my spirit into the four rivers of Paradise, into wine and milk and honey and water. Every moment He dips the bowl of my spirit into the river of joy, and pours that draught of joy from every side into the bowl of my head with its ten handles—eye, ear, tongue and the rest of the senses—so that I may convey it to another. I see too that all my joy springs from the water of my life, like life from the divers waters of Paradise; and this life of mine too waxes greater out of the water of my life, and my ease ever augments.

16

I began, 'Glory be to Thee, O God!' I saw that it was God who was saying this through me, and that God was bringing into being in me this form of reverence, so that my fancy ceased the expression of which was 'God'. It was God who in that spiritual state was saying 'God' and 'O God' and 'Glory be to God'; this He was saying through me because of the marvels that were in me, and the cessation of all fancies. Now the expression 'Glory be to Thee, O God' is an expression of colloquy; no one would ever say that it is a lie and not colloquy, and colloquy cannot take place without presence.

When I gaze at God I become effaced and naughted; again, when I gaze at my own servanthood God restores me to existence. I said, *Thee*—that is, I assert His existence and gaze only on Him—*we serve* (Koran I: 5); I said, I assert myself as being His servant. If in the moment of recollection I gaze upon my own servanthood and freewill, a sense of abjectness and meanness overcomes me and in the course of my recollection I say, 'I am Thy wretched slave, I am Thy miserable sinner.' Again, when I gaze upon God and gaze upon God's sovereign decree, my freewill departs and I fall into distraction; then my meanness departs, and I become lost in wonder.

Now in the moment of recollecting God I gaze on my own freewill, and I gaze on my servanthood, so that I may not become forspent. When I become forspent and incapable of further effort, I gaze on God, and gaze on God again, till I am lost in wonder. In one gaze I am a slave, and in one gaze I am a castaway. Again I cleanse my gaze in the moment of gazing, because the gaze itself is the property of God, and it is God who is gazing upon us.

So I say to all my parts, 'Since God is gazing upon us, come, let us be naughted in reverence of God.' That very instant I saw that all my parts were standing in a circle about my spirit and were following my spirit's lead, just as men follow the lead of the imam in the Kaaba. All were becoming effaced in prayer in the presence of God, and my spirit was an elder seated in the middle of the circle; while my parts were travellers who had journeyed hard about the world and had now all returned to my spirit, heads dropped upon knees, absorbed in ecstasy, all speaking yet silent. So the revering of God must be sweeter to my parts than every manner of food and drink, and its intoxication more powerful than the intoxication of all intoxicants.

Again I examined my spirit and the locus of my knowledge, to see precisely how God inscribes so many kinds of knowledge in me and other spirits. God inspired me saying, 'It is necessary to gaze upon the discriminate perception and knowledge and wisdom, so as to see marvels.' Again in prayer I recollected God, saying, 'O God, I desire to behold Thy modality.' I saw that there appeared the form of a cage, so that I might see nothing. I said, 'Then forms are like a cage, and this bird of the spirit must surely escape from here.' I saw that every form comes into being out of God and returns again to God and is naughted, *and to Him is the homecoming* (Koran V: 18). I said, 'Then there was Something anterior to the forms, from which the forms became compounded and acquired colour and became visible. Now I see that that Forerunner has no quiddity; even as no number existed without one, so no form or visible thing existed without That.'

I saw thereafter that my spirit was a sun; until the wall of the forms and the air of desire existed, my spirit would not manifest; and so long as the tablet of the forms was not in being, the writing and inscribing of my spirit would not appear.

Now, O God, shelter the blossoms of my spirit from the cold blast of the thoughts of those mortals and those creatures with whom I keep company, who are immersed in their own frozen pleasures and know nothing of my joys and savours. Or if not this, then do Thou, God, make my spirit unaware, that its gaze may in no wise light upon them, neither upon their joys nor their sorrows. O God, preserve the petals of my spirit's blossoms from the heat of their pleasures, that they may not turn black and withered in the cold blast of spurning and exclusion and estrangement.

17

I rose up in the night. I fixed my gaze on my own perceptions, and saw that my perceptions like hand-trained birds were departing to the essence of God. Their feathers and wings were burning, and the effect of that was beating at my brain and bones; and my head and teeth began to ache. I could neither endure without God's passionate madness, nor could I reach him.

Next morning when I entered mosque the imam began to recite the Koran. He started chanting of Paradise maidens and palaces; that is to say, 'God says, If you love me, who have manifested My love in those, take the amorous play of My love from the brows of the bright-eyed Paradise maidens and the limpid water of the heart, and contemplate Me in the delicious fountain of these. Behold My heart-ravishing charm in these, for without these you will never attain to My beauty. In the present world I have created these delights appropriate to natural instinct and passion, whereas in the other world I have created those delights as a reward for My good pleasure; so that you behold in both worlds faces in the remembrance of My love. All this that is in this world is the cheeks of Me; and all that that is in the other world is the beauties of Me. So keep your eyes fixed on the forms of God, and in your heart go about the realities. When you draw strength in those assemblies from beholding the beauties of lovely ones and fair maidens, then you will be able to see My beauty. Keep your heart fixed on the spirit of God, and in the forms keep your eyes fixed on the beauty of God.'

I kept gazing on my own perception. I saw that perception was not in me, it was elsewhere; and that coming and going of perception was not at my control and freewill. I saw again that I was that perception. Hence God was bringing me hither and carrying me thither, and the whole time I was as it were glued to God. Whenever God came, He brought me, and I was God's attribute; and whenever God departed He took me away—*and I breathed into him of My spirit* (Koran XV: 29).

Now I am quit of my own existence and change of moods, since I am the attribute of God. In the time of death God departs from me altogether; in the time of sleep He departs in part; in the time of my distraction and heedlessness, when nothing is precisely fixed, He departs a little. Again, in the time of my fixed perception like-wise, when God displays perception to me, many things become known to me; and so forth. So it is with the sun, which has the moon and the stars for followers—when it sinks in the west the world becomes darkened; then, when the stars and the moon scatter abroad, the world is brighter; again, when the trace of the sun appears and mounts on high, the world becomes brighter still. In like manner, in the time of not-being I am darkened indeed; in the time of sleep I become brighter; in the time of distraction I become brighter again; then in the time of my fixed perception I become brighter again by God's favour.

A guidance to the godfearing who believe in the Unseen (Koran II: 3). I said, 'O God, I am wholly perception, and I have attached my perception to Thee in the Unseen, and to the recollection of Thee I have devoted my perception. *And perform the prayer* (Koran II: 3)—that is, in performing the prayer I have devoted my perception to humility before Thee. *And expend of that wherewith We have provided them* (Koran II: 3): and I have expended my perception upon Thy way, since the best of me is my perception. O God, I have devoted all to Thee, since blood and humour and flesh are not worthy of Thy presence.' God inspired me, saying, 'We have accepted thy blood and veins and sinews, and pardoned thee, by the blessing of the devotion of Thy perception to Us: *God has bought from the believers* (Koran IX: 111).'

I was upon this train when Zain recited the Koran. I was observing the inner meanings of the Koran, and also beholding the works of God. The idea came to me that I would look upon the world and view God's compassion and goodness, His wrath, His beneficence and blessings, simply to see what would happen, what wise purpose of God would arise out of this, what benefit I should derive from this examination. God inspired me, saying, 'When you gaze upon the world of Our attributes, you come to know Our perfection, and conceive a desire for My blessings and a yearning to seek after Me; you are humble before Me, and become My lover. And when you examine the disagreeable things, you become afraid of My chastisement and fearfully observe My acts; and these acts are conjoined with My good pleasure. But whoso gazes not upon the pomp of My heavens and earths, he will be rejected of Me. The latter I chastise, the former I cherish; the one I uplift, the other I cast down. I am the Caster-down and the Uplifter, the Cherisher and the Chastiser; I reprove all idolaters and star-worshippers; that all men's gaze may be turned upon My noble countenance. If you should ask what wisdom there is in this, why a beneficent one should act thus and a wise one behave thus, I reply: How else do you recognize wisdom in any man? To what other end do they act, save to cherish their friends and dissolve their enemies, and to display their own pomp? To love those who seek after them, and to abandon them that heed them not?'

I saw moreover that my gaze was God's own indication, and the simple act of God. I saw too that when my gaze fell upon my brain and my head in time of pain, it was as though God was looking down on them. All my parts rise up and stand reverently in service before God, weeping and wailing. Likewise in time of happiness when my gaze falls upon my own parts, I see that all my parts rise up in loving fashion and do service to God; songs of praise are put upon my tongue. Likewise my gaze falls upon every part of my body and all the parts of the world; I see them swiftly rising up to stand reverently in service before God.

I said then, 'I will return to myself and will observe myself, that is, I will observe my own spirit, to see what perception and what attribute rises out of it, with what it conjoins itself and collides.' I saw in my spirit, how that my five senses issued out of my spirit like five rivers of milk and honey and water and wine; all these I saw issuing out of my spirit. And I saw whence this spirit of mine had flowed with so many branches; I saw that these had all flowed out of God. I see that my glances, and my spirit, and my very self, all flowed out of God; and I see that every spirit of every creature, together with these branches, all flowed out of God; every thing mineral and vegetable, will and desire and power, all flowed out of God. I see all these things flowed by the light of God and the attributes of God and the majesty of God and the non-modality of God; *His Throne comprises* (Koran II: 255). I see that God has set up in every place the throne of His judgment, and that He exercises judgment in every thing. I see that God is perpetually sending these forms into the water of life.

18

I went to mosque and was engaged in recollection. I saw Rashīd-i Qubā'ī; his form would not depart from before my heart. I said, 'Friend and enemy, both cling firmly to the heart. Until I become estranged from all but God I will not find deliverance, neither will my heart become whole.' I said, 'I will make an effort. I will occupy my heart with God, so that my heart may not attend to anything else.' I saw the form of my heart coming before my gaze, so that all the while I was proceeding from it to God, alike from its broad mass and from all its parts. That is to say, I was proceeding out of its crimson hue to God, to see whence its crimson hue and ruby parts derived their replenishment. Its every crimson part had five senses, clutching to God and taking replenishment from God; in like manner all the parts of my heart were taking replenishment from God. I saw all the parts of the world, accident alike and object, and every thing that is, deputies and treasurers of God, deriving these replenishments from the pure intelligences and senses. I see in this world every mental phantasy as clear as the crescent moon, surging with their hands and feet and taking replenishment from the world of spirit. Again in every phantasy that I behold another door is flung open, and so *ad infinitum*. Thus it comes to be realized, if God's door should be opened, what marvels I shall see.

So first we proceeded from the world of parts to the world of accidents, then we proceeded from the world of accidents to the world of intelligences and senses. Then this world takes replenishment from the world of spirits, and the world of spirits takes replenishment from the world of God's attributes. Every world is begging from another world, hands spread open like a mendicant, hoping to be given into its palm something from that other world. So the nearer one comes to the presence of God, the purer that world is: first the world of intellect, then the world of spirit, then the world of God's attributes; then beyond God's attributes is a world of a hundred thousand spirits, surging in an ecstasy of joy and ease inconceivable. Of course the presence of God is ineffable and indescribable.

Then I gaze upon every part of my heart, how each takes replenishment from God, each separate fragment spinning like a bright phantasm and tumbling over and over, snatching immortality. All that I see. Then, when I behold how God makes my gaze to be, clearly I see that my gaze is the gazer of God. It is amazing how, when my gaze looks in a direction other than God, it is seized with the pain of jealousy; then, as soon as it looks towards God, that pain of jealousy remains no more, and it comes forth from that imprisonment.

I am amazed at the Mu'tazilite who denies the vision of God. He says, 'I cannot picture God; so there is no such thing as the vision of God.' We say, 'Though we cannot picture God, that does not prove that the vision does not exist. For this gaze of ours is given existence and created by the act of God; but it is neither joined to God nor separated from God. Any other relationship than these two is inconceivable to us; yet for all that it exists, this gaze of ours, by the act of God. In like manner the real essence of God and the attributes of God exist, for all that they cannot be pictured by us; so too our spirit.'

Again, in the time when I had become incapable of perceiving God, I saw that same non-entity and stripping and effacement. I said, 'So God is this non-entity and effacement and stripping too, inasmuch as all these come into existence out of Him, out of power and knowledge and beauty and love. So this stripped non-entity contains and comprises all things created in time and is itself eternal; things created in time are within it as a pebble in the sea.' I also said, 'O God, excuse me; because Thou didst not show Thyself to me, I saw this stripped non-entity proceeding from Thee.'

Now the concept of the spirit is among the actual concepts; whatever belongs not to actual concepts cannot be conceived by the spirit—like God and His qualities and things in the Unseen. That which is inconceivable however is not therefore impossible.

19

I said 'God' in this sense, that all choice and will and power and action belong to God, and all joys are in this choice and power and action. The term 'predestined' carries its own label; it means that such a man is without choice, helpless, powerless, savourless; the 'predestinarian' has no life left in him. When I recollect God, I gaze upon God saying, 'O God, give me a free-will, bestow some action and choice on me.' If God bestows on me action and free-will, I offer Him thanks for such a benefit and so continue. If God does not give me free-will, I gaze upon God saying, 'O God, Thou art absolute in free-will and choice and action.'

Now in the time of recollection and meditation I do not suffer every thought to emerge; for thought is like speech. Joy resides in action and free-will, proving that the term 'predestination' is used for the absence of choice. So I said, 'One must not speak words to every man, or he will be bewildered.' So I said, 'I will look into my mouth, which is a triple veil over the speaking of words, and I will look into my heart, which is so many veils over the thought of speech, so that I may not recklessly produce the words out of these veils. Yes, the tongue is a narrow way for the operation of the heart; if I block this way, the words will not emerge but will go back.'

Speech is the marrow of the heart, which comes out by way of the tongue. Whenever the speech is true, the heart also must be true. Perchance speech is like the bridge of Sirat, narrow and sharp; its sharpness is truthfulness—set it against a mountain and it will pass through it; narrow, in that not every man can find the way to it. To whatever extent you travel on this way of speech, to that extent you will pass over Sirat. It is because of the preciousness of a thing that the way to it is made narrow; that is, it is difficult to reach a treasure, for the treasure has watchmen and guardians, and the place where it is stored is also strong. When however it is a waste, it is easy to go thither.

Ah, what a treasure is Paradise and the unseen world, full of magic alchemy indeed! When one grain of that alchemy was rubbed on the glittering orb of the sun and moon and stars, the base copper of their being shone like golden pieces on the azure chessboard of heaven; but in the moment that God takes that alchemy away from them, they all come out black as a frying-pan.

In the night when I awake from sleep, I gaze upon all my parts, my joy and sorrow, my thought and perception, my heart and all my other members outward and inward altogether; and I see that all these owe their existence and being to God. In the time of sleep God gives me repose; in the time of waking He gives me awareness. That He gives me, to the end that I may know Him and love Him, and seek my desire of Him. Every part of me says 'I take refuge with God'—that is, 'I seek all rest from God, and all relief from the vision of God. All my hopes and joys are in God.' When I remember God, I know that God draws me unto Him and is calling me to Him lovingly and graciously. In that instant I see my own spirit bowing low, humbly coming into the presence of God, rending asunder all the garments of heedlessness and the forms that wrap it, hastening like a lover and performing every duty with vigour and earnestness, with reverence and obedience and compassion and kindliness to every creature. I gaze again, and see that all these intentions and acts of mine are by God's will and act; not dead like the predestinarian, however—I am bold and free.

Again I meditated to myself, saying, 'My spirit reveres God, and meditates upon the work of God, labouring that my love for God may ever increase.' In no manner did it appear whether these states were pleasing to God or no. Then God inspired me, saying, 'Love is never one-sided. Suppose a second time that the spirit of someone else is in bond to your love, and in bond in the sense that, when your love reaches out to that man, then love is truly established.' Then I realized that my labours to love God were pleasing to God.

20

I gazed at all the fair and lovely creatures which God has created with such delicate charm. I gazed again, and saw that God has created in such beauty these lovely ones, whom He has appointed as it were a veil of workmanship and a veil of the soul. I said, 'If His workmanship is so heart-ravishing, what must God Himself be like?'

I saw moreover that the composition of forms was like the composition of words. By the utterance 'Be!' every thing is brought into existence. Therefore the whole world is speech, brought into being by the one 'Be!' If His speech is so fair, what must His essence be like?'

So every day I cock my ear and listen to His words, and gaze and see these words of His which have been brought into existence. For I am this same intelligence and discrimination and perception, these savours and joys; this identity of mine is not compounded of bodily parts, rather it is compounded of these essential elements. Whence comes this ego of mine? It comes from God. Who is God? God is He whose handiwork these essential elements are. Just as God is without modality, so His handiwork is without modality. You might say that our 'I' and 'thou' both subsist through God's 'Thouness', being the handiwork of God.

So I am constantly busied with God, and remember no other thing but God; for 'the remembrance of solitude is itself a solitude.' If I see perfection I say, 'Praise belongs to God'; if I see imperfection I say, 'Surely we are God's.'

If any man says, 'I have no savour of God,' I say, 'It becomes clear in time of separation whether there has or has not been savour.'

I saw again that God's hearing and sight and act are all without modality. For shape and form belong not to the bounds of hearing and sight and act; form and shape are mutually opposed and exclusive, whilst hearing and sight and act are eternal. Accidentality, shape and form—these three are destruction and deficiency; beauty and charm and love likewise are essential elements whereof accident is the destruction. Form and modality are irksome to love and beauty; wherever passion and love exist in perfection, there one cannot speak of modality; whenever modality begins to arrive on the scene, passion and love begin to depart, and beauty begins to diminish. So since God's act and attributes and beauty are perfect, God has no modality. Therefore God designated forms and beauties and modalities to be as it were the walls and perimeter of His being, that is, all beauties subject to modality are like a crumbling salt-marsh encircling a city: in what respect do these resemble the act and attributes of God? *Like Him there is naught: He is the All-hearing, the All-seeing* (Koran XLII: 11). So God is veiled by shape, form and modality.

If a gnostic sighs, say not to him, 'Why did you sigh?' For he cannot explain that sigh, because that sigh is for a modeless beauty; how then should modality affect his sigh? If tears rain from his eyes, they rain for the modeless; enquire not after their modality. I myself, when I recollect God and gaze at God and God's act and beauty, also sigh, and bid my disciples to sigh too, and not to enquire after the modality of this sigh.

When I am silent, not mentioning God's name, not sighing nor meditating, the earth and the shape of heaven and other things come into my thoughts. It is as though God has done to death my spirit and my gnosis and levelled them with the earth. Then, when He dilates my spirit with repose and ease, it is as if He has raised me up from the earth in resurrection, giving me life after death. So every moment goodly thoughts come to me, and because of each joyous thought I am raised from the dead.

When I say 'God' I understand and contemplate the Godhead and attributes of God, the traces of His handicrafts and wonders. When I say 'God' I see that my saying 'God' is beyond my voice and words, and that tenuous veil of the voice is an intermediary between God. So the intermediary between God and the being of the world and the parts of the world, and between me and my thoughts, is that tenuous veil, no more, which is the voice. God I see operating behind that veil in all the parts of the world.

I said, 'I will gaze upon myself, that by way of my parts and states and thoughts I may see God.' My heart went out to the form of my thoughts. I said, 'All the joys they impart are not worth withholding me from gazing at God. They are like straws in this warm pool of my gaze.' God said, 'Since thou yearnest for Our presence to bear them provision to reinforce their love, We too are sending thee unto them again to convey to them provision: *Him We shall turn over to what he has turned to* (Koran IV: 115).

I descended again into my own thoughts and states; as a man examines gold to descry its pure element, even so I began to examine the whole of me, to descry where this sum of me was reaching to God. The farther forward I went, I saw light like as it were multifarious rays intertwining. The deeper I descended, what wonders I saw enacted! Indeed, these lights and states which became visible I contemplated sensibly and visibly as the traces of God's handiwork, and saw them just as I see the day. If I should think fit to doubt this vision, equally well would I think fit to deny the day.

I said, 'God is greater'—that is, 'God is too great and mighty for me to have knowledge of Him and to know Him. His kingdom surpasses and transcends all that I can conceive.' It is as though my saying 'God' is as the seed of all the infinite multitude of existing things, whence sprout a hundred thousand sprays of different flowers, each petal thereof reason, discrimination and power.

Now God is living, and all things fair derive from life. Each part of the world that appears unpleasing to any man derives from deadness, the mineral and the vegetable; but from the aspect of life every thing is beautiful. The ninety-nine Names of God are the very essence of God: He is all love, He is all beneficence, He is all life; but to them that are veiled He is all wrath.

(*Ma'ārif.*)

NINE

Lyrical Interlude

The Arabs always looked back upon their ancient desert poetry with fierce if sometimes uncomprehending pride; the *Seven Odes* were for them unsurpassable models of eloquence and energy. This living record of long-forgotten feuds, with the lovingly meticulous descriptions of desert scenes, inevitably left its impress on all the poetry which succeeded it. But when the Arabs became a civilized and settled people, heirs to the urban culture of Rome, Byzantium and Persia, it seemed increasingly absurd for the elegant poet to pretend that he spent his life in the saddle; though he loved to picture his royal patron as so occupied. In the revolution which transformed the old style into the new, poetic values underwent a profound change; yet the change was a change within the established canon, revitalizing without destroying. Metre, rhyme, and heightened language: these continued, as they still continue, to provide the essential framework within which the poem was constructed.

The most striking feature of this revolution of style was the elaboration of poetic images. Simile and metaphor were indeed the bread and butter of the desert poet; now they provided the entire menu. Creative writing was accepted as a search for new themes, and new treatments of old themes. In this essay we shall attempt briefly to indicate and illustrate a few of the many novel subjects which the poets took into their repertoire; basing our observations upon a valuable anthology of Moorish poets compiled during the thirteenth century in Spain.[1] But first it should be remarked that in the new style, poems were assessed by the excellence of their component elements, so that the anthologist generally quoted not more than five or six lines of what was originally in most cases an extensive composition. For the Arab poet thought out his work line by line, and strove to crowd into each couplet all the wealth of idea

[1] Ibn Sa‘īd, *Rāyāt al-mubarrizīn wa-ghāyāt al-mumaiyizīn*. Edited with a Spanish translation by E. García Gomez. Madrid, 1942. English translation by A. J. Arberry. Cambridge, 1953.

and expression he could muster; poetry was an arabesque, and the art of the miniaturist ruled supreme.

In translating these verses one is confronted by the curiously difficult problem which all Arabic poetry poses, and this new style of poetry in a remarkable degree of complexity. The Arab poet, accepting without question the constricting conventions of his art, proved his skill and his originality by the success with which he mastered his handicap. His style was therefore characterized by a quite extraordinary concentration and intensity; we have called this poetry arabesque, and indeed it is fully as exquisitely and delicately ornamented as the finest Saracenic architecture. Brevity of expression was a traditional requirement of Arab eloquence: the thirteenth century poet Ibn al-Khabbāza referred to this fact in an elegy on a king who died young, using the comparison as a curious conceit.

> Your life was of the order true
>   Of Arab eloquence;
> The tale was brief, the words were few,
>   The meaning was immense.

The Arab poet of this period—from the ninth to the thirteenth century—prided himself on his capacity to weave the intricate pattern of his thought in words as few and as choice as possible. Sometimes the images are so novel and so alien to our experience, that the translator stands almost helpless before his model, at a loss how to depict so much exotic beauty upon so small a canvas. To give a literal translation is worse than useless; the perfume is the essence, and the essence is volatile in the extreme. It is essentially a task of re-creation, so far as may be within the same narrow compass of brevity and concentration. Failure is almost inevitable; success can never be more than partial. But all this is best shown by illustrations.

Ibn al-Ṣābūnī, who lived at Seville in the thirteenth century, composed the following description of a beautiful girl in a red gown.

> She is coming, coming,
> So soft her tread,
> A moon in gloaming
> Rose-garmented.
>
> As if her glances
> My lifeblood shed,
> And wiped their lances
> In her robe of red.

This is a very short poem, and at first reading perhaps appears very simple; the simplicity is a delusion. Take the phrase 'a moon in gloaming': this conjures up images which only a familiarity with Arab convention can illuminate. The 'moon' is the accepted metaphor for a beautiful face, pale and glowing; the 'gloaming' is a reference to the dark tresses which throw into relief the brilliance of the 'moon'. In the second stanza the poet elaborates the well-loved comparison of the glances of the beloved with spears aimed at the lover's heart; his heart is pierced by them, and her robe is crimsoned with his lifeblood. The poet, using hackneyed themes, has combined and refined them into a new and satisfying synthesis.

Here is a poem by al-Isrā'īlī, who died at Seville in 1251.

> Elms in the meadow springing,
> Silken pennants swinging
> On tawny lances;
> The river dances. . . .
>
> Ripple of mail rises
> To war; no surprise is
> The elms stand steady,
> Line of combat ready.
>
> Wave on wave surging,
> To the ramparts verging;
> The bent elms prattle
> And cry, 'To battle!'

The images are conventional. Tall trees are 'tawny lances', a stock phrase; the poet sees the topmost twigs fluttering in the light breeze, and compares them with the pennants swinging on the spears of Arab horsemen. The breeze rises, and ripples the surface of the dancing river; the comparison of rippling water with a coat of mail is not new—it has been used by many poets since its invention in pre-Islamic times. The rest of the poem is novel, and the picture when completed is a masterpiece of concentration.

Among the writers who had already used the simile of the coat of mail was blind 'Aṣā of Sharish, a suburb of Seville; he lived in the twelfth century, and is best remembered for this striking vignette.

> That mighty smith, the wind,
> Is at his task assigned;
> The smooth wave crinkles,
> Hammered into wrinkles.

Ring by ring
The mail is fashioning;
Nail by nail the rain
Rivets the forged chain.

Abu 'l-Ḥasan of Badajoz, a contemporary of 'Aṣā, recaptures the martial spirit of ancient Arabia in a brief poem in which he uses a series of conventional images—the 'fire' of battle, the 'flames' of love, the 'spears' of the beloved's glances.

I recalled my heart's desire
While the flames of battle darted,
And remembered how love's fire
Burned my body, when we parted.

As the foemen shaft on shaft
Thrusted, I descried her glances
Gleam among them, and I laughed
Running to embrace their lances.

Some of the subjects treated by the Arab poets of Spain were chosen deliberately for their novelty, and the resulting compositions are a pleasing combination of amusing grotesqueness and refined charm. Thus, al-Ṭulaiṭilī who lived at Lisbon in the twelfth century etches the following picture of an ant.

Slender her flank,
Narrow her shank,
Carved to design
Exceedingly fine.

Ethiop-hued,
Lugging her food
Gripped between claws
Like a pincer's jaws.

Look at her rump:
A little lump
Of blackness, which
Is new-dripped pitch.

Or you may think
It's a blot of ink,
The hasty smudge
Of a learned judge.

Abū Yaḥyā of Cordova, who flourished a century later, saw a moth beat its wings against a flask of wine, and then fall dead upon the carpet. Knowing that wine had often been compared by earlier poets with flame, he invented this poem to establish the causation.

> The moth a merry caper
> Around my flagon turned,
> Supposing it a taper
> That in the shadow burned.
>
> With beating wings he hung him
> About the flame it shed,
> Until the flagon flung him
> Upon the carpet, dead.

Ibn Shuhaid of Cordova, who died in 1034, has a brief poem in description of a storm.

> Mouths half-open, in their shrouds
> The parched blossoms
> Pressed their lips against the clouds'
> Brimming bosoms.
>
> Then the rains in majesty
> Enfiladed,
> Abyssinian soldiery
> Golden-bladed.

Poets had before compared flowers with thirsty mouths, and clouds with teaming breasts; rain had been likened to arrows, and lightning to flashing swords; but it was new to think of the black clouds as Abyssinian soldiery, and of course the ensemble is an original creation. The same poet similarly crowds a series of familiar images into an even shorter composition of astonishing pregnancy.

> The sword is a sheathed rivulet, to whose brink
> Death comes to drink,
> The lance a bough, that drips a crimson flood
> And fruits in blood.

Mosquitoes supplied al-Sumaisir of Cordova (eleventh century) with an extremely novel and diverting idea.

Mosquitoes are sucking
My blood like sweet wine,
And hey noddy-noddy
They merrily sing.

How nimbly they're plucking,
These minstrels divine!
Their lute is my body,
Each vein is a string.

Ibn Darrāj of Castalla, a suburb of Jaen, who died in 1030, compared
lilies with the white castles which Moorish princes built for themselves high upon the hills of Andalusia and having thought of this
likeness he delighted to develop it with further fancies.

Lily castles gleam
Engineered, supreme
On their stems to swing,
By the hand of spring.

Silver battlements
And, to their defence,
Round the prince, his bold
Knights, with swords of gold.
(From *Poetry*, Vol. 3, No. 11, pp. 2–6.)

Let us consider a few more examples of poetic arabesque from Ibn
Sa'īd's anthology. The first poem in the collection is as good a point
of fresh departure as any.

Sweet night of joyous merriment
Beside the swerving stream I spent,
Beside the maid about whose wrist
So sweetly swerved her bracelet's twist:

She loosed her robe, that I might see
Her body, lissom as a tree:
The calyx opened in that hour
And oh, the beauty of my flower!

The author is al-Mu'tamid, who was king of Seville from 1068 to
1091 and was thus an exact contemporary of William the Conqueror.
In *Night by the River* he takes as his theme a beautiful concubine,
whose attractions he depicts briefly and in conventional terms; she

is compared with the bough of a *ban* tree, a species of meringa, of which the lexicographers remark that it 'grows tall, in a straight, or erect, manner, its wood having no hardness; on account of the straightness of its growth and of the growth of its branches, and their length and tenderness, the poets liken thereto the tender girl of tall and beautiful stature.' The comparison is already found in the poetry of Imr al-Qais, who lived in the sixth century and is esteemed as one of the great patriarchs of Arabic literature; it is one of the commonest similes in Arabic poetry. But al-Mu'tamid develops the image and gives it new life by picturing the concubine's naked charms as a flower on the *ban* tree, now first revealed and enjoyed with the opening of its calyx, by which he represents her soft, clinging gown as it is loosened for him. The scene is enacted on the banks of a winding river; a river is not infrequently compared by the poets with a gleaming wrist seen emerging from the fringes of a green cloak; al-Mu'tamid observes that his concubine is wearing a twisting bracelet, and he therefore refines the stock image by showing both elements of the comparison together—the river itself, and the gleaming wrist adorned with the bracelet.

The second poem, *The Handsome Knight*, is constructed around the extremely stale and hackneyed comparison of a beautiful face with the noonday sun.

> And when, accoutred in your mail
> And with your helmet for a veil
> That hid your beauty from the day,
> You charged into the fray,
>
> We deemed your countenance to be
> The noonday sun, now suddenly
> Occluded by an amber cloud
> Its radiance to shroud.

To apply this image to a knight in battle is particularly appropriate, because the field of combat is commonly represented as being dark and shrouded in a veil of dust, and the gay and reckless demeanour of the hero facing mortal danger readily brings to mind the laughing sun. By a brilliant improvisation al-Mu'tamid likens the helmet which the handsome knight is wearing to a cloud covering the face of the sun. The cloud is said to be of ambergris, of which the best quality as the dictionaries inform us is the white or whitish; it is therefore a light heat-cloud, and indeed the gleaming steel helmet is seen to be white.

Let us pass to the single poem representing the lively humour of Ḥabīb, who was vizier of Seville in the early part of the eleventh century and wrote a book *On the Excellence of Springtime* which has survived.

> And when you passed, for all to seek,
> The winecup of your blushing cheek,
> Assuredly I was not slow
> To quaff that wine aglow.
>
> The tender grape is pressed below
> Men's feet, to loose its precious flow;
> The wine that in your soft cheek lies
> Is quickened by men's eyes.

This gay trifle is based on the interminably-repeated comparison of the saki's blushing cheeks with the glowing red wine; the theme occurs often enough in Ibn Saʿīd's anthology, and desperately requires some variation or other to make it acceptable once more at this late hour. Ḥabīb gives the image freshness with a pleasing turn of wit; he observes that the shy young saki blushes before the admiring gaze of the amorous drinkers, and logically concludes that it is their eyes which have expressed the wine in his cheeks, whereas the wine in his flask was the produce of men's feet trampling the grapes. The light humour of this comparison may be usefully compared with the somewhat heavier touch shown by Abu 'l-Ḥasan in his *Golden Glow*.

> See, his slender fingers shine
> In the sunlight of the wine,
> As the wild narcissus tips
> With its gold the oxen's lips.

He pictures the reflection of golden wine on the saki's fingers—and he uses language which recalls the familiar likening of golden wine to the sun—as resembling the saffron of the wild narcissus which colours the lips of browsing cattle; this bizarre comparison, all the more appealing to the taste of the period for its unexpectedness and suggestion of bathos, must surely have been unprecedented and therefore admired for its originality.

Ibn ʿAbd al-Ghafūr's *Coat of Mail* introduces us by inversion of image once more to the very beautiful but by his time commonplace likening of a river rippled by the breeze to chain armour.

A coat of mail, that sprays from me
The glancing shafts, as if they be
Reproaches scattered from the ear
Of lovelorn swain, too sick to hear.

And when I cast it down outspread
Upon the field, I would have said
Its links flow rippling o'er the net
Like rivulet to rivulet.

But when I clothe myself therein,
All emulating eyes to win
For my resolve and ardour high,
No water-armoured knight am I!

The comparison is worked out in the second of the three stanzas, but the poet feels that the simile, though perfect in its normal form, is seriously defective in strict logic when inverted after the way he has in mind; he therefore protects himself from criticism by first emphasizing the invulnerability of the armour he is describing, and this he achieves through the skilful and surprising introduction of the hackneyed theme of a lover deaf to all reproaches; he reinsures against misunderstanding by adding a final stanza in which the coat of mail is shown upon the warrior's body to have nothing whatsoever in common with the water to which he has likened it.

Besides refining and revitalizing the well-loved and all too familiar images, the poets of this period also looked, as we have remarked above, to prove their originality and wit by describing scenes and sensations which had never been treated before. This was no new impulse of the Arab genius, for the old desert poets had been pleased to observe and record whatever took their fancy, and the attentive eye with which they recognized minute differences between the homogeneous features of their austere environment only needed a change of circumstance and outlook for it to see beauty and oddity in such things as a walnut, an aubergine, a thimble, a radish, an ant, or an unripe orange. Nor is it to be supposed that the flashing wit which so enlivens the sophistication of this writing was something fresh to the Arab mind; the boisterous repartee of desert life, sometimes expressed in cruel and biting satire, sometimes released in gentle and loving raillery, had predisposed the Moors to the enjoyment of humour, and the pregnant brevity of Bedouin eloquence had prepared the way for the perfect epigram.

Consider Ibn Ḥaiyūn's *Inverted Eyelids*, which must assuredly be almost if not wholly unique.

Is a welling fountain hid
In your eye's inverted lid,
That your tears, o'erflowing it,
Run cascading through the slit?

It is curved (think I) as if
On the billows rode a skiff,
And the breeze has made it heel
Over almost to the keel.

And the man, its mariner
(So to the pupil we refer)
Fearing he may drown, no doubt,
Bales the brackish waters out.

Very few other poets of whatever language could have attempted, or thought to attempt, such an unpromising subject, and none but an Arab could have treated it with equal delicacy and humour. The phenomenon is not uncommon in the lands of the southern Mediterranean, scourged still by a multitude of painful and disabling diseases of the eye. The poet knew that tears had often been compared in the hyperbole of passionate lyric with a flooding ocean; he was also familiar with the convention of calling the pupil the 'man' of the eye. Looking at a man suffering from this affliction, he suddenly noticed that the exposed membrane of the eye was shaped like a curved skiff; this discovery, evidence of his inventive genius, enabled him to construct a little poem of most curious charm; one can sense the delight with which he added one arresting image to another, to paint a novel, humorous, and at the same time strangely beautiful picture.

Ibn Sa'īd fortunately did not feel embarrassed about including in his anthology, compiled to prove to the Arabs of the East that the Arabs of the West could also write fine poetry, specimens from his own composition. He was especially sensitive to the beauty of running water, the abundance of which in Andalusia came as a grateful consolation to these Arabs so far from their barren original homeland.

The river is a page
Of parchment white;
The breeze, that author sage,
There loves to write.

And when the magic screed
Is finished fair,
The bough leans down, to read
His message there.

As if stimulated to further inventiveness by the novelty of this idea,
the poet writes another epigram having a different and even more
bizarre point to make.

The jealous breeze, a-shiver
Lest envious glances harm
The beauty of the river,
There writes a magic charm.

The following three little pieces well illustrate his versatility in
painting waterscapes.

Wave Wing

The languid river, like
A bird upon the wing,
Lifts up its wave, to strike
The zephyr flurrying.

The Setting Sun

The sun, about to part,
Sad and sick of heart,
Stretches out his hand, to take
Farewell of the lake.

Sunlight on the Sea

The sun, that bright swan, stoops
Serenely to the west
And, slowly sinking, droops
Its wing on the sea's breast.

Preoccupation with the same fertile source of images causes Ibn
Sa'īd to see a seascape in the night sky.

The stars are foam-flecks, white
Upon the sea of night;
The moon, a frigate proud,
Tosses on a cloud.

When he comes to treat the popular theme of the aubade after a night of carousing, he crowds his lines with the usual but subtly varied images.

> Rise, and pour me rosy wine,
> Dawn aglow at morning shine;
> Wine of daybreak, cool to sip,
> Crimsons the horizon's lip.
>
> See, the lightnings shake their spears
> And the clouds are cavaliers;
> Swift their showering arrows come
> As the thunder rolls its drum.
>
> And the rivers, rightly pale,
> Clothe themselves in coats of mail;
> Pardonably do the trees
> Sway and shiver in the breeze.

Another aubade included in the anthology, the work of Ibn Hāni' who died in 973, is in fact the long and elaborate prelude to a panegyric to the poet's royal patron. The poet has crammed his stanzas with an astonishing wealth of learned reference and varied imagery.

> Wonderful night, that sent to me
> And you a black-tressed messenger,
> What time we watched the Gemini
> Pendant in the ears of her!
>
> And our saki all the night
> Launched against the shadows grim
> His lantern, red as dawning light,
> Never extinguished, never dim.
>
> Softly humming, cheeks aglow,
> Slender his stature, slim and fine,
> Thick-lashed eyelids, drooping low
> With the burden of the wine.
>
> The brimming liquor, tremulous,
> Scarcely leaves him with a hand;
> So constantly he bows to us,
> Scarcely has he strength to stand.

They say, 'He is a lissom reed
Waving on a sandy dune';
Know they not a dune indeed,
Do they forget a reed so soon?

For our bed, to couch us in,
The garments of the wine we take;
The harsh shadows tear its skin
Our warm coverlet to make.

Passionate heart to passionate
Heart draws nigh, and lip to lip
Presses; for hearts are yearning yet,
And mouths would honeyed kisses sip.

I beg you, rouse his idle cup
And bid his sleepy eyelids wake;
The drowsy flagon tumbles up,
Mindful our dry throats to slake.

Darkness has already snapped
A stretch of his constricting chain;
Night's army stands to order, apt
To contend with dawn again.

The stars that crown the Pleiades
Turn their backs on all the land
And vanish; gleaming rings are these
On fingers of a hidden hand.

And in their wake Aldebaran
Lumbers on his plodding way
Like a laden journeyman,
Whose beasts are spirited astray.

Yonder shining Sirius
Advances with more urgent stride,
Spurring on impetuous
His steed Mirzam at his side.

And his sister from behind
Ere the rising of the day
Hurries to him, to unwind
Their veil that is the Milky Way.

She fears the Lion's dreadful roar
As he flashes through the night,
Nathra, his muzzle, thrust before,
And rends the darkness at a bite.

Yet, it seems, the Fishes twain
Swimming broadly down the sky
Make to clutch him by the mane,
And undertake that he shall die:

One, the Lancer, aims his dart
And strikes, until his lifeblood drips;
Unarmed, the other in his heart
Raging, gnaws his finger-tips.

Ursa's stars, methinks, are roes
Of Wajra, searching till the dawn
A wild wilderness, where those
Seek their lost and straying fawn.

And Canopus on the rim
Ot his horizon, torn apart
From a loved friend, finds after him
No other, to console his heart.

Dim Suha, that wasted swain
With his visitors, this night
Now is visible, again
And again is lost to sight.

Aloft the Pole-star, cavalier
Supreme, with pennants twain arrayed,
Very scornful seems to peer
At the stars' slow cavalcade.

Aquila, his pinions clipped,
Drops vertiginous through the skies;
His wings, no more feather-tipped,
Fail him, and he cannot rise.

His brother, wheeling yet on wing
Sublime, unwearied to the prey,
Suddenly appears to spring
And snatches half the moon away.

Night, circumferenced in profound
Darkness, black as ebony,
Presently is swathed around
In purple weave of majesty.

As her shadows now decline
Swaying slantwise o'er the earth,
Meseems she passed the night with wine
And staggers in her drunken mirth.

> Dawn, lifting up his pole of light,
> Is a Turkish monarch, who
> Challenges that Ethiop night,
> And he vanishes from view.
>
> The sun's standard fluttering
> Is Jaafar, my Lord-Emperor
> Who, looking on a rival king,
> Only laughs, and laughs the more.

After this lengthy prelude the poet swung into his main theme, the praises of his monarch whose bounty he doubtless craves; but the remainder of the ode is lost.

One remembers with affection other poems from this choice anthology, witnesses to the varied talents and interests of old Andalusia. Thus, al-Munfatil, who flourished in the eleventh century, describes his mistress.

> Friends, hear the story of
> My heart's only love:
> Lissom is she,
> And, as she sweetly sways,
> My fond heart obeys
> Her witchery.
>
> So sweetly she enchants;
> Each firm breast a lance
> Pointed at me,
> And pointed, guarding yet
> Her inviolate
> Virginity.

Abū Ja'far of Alcala La Real, who died in 1163, was in love with the poetess Ḥafṣa and sent her the following verses.

> God ever guard the memory
> Of that fair night, from censure free,
> Which hid two lovers, you and me,
> Deep in Mu'ammal's poplar-grove;
> And, as the happy hours we spent,
> There gently wafted a sweet scent
> From flowering Nejd, all redolent
> With the rare fragrance of the clove.

High in the trees a turtle-dove
Sang rapturously of our love,
And boughs of basil swayed above
A gently murmuring rivulet;
The meadow quivered with delight
Beholding such a joyous sight,
The interclasp of bodies white,
And breasts that touched, and lips that met.

Ḥafṣa sent her lover a playful reply.

Do not suppose it pleased the dell
That we should there together dwell
In happy union; truth to tell,
It showed us naught but petty spite.
The river did not clap, I fear,
For pleasure that we were so near,
The dove raised not his song of cheer
Save for his personal delight.

Think not such noble thoughts as you
Are worthy of; for if you do
You'll very quickly find, and rue,
High thinking is not always wise.
I scarce suppose that yonder sky
Displayed its wealth of stars on high
For any reason, but to spy
On our romance with jealous eyes.

Abū 'l-Baḥr of Murcia, who died in 1202, remembers with understandable self-satisfaction a night of masterly self-control.

Beautiful is she,
Beauty all excelling,
A world of witchery
In her gestures dwelling.

Fairer than the moon
Which, her charms so slender
Beholding, craves the boon
Humbly to attend her.

See, the shining grace
Of its crescent golden
Is but her radiant face
In a glass beholden.

On her cheek the mole
Punctuates and stresses
The calligraphic scroll
Lettered by her tresses.

As I lay at night
Nigh to her, night fashioned
Two fires: her beauty bright,
And my sighs impassioned.

Like as o'er his gold
Palpitates the miser,
So yearned I in my hold
Wholly to comprise her.

Yea, I bound her well
In my ardent rapture,
Afraid lest my gazelle
Should escape my capture.

Yet I kissed her not,
Chastity denying
My lust, a furnace hot
In my bosom sighing.

Marvel, if you will:
I, of thirst complaining,
While yet the healing rill
On my throat was raining.

Ibn al-Ḥammāra, a notable of the twelfth century, penned these
lines on the death of his wife.

Zainab, if you have departed,
Yet the selfsame back you rode
Shall transport this broken-hearted
Lodger from his lone abode.

With what ardour should I cherish
Other women for my lust,
While you bloom and beauty perish,
And your charms are turned to dust?

When you fell to the embraces
Of the dusky earth, I cried:
'Lo, the stars have lost their places,
And the sun of love has died.'

O most fair and fragile flower
Withering so soon to death,
Did the heavens grudge a shower?
Could the breeze not spare a breath?

(From *A Moorish Anthology*.)

As a tail-piece to this selection of Andalusian poems we append a
handful of the compositions of one of the greatest writers of Moorish
Spain, translated on the occasion of the ninth centenary (Muslim
reckoning) of his death. Ibn Zaidūn, born at Cordova in 394/1003
of a noble family and orphaned early, had gained celebrity as a poet
before his twentieth year. A passionate attachment to the poetess
Wallāda brought him to prison through the machinations of a
powerful rival. Later in his life he migrated to Seville where he
became vizier to al-Mu'taḍid and his successor al-Mu'tamid, some
of whose verses have been quoted above. Ibn Zaidūn died at Seville
in 463/1071.

Fidelity

Say what thou wilt to me, thou'lt never prove
Inconstancy or fickleness in me:
For how should I betray, or changeful be,
Since all my joy in living is thy love?
No passing consolation can remove
The paint hy parting wrought, the misery
Of passion thwarted, the infirmity
Of this sick heart condemned uncured to rove.

Heed now my prayer: if ever I betrayed
The troth I pledged to thee; if I have ta'en
Delight in other lips; if I have made
New secret loyalties to be obeyed—
Then let my fondest hopes be proven vain,
Nor may thy presence gladden me again.

A Song for the King

O let our tongues thy power proclaim,
Great king, and celebrate thy name!
Behold, thy presence in this place
Doth lend our vast assembly grace.

Within this cool and watered glade
We bask in thy protective shade;
Thy bounteous gifts our spirits bless,
Thy virtues are our happiness.

Fill Every Glass

Fill up, and let the wine run free,
For merry is our company;
No gayer season could be found
To give the brimming beaker round.

Small cause is there, though spring be fled,
For hearts to be dispirited;
The tender beauties of these bowers
Excel by far his faded flowers.

My Life for Thine

Can time cast sorrow in my heart
When thou my joyous comrade art,
Or shall my day be turned to night
While in thy radiance I delight?

I set my seed in thy love's bower,
And watched to see my fond hopes flower;
But all the harvest of my faith
Is withered dreams and fancy's death.

'Twas faithlessness I won from thee
As wage for my fidelity;
My gift of love by thee was sold
For little gain of yellow gold.

Yet, though thy wilfulness and sin
Are proved my woes' sole origin,
This one reward I seek to take—
To yield my life for thy dear sake.

Fair of Heart

Thus thou hast rewarded me—
Exile for fidelity;
For a constant heart and true
One brief joy, and then, adieu!

Tell me this, and tell me plain:
I that was by passion slain—
Was it chance that ruled my fate,
Or design deliberate?

When my love was strong and hale,
Then did thine grow faint and ail;
When I speeded to obey,
All the more thou saidst me nay.

Loveliest of beings, thou,
Soft to touch, divine to view,
Glance that all enchantment knows,
Breath more fragrant than the rose;

Very fair God fashioned thee:
Fair let all thy dealings be;
If thou prove not fair of heart,
What care I, how fair thou art?

Parting

And when we met at morn to say goodbye,
And the bright pennants fluttered to the sky
Above the castle's towering battlements,
And the proud steeds were matched, and through the tents
The drums of parting rolled, what tears of blood
Streamed from our eyes, as if their crimson flood
Welled from deep wounds that seared the very heart.
And then I said: 'If now we have to part,
Yet in three days I look for thy return.'
So spoke my hopes: but now my heart doth burn
These thrice three nights, and still no sight of thee;
And ah, the anguish that consumeth me!

The Truth is Out

Now the truth at last is out,
Certainty has banished doubt;
Now mine enemies have seen
How deluded they have been,
And that when with morbid will
They desired my utmost ill,
Hoped that I, the staunchly true,
Should prove false, and traitor too,
They accounted far too light
Duty's call and friendship's right.

Fair Gazelle

O fair gazelle
Whose charms do dwell
Within mine eyes, my heart, my soul,
My love for thee,
As all may see,
Is single, pure, entire, and whole.

So all declare
Who witness bear,
And thou thyself a witness art;
Let envy blind
The jealous mind,
It cannot hurt the loving heart.

If half the fire
Of my desire
Had burned and blazed within thy breast,
There never were
A barrier
Betwixt my yearning and my rest.

Passion's Lay

Ah, when will our long parting cease?
And shall I ever win to peace,
That I may pour into thine ear
My anguished tale of yearning drear?

I pray God grant us such a day
When I may chant my passion's lay,
And from mine eyes the salt tears start
To witness to a loyal heart.

Thy Will be Done

Sweet gazelle that castest me
Fettered in affliction's keep,
Not an hour, since losing thee,
Have I culled the sweets of sleep.

Ah, that I might have a sign,
Just one glance of thy dear face!
Of my tortured love I pine;
Let my pleader be thy grace.

Formerly I dwelt alone,
   Innocent and fancy-free;
Since thy beauty I have known,
   Whither fled my liberty?

Once my secret was mine own;
   Now it stands for all to know:
Then let all thy will be done,
   For I cannot let thee go.

Prove Mankind

So, thou hast betrayed my trust,
Trailed my honour in the dust;
Ta'en my heart, that loved thee well,
At the cheapest price to sell.
'Ho, a bargain!' thou didst cry,
'Come, what offers? Who will buy?'
Thou, who wert my armoury
In the strife with destiny,
Faithless proved and renegade
Common cause with fate hast made.
Sell me then what price thou wilt:
Thou shalt soon repent my guilt—
Others will thy torment be:
Prove mankind, and thou wilt see.

A Cup

A bowl am I, dispensing joy
To pretty maid and mirthful boy;
Within my guardian grasp I hide
A noble vine's empurpled tide—
A subtle spirit, nursed to rest
Within my soft, embracing breast.

Life has of boons a thousandfold,
And all lie here within my hold,
In sweetest harmony combined:
What loveliness was e'er designed
That with my loveliness could vie,
In saki's hands now borne on high?

Reproach

O thou that mockest at thy lovers
And makest light of thy reprovers,

Since thou my slanderers hast heeded,
No longer is my fond love needed:

Thanks be to God, for He doth prove me
The falseness of thy claim to love me;
And I will win fine consolation
In truer lips for thy lost passion.

Nights of Joy

Ah, many the long night thou and I
   Have passed at ease with the wine-crowned cup
Till the red dawn gleamed in the night-dim sky
   And the stars of morn in the east rose up,
And along the west the stars of night
Like defeated armies pressed their flight.

Then the brightest of joys were ours to gain,
   With never a care in the world to cloud,
And pleasure untouched by the hand of pain,
   Were delight with eternal life endowed.
But alas! that even the fairest boon
Is doomed, like night, to be spent too soon.

Evil Flame

What evil flame my soul hath fired,
Desirous still, yet undesired!
My love is pure, without alloy,
But she is wanton, though so coy.

Since she both lovely is and vain,
Each moment newly I am slain;
Yet how can I endure to part
From her whose dwelling is my heart?

Wine and Roses

'Bring wine!' I said;
But she that sped
Bore wine and roses beautiful.
Now from her lip
Sweet wine I sip,
And from her cheeks red roses cull.

(From *al-Adab wa'l-Fann*.)

TEN

Faith and Doubt

What things is it necessary for a Muslim to believe, in order that he may by God's grace by saved? From this question 'the Two-and-Seventy jarring Sects' arose, threatening down the bloody centuries to tear to pieces the body of Islam. It is true that the Koran could always be cited for simple statements of the articles of faith.

> The Messenger believes in what was sent down to
>   him from his Lord,
> and the believers; each one believes in God
>   and His angels,
> and in His Books and His Messengers; we
>   make no division
> between any one of His Messengers. They say,
>   'We hear, and obey.
> Our Lord, grant us Thy forgiveness; unto Thee
>   is the homecoming.'   (Kor. 2: 285.)

And it is true that the 'attestation of faith' which sums up the teaching of Islam contains only two clauses: 'I testify that there is no god but Allah. I testify that Muhammad is the Messenger of Allah.' The example of the wranglings of Christian theologians before them should have sufficed to warn their Muslim colleagues what to expect when it is proposed to define the boundaries of orthodoxy.

Coming into the field at the end of three centuries of impassioned contention, the Sufi peace-maker al-Kalābādhī in his *Doctrine of the Sufis* summed up the formulations of the by then most generally accepted theology, as an essential introduction to his argument that the Sufis, who had lately been heavily attacked and persecuted, were after all the most moderate and orthodox of believers. The following passages from his book present a fair and clear picture of Sunni doctrine after the defeat of the Mu'tazilīs and the discrediting of the more extreme anthropomorphism.

The Sufis are agreed that God is One, Alone, Single, Eternal, Ever-lasting, Knowing, Powerful, Living, Hearing, Seeing, Strong, Mighty, Majestic, Great, Generous, Clement, Proud, Awful, En-during, First, God, Lord, Ruler, Master, Merciful, Compassionate, Desirous, Speaking, Creating, Sustaining; that He is qualified with all the attributes wherewith He has qualified Himself, and named with all the names whereby He has named Himself; that since eternity He has not ceased to continue with His names and attri-butes, without resembling creation in any respect; that His Essence does not resemble the essences, nor His Attributes the attributes; that not one of the terms applied to created beings, and indicating their creation in time, has currency over Him; that He has not ceased to be Leader, Foremost before all things born in time, Existent before everything; that there is no Eternal but He, and no God beside Him; that He is neither body, nor shape, nor form, nor person, nor element, nor accident; that with Him there is neither junction nor separation, neither movement nor rest, neither augmen-tation nor decrease; that He has neither parts nor particles nor members nor limbs nor aspects nor places; that He is not affected by faults, nor overcome with slumbers, nor alternated by times, nor specified by allusions; that He is not contained by space, nor affected by time; that He cannot be said to be touched, or to be isolated, or to dwell in places; that He is not compassed by thoughts, nor covered by veils, nor attained by eyes.

They are agreed that He is neither perceived by the eyes, nor assailed by the thoughts; that His attributes do not change, and that His names do not alter; that He has never ceased thus, and will never cease thus; that He is the First and the Last, the Outward and the Inward; that He is acquainted with everything, that there is nothing like Him, and that He sees and hears.

They are agreed that God has real qualities, and that He is quali-fied by them, these being: knowledge, strength, power, might, mercy, wisdom, majesty, omnipotence, eternity, life, desire, will, and speech. These are neither bodies nor accidents nor elements, even as His essence is neither body nor accident nor element. They also agree that He has hearing, sight, face, and hand, in reality, unlike ordinary hearing, sight, hands, and faces. They agree that these are attributes of God, not members or limbs or parts; that they are neither He nor other than He; and that the assertion of their being does not imply that He is in need of them, or that He does things with them. Their meaning is the denial of their opposites, the assertion that they both exist in themselves, and subsist through Him.

They also agree that His attributes are neither diverse nor similar: that His knowledge is not the same as His strength, nor other than His strength; and so with all His attributes, such as hearing, sight, face and hand—His hearing is neither the same as His sight, nor other than His sight, in the same way as His attributes are not He, nor other than He.

They are at variance as to whether or not God has ceased to create. The greater part of them, and the majority of their leaders and foremost men, say that it is not possible for an attribute to come to God in time which He has not the right to claim in eternity. He did not deserve the name 'Creator' because of His creating creation, or the name 'Maker' because of originating mortal beings, or the name 'Former' because of forming the forms: if this had been so, He would have been eternally deficient, only becoming complete through the act of creation—far removed is God above that!

They hold that God is eternally the Creator, Maker, Former, Forgiving, Compassionate, Grateful, and so on, through all the attributes wherewith He has qualified Himself, being qualified by them in pre-eternity. As He is qualified by knowledge, strength, might, majesty and power, so He is similarly qualified by making to be, shaping and forming, as well as by desire, generosity, forgiveness and gratitude. They do not differentiate between a quality which is an act, and a quality which cannot be described as an act, such as greatness, splendour, knowledge, strength.

They are agreed that He is without ceasing Ruler, God and Lord, without subject or slave: it is therefore in the same way permissible to say that He is Creator, Maker and Former, without any thing created, made or formed.

They are at variance concerning the names of God. Some of them maintain that the names of God are neither God, nor other than God: this is parallel to their doctrine concerning the attributes. Others hold the view that the names of God are God.

They are agreed that the Koran is the real word of God, and that it is neither created, nor originated in time, nor an innovation; that it is recited by our tongues, written in our books, and preserved in our breasts, but not dwelling therein. They are also agreed that it is neither body, nor element, nor accident.

They are at variance concerning the nature of God's speech. The majority of them hold that the speech of God is an eternal attribute of God contained in His essence in no way resembling the speech of created beings; and that it possesses no quiddity, just as His essence possesses no quiddity, except for the purpose of affirmation. The greater part of them are agreed that God's speech does not consist of letters, sound or spelling, but that letters, sound and spelling are indications of His speech, and that they have their own instruments and members, to wit, uvula, lips and tongue.

They are agreed that God will be seen with the eyes in the next world, and that the believers will see Him but not the unbelievers, because this is a grace from God. They hold that vision is possible through the intellect, and obligatory through the hearing. They are agreed that God is not seen in this world either with the eyes or with the heart, save from the point of view of faith. They are at variance as to whether the Prophet saw God on the night of the heavenly journey. The majority of them, including the most important Sufis, declare that Muhammad did not see Him with his eyes, nor any other created being, in this world.

They are agreed that God is the Creator of all the acts of His servants, even as He is the Creator of their essences: that all that they do, be it good or evil, is in accordance with God's decree, predestination, desire and will; otherwise they would not have been servants, subject to a Lord, and created.

They are agreed that every breath they draw, every glance they make, and every motion they perform, is by virtue of a faculty which God originates in them, and a capacity which He creates for them at the same time as their actions, neither before them nor after them, and that no action can be performed without these. They are agreed that they are accredited with acts and merit in a true sense, for which they are rewarded and punished, and on account of which God issued command and prohibition, and announced promises and threats.

They are agreed that God does with His servants whatever He wishes, and decrees for them however He desires, whether that be to their advantage or not: for the creation is His creation, and the command is His command. They are agreed that all God's dealings with His servants—kindness, health, security, faith, guidance, favour—are only a condescension on His part: if He had not acted thus, it would still have been quite feasible. This is in no way incumbent upon God: for if God had been obliged to follow any such course of action, He would not have been deserving of praise and gratitude.

They are agreed that reward and punishment are not a question of merit, but of God's will, generosity and justice: men do not deserve eternal punishment on account of sins from which they have afterwards desisted, neither do they deserve eternal and unlimited reward because of a limited number of good deeds. They are agreed that if God should punish all who dwell in heaven and earth, He would not be unjust to them, and that if He should bring every unbeliever into Paradise, it would not be an impossible thing: for creation is His creation, and command is His command. But He has stated that He will bless believers eternally, and punish unbelievers eternally, and He is true in what He says, and what He states is the truth.

They are agreed that the absolute threat of God applies to unbelievers, and the absolute promise to those who perform good works. Some have maintained that remission of minor sins is secured by the avoidance of major sins. They make the possibility of the remission of major sins to depend on the Divine will and the Prophet's intercession. They are agreed upon confirming all that God has mentioned in His Book about intercession, and all that has come down in the stories told of the Prophet.

They believe in the Path, holding that it is a bridge stretched over hell. They believe in the Balance, holding that the deeds of men will be weighed. They believe that God will deliver from hell every man in whose heart there is an atom's weight of faith, in accordance with the Tradition. They believe that heaven and hell are eternal, but created, enduring for ever and ever without passing away or being destroyed; and similarly that their inhabitants continue in them eternally, blessed or punished for ever, with a bliss that never ends, or a punishment that never ceases.

According to their view, those Muslims who commit major sins are believers by virtue of the faith which they possess, but evil-doers because of the corruption which is in them. They hold that it is right to pray behind any Imam, whether he be a man of piety or a sinner. They also hold that it is right to pray for every person who dies, provided he be one of those who turn to Mecca. They hold that the observance of Friday, and the assemblies of Muslims, and feasts, is binding upon every Muslim who has no legitimate excuse, under the leadership of any Imam, be he pious or sinful; and likewise the Holy War and the Pilgrimage. They hold that the Caliphate is true, and that it resides in the house of Quraish. They are agreed on the precedence of Abū Bakr, 'Umar, 'Uthmān and 'Alī. They hold that it is right to imitate the Companions and the holy men of old, but are silent as to the disputes which existed between them, holding however that these in no way detracted from the 'better portion' foreordained to them by God.

They believe that every man concerning whom the Prophet testified that he would enter Paradise is in fact in Paradise, and that such a man will not be punished in hell. They hold that it is not right to take the sword against governors, even though they commit wrong. They hold that it is the duty of all, so far as they are able, to do good, and to refrain from doing evil, with kindness, mercy, considerateness, compassion, goodness, and gentleness of speech. They believe in the punishment of the grave, and the inquisition of Munkar and Nakīr. They believe in the ascension of the Prophet, and that he was carried to the seventh heaven, and to whatever God willed, in a single night, while waking, in the flesh. They attest the veracity of visions, holding that they are tidings of good cheer to believers, or warning, to give them pause. Lastly, they maintain that when a man dies, or is slain, it is in the fullness of his destiny: they do not agree that a man's destiny can be thought of as falling suddenly, but hold that when it comes, it comes at its proper time, and cannot be put back or forward a single hour.

(From *The Doctrine of the Sufis*.)

Of the many issues dividing the 'rationalist' Mu'tazilites from their fundamentalist opponents, embodied most forcefully in the person of Aḥmad ibn Ḥanbal (d. 241/855), none was felt to be more crucial than the question whether the Koran was eternal or created. Though rationalistic argument was advanced by both sides to support their respective positions, what was at stake was far more than the formulation of an intellectually acceptable theory. If the Koran were allowed to be created, the danger was great that it might next be alleged by those steeped in Neoplatonist thought that God's Word as revealed to Muhammad through the mediation of the archangel Gabriel shared with all created things the imperfection arising from their association with matter.

The Koran itself provides no clear lead to those anxious to prove its eternity, for all the ingenious interpretations of

> Nay, but it is a glorious Koran,
> in a guarded tablet.

The best that al-Ash'arī (d. 324/935), the ex-Mu'tazilī who did more than any other man to defeat the school of theology to which he formerly belonged, could do by way of enlisting scriptural authority was to quote Koran 16: 42:

> The only words We say to a thing, when We
> desire it, is that We say to it, 'Be,'
> and it is.

Upon the thread of that slender text he hangs a wonderfully ingenious scholastic argument. 'If the Koran had been created, God would have said to it "Be!" But the Koran is His speech, and it is impossible that His speech should be spoken to. For this would necessitate a second speech, and we should have to say of this second speech and its relation to a third speech what we say of the first speech and its relation to a second speech. But this would necessitate speeches without end—which is false. And if this is false, it is false that the Koran is created.'[1]

The theologians, particularly those of the Ḥanbalī school, turned to the reported sayings of Muhammad to buttress their argument that the Koran was uncreated. A tract composed by the eminent Ḥanbalī Ḍiyā' al-Dīn al-Maqdisī of Damascus (who was born in 569/1174) shows that the controversy was still alive so long after al-Mutawakkil proscribed the Muʿtazilī view as heresy. In or about the year 630/1232 al-Maqdisī received a letter from a correspondent in Amid (Diyarbekr) informing him that a man had come to that city who denied the authenticity of the statement that 'the Koran would return to God.' The doctrine thus summarized was felt to be consequential upon the major thesis that the Koran is uncreated and that it 'originated' out of God.

Ḍiyā al-Dīn begins his defence of the orthodox position by quoting two very familiar Traditions of the Prophet: (1) 'The religion issued a stranger, and shall return as it issued.' (2) 'The Hour shall not strike until there is no more said on the earth, God, God!' He claimed that these Traditions justified acceptance of the pronouncement reported on the authority not only of the Prophet himself but also of several Companions, Followers, and other leaders of Islam. This statement is contained in the words ascribed to ʿAmr ibn Dīnār al-Makkī (who died about 125/742–3): 'I have found our shaikhs since the last seventy years saying, The Koran is the Speech of God, from Him it issued and to Him it shall return.'

The author gives the names of ten Companions whom ʿAmr ibn Dīnār definitely met; he also mentions as an authority—independent of Sufyān ibn ʿUyaina (d. 198/813–14)—Abū Jaʿfar Aḥmad ibn Sinān al-Wāsiṭī, the date of whose death is variously given as between 250/864 and 259/872–3. In a marginal note he cites five additional authorities for the statement; the list is slightly puzzling, for whereas the last four were more or less contemporaries and of an age to report from ʿAmr ibn Dīnār, the first, ʿAbd Allāh ibn Masʿūd, was of course a Companion and died in 32/652–3, before ʿAmr ibn Dīnār was born. This later insertion, to which the author specifically

[1] *Revelation and Reason in Islam*, pp. 24–5.

refers in one of his autograph entries in the unique manuscript in which the tract is preserved, concludes with a closely similar statement put into the mouth of Aḥmad ibn Ḥanbal by his closest disciple Abū Bakr Aḥmad ibn Muḥammad ibn al-Ḥajjāj: 'I have met Traditionalists, theologians, and lawyers at Mecca, Medina, Kufa, Basra, Damascus, the Frontiers, and Khurasan, and I have seen them to be orthodox; I asked the lawyers concerning it, and every one said, The Koran is the Speech of God, uncreated, from Him it issued and to Him it shall return.'

This concludes the introductory exposition. The author next states that this question—the eternity of the Koran and its return to God—was debated at Baghdad during the time of 'the shaikhs of our shaikhs,' and that a comprehensive answer was written in a book called *al-Burhān fī nuṣrat al-Qur'ān* by Abū Zaid Ja'far ibn Zaid ibn 'Abd al-Razzāq al-Sha'mī al-Baghdādī. There now follows the author's presentation of his chains of authority for various versions of the formula.

(1) 'Alī ibn Abī Ṭālib, the Prophet's kinsman and fourth caliph, is reported to have said: 'It (sc. the Koran) is neither creator nor created, but it is the Speech of Almighty God, from Him it issued and to Him it shall return.' The author's immediate authority for this report is Ibn Sukaina of Baghdad (519–607/1125–1210), a most eminent Traditionist under whom he once studied. Ḍiyā' al-Dīn adds that the narration is given in the *Kitāb al-Sunna* of al-Lālakā'ī (d. 418/1027), a work no longer extant.

(2) 'Abd Allāh ibn 'Abbās, the Prophet's cousin (died between 68/687 and 70/689), is reported to have said to a man whom he heard using the expression O Lord of the Koran, 'Fie! The Koran is the Speech of God, and is not subject to a Lord; from Him it issued and to Him it shall return.' The report was received by the author from Abū Ja'far al-Ṣaidalānī (509–603/1115–1207) at Isfahan; it is also stated to occur in al-Lālakā'ī's *Kitāb al-Sunna*, and to be celebrated.

(3) 'Amr ibn Dīnār is quoted for the saying first reported above, with Sufyān ibn 'Uyaina as the transmitter. The author's immediate informants are Ibn Abī Jamīl al-Qurashī (499–580/1106–84) whom he heard at Damascus, and Ibn Sukaina. Sufyān ibn 'Uyaina was in the Great Mosque at Mecca, when the celebrated Bishr al-Marīsī (d. 218/833) entered, the redoubtable champion of the doctrine that the Koran was created. A man said to Sufyān, 'O Abū Muḥammad, do you know this man?' Sufyān said, 'Who is he?' The man replied, 'Bishr al-Marīsī.' 'And what does he say?' asked Sufyān. The man answered, 'He says, the Koran is created.' 'Glory

be to God!' Sufyān exclaimed. 'I heard 'Amr ibn Dīnār sixty years since say, God is the Creator and all beside Him is created except the Koran; verily from Him it is issued and to Him it shall return.' Since it was in 124/741–2 that Sufyān, then a lad of 14, met 'Amr ibn Dīnār, we are able to date this incident at about the year 184/800. Apart from certain weaknesses in the chain of transmission, it seems unlikely that Sufyān could at this date have been in ignorance of the notorious views of al-Marīsī, seeing that the latter admitted, certainly before his death in 218/833, that he had been holding them for forty years; in another story Sufyān is reported as urging that al-Marīsī should be killed.

The next section, where the author again draws upon Ibn Sukaina back to al-Khallāl (d. 439/1047), and therefore conceivably upon the latter's writings, gives the text of the pronouncement of Ibn Sinān al-Wāsiṭī to which he had referred earlier. This strongly anti-Muʿtazilite statement of a man whose respectability as a Traditionist is widely attested is as follows: 'Whoever asserts that the Koran is two things, or that the Koran is a relation by God, he is a heretic and an unbeliever in God. This Koran is the Koran which God sent down by the tongue of Gabriel upon Muhammad, God bless him and give him peace; it is neither changed nor substituted; *falsehood comes not to it from before it nor from behind it; a sending down from One All-wise, All-laudable* (Kor. 41: 42), as Almighty God said, *Say: If men and jinn banded together to produce the like of this Koran, they would never produce its like* (Kor. 17: 90). If any man were to take an oath that he would not speak that day, and then recited the Koran, or prayed and recited the Koran, or used the Muslim salutation during prayer, he would not have broken his oath. Nothing can be held comparable with the Speech of God. The Koran is the Speech of God; from Him it issued, and to Him it shall return; nothing belonging to God is created, neither His Attributes, His Names, nor His Knowledge.'

The last paragraphs of the tract are concerned with the problems of the manner in which the Koran shall return to God. The author begins with a Tradition, which is included by Ibn Māja (d. 273/886) in his *Sunan*: 'The Book of God shall be come upon one night, and in the morning the people shall find that not a verse of it is left, either in the earth or in the heart of any Muslim.' The analysis of the double chain of authorities cited by Ibn Māja reveals two weak links at the same spot, namely the immediate transmission from Abū Mālik al-Ashjaʿī, held inclined to be apocryphal as professing Murji'ite views.

The doctrine of the uncreated nature of the Koran was one of the many matters which engaged the attention of that greatest of Ḥanbalī scholars, the courageous and indefatigable Ibn Taimīya (661–728/1263–1328). A very useful summary of his views on this matter is given in a *fatwā* (legal pronouncement) which he issued in reply to the following question: 'A certain man has stated that God did not speak to Moses directly; He only created the speech, and the voice in the bush, and Moses heard the bush speak, not God; he has also asserted that God did not speak the Koran to Gabriel, but that he merely took it from the Preserved Tablet. Is he right or not?'

Ibn Taimīya naturally condemns this view; the man holding it is to be called upon to repent, and if he refuses, he is to be slain. The first person in Islam to utter this heresy was al-Jaʿd ibn Dirham; he was slaughtered at the ʿĪd al-Adḥā by Khālid ibn ʿAbd Allāh al-Qasrī (d. 126/744). Thereafter the same view was taken up by Jahm ibn Ṣafwān, the eponymous founder of the Jahmīya sect, who was put to death by Salama ibn Aḥwar in Khorasan (in 128/746); it was an element in the wider Jahmīya denial of God's Attributes, so that they asserted that God had not the attributes of knowledge, life, omnipotence, and speech, and stated that the Koran was created. The Muʿtazilites who followed ʿAmr ibn ʿUbaid (d. 145/762) thereupon adopted this doctrine to which they added other heresies; God really spoke to Moses, but He created speech for this purpose, either in the bush, the air, or something else; they would not allow to God any attributes, including speech.

All orthodox theologians are agreed that God actually spoke to Moses, and that the Koran is the uncreated Speech of God. Abu 'l-Qāsim al-Ṭabarī (i.e. al-Lālakāʾī) enumerated some fifty-five or more Followers and religious leaders—apart from Companions—who supported this doctrine in different ages; if he had cared to collect the names of Traditionists who subscribed to it, his list would have run into thousands. He quoted on two chains of tradition the remark made by ʿAlī ibn Abī Ṭālib at the battle of Siffin: 'I have not appointed as arbitrator any created being; I have appointed as arbitrator naught save the Koran.' He also cited various other stories as supporting evidence, including the incident of Ibn ʿAbbās at the funeral, and the remark of ʿAmr ibn Dīnār about the shaikhs since seventy years.

Ibn Taimiya then lists many prominent theologians and lawyers who have condemned the heresy of a created Koran, including the four founders of the orthodox schools of jurisprudence, and the great al-Bukhārī; Abu 'l-Ḥasan ʿAlī ibn ʿĀṣim (105–201/723–816) is even reported to have said that those who asserted that God had a son (sc. the Christians) were not more infidel than those who denied that God spoke. After a subtle theological discussion of the claim that it was the bush and not God which spoke to Moses, he returns to the ancient formula that 'the Koran is the Speech of God, from Him it appeared and to Him it shall return,' a formula which we have seen to rest ultimately on 'Amr ibn Dīnār's reported statements. This he describes as the meaning of Aḥmad ibn Ḥanbal's assertion that 'the Speech of God is of God and is not separate from Him.' Ibn Taimīya quotes in support of this formula the Tradition, accepted by Aḥmad ibn Ḥanbal and others, 'Ye shall not return unto God with anything more excellent than that which issued from Him,' which is glossed as being a reference to the Koran.

The rest of the *fatwā* is taken up with a theological discussion of the true meaning of the expression—now assumed as invulnerable—that the Koran issued from God. It is not correct, Ibn Taimīya asserts, to argue that the Speech of God by issuing from God departed out of His Essence and dwelt in another. When a mortal speaks, his speech does not depart out of his essence and dwell in another; when the discourse of the Prophet is quoted, this does not make the discourse any other man's but the Prophet's; therefore the same reasoning is *a fortiori* applicable to God's Speech. When the Koran is recited, the voice is that of the reciter but the Speech is God's.

(From The Islamic Quarterly, Vol. III, pp. 16–41.)

When Abū Ḥāmid al-Ghazālī took the decision to throw in his lot with Sunnite theology and to condemn philosophical speculation, he did not hesitate to demand execution as the right penalty for holding the following opinions: that the world and all substances are eternal; that God's knowledge is universal and does not extend to particular events occurring to individuals; and that there is a resurrection of the soul but not of the body. This declaration by the champion of Revelation against the advocates of Reason, a turning-point in the intellectual history of Islam, took place in the very province and during the selfsame generation as produced the man universally famed as the great spokesman of scepticism, that sad hedonist and gay parodist, mathematician, astronomer, metaphysician and occasional poet, 'Umar al-Khaiyām or, as FitzGerald advertized his name, Omar Khayyám. It is necessary to keep in mind the circumstances of his half-despairing, half-indifferent defence of traditional Persian doubt, if one is to savour to the full the subtle qualities of his poetic sallies.

1

All they who threaded meaning's gem
   Upon the cord philosophy
   Spake much upon the Deity;
But little knowledge was in them.

Unravelling those secrets' skein,
   None ever found its origin,
   But having each his tale to spin
Each fell at last asleep again.

2

And these, the choicest and the best
   Of lowly Earth's ingenious breed,
   Mounted on speculation's steed
Still strive to scale Heaven's highest crest.

But Thou, sublime upon Thy throne,
   Beholdest with indifferent eyes
   Their reasons, reeling like Thy skies,
Defeated by the great Unknown.

3

Thou, Lord, didst mingle of Thy skill
   The dust and water of my clay;
   Thy fingers spun, for my array,
Wool or fine linen, at Thy will.

Since Thou hast written long ago
   Whatever good I may have sought,
   Whatever ill through me is wrought,
What, Lord, remains for me to do?

4

Ah, that at Fortune's fickle lust
   We waste and wither to no goal,
   That in the wide inverted bowl
Of Heaven we are ground to dust.

Woe and alas, that as the eye
   This instant flickers in its lid
   We, who were pleased in naught we did,
Unwilling born, unwilling die.

5

Though never face more radiant were,
   No tresses lovelier than mine,
   My cheeks the tulip's glow outshine,
My stature slender as the fir:

'Tis still unclear, for what sublime
   And purposed end so cunningly
   The Artist of Eternity
Arrayed me in the bower of Time.

6

What hath befallen Heaven's wheel
   That ever on the base bestows
   Great mills of gain, cool porticoes,
Warm pools their weariness to heal?

The noble, thanks to those same skies,
   Must pledge their all, to get them bread
   Before they mount their narrow bed:
Such justice justly I despise.

7

Surrender not thy flesh to woe
   For the injustice of Man's fate,
   Nor yield thy soul inconsolate
To grieve for friends lost long ago.

Give not that precious heart of thine
   Save to the loved one's locks, to bind:
   Scatter not life upon the wind,
Nor live one moment without wine.

8

Thou who art wholly unaware
   How the world's order is designed,
   Since thy foundations are the Wind
Thy structure is no more than Air.

Thy being is a boundary
   That runs betwixt twain nothingness:
   About thee all is substanceless,
Thyself, therein, Nonentity.

9

Ah, that life's precious capital
    Was spilled so soon and drained away,
    That Destiny in ambush lay
For many hearts, to slay them all:

And, for the world that after waits,
    No man has ever come from there
    To bring us tidings, how they fare
Whose journey lies beyond its gates.

10

I never sipped, as I recall,
    The limpid wine of glad relief,
    Without the hand of sudden grief
Poured me its cup of bitter gall.

I never dipped in joy my bread
    Into the salt of any friend,
    But that as surely in the end
My heart in sorrow broke and bled.

11

I cannot count what profits Doom
    Our coming here, our being sped,
    Nor tell the pattern that our thread
Of Being weaves upon life's loom.

I only know the brazen Sky
    Whose conflagration fires the air
    Burns all things lovely, and the fair
Converts to dust, without one sigh.

12

The secrets of Eternity
    Are far beyond our finite ken:
    We cannot riddle what the Pen
Of Fate has scribed for you and me.

In casual converse we engage
    Behind the curtain of our day;
    But when the curtain falls, the play
Is done, and desolate the stage.

13

Look not for happiness from Fate,
　For all life's yield is but a breath:
　Each grain of dust records the death
Of some once lordly potentate.

The world's affairs, as so they seem,
　Nay, the whole universe complete
　Is a delusion and a cheat,
A fantasy, an idle dream.

14

Since God desired not in His might
　What in my weakness I designed,
　I do not think that I shall find
What I have willed to be the right.

If rectitude doth all belong　.
　To what He only wished to be,
　What I desired, as now I see,
Could scarce be otherwise than wrong.

15

They who encompassed all high wit
　And of fine words the mastery bore,
　Who in discovery of deep lore
A lantern for their fellows lit:

Those never won to find a way
　Out of the darkness of our night:
　They had their legend to recite,
And then in endless slumber lay.

16

Grave cadi of the learned brow,
　We idlers far outlabour thee;
　And, spite our drunken revelry,
We are still soberer than thou.

We drink the liquor grapes have bled,
　But thou the blood of fellow-men:
　Justly declare—which of us, then,
The greater share of blood has shed?

17

How long, O Lord, must I endure
    Life's mean deceits and trickeries?
    How long must I consume the lees,
And never taste the liquor pure?

I would Life's saki, with his hand
    Still dripping with foul treachery,
    Might pass my bowl of life to me,
To pour its dregs into the sand.

18

This little while, till Fate shall smite
    And life's last fever burn the brow,
    Come, let us drink, today and now,
This wine of our supreme delight.

For when the heavens do their worst,
    In the dread hour when we must leave,
    No quarter will the heavens give
Nor even water for our thirst.

19

Much have I wandered o'er the face
    Of earth, by mountain and by plain,
    And all my wandering was in vain:
The world is not a better place.

Though pain has plagued my every day,
    I am contented, truth to tell;
    For if my life passed never well,
At least it passed right well away.

20

Khayyám, he earns the high disdain
    And merited contempt of doom
    Who impotently sits in gloom
Beneath Time's avalanche of pain.

Then fill the crystal beaker up
    And drink to the lamenting lute,
    Before the day its voice is mute,
And shattered on the rock thy cup.

21

Yon brave inhabitants who lie
    All turned to dust and in the tomb
    Fulfil their dark and dusty doom:
Their scattered motes asunder fly.

What was the potion they partook
    That, till the Day of Reckoning,
    Lost to themselves and everything,
All loves, all labours they forsook?

22

Wine is a ruby liquefied,
    Quarried within the hollow bowl;
    The cup's a body, and its soul
The liquor's coruscating tide.

Yon gleaming glass of crystal clear
    Now laughing with the crimson wine
    Enshrines the life-blood of the vine,
And all its glitter is a tear.

23

No man hath ever found the way
    Behind this veil of mystery,
    No mind unravelled utterly
The tangle of the world's array.

No other lodging-place know I
    Except the earth's heart, dark and cold:
    These fables are not quickly told—
Drink, these brief moments ere we die!

24

Riddle me this: a bowl I know
    Which Reason doth high praise allow,
    And in affection on its brow
A hundred kisses doth bestow.

Yet Time, the fickle potter, who
    So skilfully designed a cup
    So fragile, loves to lift it up
And dash it to the earth anew.

25

Now, in this hour ere night descend
   And griefs assail and slay the soul,
   Bid them bring forth the crimson bowl
And pour the wine, beloved friend.

Think not, my foolish, silly swain,
   Thou art as gold, that on a day
   Men should commit thee to cold clay
Thereafter to bring out again.

26

The wine and the beloved for me!
   Take you your convent and your church,
   If after Paradise ye search:
If I'm for Hell, so let it be.

Declare, what shortcoming ye see
   Me guilty of, since long ago
   The Eternal Artist drew me so
Upon the Slate of Destiny.

27

The several particles discrete
   That in the crystal cup unite,
   No drunkard's hand would deem it right
To take and shatter it complete.

Whose was the tender love that made
   Those lovely hands, so soft and white,
   Those beauteous faces? By whose spite
Were they in utter ruin laid?

28

Those venturers who took not rest
   But wore the world out with their feet,
   And measured Earth and Heaven complete
Still urgent on their boundless quest:

I do not know, when all was done
   And their far labours left behind,
   If they more clearly had in mind
God's Truth, than when they first begun.

29

O Time, who dost thyself confess
  The wrongs by mortal men endured,
  The convent where thou art immured
Is dedicate to ruthlessness.

Thy blessings on the base alone
  Are showered; men of nobler part
  Thou punishest; which proves thou art
A donkey, or a doting crone.

30

Lovers, and all in disarray,
  Dishevelled, drunken and distraught
  Where the fair idols dwell, and naught
But wine to worship, this glad day—

With selfhood to oblivion hurled
  We stand emancipate, alone
  Attached to God's eternal Throne
As at the dawning of the world.

31

If I have never sought to thread
  The pearl obedience on life's cord,
  If I have never swept, dear Lord,
The dust of sin from my hoar head:

Yet I despair not to attain
  The threshold of Thy throne of grace,
  Since at no time, and in no place
I ever said that One was twain.

32

There shall be Paradise, men say,
  With dark-eyed maidens of delight,
  Tart wine to taste through all the night,
And honey sweet to suck all day.

If then the wine and well-loved friend
  We worship, wherein lies the shame,
  Seeing that there awaits the same
When all life's tasks are at an end?

33

The pious say, all sinful men
   Who dare God's holy Laws defy,
   In whatsoever guise they die
Shall likewise be raised up again.

Wherefore we pass our lives away
   With the beloved, and the cup,
   That haply so we may spring up
When breaks the Resurrection Day.

34

A stark and solemn truth I say,
   Not as in parables to preach:
   We are but counters, all and each,
That Heaven moveth at its play.

We stir awhile, as if at will,
   About the chessboard of the days,
   Till in the box of death Time lays
Our pawns, to be for ever still.

35

If thou shouldst win into thy grasp
   A goodly bowl from niggard Fate,
   Drink wine, where good men congregate,
Drink ever, where the thirsty gasp.

For He, Who this world's palace reared
   In splendour, small attention owes
   To thy puffed-out mustachios
And my pathetic, blustering beard.

36

One hand the Holy Book doth hold,
   One clasps the bowl of flaming wine:
   Now only lawful joys are mine,
Now with the lawless I make bold.

Beneath the skies' uplifted span,
   The turquoise-marbled dome on high,
   Not utter infidel am I
And neither wholly Mussulman.

37

The manner that I look upon
 This life's affairs, and analyse,
 The whole round world, as view my eyes,
Is vanity, and better gone.

Then to Almighty God be praise,
 For truly, wheresoe'er I turn,
 Naught but vexation I discern,
And disillusion all my days.

38

I know not why the Hand whose joy
 Was to create in order due
 The temperaments, exact and true,
Is pleased to sap them and destroy.

If they were well, as was His aim,
 Why did He shatter them again?
 And if they were not well, why then
Since He designed them, who's to blame?

39

Old Age, that all injustice wreaks,
 Experienced in human hurts,
 To quince-like pallor now converts
The faded cherries of my cheeks.

Life's corner-stone, the roof and walls
 And gates of its proud edifice
 Crash down; my tenement of bliss
In utter desolation falls.

40

Best of all friends I ever had,
 Give heed to this my counsel wise:
 Think not on the unrooted skies,
Let not their swivelling make thee sad.

Best in contentment's quiet court
 Choose thou thy corner, and there squat,
 Regarding with amusement what
The heavens contrive in their poor sport.

(From *Omar Khayyám: a New Version*.)

The argument between sect and sect within Islam was paralleled by
a polemic between Islam on the one hand and the 'unbelievers' on
the other. The attacks on Christianity and Judaism were particularly sharp, having begun, as we have seen in an earlier chapter, in
the Koran itself. Ibn Ḥazm when he entered these lists became a
very different character from the gentle amateur of the Art of Love
as revealed in *The Ring of the Dove*. Abū Ḥāmid al-Ghazālī, having
sharpened hs dialectic claws in the battle against philosophy and
the campaign against the Ismāʿīlī heresy, turned with an almost
casual air to the easy task of demolishing the Christian doctrine of
the Divinity of Jesus. This little labour he accomplished to his
evident satisfaction in a curious commentary on the opening verses
of the Gospel of St John. What makes his essay even more bizarre
is that he appears—as the following extract demonstrates—to have
laboured under the delusion that the language in which that Gospel
was originally composed was Coptic!

That Jesus was not Divine

We now turn to a final point, and shall examine one of their greatest
cruxes on which they (the Christians) rely to prove the Divinity of
Jesus, upon whom be peace—the opening verses of John's Gospel:
'In the beginning was the Word, and the Word was with God, and
the Word was God. The same was in the beginning with God. All
things were made by him; and without him was not anything made
that was made.' So on and so forth, to the end of the passage: 'And
the Word was made flesh, and dwelt among us, and we beheld his
glory.' (John 1: 1–14.)

The opening of this passage has no connexion at all with establishing the Divinity of Jesus, upon whom be peace. For they believe
that the Essence of God is one in substance, but that it possesses
various aspects. If it be considered as determined by an attribute
whose existence does not depend upon the prior existence of another
attribute—such as existence itself—then that is what is called by
them the Person of the Father. If it be considered as qualified by
an attribute, such as knowledge, whose existence does depend upon
the prior existence of another attribute—for the attribution of
knowledge to an essence in fact depends upon its being already
qualified by existence—then that is what is called by them the
Person of the Son, and the Word. Finally, if it be considered as
determined by its Essence being intellected by itself, then that is
what they call the Holy Ghost. So the Father connotes the idea of
existence, the Word (or the Son) connotes the idea of a Knower,

and the Holy Ghost connotes the idea of the Essence of the Creator being intellected by Itself. Such is the purport of this terminology: the Essence of God would be One in substance, but is qualified by each of these three hypostases.

Others say that if the Essence is considered *qua* Essence, without account being taken of any attribute, such an approach would see It as Pure Intellect, and this is what is called the Person of the Father. If It is considered as intellecting Itself, then this would give the idea of the Intelligent, what is called the Person of the Son, or the Word. If It is considered as determined by Its Essence being intellected by Itself, then that corresponds with what is called the Person of the Idea of the Intellected, or the Holy Ghost. According to this terminology the Intellect represents the Essence of God alone, the term 'Father' being a synonym for the Intellect; the Intelligent equals His Essence as determined by Its intellecting Itself, the 'Son' or the 'Word' being synonyms for the Intelligent; Intellectedness is equivalent to God whose Essence is intellected by Him, with the synonym 'Holy Ghost'.

Both these terminologies establish the Word as expressing the Essence qualified by knowledge and intellect, and likewise the Son. Each, the Word and the Son, would therefore be a 'Person' by which is indicated the Knower or the Intelligent. So the phrase 'In the beginning was the Word' means, 'In the beginning was the Knower'; the phrase 'and the Word was with God' means, 'and the Knower never ceased to be an attribute of God,' i.e. this attribute never ceased to appertain to God; 'was' here means 'never ceased to be.' The phrase 'and the Word was God' means, 'this Word—by which is indicated the Knower—that Knower was God.' The phrase 'The same was in the beginning with God' means, 'God never ceased to possess the attribute of what is indicated by this expression, namely the Knower, which is what is indicated by the term "the Word." ' It *is* God, because we are informed expressly that 'the Word was God'; this is intended to put an end to the speculation of those who may believe that the Knower—what is indicated by the term 'the Word'—is other than God.

Such is their belief regarding these Persons; such are the words of the commentator on their Gospel in the opening of this chapter. If the ideas are correct, there is no need to quarrel about phraseologies or terminologies. It is clear from their comments that the opening of this chapter contains no indication whatever of the Divinity of Jesus, upon whom be peace.

There remain two ambiguous passages in this chapter which give rise to misapprehension. The first is: 'There was a man sent from

God, whose name was John. The same came for a witness, to bear witness of the Light, that all men through him might believe. He was not that Light, but was sent to bear witness of that Light. That was the true Light, which lighteth every man that cometh into the world. He was in the world, and the world was made by him, and the world knew him not.' (John 1: 6–10.)

We would observe that the one described in these words as never ceasing to be in the world, and the world having been made by him. is *either* the Manhood isolated from its connexion with the Godhead (or in respect of its connexion therewith), *or* the Godhead *qua* Godhead (or in respect of its connexion with the Manhood, i.e. its manifestation therein), *or* the Third Reality.

The only one of these alternatives which is correct is the Godhead *qua* Godhead. The idea that it should be the Manhood necessarily fails, alike whether we hold it isolated from its connexion with the Godhead or in respect of its connexion therewith. The former of these two alternatives is obviously incorrect; the latter equally so, since its connexion with the Godhead occurred in time; for that connexion only took place after it had been created. How therefore can the Manhood be described as having made the world, and as having never ceased to be in it? The same may be said of the Third Reality: óne of the two parts of the Third Reality is the Manhood, which was created in time; therefore the Third Reality was non-existent before the Manhood was created; so it cannot possibly be described as above-mentioned. The identical verdict applies to the Godhead as manifesting in the Manhood: its manifestation therein only took place when it created the Manhood; so if we judge the Godhead as above-mentioned in respect of this connexion which took place in time, it becomes impossible to hold it qualified in the manner mentioned.

These attributes therefore refer only to God, glorious is His Name, *qua* God, not in respect of His conjunction with the Manhood, and not in respect of the conjunction of the Manhood with Him. These words of the Gospel must therefore be taken as applying to God, great and glorious is He. So the words amount to the following: 'but was sent to bear witness of that Light. That was the true Light, by which the Truth lighteth every man; because the Truth, glorious is His Name, is He who guideth every man by the Light of His knowledge unto the real knowledge, and, in lighting him, maketh him aware of the subtle secrets of all that He hath made, secrets which cannot be attained by any intellect save by the Light of His guidance.' This meaning is so clear that it requires no long exposition. The term 'Light' is used elsewhere in the Gospel with the meaning of 'guidance', as when Jesus says: 'As long as I am in the world, I am the light of the world' (John 9: 5); John declares this in the 22nd chapter. The same declaration occurs in chapter 25: 'I am come a light into the world' (John 12: 46). These declarations confirm our interpretation of 'light' as connoting 'guidance'.

The second ambiguity occurs at the end of the chapter: 'And the Word was made flesh, and dwelt among us, and we beheld his glory' (John 1: 14). It is necessary to quote the phrase as it occurs in the Coptic, in order to show how they have slipped up and deviated from its original interpretation, diverting the text from its corresponding meaning into one that is diametrically opposed to intuitive reason. The Coptic reads: *ow oh pysagy afer ow sarks*. This means: 'And the Word made flesh'; for *afer* in Coptic means 'made'. Taken in this original sense there remains no difficulty at all; the phrase declares explicitly that the Knower, who stands for the hypostasis of the Word (identified as God—'And the Word was God'), 'made flesh, and dwelt among us, and we beheld his glory'—i.e. that flesh which God made was none other than Jesus, upon whom be peace; it was he who appeared, and whose glory was seen.

They excuse their deviation from this manifest sense by arguing that the word *afer* is used in Coptic to mean both 'made' and 'was made'. Their viewpoint certainly calls for some excuse. But indeed it is quite laughable; for when a word is equivocal, its meaning in a given context is specified as the simplest alternative indicating that the intention is that particular sense. Then what are you up to, my friend, contesting with reason which requires the word to be taken in the sense we have pointed out? Again, even allowing for the fact that this word in the original Coptic has a double meaning, the translator has here undoubtedly transgressed against the rule governing equivocal expressions. In cases of doubt, the meaning of an equivocal expression is determined by its context; in the present instance however the translator decided to divert the expression from what *must* be its intention and to take it in a sense which reason declares could *not* have been intended. In that way he was able to get the interpretation that God the Knower 'was made flesh'.

I know of nobody who has been so impudent towards God as this sect. No, by God! There is no disgrace more shocking than that of a people who believe that God the Knower was buried. They affront God by actually making that statement, saying that one should fast on a particular Saturday 'because the Maker of the world was buried on that day'; that is explicitly stated in their canons as recorded on the authority of their leaders and apostles.

> And whomsoever He leads astray, thou
> wilt not find for him a protector to
> direct.   (Kor. 18: 16.)

'But we take this passage in that sense because the context swings preponderantly in that direction.' So someone may say. To this we reply that when a preponderant probability conflicts with reason, it should be rejected as unreliable. Incidentally, to call such an interpretation 'a preponderant probability' is sheer ignorance, and whoever propounds such a view has no scientific guide to put him on the path of truth.

It would be quite sufficient to dispose of this ambiguity if we confined ourselves to this clear exposure of the way they have tampered with the text, so making it ambiguous. However, if we desire to settle the quarrel once and for all, we will concede that the word at issue has been used equivocally, and that the context surrounding it makes it probable that it should be taken as meaning 'was made' rather than 'made'. Even so, the solution of the ambiguity is clear enough; on this reckoning too, no intelligent man will hesitate for a moment to divert the word from its literal meaning. It is declared that the 'Word' mentioned at the beginning of the chapter is God: 'and the Word was God'. How then can one pronounce concerning God, that He *became flesh*?

This is how this statement is to be corrected. The 'Word' in their system stands for the Essence regarded as the attribute of knowledge or speech, as explained at the beginning of the chapter. It therefore indicates the Essence qualified by knowledge or speech. This usage is by no means peculiar to God; a dubious expression, however confused it may be, may quite properly and accurately be used to denote each particular thing to which it is applied. So 'the Word' can be employed to connote the Essence as defined by knowledge or speech, without any implication of the Essence having the attribute of corporeality or being disjoined from that attribute. Consequently, at the beginning of the chapter 'the Word' is applied to the Knower as disjoined from corporeality in fact, sc. God; while at the end of the chapter the same term is also applied to the Knower or the Speaker as having the attribute of corporeality in fact, sc. the Messenger. Therefore the phrase 'And the Word became flesh' means 'That God-Knower who was indicated by the term "the Word" was disjoined from corporeality, but now that indicated by the term has become a Knower having the attribute of corporeality, sc. the Messenger.' For when this term is employed to connote the Essence as defined by knowledge, it necessarily loses the meaning of the Knower.

All this depends on the concession that 'the Word' has been employed to connote the Essence *qua* Essence, as defined by an attribute. If it is claimed that that belongs exclusively to the Essence of God, then its application to Jesus, upon whom be peace, can only be metaphorical. That the meaning of the term is shared equally by both is fully established; that is one of the greatest justifications for the use of the metaphor. This interpretation is not rebutted by the objection that it runs contrary to the literal sense of the text; allegorical interpretation has no other purpose than to divert an expression from its literal sense, when there exists a substantial indication forbidding the expression to be retained in its proper connotation.

It may be objected that this interpretation is acceptable only if the discourse is then coherent, particularly in the case where God, glorious is His Name, is speaking. But when reason (we reply) decrees that it is impossible for the expression to retain its literal sense, then it must be interpreted allegorically. If such interpretation diverts the expression from its literal sense in the manner mentioned, and gives it a meaning which may well be that intended, then the literalist has no excuse left for opposing reason and the possibility of allegorical interpretation.

We will now demonstrate that the words of this text are in fact not incoherent, and that they can be construed as giving a perfectly plausible meaning on the lines of our interpretation. It is established that it is the Truth, glorious is His Name, who lightens with His Light 'every man that cometh' and unveils for him every secret; that much is clearly stated in this text: 'to bear witness of the Light. That was the true Light, which lighteth every man.' The phrase 'He was in the world' may well qualify 'the Light', and also the Truth, glorious is His Name; for Almighty God's guidance, His making clear every secret and His unveiling every ambiguity—that has never ceased to dwell in the world. The words 'and the world was made by him' qualify the Truth, glorious is His Name; that has been explicitly stated at the beginning of the chapter: 'All things were made by him.'

I should like to know what excuse there is for taking this to refer to Jesus, upon whom be peace, in the face of the clear statement occurring at the beginning of the chapter, describing God: 'and without him was not any thing made that was made.' The words 'he came unto his own' mean 'to the Truth's own appeared His Light', sc. His guidance and direction; since it is by His Light that every man is guided who follows the right path. The 'coming' of the Light here means its manifestation, since to describe abstract things as 'coming' can be taken as meaning their 'manifestation'. As for the words 'and his own received him not', the meaning of 'his own' is 'those who were called to guidance', i.e. 'His own who were called to His guidance did not receive His guidance'. The words 'But as many as received him' mean 'As for those who received His guidance', and these were not the same as those who did not receive it; this is proved by the use of the word 'as' to introduce the statement, for 'as' is a disjunctive particle. 'To them gave he power to become the sons of God': it would have been more natural to say 'to become His sons', only the writer avoided that preferring the explicit mention of the revered Name God, because of the noble relationship, in order to make a deeper impression on the souls of his readers. After that he said: 'even to them that believe on his name: Which were born, not of blood, nor of the will of the flesh, nor of the will of man, but of God', meaning that this sonship by virtue of which they obtained that noble relationship was not of the order of those sonships which are apt to result from the wills of men and their attention to women, with the resultant formation of flesh and blood, but rather the meaning is that extreme nearness and compassion of God towards them, as has been described above. Finally the writer connects up again with the beginning of the chapter, making it clear that it is a property of the Word, from which the idea of the Knower is derived, to be applied to the Knower alike whether He is disjoined from corporeality—such as the Essence of the Creator—or not disjoined, as with the essence of the Messenger.

In interpreting the doctrine of the hypostases, the Christians have followed a procedure which has obliged them to proclaim the existence, conceptually and objectively, of three Gods, distinct in their essences and natures, or else to deny the Essence of God, glorious is His Name. For they use the term 'Father' for the Essence as defined by fatherhood, 'Son' for the Essence as defined by sonship, and 'Holy Ghost' for the Essence as defined by the aspect of 'proceeding'. And after all that they still speak of One God!

If they are cornered in this matter and realize that the Essence of the Father as particularized by the attribute of Fatherhood cannot admit the attribute of Sonship—and the same argument applies to the Son and the Holy Spirit—and that it is not one of those *relative* essences, so as to be considered a father to one person and a son to another, they then state that the Essence is one, but that it is perfectly possible to describe it by all those attributes;

only 'when we describe It by one attribute, we imply the negation of whatever is different from it.' That is the pitch of their ignorance and stupidity: they proclaim the pre-eternity of these Essences and of their attributes. So the Essences are inseparably attached to the attributes, and the attributes are inseparably attaching to the Essences: whenever the thing attached to exists, the thing attaching to exists also, and whenever the thing attaching to is removed, the thing attached to is removed also. So if we suppose that the attribute attaching to the Essence is negated, we must also suppose the Essence Itself to be negated.—This is the meaning behind that solemn reference in the Holy Book:

> They are unbelievers
> who say, 'God is the Third of Three.' (Kor. 5: 73.)
> (*al-Radd al-jamīl.*)

ELEVEN

Parable and Anecdote

The purveying of fiction, and its application to various uses, had long been established as an entertainment and a method of moral and religious instruction in many of the lands which came to be united, whether closely or loosely, in Islamic civilization. Greece, Egypt, Mesopotamia, Persia and India all poured their tributaries into the Ocean of Story, to be drawn upon in turn by the Arab and Persian writers and poets. In this chapter we shall gather a few examples of parable and anecdote culled from the immensely rich literature of Islam. These apologues, myths, legends offer ample material for those interested to study the psychoogy and sociology of the peoples who loved and transmitted them, quite apart from their value and qualities as specimens of creative writing.

In the *Naurūz-nāma*, a learned and diverting dissertation on the history of the Persian New Year festival attributed to Omar Khayyám, we read the following fable.

The Invention of Wine

In the histories it is written that there once reigned in Herat a powerful and absolute monarch, having much treasure and property and a countless army; Khorasan was also under his sway. He was of the family of Jamshid, and his name was Shamiran; the village of Shamiran by Herat which is still extant was founded by him. He had a son called Bagham who was very brave, manly and strong; in those times there was no archer like him.

Now one day King Shamiran was seated on his veranda in company with his nobles, his son Badham also being in attendance on him, when by chance a phoenix came upon the scene; it uttered a loud cry, fluttered down and landed in front of the throne, a little way off. King Shamiran looked and saw a snake coiled around the neck of the phoenix; its head thrust down, it was set upon biting the phoenix.

'Heroes!' the king cried out. 'Which of you will rescue this phoenix from this snake and shoot an arrow straight at it?'

'It is your servant's task,' Badham replied, and he shot an arrow in such wise that he fastened the snake's head to the ground, no harm befalling the phoenix. The phoenix escaped, fluttered around there for a while, and then flew off.

By chance the next year on the same day King Shamiran was seated on his veranda, when that phoenix came again, fluttered over their heads, and landed on the very spot where the snake had been shot. He placed something on the ground with his beak, uttered a few cries, and flew off. The king looked, and saw the phoenix.

'What do you think?' he addressed the company. 'Is that the same phoenix as the one we rescued from the snake, and now it's returned this year and brought us a present by way of repayment? Look, it's hitting the ground with its beak. Go and see, and bring me what you find.'

Two or three of his courtiers went, and saw two or three seeds in all placed there. They picked them up, and brought them before King Shamiran's throne. The king looked, and saw that the seeds were very hard. He summoned the scholars and viziers and showed them the seeds.

'The phoenix has brought us these seeds as a present,' he said. 'What do you think? What ought we to do with these seeds?'

They all agreed that the seeds should be sown and carefully tended, to see what would appear by the end of the year. So the king gave the seeds to his gardener.

'Sow them in a corner of the garden,' he told him. 'And put a fence round them, so that no animals may get at them. Look out for birds too, and report progress from time to time.'

The gardener did as he was ordered. That was in the month of Nauruz. After some while a shoot sprang up from the seeds. The gardener informed the king, and the king and the learned men came and stood over the seedling.

'We've never seen such a shoot or such a leaf,' they stated. Then they went back.

In the course of time the shoots multiplied, the eyes became swollen, and clusters hung down from them resembling millet. The gardener came to the king and told him that there was no tree in the garden that looked more cheerful. The king went again with the scholars to look at the tree. He saw that the shoot had become a tree, and the clusters were all hanging down from it. He stood marvelling.

'We must be patient,' he said. 'We must wait till all the trees are in fruit, to see what sort of a tree this is.'

The clusters grew large, and the unripe grapes matured. Still they did not dare to touch them until autumn came, and the other fruits such as apples, pears, peaches and pomegranates were ripe. Then the king came into the garden and saw the grape-tree looking like a bride adorned. The clusters had grown huge and turned from green to black; they shone like agate, and one by one the grapes poured from them.

The scholars were all unanimous that these were the fruit of the tree. The tree was fully mature, and the grapes had begun to pour from the clusters. That was a sure sign that the virtue of the fruit lay in its juice. The juice must be gathered and put in a vat, to see what the result would be. No one dared put a grape into his mouth; they were afraid it might be poison and they would all be dead. So they put a vat in the garden and collected the grape-juice until the vat was full.

'Whatever you see happen, you're to let me know,' the king ordered the gardener. Then they went back.

When the grape-juice in the vat fermented, the gardener came and told the king.

'This is what's come from that tree. But I don't know whether it's poison or antidote.'

So they decided to take a murderer out of prison and give him some of the liquor to see what would happen. They acted accordingly; they gave some of the liquor to the murderer, and when he had drunk a little he made a wry face.

'Would you like some more?' they asked him.

'Yes,' he answered.

They gave him another drink, and he began to make merry and sing and dance about. He wasn't at all overawed by the king's presence.

'Give me one more drink,' he shouted. 'Then you can do what you like with me. Men are born to die.'

So they gave him a third drink. He swallowed it down, and his head became heavy. He dropped off to sleep, and did not come to his senses until the next day. When he had recovered consciousness they brought him before the king.

'What was that you drank yesterday, and how did you feel?' they asked him.

'I don't know what it was I drank, but it was delicious,' he replied. 'I wish I could have three more glasses of it today. The first glass I had some trouble swallowing, because it tasted acid, but when it

had settled in my stomach I found I wanted to have another. When
I drank the second glass I felt lively and merry. All my shyness
disappeared, and the world seemed a wonderful place to live in.'

So King Shamiran learned what drinking was. He made a great
feast, and instituted the noble custom of wine-bibbing.

An almost exact contemporary of Omar the Epicurean, Sanā'ī the
moralist and mystic composed many poems including an epic of the
religious life, the *Garden of Reality*. In this pioneering work he set
a fashion, followed by many poets after him, of relieving the
austerity of his discourse with illustrative anecdotes, much as your
Christian preacher will do. In these Muslim parables it is not
infrequent to come upon apocryphal legends of Jesus.

Jesus and the Devil

In a book I once read that the Spirit of God
went forth one night into the wilderness.
A watch had passed when, suddenly seized by sleep,
he made haste to find himself a slumbering-place.
Seeing a stone cast down, he took it for his pillow,
fared on no farther, and soon was fast asleep.
A while he slept; then hastily he awoke
to see the Devil standing above his bed.
'You outcast, you accursed dog,' he cried,
'upon what business do you come slinkingly here?
The place that is the sanctuary of Jesus,
how do you think to find yourself a shelter there?'
'Well, you have given me much trouble,' replied
the Devil, 'meddling about in my domain.
Why do you want to interfere with me?
Why do you meddle about in my domain?
The kingdom of this world is all my domain;
you haven't any place there; it's all my place.
First you plunder me of what's mine by right,
then you abuse me in your sanctuary.'
'How have I given you trouble?' Jesus asked.
'When did I make assault on your property?'
'That stone you have as your pillow,' the Devil replied,
'isn't it of this world? Then how did you filch it?'
Jesus in all haste flung the stone from him;
the Devil's phantom thereupon melted away
saying, 'You've saved yourself, and driven me off.

Henceforward I shall not interfere with you;
you for your part leave my property to me!'

Shihāb al-Dīn Suhrawardī Maqtūl, learned in Greek philosophy and
Magian learning, author of deeply metaphysical treatises in Arabic,
was only thirty-seven when he was executed at Aleppo by command
of Saladin's son al-Malik al-Zāhir on a charge of blasphemy. In
Persian he composed a great number of charming allegories which
seem to be in true line of succession to Plato's myths. In the following legend, symbolizing the descent of the soul into the material
world, Greek philosophy and Islamic dogma are brought together
by the skilful use of Koranic quotations, and Arabic verses are
cited to heighten the discourse.

The Peacock

A certain king possessed a garden which through all the four seasons
never lacked for fragrant herbs, verdant grasses and joyous
pleasances; great waters therein flowed, and all manner of birds
sitting in the branches poured forth songs of every kind. Indeed,
every melody that could enter the mind and every beauty that
imagination might conceive, all was to be found in that garden.
Moreover a company of peacocks, exceedingly graceful, elegant and
fair, had there made their abode and dwelling-place.

One day the king laid hold of one of the peacocks and gave orders
that he should be sewn up in a leather jacket, in such wise that
naught of the colours of his wings remained visible, and however
much he tried he could not look upon his own beauty. He also
commanded that over his head a basket should be placed having
only one aperture, through which a few grains of millet might be
dropped, sufficient to keep him alive.

Some time passed, and the peacock forgot himself, the garden-
kingdom and the other peacocks. Whenever he looked at himself he
saw nothing but a filthy, ugly sack of leather and a very dark and
disagreeable dwelling-place. To that he reconciled himself, and it
became fixed in his mind that no land could exist larger than the
basket in which he was. He firmly believed that if anyone should
pretend that there was a pleasurable life or an abode of perfection
beyond it, it would be rank heresy and utter nonsense and stupidity.
For all that, whenever a breeze blew and the scent of the flowers
and trees, the roses and violets and jasmine and fragrant herbs was
wafted to him through the hole, he experienced a strange delight
and was curiously moved, so that the joy of flight filled his heart.
He felt a mighty yearning within him, but knew not the source of

that yearning, for he had no idea that he was anything but a piece of leather, having forgotten everything beyond his basket-world and fare of millet. Again, if ever he heard the modulations of the peacocks and the songs of the other birds he was likewise transported with yearning and longing; yet he was not wakened out of his trance by the voices of the birds and the breath of the zephyr.

One day he was enjoying these sounds and scents—

> The zephyr wafted o'er me, as if to say
> 'I bring you news of your love, so far away.'

For a long while he meditated upon whence this fragrant wind and these sweet voices might be coming—

> O lightning-flash, illumining the sky,
> From what remote enclosure do you fly?

He could not understand; yet at such moments an involuntary happiness possessed him—

> If Laila the Amirite should whisper to me
> Greetings, when I am laid in the stony tomb,
> I would answer her with joy, even though it be
> But the screech of an owl issuing out of the gloom.

This ignorance was because he had forgotten himself and his original homeland—

> *as those who forgot God, and so He*
> *caused them to forget their souls.*

Every time a breeze or a sound reached him from the garden he was moved with longing, yet he did not realize the reason or know the cause—

> The lightning sped from Ma'arra deep in the night
> And tarried at Rama, weary of so long flight,
> Stirring the camels, the horses, the cavalry
> Till the very saddles wellnigh leaped for glee.

For many a long day his bewilderment continued. Then one day the king commanded his servants to bring the bird and release it from the leather jacket and the basket—

> *For it is only a single scaring—*
> *then behold, they are sliding down*
> *from their tombs unto their Lord—*
> *when that which is in the tombs is overthrown*
> *and that which is in the breasts is brought out—*
> *surely on that day their Lord shall be aware of them!*

When the peacock came forth out of the veil he saw himself in the midst of the garden. He beheld the hues of his wings, the garden, the flowers, the various forms, the world's expanse, the wide arena to wander and fly in; he heard the voices and songs of every species; and he was seized with wonder at his own estate, and overcome by vain regrets—

> *'Alas for me*
> *in that I neglected my duty to God'—*
> *'We have now removed*
> *from thee thy covering, and so thy sight today is piercing'—*
> *Why, but when the soul leaps to the throat of the dying*
> *and that hour you are watching,*
> *and We are nigher him than you, but you do not see Us—*
> *No, indeed: but soon you shall know.*
> *Again, no indeed: but soon you shall know.*

Here is another Jesus-legend occurring in the *Storehouse of Secrets*, the first of the five epics composed by Niẓāmī, born at Ganja in 1140.

> The Messiah's foot, which ever described the world,
> one day adventured into a little bazaar;
> he saw a dog-wolf fallen upon the pathway,
> its Joseph having emerged out of the well,
> and over that carcase a throng of sightseers
> hovering like a carrion-eating vulture.
> One said, 'The disgustingness of this to the brain
> brings darkness, like a puff to a lantern.'
> Another said, 'That isn't all it produces;
> it's a blindness to the eyes, a pain to the heart.'
> Each man played a variation upon that theme,
> cruelly abusing the wretched carcase.
> When the time for speaking came to Jesus
> he let go the faults, and went straight to the substance.
> He said, 'Of all the engravings within His palace

no pearl is there so white as that dog's teeth;
yet these two or three men, out of fear and hope,
whitened their teeth with that burnt oyster-shell.'

The *Marzubān-nāma* of Warāwīnī, 'modernized' early in the thirteenth century, is a collection of animal fables much in the tradition
of the *Kalīla and Dimna*.

The Thief and the Flea

Once upon a time a thief resolved to cast his noose over the battlements of the palace of the Chosroes and nimbly to creep into his
treasury. For some while the tumult of this melancholy passion had
besieged the door and roof of the thief's brain, and the vessel of his
thoughts was filled with this idea, so that at last he could conceal
it no longer; for 'unless a man with bronchitis coughs, he soon
becomes a consumptive'. In all the world he could not descry any
suitable intimate or congenial confederate with whom to share his
secret, apart from a flea that he discovered in the midst of his
garments.

'This feeble creature has no tongue to speak with,' he observed.
'And even if it could, seeing it is aware that I nurture it with my
own blood, how could it ever approve of disclosing my secret?'

The soul in his body, like a flea in the drawers or a pebble in the
shoe, so tormented the hapless fellow with the importunity of its
nagging that he told his secret to the flea. Then one night fate made
assault against him and incited him to embark upon that perilous
emprise. By a variety of cunning devices he hurled himself into the
Chosroes' palace. By chance he found the bedchamber void of the
presence of any servants, and he secreted himself underneath the
couch. The Chosroes entered and went to bed. No sooner had he
laid his head on the pillow with the intention of sleeping, than the
flea transferred itself from the thief's garments to the royal bedclothes, and there created such a disturbance that the Chosroes
became extremely vexed. He ordered lights to be brought and a
good search made in the folds of the bedclothes. The flea jumped
out and hopped under the bed. As a result of the flea's leap the thief
was discovered and duly punished.

(From *Classical Persian Literature*.)

In the same highly productive period of Persian literature Farīd
al-Dīn 'Aṭṭār of Omar's Nishapur was writing a succession of epics
with mystical meaning, most famous of which is that epitomized by

FitzGerald in his *Bird-Parliament*. Here follows a story from the *Ilāhī-nāma* ('Divine Epopee').

The Pious Wife

Once there lived a woman fair and lovely, her cheeks bright as day and her tresses black as night, possessed alike of goodness and benignity, righteous and religious withal. Her goodness was famous throughout all the world; her charm was equalled only by her sweetness. Fifty or sixty-fold clustered the curls of her tresses; her eyes were two *sads*, her brow a *nun*, spelling out the proof irresistible of a curved scimitar. When she parted her pearl-scattering cornelian lips, she slew with their immortal water all who would resist her; or you might say that her smiling mouth was an oyster-shell, its pearls her gleaming teeth—behind the laughing rubies of her lips her teeth glittered like flashing pearls. Her chin was a silver apple, bringing only calamity on those who would gather it. Heaven itself, beholding her countenance, span distraught like a heart-sick lover. Those familiar with the magic of language called her by the sweet name of Marhuma. Albeit a woman, the wheel of turning fortune reckoned her in the number of valorous men.

It chanced that her husband one day suddenly set forth on the road to perform the pilgrimage. Now the good man had a younger brother, but he was by no means a noble character; to him the husband entrusted his lady, charging him to watch over her faithfully. Having delivered himself of this speech, he departed. His brother accepted to do all that he bade him, and indeed devoted himself to his charge, showing great solicitude for his brother's wife. Night and day he applied himself to her interest; every moment that passed he sent her a new present.

Early one day repairing to her presence, the brother beheld the heart-ravisher unveiled. He lost his heart to her immediately, utterly overthrown, bleeding inwardly; so headlong he fell into that enchantress' snare that in a single instant he suffered the pains of a hundred lives. He wrestled strenuously with his reason, but every moment his passion grew fiercer. Being wholly unable to do without her, having lost control of himself completely, conquered by passion and by reason deserted, he forthwith disclosed to her how things stood with him. He wooed her with violence, gold and entreaties; the woman drove him from her presence with contumely.

'Have you no shame before God?' she cried at him. 'Is this all the respect you show to your brother? Is this all your religion and mosque-going mean to you? Is this the way you keep faith with your brother? Away with you! Repent, and repair to your Maker; put out of your mind these wicked thoughts.'

'This attitude,' the man replied, 'will yield you no profit. You must satisfy me this very instant! If you refuse me, I will have done with tenderness; I will dishonour you, and then abandon you. This very hour I will cast you into destruction; I will bring down on you a fearful calamity.'

'I fear not your threats of destruction,' the wife retorted.' Better destruction in this world than in the world to come.'

The evil wretch thereupon feared that the wife would report to his brother all that had transpired. Scoundrel that he was, he made ready his defence, purchasing the testimony of four rascals who bore witness that the woman had committed the sin of adultery. The judge, accepting his deposition, immediately sentenced her to be stoned. Dragging her out of town, they let fly at her with stones from all sides. The woman being pelted with countless missiles, they deemed that her spirit had departed from her; they left her where she lay, to be a lesson to all the world.

The unfortunate woman remained there in the desert, weltering in her own blood amidst the sands. When night had passed and day began to dawn, the woman recovered her senses a little. She sobbed in her misery and exhaustion; the narcissus of her eyes bedewed the saffron of her cheeks.

By chance a Bedouin, abroad upon his camel so early in the morning, heard her groans. Dismayed, he alighted from his beast and approached the woman.

'Woman, who are you, lying here like one dead?' he enquired.

'I am sick and suffering,' the woman replied.

'I will look after you,' the Bedouin comforted her.

He seated her upon his camel and conveyed her swiftly to his dwelling. There he took great care of her day and night, till that heart-ravisher had recovered her strength. Once more her charms returned; once more she became an agreeable companion. The pomegranate-blossom of her cheeks flowered anew; once more her tresses wove their girdle of curls. Out of the lapidation she emerged freshly radiant as a ruby wrested from the granite rock. The Bedouin, beholding her beauty, knew that she was ruler absolute over his life. Entranced by her loveliness, he swooned; in his agony the shirt upon his body became his winding-sheet.

'Be my lawful wife,' he begged her. 'I am dead; unite with me, and restore me to life.'

'I have a husband already,' she answered him. 'How can I take another spouse?'

His affection for her passing beyond all bounds, at last he invited her to him privately.

'Why,' she exclaimed, 'now you have forsworn the Faith. Are you not afraid of the wrath of the Judge Divine? Then you cared for me for the love of God; now you would execute the commands of the Devil. Convert not to evil the good which you have done; do not sap the edifice of the temple of the Faith. When I rejected a like invitation I suffered much injury and was sorely stoned; now you would tempt me to the selfsame sin. Do you not realize that, because I am pure in heart, even though you should rend my person into a hundred pieces, no injury will befall my holy body? Be gone! Purchase not your soul's everlasting torment for the sake of gratifying a casual lust.'

Moved by the sincerity of that chaste woman, the Bedouin adopted her as a sister. He repented of harbouring such thoughts, to engage in which traffic was the Devil's work.

Now the Bedouin owned a negro slave, who chanced unexpectedly to return from a journey. Seeing the woman's beauty, he yielded his heart to her; heart and soul enflamed, he surrendered to her completely. Desire for union with her surged up in his heart, but it was a desire that could not be fulfilled.

'I am black as night, and you are like the moon,' he addressed her. 'Why should you not share my night with me?'

'That can never be,' she answered him. 'Why, your master himself made the same proposal often enough. Since he, whose face is like the moon, failed to achieve me how should you, you blackamoor, expect to succeed?'

'So you turn me away?' said the slave to her. 'You will not escape from me until you deliver me. Else, I will devise a cunning ruse to drive you out of the house immediately.'

'Do what you will,' said the woman. 'What is that to me? I am not afraid, even if my destiny is to die.'

This enraged the slave against her; his tremendous passion for her turned into terrible hate. Now his master's wife had a lovely child; in his anger the slave rose up one night and slew the infant as it lay in its cradle. Then he carried forth the bloody dagger and hid it under the pillow of the good woman to create the impression that she was the murderer.

Next morning the mother of the slaughtered child rose up to give it her milk. She beheld the child, its head severed from its body; she raised from her agonized heart a cry. Her shrieks and lamentations filled the whole world; she cut her hanging tresses and bound them about her waist. A search was set on foot to discover the perpetrator of that atrocious crime. Under the pillow of the good woman lay bare, for all the world to see, a bloodstained dagger.

'The woman did this deed,' went up the cry. 'She is the criminal who slew the child so miserably.'

The slave and the child's mother beat the young woman beyond all description. The Bedouin now entered on the scene.

'Woman,' he shouted, 'what evil did I ever do you, that you should slay such a beautiful child? Did you not shrink from shedding innocent blood?'

'Who in the world could make such an allegation?' she answered. 'God, my brother, endowed you with reason to the end that you should think rationally and coherently. Consider with the eye of reason, virtuous sir. You have been so good to me. You took me as your own sister for the pure love of God. You showered so many benefits on me. Should this be your repayment? Just think a little; how should I hope to win greater respect from you by committing this murder?'

The Bedouin, being a man of uncommon wisdom, accepted the woman's words. He was convinced that she was innocent; at the same time it was out of the question that she should live in his house any longer.

'After such a happening,' he said to her, 'you would have a very heavy load to bear. My wife will always suspect your guilt. Every time she sees you, she will remember the child; her grief will be renewed every moment, her suffering will surpass all measure. She will curse you; she will never wish you well. However good I may be to you, she can never be the same. You must leave the house forthwith.'

So saying, he handed her privily three hundred dirhams.

'Spend these on the journey,' he said.

The woman sorrowfully accepted the gift and set out on the road. She had walked some distance, when suddenly a village appeared in the distance. She saw a gallows erected by the wayside; men had come from all parts to stand around it. A young man, heartbroken and anguished, was being hanged that day.

'Who is this man?' the woman enquired. 'Tell me, what crime has he committed?'

'This village,' they answered, 'is the property of a prince who is unequalled in injustice. If you want to know, it is the custom in this village that if any man is unable to pay his taxes, the tyrant has him strung up on the gibbet. That is why he is being hanged just now.'

'What taxes does he have to pay? How much does he need this moment?' she asked.

'The facts are simple,' they told her. 'Every year he must pay three hundred dirhams.'

'Ransom his life,' the compassionate woman said to herself. 'You have escaped with your life from stoning and hanging; now redeem the poor fellow from the gibbet. If,' she addressed the bystanders, 'I give this money myself, will they sell him to me?'

'At once,' they replied.

Forthwith she gave them the three hundred dirhams and freed the young man from his anguish. As soon as she had handed over the money she set out once more. Swift as an arrow the youth ran after her. When he saw her face, his heart leaped into his mouth; lovesick, his lamentations mounted to high heaven.

'Why did she liberate me from the gallows?' he cried distraught. 'If I had yielded up my life suddenly on the gibbet, I would never have suffered the agonies of love for such a beauty.'

For all that he pleaded with her, his words brought him no profit; of what use was his smoke, seeing the woman would not be set on fire? He argued long with her and wept in supplication, but all that he gained for his pains was abject humiliation.

'Is that all the consideration you have for me?' the woman demanded. 'Is this your recompense for what I did for you?'

'You have stolen away my heart and soul,' the youth replied. 'How can I renounce you for a single moment?'

'Renounce me not if you will,' the woman answered, 'you will never get anywhere with me.'

So arguing, they walked and walked until presently they reached the sea. By the shore a ship was lying heavily laden with goods and many merchants. The youth, by now despairing of having his way with the woman, called to one of the merchants.

'I own a beautiful slavegirl,' he told him. 'Her only fault is that she is uncontrollable. I have never seen the like of her indiscipline. How much longer must I put up with her rebellion? Though otherwise she is nonpareil, I am not enamoured of her bad temper. I have striven enough; how long must I go on striving? If you are willing, I am prepared to sell her.'

'Be on your guard!' the woman advised the merchant. 'Never purchase me from him, for I have a husband, I am a freewoman. I protest against his wrongdoing.'

The merchant did not heed what she said; he bought her from the youth for a hundred dinars. Very roughly she was made to embark, and the ship set sail immediately. When the purchaser inspected her face and figure he at once fell desperately in love with her. On that tossing sea his heart surged with passion; the monster of lust reared its ugly head. He took steps towards her.

'Help, help!' the woman cried. 'You are Muslims, and I am a Muslim. You are believers, and I am a believer. I am a freewoman; my husband is living. God be witness to the truth that I declare. You doubtless have mothers and sisters of your own, daughters besides modestly veiled. If anyone meditated such evil against them, you would surely be in a state of agitation. If you would never consent to their being insulted, how can you acquiesce. in my suffering the like indignity? I am an exile, a woman alone, poor and friendless; I am weak and helpless, wretched, in distress. Do not occasion further pain to my broken heart; remember that after today there will be a morrow.'

Moved by her eloquence and evident sincerity, the sailors pitied her predicament. They resolved unanimously to give her succour, becoming her protectors and sympathizers. Each man however, as soon as he saw her face, fell hopelessly in love with her, until every man jack of the company—to cut a long story short—was her abject admirer. Much they conversed about her, much they strove to conceal their feelings from her. Finally, since all their hearts throbbed with intolerable longing, they came to a common decision; they would seize the woman suddenly and have their pleasure of her by force.

The woman, becoming apprised of their nefarious design, it seemed to her that the whole sea was filled with her heart's blood. She opened her lips in prayer.

'Knower of all secrets, protect me against the evil of these wicked men. No other have I but Thee in either world. Expel from their heads this unlawful design. Or if Thou wouldst slay me, that Thou canst do; death would be preferable to such a life. Either save me, or let me die this day, for I can no more endure this burden of anguish. How long wilt Thou make me to wallow in my own gore? Thou wilt surely never find any more overthrown than I.'

So saying, she fainted. The sea surged on account of her. A raging fire broke forth from the waves, so that the whole ocean was set ablaze. The entire ship's company was pitched headlong into the flames, and at once reduced to ashes; but their goods survived unscathed. Then a wind blew from the horizon and sped the ship to port.

Sweeping the ashes overboard, the woman dressed herself like a man, hoping thus to escape from the attentions of the amorous, to hold her head manly on high. Many people hurried from the city to greet the ship; they saw a youth of moonlike beauty seated on board alone, surrounded by a vast fortune. They questioned the bright young 'man'—how had he come to arrive alone with all those possessions?

'Not until the king himself arrives,' she answered. 'I will not tell my story to anyone else.'

They carried the news to the king.

'Today a youth has arrived, a veritable charmer. All alone he has brought to harbour a ship laden with wealth. For the rest he refuses to say anything. Only to you is he willing to tell his tale, to relate the story of the ship and its cargo.'

Wonder-struck, the king hurried to the port. Saluting the hand-some 'youth', he enquired politely after his circumstances.

'There were many of us on board,' the woman recounted. 'We had voyaged a good distance, sailing continuously by day and night. Then the sailors caught sight of my face, and lusted after me. I prayed to God, and God so wrought as to ward off from me the evil of that handful of villains. Fire broke out and consumed every one of them, delivering me and reviving my soul. See, here is one of them still *in situ*, no more a man but a heap of black. I take this as a visible warning; I am not avid for worldly possessions. Take the lot; it is of incalculable value. There is only one thing I would have you do for me—to erect this very day on the seashore a shrine for me where I may worship, to order that no man, be he pure or impure, is to interfere with me. Let me be granted but to sit in peace here, and I will devote myself to God night and day.'

King and army on hearing this speech realized her saintliness and miraculous grace. They believed in her absolutely, and thence-forward opposed not her slightest command. The temple which they erected for her might well be said to rival the Holy House of Mecca. She entered it and gave herself up to devotion, pursuing a life of divine contentment.

In time the king falling into the snare of death, he summoned his ministers and officers and thus addressed them.

'It seems good to me that, when I turn my face from this lower world, this young religious should rule over you in my place as king, so that through him my people may enjoy tranquillity. People, execute this my testament!'

With these words he yielded up the ghost. His body was com-mitted to the earth.

Ministers, princes and commons assembled together and took their way to the woman. They told her the secret of the king's testament.

'Whatever it pleases you to command, you have the power, for the throne has passed to you.'

The woman had no desire for such elevation.

'How can a hermit rule the world?'

'You, hermit, are the one indicated,' they cried. 'Take the sovereign power. Enough of excuses!'

'Since I have no option,' the woman answered them, 'I require a woman beautiful as a moonbeam, to be my lawful spouse. For I have grown weary of solitude.'

'Your majesty, choose the daughter of whomsoever of us you please,' the nobles cried.

'Send me a hundred girls,' she said. 'But send them accompanied by their mothers, so that I may examine each one in turn and make my choice out of them all.'

The nobles that very day with all their heart's love sent her a hundred dazzling girls. They entered her presence accompanied by their mothers, beside themselves with shyness and eager expectation who should please the king best, and on whom his choice would fall. The good woman revealed herself to them.

'How,' she asked, 'can kingship be appropriate to a woman? Carry these words back to your husbands. Deliver me from this heavy burden.'

Dumbfounded, the women left the temple and informed the nobles of what had transpired. All, humble and great alike, on hearing the truth about the woman were amazed. They despatched a woman to her by return.

'Since you are the heir-apparent, appoint someone to be king over us, or else shoulder the sovereignty like a man.'

She chose a suitable candidate from among them, and then once more occupied herself with her devotions; she acted as kingmaker, rather than moving to the throne herself. Her fame spread abroad to all parts of the world.

'A real phenomenon,' people commented. 'No one possesses anything like the efficacy of her prayers. A woman, and no man alive approaches anywhere near her! Her holy breath exercises such virtue on the paralysed that they recover their powers and walk again.'

So great was her renown throughout the world, yet still none knew her true measure.

Her husband, returning at last from the pilgrimage, was surprised to find no sign of his wife. He discovered his hearth and home desolate, his brother blind and out of his wits, having lost the use of his hands and feet, unable to stir from his bed. Night and day he suffered the torments of hell, grieving after the woman; his soul flamed alternately on account of his brother's injured rights and by reason of his incurable malady. His brother asked him about his vanished wife; he opened his mouth and told his tale.

'That woman committed adultery with a negro. Amazing, yet many bore witness. When the judge heard their testimony he was pleased to condemn her to be stoned. So she was stoned miserably. May you live for ever! but your wife has vanished.'

When the husband, long separated from his family, heard these words he was sorely distressed to learn of his wife's sinfulness and death. He wept and beat his breast; then he withdrew into a corner, and with patient resignation gave himself over to mourning. Presently, seeing his brother in so lamentable a state, the only member of his body still functioning being his tongue, he thus addressed him.

'Poor soul, paralysed hand and foot! Listen; I have heard tell of a certain woman, famous as the sun, who lives in such and such a place. It seems that God answers all her prayers. Many blind folk have regained their sight by her prayers, many paralytics have walked again. If you like, I will take you to where she dwells; perhaps she will put you on your feet.'

The brother rejoiced to hear this news.

'Make haste,' he cried. 'I am done for. Save me, if you will.'

Now the good husband chanced to own an ass. He bound his brother on the beast, and set forth. Fate brought them one day, at nightfall, to the house of the Bedouin. The latter, being a generous soul, invited them to be his guests for the night.

'Where are you making for?' he asked.

'I have heard tell of a religious woman,' said the husband. 'By her prayers and incantations many blind and afflicted folk have been healed. My brother here is also fallen sick, struck blind and paralysed. I am taking him to this woman, that haply he may walk again and see.'

'A certain woman, very wise, inhabited these parts for a while,' said the Bedouin. 'My slave falsely accused her, and in consequence the miscreant was paralysed and struck blind. Now I will bring him along with you; perhaps her prayers will restore him also to health.'

They set out, and covering many stages arrived at the village where the young man had been strung up on the gallows. There they alighted in a dwelling suitably furnished for such a caravan, belonging as it did to the wicked youth who, wondrous to relate, now dwelt there, blind and unable to stir hand or foot.

'We are in the same plight,' the travellers told him. 'We share the same portion, the same pain. Since we are partners in this harvest of grief, it is only fitting that we should lodge in this place.'

The young man's mother was present. When she beheld the pair of paralytics she demanded the story of their pain and affliction. They promptly told her their tale of woe, and she wept copious tears.

'My son is in the same predicament,' she cried. 'I will accompany you.'

She sprang up and seated her son firmly on a mule, and the three couples set out on the road. They reached the good woman's retreat at dawn. With the soft sigh of that auspicious daybreak the woman religious emerged from her cell. Sighting her husband from afar, she prostrated herself for joy, and wept tears of gladness.

'How can I emerge? Bashfulness restrains me,' she mused. 'What shall I do? What shall I say to my husband? I cannot show my face.'

Gazing further, she observed the other three men who had been the enemies of her life.

'Ah!' she exclaimed. 'It is good that my husband has brought with him witnesses. Their paralysis is sufficient testimony against those three sinners. Now that I see all three are blind, what more do I want? What, Lord, need I say? The testimony is enough.'

She came forward and gazed at her husband, but kept her face veiled.

'Say what you want,' she said to her husband.

'I have come here in quest of a prayer,' replied the godly man. 'I have a brother blind and afflicted.'

'If the sinner will acknowledge his sin,' she assured him, 'he will obtain deliverance from his untoward suffering. Otherwise he will remain blind and afflicted.'

'Impotent and in desperate need as you are,' the pilgrim said to his brother, 'confess your sin that you may be saved. Otherwise you will be tied to your troubles forever.'

'I would rather suffer a hundred years than disclose my story,' the brother replied.

They argued back and forth, till finally to his confusion he related the whole affair.

'My paralysis is a punishment for that crime,' he ended. 'Now slay me, if you will—or forgive me!'

The husband considered a while. Then, though the news was bitter indeed to stomach, he made up his mind.

'Since my wife has vanished, at least I can save my brother.'

So he forgave him. The woman prayed, and in a trice delivered him out of a hundred pains. He recovered the use of his hands and his feet; the veil was lifted from both his eyes.

The Bedouin next commanded his slave.

'Now confess your sin!'

'Though you should propose to slay me, I cannot declare my crime,' the slave replied.

'Tell the truth!' his master repeated. 'Today you have no cause to fear me. I have pardoned you once and for all, so what are you afraid of? What excuse have you now?'

So the slave brought his guilty secret to light.

'*I* slew the infant in the cradle. The woman was innocent of the murder. I was caught in the toils of my own evil making.'

Perceiving his sincerity, the woman prayed for him; she restored his sight and fulfilled all his wants.

The old woman then advanced her son in turn. He too confessed his crime.

'A certain woman came to my succour, redeeming me surprisingly from the gallows. Yes, she ransomed my life, and then I sold her. That briefly is my story.'

The woman prayed for him, and he likewise saw again and could walk once more. She then sent them all outside, but detained her husband, to whom she unveiled. Thereupon he cried aloud, and fainted. When he regained consciousness, the good woman approached him.

'What befell you,' she asked, 'that suddenly you shouted and fell down?'

'Once I had a wife,' he answered. 'This moment I thought you were she, for you are so like her that one cannot tell a hair's difference between you and her. Voice, face, figure, walk—you are her living image. Were she not crumbling in the grave, I would have sworn you were she, chaste lady.'

'Prepare for good news, man,' the pious wife exclaimed. 'That woman committed no fault. She did not commit adultery. I am that woman. I have walked in the faith. I was not slain by the stoning. I did not die. God delivered me out of many pains; by His grace he brought me to this safe refuge. Now let us give thanks a hundredfold to Him, for that He has vouchsafed us this reunion.'

The husband prostrated himself to the ground. He loosed his tongue.

'Holy art Thou, who all possessest! How can my tongue tell the thanks due to Thee? Truly it transcends my heart and soul.'

He went forth and called to his fellow travellers. He told them the whole history, good and bad together. In short, from every tongue went up a shout and a clamour that reached to high heaven. The brother, the slave and the youth alike felt at once shame and joy.

The woman first put them to shame, then in the end she forgave them and showered presents on them. She designated her husband as king, and appointed the Bedouin to be his prime minister.

Having thus laid the foundations of perfect felicity, she withdrew from the scene and devoted herself to God's service.

(Ilāhī-nāma.)

Jalāl al-Dīn Rūmī, son of Bahā' al-Dīn Walad from whose meditations we have quoted in a previous chapter, having founded the famous Sufi Order of Whirling Dervishes died at Konia in 1273, honoured as a saint and a great teacher in the land of his adoption. His poetry, thanks largely to the scholarly labours and brilliant interpretation of R. A. Nicholson, is now famous throughout the world. His principal work, the immortal *Mathnawī* in which he set out to expound his mystical ideas, albeit in somewhat chaotic fashion, holds embedded in its 25,000 couplets more than two hundred tales and parables intended to illustrate his theosophic doctrine. In the following story, meant to point a warning against the mortal peril of greed, Rūmī parodies comically the life of the Sufi convent.

The Sufis and the Dervish's Ass

A dervish on his wanderings arrived at a certain hospice. He led his beast along into the stable, where with his own hand he gave it a little water and some fodder—a very different dervish from the one we spoke of before. This man took due precaution against neglect and muddle-headedness; but what profits precaution against the inexorable march of destiny?

The Sufis dwelling in that hospice were poor and destitute: poverty, goes the saying, wellnigh encompasses soul-destroying disbelief.

Rich man with your full belly, beware, do not laugh at the crookedness of the suffering poor.

Because of their destitution that flock of Sufis resolved unanimously upon selling the ass.

'In time of necessity,' they said, 'carrion is lawful meat. Many a corrupt act has become, through necessity, a righteous deed.'

In that very instant they sold the poor little ass, fetched fine pastries and lit candles; the hospice rang with great merriment.

'Pastries to eat tonight, music and dancing, plenty to eat! How much longer must we go begging with our wallets? How long endure hardship and three-day fasting together? We too are God's creatures,' they cried. 'We too have souls. Luck is with us tonight: we have a guest.'

After this manner they were sowing the seed of falsehood, deeming to be the soul that which was not the soul. The traveller for his part, worn out by the long journey, took what he saw as a fine reception and the fondest welcome, for the Sufis made a great fuss of him one after another, playing well the backgammon of flattering attention.

Seeing them so affectionate towards him, the dervish exclaimed, 'If tonight I do not make merry, pray, when shall I do so?'

They ate the pastries, and began the music and dancing; the hospice was filled to the rafters with smoke and dust—smoke from the kitchen, dust from the stamping of feet, every soul in a commotion of yearning and ecstasy Now, fluttering their hands, they would stamp their feet; anon in deep prostration they swept the floor with their brows.

When the spiritual concert had run its full course, the minstrel struck up a deep and solemn air.

'The ass is gone, the ass is gone'; so commenced his song, stirring up all present to an equal share in the ditty. To this same rhythm they continued stamping their feet till dawn, clapping their hands and shouting, 'The ass is gone, the ass is gone!'

The dervish, imitating the others, also began to chant impassionately, 'The ass is gone!'

At last the joyous excitement passed. The music ceased. It was dawn. All cried, 'Farewell!' The hospice was deserted. The dervish found himself alone.

The traveller set to work to shake the dust off his baggage; he humped the baggage out of his cell to tie it on his ass. Not wishful to journey alone, he was hurrying to rejoin his fellow-travellers. He entered the stable, but did not find his ass.

'That servitor has taken it to water,' he said. 'It drank very little water last night.'

The servitor came along then, and the dervish asked him where his ass was.

'Look at your beard, you silly old man!'

The servant's answer set off a fine quarrel.

'But I entrusted my donkey to you. I put my ass in your charge. Come, straight to the point,' cried the dervish. 'No arguing. Hand back to me what I entrusted to you. I am simply asking for what I gave you. Return immediately what I sent you. The Prophet said, "Whatever your hand has taken must in the end be given back." If that does not satisfy you, with your impudence, come, let us go together and call on the Cadi.'

'I was overpowered,' the servitor replied. 'The Sufis all rushed on me, and I was afraid for my life. Do you fling liver and lights at a pack of cats and then expect to find any trace of it? One loaf of bread among a hundred hungry mouths? One mangy cat before a hundred dogs?'

'I take it they seized the ass from you by force intending to spill my blood, poor wretch that I am. So,' the dervish concluded, 'you did not dare to come and tell me they were carrying off my donkey. If you had, I could have bought it back from whoever had it, or they might have made a round robin for my benefit. There were a hundred ways of making good the damage when they were here; now every one of them has gone off in a different direction. Whom can I set hands on and hale before the Cadi? It is you yourself who have brought this judgment upon me. Why did you not come to me and tell me, "Stranger, such a terrible wrong has been committed"?'

'By Allah, I came many times to inform you of what had occurred,' said the servitor. 'But you kept on saying "The ass is gone" with greater gusto than any of them. Consequently I returned again, thinking, "He knows all about it; he is content with this judgment; he knows the mind of God." '

'They were all chanting the words so merrily,' said the dervish, 'that I too found enjoyment in chanting them. Blind imitation of them has destroyed me entirely; two hundred curses on that blind imitation!'

(From *Tales from the Masnavi*, pp. 101–3.)

One of the most popular sources of legend, based in part upon historical fact, was the celebrated love-affair between 'the mighty Mahmúd, the victorious Lord' and his slaveboy Ayāz. The Sufis delighted to interpret this scourge of India's paederasty in transcendental terms, and Rūmī was following an established tradition when he recounted his tale of

King Mahmud and Ayaz

Instigated by spiritual insight, Ayaz hung up his sheepskin jacket and rustic shoes. Every day he would enter his private chamber and remind himself, 'These are the shoes you once wore; regard not your present elevation.'

His enemies told King Mahmud, 'He has a chamber apart where he keeps gold and silver and a crock of jewels. He lets no one into it; he keeps the door always locked.'

'I wonder now what that servant of mine has got, kept hidden and secret from me,' pondered the king. 'Go,' he commanded one of his generals, 'at midnight; open the door and enter the chamber. Whatever you find shall be yours. Plunder him, expose his secret to all the courtiers. Does he basely conceal silver and gold from me, in spite of my countless kindnesses and favours? He makes a show of loyalty and love and ardour, and all the time he is like a chandler displaying corn and selling barley! In the eyes of him who discovers the whole of life in love, anything but unquestioning service is rank infidelity.'

The general with thirty reliable officers set forth at midnight to open the door of his chamber; so many champions, torch in hand, proceeded towards the chamber gleefully.

'It's the Sultan's orders,' they cried. 'Let's break open the room and each grab a purse of gold.'

'Why bother with gold?' said one. 'Speak rather of cornelians and rubies and jewels! He's the Sultan's very personal treasurer; indeed, now he's as dear to the king as life itself.'

To one so beloved of the king what value would rubies and jacinths have, emeralds or cornelians? The king for his part harboured no evil thoughts of him; he was mocking at his courtiers, to test and prove them. He knew that Ayaz was innocent of deceit and guile; yet his heart trembled with misgiving lest the charge be true, and Ayaz feel hurt.

'I would not have him put to shame,' thought the king. 'He has surely not done this; and even if he has, it is well. He is my beloved; let him do whatever he will. Whatever my beloved does, it is I who have done it. I am he, he is I; what if I am in the veil? He is far from being of such a disposition, such attributes; to compound such a story is raving and utter fantasy. For Ayaz to be guilty of this is absurd and unthinkable, seeing that he is an ocean whose depths none can plumb.'

Meanwhile the trusty officers proceeded to the door of the chamber and began their quest for treasure and gold and the crock of jewels. Greedily and with infinite skill and cunning, two hundred of them contrived to open the lock. For it was a difficult and intricately-bolted lock, chosen by Ayaz out of many locks; not that he was miserly with silver and wealth and crude gold, but he desired to hide his secret from the vulgar, 'lest some' (so he thought) 'should vainly imagine evil, others name me hypocrite.'

So, inspired by greed and manifold foolish eagerness, the raiders at last burst open the door of the chamber. They tumbled in through the doorway jostling each other, like insects swarming on putrid whey. Hurriedly they looked to left and right. Nothing was there but a torn pair of shoes and a sheepskin jacket.

'There must be some treacle in this place,' they assured themselves. 'These clodhoppers here are only a blind. Hey, fetch sharp picks; try digging and tunnelling.'

They dug and they searched here, there and everywhere, excavating holes and deep hollows, whilst the very holes shouted at them, 'We are but empty holes, you filthy stinkers!' So they became ashamed of their evil thoughts, and filled in the holes again. Then they returned to the king, grimy and pale of face and ashamed.

'Well, what is the situation?' the king asked pointedly. 'Your arms are empty of gold and purses. If you have secreted the sovereigns and coppers, where is the shining joy that should show on your cheeks?'

The trusty officers with one accord began to excuse themselves, falling prostrate like a shadow before the moon. To exculpate their impetuousness and bluster and self-conceit they brought before the king sword and winding-sheet. All bit their fingers from shame.

'King of the world,' they cried every one of them, 'if you shed our blood, it is lawful and just. If you forgive us, it is grace and favour. We have done such deeds as became us; so what is your pleasure, glorious king? If, heart-gladdener, you remit our crime, night will have done the things of night, day the things of day. If you forgive us, despair will be dissolved; if you forgive us not, may a hundred like us be a ransom for the king!'

'No,' answered the king. 'I will not determine between this comfort and cruel chastisement. That is for Ayaz to decide. Ayaz, pass judgment upon the sinners! Ayaz, careful a hundredfold to keep yourself pure, though I boil you two hundred times in action, I find no dregs in the foam of your boiling.'

'I know that this is your gift,' said Ayaz. 'Else all that I possess is these peasant's shoes and sheepskin jacket.'

'Come now, Ayaz, dispense justice,' the king repeated. 'Lay the foundations of a justice rare in the world. Those who have sinned against you surely deserve to be slain; yet they are hopefully hanging upon your forgiveness and clemency, waiting to see whether mercy or wrath, whether the waters of Kauthar or the fires of Hell prevail. Ayaz, execute this matter speedily, for anxious expectancy is a kind of vengeance.'

'King, the command is wholly yours,' Ayaz replied. 'When the sun is present, the star is annihilated. Who is Venus, or Mercury, or a meteor, to venture forth in the presence of the sun? Had I forsaken the rustic shoes and sheepskin jacket, I would never have sown such seeds of reproach. What was the point of putting a lock on the chamber door, when beset by a hundred imaginative and envious rivals?'

'Ayaz, what mean these marks of affection for an old shoe, like a lover idolizing his beloved?' the king demanded. 'You have made of a shoe your religion and cult, as did Majnun the face of Laila. You have mingled your soul's love with two ancient objects which you have hung up in your chamber. How long will you converse newly with two ancient articles, breathing the ancient secret into inanimate things? Like the Bedouin bards you are drawing out your long tale of love to the deserted abode and the traces of bygone habitation. Your rustic shoes—of which Asaf are they the ancient abode? Your sheepskin jacket—one might say it is the shirt of Joseph! Expound, Ayaz, the mystery of the shoes and why you abase yourself so much before them, so that Sunqur and Bakyaruq may hear the innermost secret of the sheepskin jacket and rustic shoes.'

One day the king hastened to his council-chamber, where he found all his ministers assembled. He brought forth a lustrous pearl and placed it swiftly in the palm of the vizier.

'What do you think of this pearl? What is it worth?' he asked.

'It is worth more than a hundred ass-loads of gold,' the vizier replied.

'Break it,' ordered the king.

'How should I break it?' cried the vizier. 'I am a well-wisher of your treasury and wealth. How should I deem it right that such a pearl beyond price should be squandered?'

'Admirable!' the king exclaimed, bestowing on him a robe of honour and taking back the pearl. Then, after an interval of conversation with his courtiers on the latest events and ancient mysteries, he put the pearl in the hand of a chamberlain.

'What would this be worth to one eager to possess it?' he demanded.

'Half a kingdom—God guard it from destruction!' the chamberlain answered.

'Break it,' the king ordered.

'King, whose sword shines as the sun,' said the chamberlain, 'it would be a great pity indeed to break it. Pass over its value, and consider its lustre and brilliance that outshines the light of day. How should my hand move to shatter it? How should I be the enemy of the king's treasury?'

The king gave him a robe of honour and increased his allowance, then opened his mouth in applause of the chamberlain's intelligence. After another interval the king, continuing his experiment, handed

the pearl once again to the Minister of Justice. The latter spoke to
the same effect, as did all the other ministers. The king bestowed a
costly robe on each one of them, and raised their salaries.

'Now, Ayaz, will you say what this fine and lustrous pearl is
worth?'

'More than I can tell,' responded Ayaz.

'Break it into little pieces at once,' the king commanded.

Ayaz, who had a couple of stones in his sleeve, speedily ground
the pearl into powder. Thereupon a great cry and clamour arose
from the courtiers.

'What recklessness is this? By Allah, whoever broke this brilliant
jewel is an infidel.'

'Illustrious princes,' Ayaz countered, 'which is more precious—
the king's command, or the pearl? In the name of God, which is
worthier in your eyes—the Sultan's command, or this excellent gem?
Having your gaze fixed upon the pearl, not upon the king, the goal
of your desire is the ghoul, not the royal road. I will never avert
my gaze from the king, I will never turn my face to a stone, like an
idolater. That soul has lost indeed the pearl of great price, that
prefers a coloured pebble and relegates my king.'

The king signalled to the veteran executioner, as if to say, 'Remove
these wretches from my dais! How are these wretches worthy to
stand on my dais, seeing that they break my command for the sake
of a stone? In the eyes of such workers of corruption my command
is become mean and worthless because of a coloured pebble.'

Thereupon the affectionate Ayaz leaped up and ran to the throne
of that puissant Sultan, prostrated himself and spoke with his hand
to his throat.

'Sovereign before whom the heavens themselves stand in wonder,
phoenix from whom all phoenixes derive their auspiciousness, all
generous men their generosity, bounteous one before whose un-
selfishness all worldly bounties are swept out of sight, beauteous one
beholding whom the red rose has rent its skirt in shame! Forgiveness
itself is sated with your forgiveness; your pardon gives the foxes
strength to prevail over the lion. Any man who treats your command
with insolence, on whom shall he rely saving your pardon? Storehouse of pardon, the heedlessness and impudence of these sinners
derive from the abundance of your clemency. Pardon them, you in
whose coffer all pardon is contained, you whose loving kindness is a
precedent for all mercy.

'Yet who am I, that I should beg you to forgive, you who are the
sovereign and quintessence of the Divine fiat? Who am I to exist
along with you, you whose skirt every "I" has seized? How should

I plead for mercy to you whose indignation is justly kindled? How should I seek to guide your clemency, which is endued with perfect knowledge? If you made me submit to cuffing, I am deserving of a hundred thousand cuffs. What should I say in your presence? Should I instruct you, or should I remind you of the rules of graciousness? What is there that is not known to you? Where in all the world is that which you do not have in mind? You who are free of all ignorance, whose knowledge transcends all chance that forgetfulness should hide aught from it, you have deemed a nobody to be a somebody, you have exalted him by your light to shine even as the sun. Since you have made me somebody, if I make supplication, of your generosity give ear to my supplication.

'Inasmuch as you yourself have brought me forth from the form to the reality, it is you yourself who have made this intercession. Since this habitation has been emptied of my chattels, naught in this house, be it wet or dry, belongs to me. You have made the prayer to flow out of me like water; give it stablishment likewise, and let it be answered. You were the inspirer of the prayer at the first; be also the hope of its fulfilment at the last, that I may boast that the king of the world pardoned the sinners for the sake of his slave.'

(From *More Tales from the Masnavi*, pp. 116–21.)

It is by common consent agreed that the supreme master of the apologue is the poet Saʻdī of Shiraz, younger contemporary of Rūmī, who died in his beloved native city in 1291 or 1292, according to the traditional accounts a centenarian. Having travelled far and wide during his youth and middle age, he returned home to distil the wisdom of experience and much study into two books, the *Būstān* in verse and the *Gulistān* in a mixture of rhymed prose and poetry. These masterpieces of literature have been transcribed lovingly down the centuries, bringing out the best skills of calligraphers and miniaturists. The following anecdote illustrating the virtue of generosity occurs in the *Būstān*.

A certain man there died, a millionaire.
A prudent man and pious was his heir;
Not miserly he fastened on the gold,
But like a noble loosed it from his hold.
From mendicants his door was never free,
Full stocked with travellers his hostelry;
He made all happy, stranger and himself,
Not, like his father, locking up his pelf.

One chided his extravagance and waste:
'Scatter not prodigally all thou hast!
It takes a year to get a harvest in;
To burn it in a moment were a sin.
Thou art not apt to bear with indigence;
So, having plenty, reckon well thy pence.
How true the peasant to her daughter spake:
"In days of wealth, for want provision make;
Keep ever charged the sheepskin and the pot,
Our village stream unceasing floweth not."
Within this world is paradise to hold:
The lion's talons may be trimmed with gold.
Go not before thy love when thou art poor,
But, having wealth, come, lay it at her door;
If empty-handed thou shouldst suppliant lie
Upon her threshold, she will not reply.
The man of gold can pluck the Devil's sight,
And snare the Demon King with cunning might.
With empty hands seek not the charming fair;
Men without silver are worth nothing there.
Hands empty have no hope to realize,
But gold will rob white devils of their eyes.
Not all thy wealth upon thy friends bestow—
Bethink thee of the malice of thy foe.
If on thy hand all winnings thou dost lay,
Thy hand in time of need will empty stay;
Beggars will never by thy help attain
To strength, and thou, I fear, wilt leanness gain!'
Thus the prohibitor of virtue spake.
The noble youth with generous rage did shake;
Confusion seized him at the critic's word.
'Utterer of confusion!' he averred,
'This property wherewith I am beset
My father from my grandfather did get.
Did they not guard it with a greedy mind,
And die in grief, and leave it all behind?
Did I not take it from my father's hand
To pass hereafter to my son's command?
Is it not better men enjoy today
What on the morrow they would steal away?
Eat then, and wear; bestow, and set at ease;
What art thou keeping back for those or these?
Such as have judgment, leave this world with gain;

> The miserly in misery remain.
> By worldly goods eternal bliss is bought:
> Then buy, my soul! or be by grief distraught.'

Here follow two of the many personal reminiscences which Sa'dī delighted to recount in the *Gulistān*.

On Listening to Music

For all that the illustrious shaikh Abu 'l-Faraj Ibn-i Jauzī (God have him in His mercy) commanded me to forsake listening to music,[1] and prescribed the life of solitude and retirement, yet the sprightly season of my youth prevailed—and being by passion and desire assailed—against my mentor's counsel I inevitably took my way—and had my pleasure of music and convivial play—and if ever I recalled my shaikh's admonition, I would say—

> If now the cadi sat with us
> He too would wax full rapturous,
> And if the censor sipped this wine
> He would remit the drunkard's fine.

But one night I came into a gathering—and there I saw a minstrel sing—

> His unmelodious minstrelsy
> Might well have burst an artery;
> Far more his anthem did displease
> Than tidings of a sire's decease.

Now my convivial friends their fingers in their ears would push—now lay on their lips, as though they would say, 'Hush!—

> Melodious music makes the heart rejoice,
> But we are joyful not to hear thy voice.

> Thy singing gives delight to none
> Save when 'tis over, and thou gone.

> When yonder harpist into song did break
> I called mine host and cried, "For God's dear sake
> Put mercury into my ears, I pray,
> Or ope thy door, and let me go away!"'

[1] Strict Muslims of the Ḥanbalī rite held that it was unlawful to listen to music.

In short, to please my friends I fell in with their wishes, and by
a considerable effort prolonged my stay until morning.

> Untimely the muezzin sounds his cry,
> Unknowing what of night is yet gone by;
> Ask of my lids how long the night has been,
> For not a moment's sleep my eyes have seen.

In the morning I loosed a dinar from my purse, a turban from
my head—and both before the singer for grace deposited—holding
him close to me—I gave him thanks repeatedly.—My friends,
regarding my devotion—to him as contrary to all accepted notion—
imputed it to feebleness of mind in me. One among them shot out
the tongue of disapprobation—and thus began his castigation:

'Your behaviour here has not been in relation to the judgment of
wise men, to give the dervish robe to such a minstrel as this. Never
in all his life did any silver into his palm come—not yet a scrap of
gold upon his drum.

> A singer? Far from this abode of grace!
> None ever saw his like twice in one place.
> When from his mouth the dreadful sounds ascend,
> The hair of every hearer stands on end;
> The sparrow flees in horror at his note,
> He robs us of our wits, and bursts his throat.'

I said, 'Best it were for you to cut short the tongue of disapprobation, for it is evident to me that this person is miraculously gifted.'

He said, 'Will you not make me acquainted with his quality in
that respect, so that I may seek to win his favour, and beg his
forgiveness for my jesting?'

I said, 'Certainly. This is my reason: my revered shaikh had many
times commanded me to forsake listening to music, and had eloquently admonished me, but I would never lend the ear responsive
to his counsel. Now this night my star auspicious—and luck propi-
tious—guided me to this spot, so that I might repent at this man's
hands, never again in the rest of my life to go about where there is
singing and conviviality.

> Sweet lip and mouth and throat,
> From you the soft voice issuing,
>   Whether or not in note,
> Beguilement to the heart doth bring.
>   But be it Lovers' Air,

> Song of Hejaz, or Khorasan,
>   What agony is there
> Mouthed by a cracked-voiced minstrel-man!'

Saʿdī and his Syrian Wife

I had grown weary of the society of my Damascus friends, and therefore made my way into the Jerusalem desert, where I enjoyed the companionship of the beasts; until the time came when the Franks made me their prisoner, and kept me with Jews in a trench at Tripoli digging clay. One of the leading citizens of Aleppo, with whom I had been formerly acquainted, chancing to pass by recognized me, and said, 'Sirrah, what manner of life is this?' I said, 'What can I say?

> I fled from men to mountain and to plain,
> For I had nothing from mankind to gain;
> How is my case? Regard me in this den,
> Where I must sweat with men that are not men.'

> Better to hang in chains, when friends are there,
> Than dwell with strangers in a garden fair.

He had compassion on my condition, and with ten dinars procured my release from bondage. He took me along with him to Aleppo, and there made me marry his daughter, adding a dowry of a hundred dinars. Some time passed. She was a woman always scowling—disobedient and growling;—she began to give me plenty of her shrewish tongue, and made life wholly miserable for me.

> A bad wife comes with a good man to dwell,
> She soon converts his present world to hell;
> Beware of evil partnership, beware—
> From hellish torment, Lord, thy servants spare!

Once in a torrent of abuse she said, 'Are you not that man whom my father bought back from the Franks?' I said, 'Yes, I am that man whom he bought back from the Frankish chains for ten dinars, and delivered into your bondage for a hundred dinars.

> A famous man delivered once a sheep
> From a wolf's hungry jaws and horrid grip.
> That night his knife upon its throat he pressed,
> Whereat the sheep expiring did protest:

"Though from the wolf today you rescued me,
You were the wolf in true reality." '

(From Kings and Beggars.)

In the fourteenth century Persia, having precariously survived the
horrors of the Mongol invasions and the despotic rule of the alien
Il-Khans, with the collapse of their central government fell once
more into the chaos of bloody civil war. Such were the circumstances in which flourished a satirist of outstanding genius in a land
never short of satirists, 'Ubaid-i Zākānī, who profitably revived the
fashion of the animal fable in a bitter commentary on the political
scene.

The Cat and the Mice

If you have reason, learning and intelligence,
hearken to the tale of the Cat and the Mice:
I will now recite for your benefit a tale
the inner meaning of which will surely amaze you.
You who are wise, intelligent and learned,
recite the story of the Mice and the Cat,
the story of the Mice and the Cat in verse—
lend me your ears—smooth as rolling pearls.

By heaven's ordinance a certain Cat
once dwelt in Kerman, mighty like a dragon,
his belly a drum, his breast as it were a shield,
his tail a lion's, a leopard's his claws.
In the time of roaring, the thunder of his voice
smote with terror even the ravening lion,
and when he thrust his paw upon the table
the lion fled incontinently before him.
One day he entered a certain wine-cellar
having in mind to go a-hunting mice;
behind a barrel he established his ambush
just like a highwayman deep in the desert.
All of a sudden a little rustling mouse
jumped nimbly from a wall on to the barrel,
poked his head in the barrel and took a swig,
got promptly drunk, and like a bellowing lion
roared: 'Where's that Cat? I'll tear off his head
and then I'll stuff his skin full of straw.
As far as I'm concerned, he's just a mail-coat
handy for unriveting in the jousting-yard!'

The Cat heard him, but didn't breathe a word;
he just whetted his claws and his teeth,
then suddenly pounced, and seized the mouse
like a panther hunting in the mountains.
The mouse whimpered: 'I am your slave:
please forgive me the sins I have committed.'
'Don't tell so many lies,' the Cat replied.
'I'm not falling for your cunning tricks.
I was listening to every word you said,
you foul cheat, you miserable Mussulman!'
With that the Cat killed and ate the mouse
and then padded delicately off to the mosque,
washed his hands and face, wiped them carefully
and recited a rosary like any Mullah:
'Creator God, behold, I have now repented;
henceforth my teeth shall not rend another mouse.
In expiation of this innocent blood I'll
give two maunds of bread in alms to the poor.'
So submissively and abjectly he prayed that
presently the tears rolled down his cheeks.
A little mouse hiding behind the pulpit
scurried out to tell the news to all the Mice:
'Great tidings! The Cat has turned a penitent,
a true worshipper, a godly Mussulman!
The admirable creature just now in the mosque was
praying, petitioning, contritely bewailing.'
When the Mice heard this remarkable story
gladness possessed them, and they laughed for joy.
Then up sprang seven most select mice,
every one of them a landed gentleman,
and out of the love they bore for the Cat
each carried a cargo of assorted presents—
one in his hand held a flask of wine,
another a dish of roasted lamb,
another a tray loaded with raisins,
another a round plateful of dates,
another a pot brimming with cheese,
another yaghourt with a round of bread,
another on his head a salver of pilau
sprinkled with the juice of best Oman lemons.
So unto the Cat those mice proceeded
uttering salaams and paeans of praise,
then with the utmost politeness made memorial:

'We freely lay our lives down before you.
Here is our oblation, worthy we hope
of your magnificence; pray to accept it.'
When the Cat set eyes on the Mice, he exclaimed:
'Surely your provision is laid up in heaven.
A long, long while I have endured hunger;
now this day I have provision abounding.
Many other days I have kept the fast
that I might be pleasing to the All-Merciful.
Whosoever faithfully does the will of God,
his daily bread shall surely be abundant.'
Then he added: 'Pray come forward
a step or two, my darling comrades!'
The little mice all of them moved forward
their hearts trembling like a linden-tree.
Suddenly the Cat pounced on the Mice
like a lone champion of the day of battle;
five most select mice he seized to him,
each one a gentleman, each an aristocrat,
two in one claw, two in the other talon,
one in his mouth, like a rampaging lion.
The other two who escaped with their lives
swiftly bore the tidings to their brother Mice:
'Why do you sit idly here, O Mice?
Dust be on your heads, you fine heroes!
Five chieftain mice he has torn to pieces,
that Cat, with his claws and his teeth.'
The Mice, sorrowing over such calamity,
straightway garmented themselves all in black
and scattering dust on their heads, they cried:
'Alas, alas for you, Chief of the Mice!'
Then with a single accord they resolved:
'We will go to the Sultan's capital
to represent our case to the Shah,
that we are victims of the Cat's aggression.'
The King of the Mice, seated on his throne,
spied from afar the Mice's cavalcade.
All bowed before him in dutiful obeisance:
'O King-Emperor of the world's ages,
the Cat has committed aggression against us:
King of Kings, succour the oppressed!
Formerly he took only one of us each year;
now his greed has become enormous—

these days he seizes five at a time
since he repented, and became a Mussulman.'
When they had uttered their sorrow to the King
the King proclaimed: 'My dear people,
I shall exact such vengeance of the Cat
as will be spoken of down the long centuries.'
Within a week he had equipped an army—
three hundred and thirty thousand mice—
all armed with spears and bows and arrows,
all accoutred with trenchant swords,
columns of infantry drawn up on the wing
and in the middle scimitars leaping.
When the great army was all assembled
out of Khorasan, Resht and Gilan,
a mouse unique, the Minister of War,
one who was clever, courageous and cunning,
cried: 'It is necessary one of us shall go
unto the Cat, to the city of Kerman,
saying: "Come to the capital to make obeisance
or else—prepare yourself for war!" '
A little mouse it was, a former ambassador,
that set forth to the city of Kerman.
Gently, so gently he addressed the Cat:
'I am an ambassador from the King.
I have come bearing tidings to you:
the King of the Mice makes ready for war.
Either go to the capital to make obeisance
or else—prepare yourself for war!'
The Cat replied: 'Straw-nibbling mouse,
never will I step forth from Kerman!'
But in the meantime surreptitiously
he mustered a terrible army of cats—
well-armed cats, fit to hunt lions,
cats out of Isfahan, Yezd and Kerman.
When the army of cats was all mobilized
he gave the order to take the field.
The army of Mice by way of the salt-lands,
the army of Cats down from the mountains—
in the desert of Fars the two armies
gave battle together like regular heroes.
The fight raged fiercely in that valley,
every one a Rustam battling in his corner;
such a mass of mice and cats were slain that

their numbers could not easily be reckoned.
Then like a lion the Cat charged impetuously,
striking directly at the heart of the Mice.
A little mouse hamstrung the Cat's steed;
the Cat tumbled out of his saddle.
'Allah, Allah!' the shout went up among
the Mice. 'Seize them, seize the brutes!'
The Mice beat on their drums, rejoicing
over a victory and enormous triumph.
The King of the Mice rode on his elephant,
before and behind him his army shouting.
He bound the Cat's two hands together
with thread and tent-ropes and pieces of string.
The King cried: 'Hang him high on the gallows,
the ignoramus, the black-faced dog!'
When the Cat beheld the King of the Mice
he boiled with rage like a bubbling cauldron;
strong as a lion, kneeling on one knee
he tore the cords asunder with his teeth;
then seizing the mice, he dashed them to the ground
so that they became one with the dust.
The army of Mice scattered in one direction,
the King of the Mice fled in another:
gone was the elephant and the elephant-rider,
gone the treasure, the crown, throne and palace.

This is a story both weird and wonderful,
a souvenir from 'Ubaid-i Zākānī:
dear heart, accept the moral of this story
and you will live happy all your days:
having heard the ballad of the Mice and the Cat
meditate well its meaning, my dear son.

TWELVE

The Art of Ḥāfiẓ

It is scarcely an exaggeration to say, that of the various important contributions made by Sir William Jones (1748–96) to the initiation and development of Persian studies in Europe, none was more felicitous, or more far-reaching in its consequences, than his early labours with the lyrics of Ḥāfiẓ; and of these labours, none bore sweeter fruit than his making of the immortal 'Shīrāzī Turk' into *A Persian Song.*

> Sweet maid, if thou would'st charm my sight,
> And bid these arms thy neck infold;
> That rosy cheek, that lily hand,
> Would give thy poet more delight
> Than all Bocara's vaunted gold,
> Than all the gems of Samarcand.

And so on for nine stanzas: the poem has been quoted twice in recent literature, and so we need not give it in full here.[1]

Jones published this famous version in his slender volume of *Poems, consisting chiefly of Translations from the Asiatick languages* (London, 1772). The book was generally well received; the *Annual Register* for 1772, noticing the publication 'by the very ingenious and learned Mr Jones, so well-known for his extraordinary knowledge of the Asiatick languages', did the author the honour of reproducing the *Persian Song* with three other poems in the collection. Horace Walpole, however, writing to his friend William Mason from Strawberry on May 25th of that year, reported to him that 'there is Mr Jones too, who has published imitations of Asiatic poets: but as Chambers's book was advertized by the tile of *Ornamental* Gardening, instead of *Oriental*, I think Mr Jones's is a blunder of *Oriental* for ornamental, for it is very flowery, and not

---

[1] *Essays and Studies by Members of the English Association*, vol. xxviii, pp. 50–1; *Asiatic Review*, vol. xl, pp. 191–2.

at all Eastern'[1]—an unworthy and rather ill-informed quip, of which
the writer no doubt repented; for in later years Walpole was glad
to place the services of his press at Strawberry Hill at the disposal
of the young scholar whose early efforts he had treated so flippantly;[2]
and after Jones's death we find him quoting his learning as proverbial—'it will require Sir W. Jones's gift of tongues to interpret
my pothooks.'[3] Walpole's crabbing of the poem was an isolated
incident; Byron evidently read and admired the verses, for he
imitated the novel rhyme-scheme in an early lyric; and Swinburne
perfected the stanza.[4] The editors of the *Oxford Book of Eighteenth
Century Verse* conferred the accolade on the poem by including it
in their anthology.

A recent criticism of the *Persian Song* by Professor R. M. Hewitt
affords an opportunity for examining Ḥāfiẓ' original afresh, and
considering how far Jones, and his emulators, have succeeded in
providing a faithful or reasonably worthy interpretation. 'As a
translation the *Song* is open to serious criticism. The rhyme system
and the stanza are remote from the original, and there is no approach
to the rhythm. The matter of the poem has been inflated by exactly
a half. . . . This poem of Ḥāfiẓ is more than usually incoherent, and
what unity it possesses comes from the rhyme which is the same
throughout and occurs ten times. There are twenty-seven rhymes
in the translation, none of them being repeated. As for the rhythm
(*amatores puellarum*), Jones has fallen back on the familiar lilt of
the octosyllabic.'[5]

The comments here offered on Ḥāfiẓ will be discussed later in this
paper; let us deal first with the faults found in Jones.

It is by now generally agreed among translators of Persian (as
well as Arabic and Turkish) lyrical poetry, that it is a mistake to
attempt to reproduce in English the monorhyme which is so
characteristic a feature of the original. Without embarking upon a
general discussion of the principles involved in this judgment, it
will be sufficient to recall that, so far as Ḥāfiẓ is concerned, the
unhappy experiment in rhymed and rhythmical imitation conducted
(at the cost of how much ingenuity and labour!) by John Payne
completely ended the argument.[6] Walter Leaf, who was more

---

[1] *Letters*, viii, p. 170.

[2] *The Muse Recalled* (1781).

[3] *Letters*, xv, p. 415.

[4] R. M. Hewitt in *Essays and Studies by Members of the English Association*,
vol. xxviii, pp. 52–3.

[5] Ibid., p. 52.

[6] *The Poems of Shemseddin Mohammed Hafiz of Shiraz* (3 vols.). London,
1901.

modest in ambition, but only relatively more successful in achievement, provided unwittingly a second witness for the prosecution.[1] The best word on this subject belongs to the Edwardian poet and critic Richard Le Gallienne, who himself, though unacquainted with the Persian language nobly essayed to make a substantial volume of translations from Ḥāfiẓ: 'So distasteful to English ideas are the metrical devices and adornments pleasing in a Persian ear that the attempt to reproduce them in English can only result in the most tiresome literary antics, a mirthless buffoonery of verse compared with which Browning at his grotesquest is endurable. Rhythms which in Persian, doubtless, make the sweetest chiming, fitted with English words, become mere vulgar and ludicrous jingle.'[2] Perhaps it was the dazzling but unparalleled success of Edward FitzGerald in imitating the rhyme—though never the rhythm!—of the Persian *rubāʿī* that led later translators astray into supposing that even more complex rhymes could be equally well copied. The truth is of course, that English is a language notoriously poverty-stricken in rhymes, whereas Persian is as conspicuously wealthy in them. This point was well understood as long ago as 1800 by John Haddon Hindley: 'The constant recurrence of the same rhyme . . . is not suited to our language, which, as has been often observed by critics, will not bear reiterated monotonies. In such cases, then, he (the translator) may surely dispense with the minutiae of punctilious imitation, provided he strictly confines himself to the prominent ideas of his original, where no eccentricities oppose him.'[3]

Professor Hewitt's second objection to the *Persian Song*—that it is half as long again as the original—is perhaps more valid, if one subscribes to the school of thought which holds, that in translating poetry from one language to another the ideal to be aimed at is that the version should come out in exactly as many lines as the original, and that the closest correspondence should be maintained line by line throughout the translation. This theory is by no means as doctrinaire as it sounds; it has been practised by some masters of the translator's craft with conspicuous success; the most recent sublime example is Laurence Binyon's *terza rima* version of the *Divine Comedy*. But most of those who have put hand to the task of rendering Persian poetry into English verse would doubtless agree, that in this case it is vain to attempt fidelity to any such strict compact; the most that one can say is, that sometimes it is possible, but more often it is not; the strangeness of the Persian

---

[1] *Versions from Hafiz*, London, 1898.
[2] *Odes from the Divan of Hafiz*, London, 1905, p. xv.
[3] *Persian Lyrics*, London, 1800, pp. 9–10.

tropes and figures often demands expansion; the exuberance of the
Persian style sometimes requires pruning; that is, if one's object, in
Le Gallienne's words, be 'to make the foreign poet a poet of one's
own country—not to present him as a half-Anglicized foreigner
speaking neither his own language nor our own.' The verdict of one
who has proved his mastery in putting Arabic and Persian poetry
into English verse is surely relevant: 'While any poem can be
reproduced in metre, few Arabic and Persian poems are wholly suitable
for English verse: we must decide what to translate, and especially
what *not* to translate, before considering how it should be done.'[1]
Jones set out in his *Persian Song* to reproduce the whole of Ḥāfiẓ'
original lyric; that he should have found it necessary to expand his
version to half as long again as his model need give neither offence
nor surprise: not offence, because the art of translation from the
Persian is not best served by establishing unalterable Median laws;
not surprise, because Jones was, after all, living in the second half
of the eighteenth century, and wrote in conformity with the taste
of his period, and that taste undoubtedly preferred an elegant
prolixity to epigrammatic succinctness.[2]

Let us now turn to the original of Ḥāfiẓ, and examine the criticism
that it is 'more than usually incoherent', and that 'what unity it
possesses comes from the rhyme'. It will be convenient to have the
text of the poem before us; fortunately there are few variants, and
the editors are in general agreement about its contents, though
differing somewhat as to the order of the lines.[3]

1 agar ān Turk-i Shīrāzī ba-dast ārad dil-í mā-rā
   ba-khāl-í Hindu-yash bakhsham Samarqand ū Bukhārā-rā

2 bi-dih sāqī mai-yí bāqī ki dar jannat na-khvāhi yāft
   kanār-i āb-i Ruknābād u gulgasht-í Muṣallā-rā

[1] R. I. Nicholson, *Translations of Eastern Poetry and Prose*, p. viii.
[2] Should translators reflect the fashion of the times in which they live, and
are their translations any the worse for their doing so? That is another fundamental question, which we cannot discuss in detail here. Jones certainly
agreed with Dryden: 'I have endeavoured to make Virgil speak such English
as he would himself have spoken, if he had been born in England and in this
present age. . . . On the whole matter, I thought fit to steer between the two
extremes of paraphrase and literal translation; to keep as near my author as I
could, without losing all his graces, the most eminent of which are in the beauty
of his words.' Commonsense and experience seem to show that most, if not
all, good translations have in them a strong flavour of the age which gave them
birth; and that every generation must make its own versions of the great poets.
[3] The text here given is that printed in the edition of Mīrzā Muḥammad-i
Qazvīnī and Dr Qāsim Ghanī (Tehran, 1320/1941). For variants, see *Fifty
Poems of Hafiz*, pp. 141–3.

3 fighān k-īn Lūliyān-í shokh. shīrīn-kār. shahr-ashūb
  chunān burdand. ṣabr az dil ki Turkān khvān-i Yaghmā-rā

4 zi 'ishq-í nā-tamām-í mā jamāl-í yār. mustaghnī-st
  ba-āb ū rang u khāl ū khaṭ chi ḥājat rūy-i zībā-ra

5 man az ān ḥusn-i rūz-afzūn ki Yūsuf dāsht. dānistam
  ki 'ishq az parda-yí 'iṣmat birūn ārad Zulaikhā-rā

6 agar dushnām. farmā'ī u gar nafrīn du'ā gūyam
  javāb-í talkh. mī-zībad lab-í la'l-í shakar-khā-rā

7 naṣīḥat gosh. kun jānā ki az jān dost.tar dārand
  javānān-í sa'ādatmand. pand-í pīr-i dānā-rā

8 ḥadīth az muṭrib ū mai gū u rāz-í dahr. kamtar jū
  ki kas na-gshūd u na-gshāyad ba-ḥikmat īn mu'ammā-rā

9 ghazal guftī u dur suftī bi-yā ū khvush bi-khvān Ḥāfiẓ
  ki bar naẓm-í tu afshānad falak 'iqd-i Thuraiyā-rā

The theory of Ḥāfiẓ' incoherency was probably first advanced by
Count Reviczki, Jones's Polish friend, in a letter to his young col-
league in orientalism, dated London, March 7, 1768: 'Ghazelam
agar an Turk non verti Latino carmine ob versuum incohaerentiam.'[1]
It may be that it was this remark Jones had in mind, when he
wrote the last verse of his *Persian Song*.

> Go boldly forth, my simple lay,
> Whose accents flow with artless ease,
> Like orient pearls at random strung:
> Thy notes are sweet, the damsels say;
> But O! far sweeter, if they please
> The nymph for whom these notes are sung.

Like orient pearls *at random* strung. An unfortunate, a most
regrettable translator's gloss; it has no justification in the original;
and it maligns the ancient skill of the oriental jeweller, who assuredly
knew well that the perfection of the necklace depends upon the
artistry with which the pearls are subtly graded, so that the double
string will exactly match in size and texture. And so the damage
was done. Ḥāfiẓ, who was using a most apt and happy (and, indeed,
most customary) image to describe his own meticulous craftsmanship, was by Jones misrepresented as confessing himself a casual,
careless jeweller of words.

[1] W. Jones, *Collected Works*, ii, p. 334.

The accusation, once made, was never afterwards repelled;[1] and indeed, the error was pardonable almost, for, as we shall see, the idea of the Persian lyric is very different from that of the Greek, the Latin, or the modern European; so that we need not wonder to find so classical a scholar as Walter Leaf—to quote a characteristic example—renewing the charge in considerable detail. 'We have learnt from our Greek masters to seek the unity of a poem in the thought or mood developed in it. Whether sensuous or intellectual, the unity is internal and essential. To a Persian poet this is not so; and that is a hard lesson which we must learn before we can do full justice to Eastern art. In the Persian ode we find a succession of couplets often startling in their independence, in their giddy transitions from grave to gay, from thought to mood. To the Persian each couplet is a whole in itself, a *nukta*, or "point", sufficiently beautiful if it be adequately expressed, and not of necessity owing anything or adding anything to that which comes before or after. It is from the common metre and common rhyme alone that the ode gains a formal unity. . . . The lyric poetry of Persia is indeed a reflection of the minds of those who sang it—sensual, mystic, recalling the voluptuous dreams of Hashish, the flashes of intuition wherein the Godhead reveals himself in moments of blinding visions to the ecstatic drunk with wine, be it of Heaven or of Earth. To this extreme discursiveness of matter the rigid frame of the metre supplies a corrective.'[2]

Of course, this is all highflown nonsense. To suppose that the Persian lyric poet—or any poet, for that matter—ever wrote in a fine frenzy of inspiration, in a sort of drunken fervour to which wine, or even hashish, may well have contributed, is to mistake the entire nature of the poetic art, and above all the poetic art as practised these thousand years in Persia. How salutary is the corrective to this absurd misunderstanding supplied by E. G. Browne! 'It will now be fully apparent how intensely conventional and artificial much Persian poetry is. Not only the metres and ordering of the rhymes, but the sequence of subjects, the permissible comparisons, similes, and metaphors, the varieties of rhetorical embellishment, and the like, are all fixed by a convention dating from the eleventh or twelfth century of our era.'[3] Although these remarks apply with

---

[1] J. H. Hindley came nearest to doing so: 'If we attend only to the time, the place, the object, the intention, and the imagery of each *Gazel*, the ideas for the most part appear to flow naturally, and without any absurd or harsh transition.' (Op. cit., p. 11.)

[2] W. Leaf, *Versions from Hafiz*, pp. 5–6.

[3] E. G. Browne, *Literary History of Persia*, ii, p. 84.

greater force, as their writer proceeds to add, to the formal ode
(*qaṣīda*) than to the lyric (*ghazal*), and are less closely applicable in
all their implications to Ḥāfiẓ than to almost any other poet, they
are far nearer the truth than anything that has been written by the
gushing romantics, and provide the only secure base for future
operations.

First it is necessary to formulate Ḥāfiẓ' theory of the lyric, so far
as it can be discovered from his practice. Ḥāfiẓ' technique is funda-
mentally thematic; by which is meant, that he constructs each lyric
upon the basis of a limited number of themes selected from a
repertory which is itself definitely restricted, and to a great extent
conventional. Having chosen his themes—as a rule not more than
two or three whole themes, with fragments of others so familiar as
to be immediately recognizable—he then proceeds to work out his
pattern. It is supremely important to understand how vital and
inevitable pattern is to the Persian poet: a people which produced
craftsmen of unsurpassed skill in the arts of line and colour might
indeed have been expected to throw up men of equal parts in the
marshalling of verbal images and sounds; and it was natural that
they should work their materials into forms essentially similar to
those invented by their fellow-craftsmen, the creators of mosaics
and miniature paintings. So it is as a mosaic of sounds and symbols
that the Hafizian lyric is to be appreciated; and its artistry, including
its unity, is to be understood as being of the order of artistic unity
that is found in the finest mosaic pattern.

Next it is necessary to recall, that in treating each theme—
chosen, as we have said, from a limited repertory—Ḥāfiẓ was well
informed of how previous poets had worked it out, and would be
striving to improve on all prior performances. It was not fortuitous
that the theorist Niẓāmī-i 'Arūḍī defined the perfect poet as one
who 'in the prime of his life and the season of his youth commits to
memory 20,000 couplets of the Ancients and 10,000 verses of the
works of the Moderns, holds them constantly before his eyes, and
continually reads and marks the *dīwáns* of the masters of his art,
observing how they acquitted themselves in the strait passes and
delicate places of song.'[1] The anthologists commonly arranged their
selections according to the subject-matter of the poems and not by
the individual poets themselves (though the other method was, of
course, also followed often enough); there is the familiar example of
Sharaf al-Dīn Rāmī who, in his *Anīs al-'ushshāq*, went so far as to
classify the verses of his choice by the particular parts of the human
body described by the poets, following the still more ambitious

[1] *Chahár Maqála* (tr. E. G. Browne), pp. 49–50.

instance of Ḍiyā' al-Dīn Nakhshabī, who in his *Juz'īyāt u kullīyāt* included prose-descriptions as well; and as recently as 1940 the contemporary writer Ḥusain Makkī published an anthology called *Gulzār-i adab* in which he assembled quotations from many dozens of poets under various thematic headings, such as 'Lailā u Majnūn', 'Sham' u parvāna', 'Gul u bulbul', 'Bīmār-i 'ishq', 'Dil-i dīvāna', 'Rūy-i māh', and so forth.[1]

With these facts in mind, let us now examine again Ḥāfiẓ' original of Jones's *Persian Song*. A complete analysis would require far more space than this article is designed to occupy, and would necessitate a meticulous examination of the complete works of dozens of poets certainly studied by Ḥāfiẓ in his formative period and always kept by him close at hand: we shall therefore restrict ourselves, as an instance of the nature and form of his technique of emulation, to the solitary but important case of Sa'dī, whom Ḥāfiẓ was understandably most ambitious to surpass.

The poem has one principal theme, one subsidiary theme, and one signature, or (to continue the metaphor of the necklace) one 'clasp' theme. All three are commonplace and frequently found in the *Dīvān* of Ḥāfiẓ. In the development and interplay of the first and second themes, the poet introduces fragments of other themes which are generally used, either fully or in part, whenever these themes are stated.

The principal theme is—the fair charmer, beautiful, proud, unapproachable, the human, this-worldly reflection of the immortal loveliness of the Divine spirit. This theme is stated in line 1; lines 3, 4, 5 and 6 develop it, introducing variations in the form of fragments and reminiscences of other themes from the general stock-in-trade: the tumult of love (line 3), the unworthiness of the lover and the self-sufficiency of the beloved (line 4), the story of Yūsuf and Zulaikhā as a myth of divine and profane love (line 5), and the sweet-bitter tongue of the beloved, symbolizing the pleasure and pain of loving (line 6).[2]

The subsidiary theme is—wine (and music) are the sole consolation of the lover, to compensate his sorrow over the incapacity of his love, and the transitory nature of mundane affairs, and to enable him to solve those mysteries of the spirit which baffle and defeat the reason. Line 2 introduces the theme; it is developed in line 7 (listen to the advice of the old man of experience who knows the

[1] The idea behind such an anthology is valuable; for if the research were ever carried out thoroughly and scientifically, we should no doubt be enabled to trace the origins and evolution of themes in Persian poetry.

[2] A reasonably close verse-translation of the poem has been appended below.

way by having trodden it) and line 8. This is perhaps the most important and characteristic of all the themes used by Ḥāfiẓ: it expresses supremely well his theory of the 'intoxicated' lover (who has in his hand the Mirror of Alexander, the Cup of Jamshīd), and symbolizes his rejection of all formal, 'sober' life, whether it be the life of the cloistered Sufi, the orthodox theologian, or the philosopher.

The foregoing analysis, brief and inadequate as it is, demonstrates the superb skill and artistry with which Ḥāfiẓ treats two typical themes separately and in close integration; it is a fair example of the technique which informs all his poetry, though it should be added that in this poem he is being comparatively simple and straightforward.

These eight lines complete the statement and development of the chosen themes, to the evident and not unjustified satisfaction of the poet; it only remains therefore to sign the poem. Ḥāfiẓ has a number of different devices for appending his signature, and a close study of his final lines brings its reward in an increased appreciation of his poetic artistry. The 'clasp' theme here used is a very common one, but its present treatment is scarcely surpassed for beauty in the whole *Dīvān*. The poet looks upon his handiwork and finds it very good: it is deserving of praise and reward.

No complete understanding and appreciation of this poem is attainable, until all prior treatments, as we have already indicated, have been examined and all images and verbal pictures drawn by earlier poets have been compared. As a fragment of such a study, we append some relevant illustrations from Sa'dī's *Ghazalīyāt*.[1]

1. Turk-i Shīrāzī (Shirazi Turk).
This phrase is used in No. 578 (p. 323) of Sa'dī's *Ghazalīyāt*, line 5:

zi dast-i Turk-i Khiṭā'i kasī jafā chandān
na-mī-barad ki man az dast-i Turk-i Shīrāzī

(No man suffers so much oppression at the hand of the Turk of Cathay as do I at the hand of the Shirazi Turk.)[2]

2. khāl-i Hindūyash (his Hindu mole).
Compare for this *Ghazalīyāt*, No. 479 (p. 266), line 9:

gharībī sakht. maḥbūb ūf.tād-ast
ba-Turkistān-i rūy-ash khāl-i Hindū

(A very beloved stranger it has alighted, the Hindu mole in the Turkistan of his face.)[3]

[1] References are to the Tehran 1318/1939 edition of Prime Minister Muḥammad 'Alī Furūghī.
[2] Turks had settled or been nomadic about Shiraz (as still now) from early times.
[3] Hindu is a symbol for blackness, Turk for fairness.

3. agar ān Turk-i Shirāzī ba-dast ārad dil-í mā-rā
   ba-khāl-í Hinduyash bakhsham Samarqand ū Bukhārā-rā
The model for this line seems to be No. 19 (p. 11), line 4:
   diyār-i Hind u aqālīm-i Turk. bi-spārand
   chu chashm-i Turk-i tu bīnand u zulf-i Hindū-rā
(They hand over the habitations of India and the regions of the
Turks when they see your Turkish eyes and your Hindu tresses.)
4. bi-dih sāqī mai-yí bāqí ki dar jannat na-khvāhī yāft
   kanār-í āb-i Ruknābād u gulgasht-í Muṣallā-rā
The idea is a commonplace, but the nearest approach to it in Saʻdī
is perhaps *Ghazalīyāt*, No. 278 (p. 149), line 10:
   sāqī bi-dih u bi-stān dād-í ṭarab az dunyā
   k-īn ʻumr. na-mī-mānad v-īn ʻahd. na-mī-pāyad
(Give, saki, and take the full measure of joy from this world, for this
life does not remain forever and this season does not last always.)
5. shahr-āshūb (city-disturbing).
The phrase occurs in No. 451 (p. 250), line 8.
6. fighān k-īn Lūliyān-í shokh. shīrīn-kār. shahr-āshūb
   chunān burdand. ṣabr az dil ki Turkān khvān-i Yaghmā-rā
At least two parallels suggest themselves. No. 5 (p. 4), line 10:
   tu hamchunān dil-i shahrī ba-ghamza-ī bi-barī
   ki bandagān-i Banī Saʻd. khvān-i yaghmā-rā
(You carry off the heart of a city with a single glance exactly as the
slaves of the Banū Saʻd carry off the table of plunder.)
   No. 252 (p. 135), line 5:
   bar ārand. faryād-i ʻishq az Khiṭā
   gar in shokh.-chashmān ba-Yaghmā ravand
(They raise the lamentation of love from Cathay if these impudent-
eyed beauties go off to Yaghmā.)[1]
7. zi ʻishq-í nā-tamām-í mā jamāl-í yār. mustaghnī-st
   ba-āb ú rang u khāl ú khaṭ chi hājat rūy-i zībā-ra
The idea in the second *miṣraʻ* is commonplace enough, cf. No. 546
(p. 304), line 9:
   dar sarapā-yí tu ḥairān mānda-am
   dar na-mī-bāyad ba-ḥusnat zīvarī
(I remain bewildered at the whole of you; no adornment is necessary
with your beauty.)
   That is the simplest possible version. Then No. 555 (p. 309), line
6:
   ḥājat-i gūsh u gardanat nīst. ba-zar u zīvarī
   yā ba-khiḍāb u surma-ī yā ba-ʻabīr u ʻanbarī

[1] Note the pun on the two meanings of *yaghmā* (Yaghma, the place in
Turkestan, and 'plunder').

(Your ear and throat have no need of gold and adornment, neither of henna and surma nor of incense and ambergris.)

And the closest parallel, No. 624 (p. 350), line 3:

ḥājat ba-nigārīdan na-bvad rukh-i zībā-rā
tū māh-i parī-paikar zībā u nigārīnī

(There is no need to adorn the cheek of beauty; you, O you with the form of a fairy, are beautiful and lovely.)

8. ḥusn-i rūz-afzūn (daily increasing beauty).

In No. 474 (p. 263), line 1 occurs the phrase jamāl-i rūz-afzūn (daily increasing loveliness).

9. agar dushnām. farmā'ī u gar nafrīn du'ā gūyam
javāb-i talkh. mī-zībad lab-í la'l-í shakar-khā-rā

This is one of the favourite ideas of the Persian poets. Sa'dī uses it often. Thus, *Ghazalīyāt*, No. 25 (p. 14), line 7:

du'ā-t. guftam u dushnām agar dihī sahl-ast
ki bā shakar-dahanān khvush buvad su'āl u javāb

(I blessed you; and if you curse me, that is easy to bear, for sweet is the question-and-answer with those of sugar-mouth.)

No. 273 (p. 151), line 3:

har-chi z-ān talkh.-tar andar hama 'ālam na-buvad
gū bi-gū az lab-i shīrīn ki laṭīf-ast u ladhīdh

(Whatever it may be, than which nothing more bitter exists in the whole world, say, so speak, for from the sweet lip it is delightful and delicious.)

No. 565 (p. 315), line 4:

agar du'ā-t. irādat buvad u gar dushnām
bi-gūy az ān lab-i shīrīn ki shahd. mī-bārī

(Whether it be your desire to bless or to abuse me, say on, for from that sweet lip you are raining honey.)

To bring this paper to a conclusion, let us review what other translators since Jones have made of this lyric. E. G. Browne went to the trouble of collecting five different verse-translations of the poem,[1] and offered a new version of his own.[2] It is not proposed here to reprint so much, but merely to quote some illustrative extracts. First, Gertrude Bell's idea of the first two lines:[3]

O Turkish maid of Shiraz! in thy hand
If thou'lt take my heart, for the mole on thy cheek
I would barter Bokhara and Samarkand.
Bring, Cup-bearer, all that is left of thy wine!
In the Garden of Paradise vainly thou'lt seek

---

[1] *The Literature of Persia* (Persia Society).
[2] *Literary History of Persia*, ii, pp. 27–8.
[3] *Poems from the Divan of Hafiz* (2nd ed., 1928), p. 90.

The lip of the fountain of Ruknabad,
And the bowers of Mosalla where roses twine.

The same in Walter Leaf:

An if yon Turk of Shīrāz land this heart would take to hold in fee,
Bokhārā town and Samarcand to that black mole my dower
should be.
Ho, Sākī, pour the wineflask dry; in Eden's bowers we ne'er shall
find
Musallā's rosy bed, nor streams of Ruknābād's delightsome lea.

In John Payne:

So but that Turk of Shiraz take
My heart within her hand of snow,
Bokhara, ay, and Samarcand
On her black mole will I bestow.
Give, cupbearer, the wine that's left;
For thou'lt not find in Paradise
The banks of Ruknabád, nor yet
Musella's rosegarths all a-glow.

Richard Le Gallienne, translating (in paraphrase) lines 1–3:

You little Turk of Shiraz-Town,
Freebooter of the hearts of men,
As beautiful, as says renown,
As your freebooting Turcomen;
Dear Turco-maid—a plunderer too—
Here is my heart, and there your hand:
If you'll exchange, I'll give to you
Bokhara—yes! and Samarcand.
Indeed, I'll give them for the mole
Upon your cheek, and add thereto
Even my body and my soul.

Come, bearer of the shining cup,
Bring the red grape into the sun,
That we may drink, and drink it up,
Before our little song is done;
For Ruknabad shall run and run,
And each year, punctual as spring,
The new-born nightingale shall sing
Unto Musella's new-born rose;
But we shall not know anything,
Nor laugh, nor weep, nor any wise

Listen or speak, fast closed our eyes
And shut our ears—in Paradise!

You little robber-woman, you
      That turn the heads of Shiraz-Town,
With sugar-talk and sugar-walk
      And all your little sugar-ways,—
Into the sweet-shop of your eyes
      I innocently gaze and gaze,
      While, like your brethren of renown,
O little Turk of Shiraz, you
Plunder me of my patience too.

E. G. Browne:

If that unkindly Shíráz Turk would take my heart within her hand,
I'd give Bukhárá for the mole upon her cheek, or Samarqand!
Sáqí, what wine is left for me pour, for in Heaven thou wilt not see
Muṣallá's sweet rose-haunted walks, nor Ruknábád's wave-
      dimpled strand.
Alas! those maids, whose wanton ways such turmoil in our city
      raise,
Have stolen patience from my heart as spoil is seized by Tartar
      band.

And P. L. Stallard[1]:

Should that little chit of Shiraz
      Bear my heart within her hand,
For her cheek's swart mole I'd barter
      Bukhara and Samarcand!

Bring me wine, boy, all remaining;
      For in Paradise no flowers
Fledge the Ruknabad, nor blossom
      Roses on Musalla's bowers.

But, ah! as the Turk his plunder,
      So my heart's ease have they ta'en
All these wantons and these fair ones,
      Wrecking cities in their train.

[1] *Renderings from the Dewan of Khwaja Shamsu'ddin Muhammad Hafiz
Shirazi* (Basil Blackwell, Oxford, 1937).

Let all these versions be taken in turn and together, and the good points from each be put into one, and the bad points excluded, they do not add up to anything approaching in excellence Jones's *Persian Song*. Miss Bell is far more faithful; Walter Leaf is astonishingly ingenious; Richard Le Gallienne is his own charming, most un-Hafizian self; yet in Jones we savour a delight complete of its kind, a gentle, flowing, distinguished style recalling the ease and spaciousness, the learning and good taste of eighteenth-century England.

Finally, lest it be said we found fault with others, while not confessing our own inadequacy, here is a new version of the 'Shīrāzī Turk' (the text is that established by Mas'ūd Farzād): we readily acknowledge that Jones's reputation has nothing to fear from it, but perhaps it adds something fresh to the interpretation of this superb example of Ḥāfiz' art.

My Shiraz Turk is she but deign
To take my heart into her hand,
I'll barter for her Hindu mole
Bukhara, yea, and Samarkand.

Wine, saki, wine! till all be gone;
Thou'lt never find in Eden's bowers
Such watered meads as Roknabad,
Nor fair Mosella's blood-rose flowers.

Ah! those provocative sweet maids,
So devastating, so adored—
They plunder patience from my heart
As Turks despoil the festal board.

When Joseph's beauty daily waxed
(So I have had it told to me)
Love lured the wife of Potiphar
To rend her veil of chastity.

The meed of my imperfect love
Her peerless beauty needeth not:
The lovely face no aid doth ask
Of powder, paint, and beauty spot.

Thou saidst me ill, and I was glad,
For well thou spakest, truth to tell:
The bitter sweetness of thy speech
Those ruby lips becometh well.

Then heed this counsel, O my heart;
Lads who would happy be, and sage,
Account more dear than very life
The ripe experience of age.

Let all our talk be wine and song,
Nor let us seek life's mystery;
For none hath solved, nor ever shall
By reason that perplexity.

Thy song is sung, thy pearls are strung;
Come, Hafiz, sweetly chant thy lay,
And soon the listening Pleiades
Will loose their jewels on thy way.

(From *Bulletin of the School of Oriental and African Studies*, Vol. XI,
pp. 699–712.)

THIRTEEN

Two Modern Egyptian Poets

In the first half of the twentieth century by far the greater part of the world of Islam, once, as we have seen, a mighty and dynamic force in the affairs of mankind, languished under foreign, non-Muslim domination. In this and the concluding chapter we shall attempt to describe how the poets of these lands, stretching from Morocco to India, reacted to the humiliating situation of their peoples, and what they said in reminiscence of past glory and as spokesmen of the liberation to come.

Ḥāfiẓ Ibrāhīm was born at Cairo, of comparatively poor parents, on February 4, 1872. After passing through the state primary and secondary schools he entered the Military Academy, from which he graduated with the rank of 2nd Lieutenant in the Artillery. His period of active service was entirely spent in the Sudan, where he was under the command of Lord Kitchener. To this period belong some of his most popular poems, poems full of yearning for his native city, poems which already breathe that spirit of patriotism which was afterwards to become a blazing flame, burning through the souls of his countrymen. In a letter to some friends in Cairo he writes:—

> From one whose weary eyelids sleep doth flee,
> Outcast of fate, and wronged by destiny,
> For ever severed from the sweet intercourse
> Of friends, heart sickened with a vain remorse,
> To you, my fellows most desirable,
> Dear boon-companions of the beaker full,
> Who swore a mighty oath ye would not rest
> Until this land holds not a soul oppressed:
> What boots the Muse of melody and song,
> What the sweet minstrel, noblest of his throng
> Than whom Abū Tammām piped not more clear,
> Since men, grown heedless of the fleeting year,

Tire the Recording Angel with their vices drear?
Greetings I send, more fair than chaliced rose,
Warmer than health that in firm body glows,
Greetings of love that ever doth augment,
A love that cannot into words be pent.
O might I know if fate will yield at last
And speed me to you, or if death shall cast
His sudden dart, and hold me evermore
In these enfolding hills, where lions roar
At their red banquet, answering the shrill groans
Of jackals battling for my whitened bones!
If my day comes, and I must yield to death,
By God's name I adjure you, and our faith,
That, when ye sit together, and the cup
Is passed by slender saki, and ye sup,
When the full moon doth cast her shadows long,
Ye will remember him who shaped this song.

In 1899 Ḥāfiẓ was transferred to the reserves, and then given a commission in the Police, with the same rank; there however he stayed only a short while, and then retired after seeing fourteen years' service in Army and Police together. He was now back in Cairo, and casting about him for means to extract full advantage from his poetical gifts. From early years he had had a passionate love for poetry, and shared that marvellous gift of committing to memory which is the common heritage of Islamic peoples. He could recite long stanzas from Abū Tammām, Abū Nuwās, al-Buḥturī, Ibn al-Rūmī, al-Ma'arrī and many others of the classical poets. To this period belongs a group of poems which make strange bedfellows with his later productions: the panegyrics, the elegies, the occasional pieces with which he sought to win the favour of the Court and the wealthy families. Skilful pieces they are, fully caparisoned with all the well-tried blandishments, all the pious hyperboles which had ever wrung a bag of dinars from a sensitive patron's hand. But Ḥāfiẓ had misjudged his age. The Court was already fully satisfied with a young man of great promise named Aḥmad Shauqī, who had been to Europe and spoke French, and could find no room for a soldier and policeman, however lyrical. Other patrons were scarcely to be found in this new ungenerous age. Only one patron remained, and to that patron Ḥāfiẓ turned at last: a fickle patron, a patron that paid ill, but a patron after his own heart. Ḥāfiẓ Ibrāhīm became the Poet of the People.

'The life of Ḥāfiẓ,' writes Ḥusain Bey Haikal the distinguished journalist, 'as it appears in his poetry, portrays an entire age in the life of the Egyptian people.'[1] 'The soul of Ḥāfiẓ,' says Ṭaha Ḥusain, 'was distinguished by two things. The first was a power and fineness of perception joined with a generous, noble character; the second was a marvellously strong attachment between this powerful soul and the souls of the masses, their yearnings and desires, their aspirations and ideals. He was not an individual living by himself for himself: all Egypt, nay, all the East, nay, all humanity was at times living in this man, feeling with his senses. . . . I know of no poet in these days who has so made his nature a true, pure mirror to his own life and the life of the people as did Ḥāfiẓ.'[2] Truly Ḥāfiẓ served his patron well. This was a patron not only to be flattered; this was a patron not only to be cajoled; this was a patron to be exhorted and entreated, to be railed at and assailed. This was a patron whom the poet must not follow, but lead. Ḥāfiẓ soon established himself as it were the standard-bearer of an army of ardent nationalists, in revolt against an alien administration. Rarely has such patriotic poetry been written. His poetry of this period, the best period of his literary life, is the poetry of a most ardent lover. So he writes, urging his countrymen to bestir themselves, if they are to attain the freedom which they all profess to desire:

> O Nile! the time of sleep is past and done.
>> While Egypt slumbers, within Egypt's shores
> Stirs an awakening; the drug-dazed brain
>> Too long has numbed her sinews. When God pours
> New life into a nation, neither might
>> Nor tyrant's threat thereafter e'er restores
> That state to death. O children of the dawn
>> So long awaited, lo, your land implores
> That ye remember. Labour now like men,
>> Be strong! Stand guard upon your homestead doors,
> Be free! If ye a Constitution seek,
>> Doubt not, nor still repine for well-paid scores:
> His right was never won, who slept on sword,
>> His never lost who flinched not from the wars.

If he could not move his countrymen with such an appeal as this, he could remind them of the past glory of Islam. If those who were now grown men would not accept his challenge, then he must put his hopes in the younger generation of boys still at school, still

---

[1] In *Dhikrā 'l-shā'irain*, p. 19.
[2] *Ḥāfiẓ wa-Shauqī*, pp. 152–3.

learning, their minds filled with the stories of the old Muslim heroes and kings. He teaches them to recite:

> Give back to us our fame and piety,
> Defend the Moslem's proud heredity.
> To God, and God alone, we bow the knee:
> Our sires were knights of war and victory.

> We ruled the world an age, and nobly bore
> A glorious name which lives for evermore:
> Came Omar, and the Chosroes' rule was o'er;
> Such were the golden days of equity.

> The skies rained tribute, when Haroun was lord;
> Men lived at leisure; laden was their board;
> And virtue found a plenteous reward.
> Our watchword echoed, 'Peace, and clemency!'

> Ask of Baghdad, 'Didst thou a rival own
> When men's religion was Islam alone?'
> Virtue had not through ease to softness grown,
> And knowledge crowned a claimed supremacy.

> We break their faith, unless we burst the bars
> That hem the East, and heal its ancient scars,
> And raise, like them, its glory to the stars,
> Or with proud spirit yield—to destiny!

It was not only the glory of Islam by which Ḥāfiẓ could conjure his followers. For centuries the Pyramids and the Sphinx had been an insoluble enigma to the Egyptians; now scholars had come from the West and resolved that riddle, and in resolving it revealed a past glory of which Egypt, the Egypt of Islam, had never dreamed. Ḥāfiẓ was quick to grasp the significance of these discoveries: he created the myth of the Immortal Egypt, an Egypt which had been highly civilized when the peoples who now ruled her were savages, an Egypt which would endure, gloriously reborn, long after the West had relapsed into its native savagery. This was a battle-cry indeed; and as a warrior he cries, through the lips of a personified Egypt:

> The people stood, for they were fain to see
> How I should build fame's firm foundations
> Alone; let those who raised the Pyramids
> In ancient times suffice me for my boast

When others strive. I am the East's fair crown,
And grace her brow, as she with myriad pearls
Adorns my throat. Can any thing be named
Whose loveliness the Western peoples boast
Wherein I have no share? My soil is gold,
My stream Euphrates, and my sky bright steel:
Where flows my runnel, vines and gilded flowers
And laurels green abound. Were justice done,
My men would lord it over old and youth
Far as the eye can reach; had they their scope,
They would discover miracles of wit
In every science. If the gods decreed
That I should die, the East must hang her head
Thereafter. Never man drew bow at me
And went unscathed: God's hand is my defence
Forever. Many an empire has designed
To work me evil, and has ceased to be:
So perish all transgressors! Say to them
Who doubt my people's glory, and deny
My sons' accomplishment: 'Have ye not stood
Beneath the Great Pyramid, and seen
What I have laboured? Have ye not beheld
Those magic carvings which defeat the art
Of any rival craftsman? Centuries
Have not assailed their pigment, though the day
Itself turn colour. Do ye understand
Those mysteries of hidden lore, which I
Hold secret in my cloak? My glory stands
Unrivalled, rooted in eternity.'

In another mood he can write, with a true poet's vision:

He mastered knowledge to his bent
That he might raise a monument
Above Nile's sloping banks, to be
A sign, a deathless memory.
What glowering frown wears yonder pile?
Fond memory doth ever smile.
What skill sublime and wondrous brave
Designed this broken tyrant's grave?
Would art had had a worthier trust
Than thus to sanctify the dust!
For they had crafts beyond our ken,

And sciences that lesser men
Lack wit to grasp; with dexterous hand
To rich invention wed, they planned
Fair idols men might be forgiven
For worshipping, in hope of heaven.
These things they planned; their day is o'er,
Time seals their secrets evermore.

So for some years Ḥāfiẓ eked out a living, constantly moving with the great though himself barely supported by the proceeds of his military pension and the meagre gleanings of his writings. In 1911, however, some influential friends found him a secure position in the Egyptian Library, where he remained until his retirement in 1932. As one of his biographers has said, his friends were probably moved to do this for him having in mind the practice which not uncommonly obtains in European countries, and more especially in France, where distinguished men of letters find refuge in libraries and museums from pressing financial problems, and there devote their quiet years to study and writing. Unfortunately, however, from one cause or another, the wells of the poet's genius appeared suddenly to dry up. Lacking the all-powerful motive of threatened penury to spur him on, Ḥāfiẓ Ibrāhīm relapsed into the fatally easy and genial life of perpetual coffee-houses and tea-parties. The flame of prophecy was swallowed up in the smoke of cigarettes.

It was on his patriotic poems that the fame of Ḥāfiẓ was built up. They were his most original contribution to Arabic literature; and there is little doubt that it will be by them, ephemeral as much of them are, that Ḥāfiẓ will live. His ode celebrating the victory of the Japanese over the Russians, which he heralds as a sign that the East is about to roll the wave of conquest back on the West, and as an encouragement to his own countrymen; the striking dialogue written after the burning of Smyrna and the defeat of the Greeks; the wrathful denunciation which he hurled at Great Britain on the occasion of the Dinshawai incident; his graceful tribute to Lord Cromer on his retirement; these and many other poems which in their day electrified his followers, will need to be taken into account by the future historian when he comes to analyse the forces and motives which underlay the Egyptian movement for independence. Nor was the skill of Ḥāfiẓ less strikingly displayed in his more strictly classical pieces. His fame as a writer of elegies is well illustrated by the following passage, the exordium of his ode on the death of Saad Zaghlul:

Night, didst thou witness what disaster sore
  Hath flooded like a torrent in our breast?
  Dawn was not risen, when from East to West
The tidings ran: 'Our leader is no more.'
Tell to the stars: 'Saad's radiant day is o'er.'
  Heaven's constellations are in sable dressed;
  White noonday is by darkness dispossessed;
Night wove a covering, which day's sun wore.

Say to the night, O sun: 'Earth's star is set
  And vanished from the earth; so I depart
From heaven, and veil my face.' In mourning weeds
  Let me be wrapped, for heavy is my heart.
Mourn thou with me awhile, lest we forget:
A noble grief is loveliest of deeds.

In February 1932 Ḥāfiẓ retired from his post in the Egyptian
Library. One of his friends tells us that he then formed great plans
of writing, of composing finer poems than he had ever penned
before But fate decreed otherwise; on a hot day of July in that same
year he was suddenly taken ill, and died that night.

Shauqī, his famous contemporary and brother-poet, lived long
enough to write an elegy for Ḥāfiẓ, which opens:

I had preferred that thou my paean hadst said,
O thou that from the living, being dead,
Takest thy wage; but thou hast gone ahead.

For, whether a man be given length of days,
Or whether sudden fortune strikes, and slays,
He knows his fate, and, being wise, obeys.

So, when God summoned thee, with little pain
Thou didst depart, and comest to that Plain
Where dwells the Prince for whom thy heart is fain.

There dwells Muhammad, with the company
Of all the saints: divine authority
Shines on his brow, and true felicity.

Now is thy longing ended; now ye tell
Of all the anguish that in time befell;
Together ye taste bliss, and all is well.

Aḥmad Shauqī was born in 1868. His father was a government
official of no very high rank. Shauqī was fond of relating that he
numbered among his ancestors, besides Egyptians, Arabs, Turks,
Greeks and Circassians. He was educated with a view to becoming

a lawyer, and in 1887 went to Montpellier to complete his studies. There he came into close contact with the French peasants, with whom he loved to live and talk; and how deep an influence those early years in Europe had on him is reflected throughout his writings, and perhaps more especially by the fact that it was at this time that he made the first draft of a drama which he did not ultimately complete until the year of his death—*Ali Bey the Great*, a historical drama of the Mamelukes.

To this period also belong some of his more curious poems, verses of great erudition which might have been written by some court-poet of the tenth century, and which in his printed *Dīwān* are furnished with copious footnotes quite indispensable to their elucidation. To this period, and to the years which followed his return to Egypt, when he became attached to the service of the Khedive, belong also his elegies and panegyrics, his set-pieces and occasional verses, which were the foundation of his fame. Excellent no doubt as much of this poetry is, judged by classical canons, yet these poems may not unjustly be said, in the words of a distinguished critic, to 'have only one merit—the merit of renovation.'[1] It is not proposed, therefore, to quote from them here.

It is a little curious that Ḥāfiẓ Ibrāhīm, who was always accounted by his countrymen by far the more revolutionary of the two poets in politics, should have spent all his days securely in Egypt, whereas Shauqī was in exile for some years. It was a fortunate chance, however, that made him choose Spain as the country where he should spend the troubled years of the 1914–18 War and after-War period. When he was allowed to return to Egypt in 1920 he brought back with him a sheaf of poems written in the true Andalusian style, as well as materials which he subsequently worked up into his only prose-drama, *The Princess of Andalusia*. His return was marked by a rapturous reception in the Cairo Opera House, at which he recited a notable poem beginning:

> So, I have come at last, when hope seemed lost,
> To thee, my country! I have found again
> My vanished youth. So every tempest-tossed
> And lonely wanderer, if God ordain,
> One day comes home. Yet, were it doomed to me,
> I should make thee my faith, and chant my prayer
> With thee my altar; yea, and I would dare
> E'en death, if I must die, defending thee.

When Shauqī is remembered as the Poet of Princes it is sometimes

[1] Ṭaha Ḥusain, *Ḥāfiẓ wa-Shauqī*, p. 9.

forgotten that he proved himself as true and ardent a patriot as Ḥāfiẓ Ibrāhīm. His intense loyalty to Islam is also displayed in many notable poems, among them his famous panegyric in honour of the Prophet's birthday. It was as a believing Muslim (for Islam honours the Founder of Christianity as a true prophet) that he composed the following Christmas carol:

> When Christ was born, a glory shone
> This whole created world upon;
> Then chivalry came down to earth
> And gentleness, to greet his birth;
> A radiance did the lands adorn
>   When Christ was born.
>
> When Christ was seen in fleshly guise
> Rose dawn suffused the night-dimmed skies;
> Then earth and heaven danced with light,
> The rippling fields were gay and bright,
> And all creation shone with sheen
>   When Christ was seen.
>
> When Christ was given, no threat was heard
> Of armèd strife, no passion stirred
> Within the hearts of warlike men;
> A monarch came to earth, and then,
> Of earth grown weary, rose to heaven
>   When Christ was given.

Apart from the very considerable bulk of poetry of the strictly classical type, Shauqī also wrote much in which he was consciously striving after the creation of something new in Arabic verse. Amongst his most interesting experiments is a not very distinguished epic on the history of the early Caliphs. This long poem is written in rhyming couplets in imitation of the Persian epic, and may fairly be regarded as marking an epoch in Arabic poetry. As an experiment it was not successful, chiefly because the theme was intolerably frigid; but at least Shauqī demonstrated that epic can be written in the Arabic language, and it is possible that what he began others will yet bring to perfection.

Shauqī indeed was by no means alone in feeling the need for some new form in poetry. Ḥāfiẓ Ibrāhīm also strove to innovate. In an early poem, which he dedicated to Poetry, he wrote:

> Physician of the soul, by virtue sired,
>   Thou art destroyed to mind and fantasy:
>   Thy East yet sleeps in leaden lethargy,

Its peoples indolent, and uninspired.
    They have debased thy art with revelry,
And drunkenness, with passion for a deer,
    Or soft gazelle, with prelude, elegy,
Paean, and satire, valour insincere,
Humiliation in the robes of pride,
And manly boast by craven deed denied.

Misprised, contemned, thou draggest on thy days
    Past buried centuries. With dolorous care
    Thou chantest Layla and her luckless fair,
Haltest at ruined camps, inditest lays
    For vanished friend, and tracks by night swept bare:
Or if but once thy art be dignified,
    'Tis on a camel's back! O Muse, prepare
To burst thy bonds preposterous! Fling wide
These doors that choke thy utterance inane,
That we may breathe heaven's air, and sing again!

Before turning to a consideration of Shauqī's more original contributions to Arabic literature, it will be sufficient to quote a single example of his admired power in elegy. This example is taken from the concluding lines of his poem on the death of Saad Zaghlul, and may be profitably compared with Ḥāfiẓ Ibrāhīm's verses quoted above, on the same theme:

Where is my pen, that was so swift to write
When I commanded, even to indite
The sun's funereal dirge? Upon Saad's day
It hath betrayed me; knowing to obey
When lesser songs were making, at the end
It stumbled, and could not bewail my friend.
Now is his soul in God's bliss, that had fill
Of earthly blessings, but remembered still
To fear its Maker. Frail intelligence
Deceived it not, nor finite cognisance
Of things unreal bemused it. Having cast
Away doubt's vain bewilderments, it passed,
In perfect faith and penitence, to God.
With weak creation for awhile it trod,
But saw, beyond this world of perishing,
The eternal Spirit. Ever swift of wing
At God's command, alas! upon this day
It heard God's last behest, and did obey.

The problems which faced Shauqī in his desire to create new forms were twofold: the problem of form itself, and the problem of prosody, with which is bound up the problem of vocabulary. Shauqī's greatest and by far most important contribution to the problem of form was his creation of the lyrical drama. Of this more hereafter: but whilst creating this new form he also went far towards producing a solution of the problem of prosody and vocabulary. We may remark similar tendencies in his later informal poetry: the use of commonplace words and expressions, the abandonment of the *qasīda* form, the dropping of end-rhymes, a deliberate attempt to colloquialize, so to speak, the austere language of classical poetry. (More daring innovations in this direction were being tried out meanwhile in the United States, by a group of Lebanese *émigré* poets.) The following poem, which in its English version follows closely the metre and rhyme-scheme of the original, exemplifies these tendencies:

> Islam, to thee be glory,
>   Thou star of fortune bright,
> Renowned in ancient story,
>   Man's guidance to the right.
>
> Upon Iran thy sway is
> And India 'neath thy ray is;
> Thy blaze that shines out stark
> Dispels our shadows dark;
> By book and pen thy mark
>   Claims armies infinite.
>
> O'er Syria thy hand is,
> Egypt thy chosen land is;
> Thy double radiance
> Destroys all ignorance,
> Thy fetter-shattering glance
>   Puts error's hosts to flight.
>
> By thee heart bound to heart is
> Past loyalty of parties:
> Thy guide and mercy true
> Shall spread the whole world through,
> Till men and nations too
>   As brothers all unite.

In creating the lyrical drama, as in creating the epic, Shauqī achieved the seemingly impossible. But whereas his experiment in epic was a failure, his lyrical drama is a contribution of unique and immortal value. The drama is a literary form which, until living memory, had taken no place whatever in Arabic literature. Religious prejudices, of course, were the prime causes of this; for the Arab is a born actor and enjoys the drama to the full. When theatres opened there was a complete lack of any material for acting; and companies still, in the 1930's, depended to an inordinate extent on translations from European languages, and more especially from French. Shauqī's plays almost alone rose above the commonplace among purely native productions. They had already created for themselves a tradition, and since his death retain the popular support which greeted their first production.

Two of the plays deal with Egypt of the pre-Islamic period: *Cambyses* and *The Fall of Cleopatra*. The former play suffered severe criticism at the hands of the well-known poet 'Aqqād, whose *Cambyses in the Balance* is a monument of ruthless and sometimes ill-natured castigation. *The Fall of Cleopatra* is not without originality, but Shakespeare and Shaw were more at home with that theme. *Ali Bey the Great* and *The Princess of Andalusia* have already. been mentioned. A fifth play, *Antara*, being based on the well-known Arab romance, has a more genuine ring. Shauqī's greatest dramatic creation, however, is without doubt his *Majnun Layla*.[1] Here he is treating a theme which goes to the very heart of Arab civilization. Poets of Persia, India and Turkey had vied with one another in the telling of the desert-romance of Qais and his unhappy passion. Shauqī approached the theme as an Arab who was fully familiar with the West. For material he drew on the version of the story as it is recounted in the *Kitāb al-Aghānī*, that massive 'Book of Songs' which is our principal source for early Arab lore; how richly he embroidered this material and what originality he displayed in the presentation of it can be fairly adjudged by comparing the story as written there with his play.

As the *Majnun Layla* is now available in its English version, it is not necessary to discuss it at great length here. It will be useful, however, to quote a few typical passages from the play, to illustrate the beauty of language, the naturalness of dialogue, and the fine poetic feeling which Shauqī there exhibits. If these speeches are compared with the speeches put into the mouths of the heroes of the story by the Persian poets, it will be realized how great an advance Shauqī has made.

In the first scene Qais describes his love for Layla:

How still the night! It stirs within me yearning
And poetry. The desert is all night,

[1] English translation published by Luzac, 1933.

And love, and poetry. God, thou hast filled
The heaven and earth with passion in this desert,
And I alone am laden with that passion.
Yearning has seized me for the tents of Layla;
I have no guide, no convoy but my passion.
At night my tent was pitched but a step from hers,
Yet all that neighbouring wrought no cure in me.
When my heart goes about her, all its passion
Suddenly swells like an upleaping stream.

Another description of his love, occurring in the second act, is also noteworthy:

Layla! A voice called Layla, and it stirred
A mad intoxication in my breast.
Layla! Go, see if the sweet sound shakes the desert,
And if a David sings there to his lute.
Layla! A call for 'Layla' fills my ear,
A loud enchantment echoing in the hearing.
Layla! She echoes in my ear and soul,
Like warblers' song that echoes in a thicket.

Even in translation the eloquence is such passages is apparent.

A good example of dialogue, highly dramatic in its context, is provided by the scene in the last act where Qais returns after Layla is dead, not knowing of her death, and asks his friend Bishr what has happened in the tribe during his absence.

QAIS: What haps in Amir, Bishr? How is my mother?
BISHR: Wearied with longing for thee.
QAIS: And my people?
BISHR: They yearn abundantly.
QAIS: The lads and girls
That once were young with me?
BISHR: All long to see thee,
And still remember thee.
QAIS: How is our tent
When the wind rises? And the starlit parties,
The talkers at the campfire? And the palm-trees,
How were they at thy leaving?
BISHR: High and green
As ever.
QAIS: And my colts I left so small?

BISHR: They are grown, Qais; they are short-haired and lean.

QAIS: 'Tis a great land; it makes the peerless champion
          To grow, brings forth the horseman and the poet.
                    (*Bishr is confused.*)
          Now, Bishr, what ails thee?

BISHR: Qais!

QAIS: Thy soul is stirred
          Most inwardly; this sobbing, like forced laughter,
          Is more akin to grief and tears.

BISHR: O God!
          What shall I answer? It is nothing, Qais.

QAIS: Thou wast so carefree yesterday: today
          It troubles me, to see thee so perplexed,
          So solemn. What has stirred thee so, my cousin?
          What are these tears that fall?

BISHR: Qais, it is nothing.

QAIS: Nay, but thou hidest something terrible:
          Thy silence is of one that cautiously
          Bears tidings of a death.

BISHR: Qais!

QAIS: Be not silent;
          Hide naught; I am acquainted with misfortune.
          Before we met, my left eye twitched, my heart
          Beat like a fluttering bird.

BISHR: Forgive me, Qais:
          Thou canst not bear what I shall say to thee.

QAIS: What, is she dead?

BISHR: Yes, she died yesterday.

Shauqī intersperses the action with songs in the true Shakespearian manner. Of these the following are examples:

Song of the Camel-Driver

Hela! Wind up wild dells,
    Bringing to home again
The wanderer. Loud bells
    Ring sadly through the plain,
Like song of birds, that trill
    On dew-bespangled tree:
Who calls in notes so shrill
    For home, so yearningly?
So deep the ringings roll,
Echoing in the soul.

Hela! Drive on apace,
　Fly to the watered meads:
Outstrip the night, and race
　To where the thicket breeds
Which Layla knew, and love.
　Driver, seek Taubed's green;
My heart doth lodge above
　Its valleys and ravine.
O moon that Nejd saw rise,
Love rules in tyrant wise.

Song of the Jinns

The firm sun flows like gold,
A wonder to behold,
　On hill and valley deep.
The dance with joy begins:
Lead on, ye Arab jinns,
　The dance of flames that leap.

We are the sons of Hell,
And with hot blood rebel
　On earth, as once our sire
In heaven, the mighty one,
Iblis, the first-born son,
　The glory of the Fire.

Gharid's Song

Valley of death, all hail! Abundant rain
　　Waters the plain:
The sacred earth becomes thy sanctuary
　　And holy sky.
Thou comest clear in stillness, and thy word
　　In hush is heard.
Thy people do not die: the night falls deep,
　　And so they sleep
Unseen; what they become, no man has guessed,
　　Nor where they rest.

The play comes to its tragic close with Qais visiting the tomb of his
beloved Layla and the successive apparitions of al-Amawī the
'genius' of Qais—according to pre-Islamic belief every poet had an
attendant spirit who inspired him—and the ghost of Ibn Dharīh a

poet of Hejaz who was seen in Layla's company in the opening
scene of the drama.

QAIS: Weep now, mine eyes; ye tears, here may ye flow;
                  For here is Layla's body, here her ashes,
                  Here is my last breath yielded to the soil.
                  Here is her pure, gay mouth that almost gleams
                  Through the affliction; here her eyelid's magic
                  Destroyed in dust, its spell was unavailing.
                  Here is the volume of my youth rolled up;
                  This field shall not unroll it. All events
                  Are here assembled: here is pleasant hope,
                  And here sweet sorrow. Outcast of the fates,
                  Will none protect thee from them, none defend thee
                  But death? Life loses its authority,
                  And yields its power to death. Outcast of life,
                  Wilt thou be never still, nor take thy rest
                  And slumber? Yea, thou hast attained a refuge:
                  Come, take thy refuge in this scattered dust.

(His 'devil' al-Amawi appears from afar, and calls him.)

AL-AMAWI: Qais!
QAIS: Ha, who calls an outcast wanderer?
AL-AMAWI: I, who revealed to thee the love of Layla.
QAIS: Go, though I know not whether thou be spirit
                  Or phantom; go, thou art not good; what devil
                  Was ever good? Thou wast an evil friend
                  To me, the evillest that ever counselled.
                  Except for thee, I would not have disclosed
                  What tore at Layla's heart, and wounded her,
                  Fouling her honour, as does oil a garment.
AL-AMAWI: Rouse thyself, Qais.
QAIS: Go, phantom. How shall he
                  Who does not sleep consort with his heart's phan-
                                                              tom?
AL-AMAWI: God grant thee mercy, Qais: spare thy reproaches,
                  Shed no repentant tears. Thou art unrivalled
                  In thy immortal sorrow, and excellest
                  In sorrow all that live. Thy doubters dwell
                  Above the dust; but thou art with the stars
                  High-throned above suspicions. Thou hast taken
                  The road to immortality, a road
                  Not trod by nations. Stand, and call to Layla,

And celebrate her praises; have thou done
With old beliefs, and pious sanctities.
Fly free of wing in air, and tramp the earth
With foot untrammelled. If men had been just
They would have let you go, even as pilgrims
Touch not the sacred dove. Rise, spread thy wings
Above the wilderness; soar in the valley,
And sink on mound; fill with ingenious lute
The heaven of palaces, the earth of tents.
Bind scattered hearts in love, and spread with song
The joy of loveliness. Still sing of Layla:
Disclose thy love, disseminate thy passion,
Make plaint of thy distemper. As a flower,
Until its scent is scattered, gives no pleasure,
So love is vain, until it is divulged.

QAIS: Shall I stand? Give me a foot. Or shall I speak?
Give me a mouth. Dost thou not see that I
Am but a broken and dismantled temple?

(Al-Amawi disappears; Qais continues.)

O God of Qais, is now my end announced?
Is the cup spilled that passed around the souls?
Why shall I care to reel beneath a frame
Where life and death make dispute? Fate this day
Has published its decree; no more, O life,
Have we defence. In death I seek for life
And, in the final agony of death,
Layla, to thee I turn. Yet how shall I
Bid life farewell, who but this morning, Layla,
Might not bid thee farewell? Alas, thy fragrance
Still haunts the plain, thy light adorns the hills,
Thy smile is on the heaven of the desert,
The sand retains thy gleam; the very mist
That hides the burning noon is but a fragment
Of thy veiled face.

(A deer passes: Qais addresses it.)

O deer, weep thou for him
Who, when thou wast a captive, ransomed thee
From those that bought and sold; who gave thy
children
His water and his food, when they were thirsty
And hungered in the wilderness. O hollow,

Be thou my coffin, winding-sheet, and tomb;
Beloved hollow, make my funeral.
Gather the deer to see me on my way:
Was ever dead man followed to the grave
By flocks of timid deer? Lo, I shall die
As I have lived, a wanderer. No men
Shall be about me, none shall follow me;
And I shall sleep alone; now nevermore
Wild beasts shall be my company, no deer
Shall graze about me here.

(*His legs tremble: Ziyad catches him. Ibn Dharih appears above one
of the tombs, weeping with downcast eyes.*)

ZIYAD: Qais, be not troubled;
           See, I am with thee.
QAIS: Be at rest, my soul:
           Thou art no more alone; there is one at hand
           Who shall design my grave, and guide the tribe
           To greet me, when I am no more. Ziyad,
           Thou art my comfort and my ransomer;
           When I was lonely, thou wast ever with me.

           (*The spirit of Ibn Dharih is seen.*)

           Ziyad, look yonder: who is this, that weeps
           Behind the grave? I am jealous for my tomb,
           Lest stranger lover wounded come to claim it.
ZIYAD: It is Dharih's son; do not fear him, Qais.
IBN DHARIH: Layla, thy grave is now become a hill
           Of immortality; with it the breeze
           Perfumes the soil of Nejd. I see an angel
           In every part; their breath is as a rose,
           Their wings are gleaming pearls, and they are
                                                 scattered
           Like to a necklace. When they meet, their greeting
           Breathes the sweet musk of 'Peace', the ambergris
           Of 'And on thee be peace'. Their conversations
           And loud magnificats are as the rain
           Of stormcloud, or the echoing of thunder;
           And there are fragrant scents such as no garden
           Has ever known. Be patient, Qais: an angel
           Attends thee, who was sacrificed to passion
           And martyred to desire. Awake, arise,

Now gaze upon the splendours of the sky,
Behold the beauty that is here revealed.

QAIS:

Where is the sky? Where is that dying man
Whom earth awaits to take into his grave?
I was afflicted long with sleeplessness:
Here is the slumber that shall be the cure
Of all my sleeplessness. When men declare
That I shall be immortal, I reply,
I shall not enter immortality
Alone: if Layla be with me in heaven,
Or in the pit, they are alike to me.
Layla is heaven, and her I have attained:
Today we slumber in the soil of Nejd.
Even in wretchedness, I love my country,
And choose her first, not immortality.

(*He hears a faint voice as if issuing from the grave.*)

VOICE: Qais.

QAIS: Ha, who calls? Alas, it is enchantment.

VOICE: Qais.

QAIS: Come, Ziyad, and listen! Bishr, give ear!

VOICE: Qais.

QAIS: Hark, my name is uttered from the grave.

VOICE: Qais.

QAIS: From her tomb she calls me by my name.
Layla, I come to thee, with soul and body!

(*He enters the last gasp.*)

What, has death healed our wounds, and gathered us
To dwell together, after so long parting?

VOICES: Qais, Layla.

QAIS: In my ears there is a ringing;
The very deserts echo 'Qais' and 'Layla'.
The world still holds us, though it pass us by:
Layla died not, her Madman does not die.

Shauqī died in the summer of 1933 at the height of his great poetic gifts. The fertility of his genius during the last few years of his life was truly amazing, and it is a melancholy reflection that his best may have remained unwritten. So great a genius, however, is never lost to literature, and the repercussions of his truly original mind will continue to be felt for many years to come.

(From *Journal of the Royal Asiatic Society*, 1937, pp. 43–58.)

FOURTEEN

The Revolt of Islam

Whether or not it may be agreed that 'poets are the unofficial legislators of mankind', there is no gainsaying the fact that poets have played a prominent, in some instances indeed a leading part in that most exciting drama of modern times, the revolt of Islam—against internal corruption, and especially and most compellingly against external domination.

> Of the hireling's blood outpoured
> Lustrous rubies makes the lord;
> Tyrant squire to swell his wealth
> Desolates the peasant's tilth.
> > Revolt, I cry!
> > Revolt, defy!
> > Revolt, or die!
>
> City sheikh with string of beads
> Many a faithful heart misleads,
> Brahman baffles with his thread
> Many a simple Hindu head.
> > Revolt, I cry!
> > Revolt, defy!
> > Revolt, or die!
>
> Prince and Sultan gambling go;
> Loaded are the dice they throw—
> Subjects soul from body strip
> While their subjects are asleep.
> > Revolt, I cry!
> > Revolt, defy!
> > Revolt, or die!
>
> Brother Moslems, woe to us
> For the havoc science does!

Ahriman is cheap enough,
God is rare, scarce-offered stuff.
Revolt, I cry!
Revolt, defy!
Revolt, or die!

The passionate shout of *inqilāb ai inqilāb* was raised by the man who was after his death to be hailed as the prophet of Pakistan. Sir Muhammad Iqbal, distinguished lawyer, distinguished philosopher, distinguished poet, as learned in Western science as in Eastern tradition, inspired millions of his fellow-Muslims in India to fight for self-reform and self-realization as a necessary prelude to freedom and independent nationhood.

Little flower fast asleep,
Rise narcissus-like, and peep;
Lo, the bower droops and dies
Wasted by cold griefs; arise!
Now that birdsong fills the air
And muezzins call to prayer,
Listen to the burning sighs
Of the passionate hearts, and rise!
Out of leaden sleep,
Out of slumber deep
Arise!
Out of slumber deep
Arise!

Now the sun, that doth adorn
With his rays the brow of morn,
Doth suffuse the cheeks thereof
With the crimson blush of love,
Over mountain, over plain
Caravans take route again;
Bright and world-beholding eyes,
Gaze upon the world, and rise!
Out of leaden sleep,
Out of slumber deep
Arise!
Out of slumber deep
Arise!

All the Orient doth lie
Like strewn dust the roadway by,

Or a still and hushed lament
And a wasted sigh and spent.
Yet each atom of this earth
Is a gaze of tortured birth:
Under Ind's and Persia's skies,
Through Arabia's plains, O rise!
    Out of leaden sleep,
    Out of slumber deep
      Arise!
    Out of slumber deep
      Arise!

See, thy ocean is at rest,
Slumbrous as a desert waste;
Yea, no waxing or increase
E'er disturbs thy ocean's peace.
Ne'er thy ocean knoweth storm
Or Leviathan's dread swarm:
Rend its breast and, billow-wise
Swelling into tumult, rise!
    Out of leaden sleep,
    Out of slumber deep
      Arise!
    Out of slumber deep
      Arise!

Listen to this subtlety
That reveals all mystery:
Empire is the body's dust,
Spirit true Religion's trust;
Body lives and spirit lives
By the life their union gives.
Lance in hand, and sword at thighs,
Cloaked, and with thy prayer mat, rise!
    Out of leaden sleep,
    Out of slumber deep
      Arise!
    Out of slumber deep
      Arise!

Thou art true and worshipful
Guardian of eternal Rule,
Thou the left hand and the right
Of the World-possessor's might.

Shackled slave of earthy race,
Thou art Time, and thou art Space:
Wine of faith that fear defies
Drink, and from doubt's prison rise!
  Out of leaden sleep,
  Out of slumber deep
   Arise!
  Out of slumber deep
   Arise!

Against Europe I protest
And the attraction of the West:
Woe for Europe and her charm,
Swift to capture and disarm!
Europe's hordes with flame and fire
Desolate the world entire;
Architect of Sanctuaries,
Earth awaits rebuilding; rise!
  Out of leaden sleep,
  Out of slumber deep
   Arise!
  Out of slumber deep
   Arise!

Sir Muhammad Iqbal died in 1938, ten years before the realization of the first part of his visionary programme, the establishment of the Islamic Republic of Pakistan. We say the first part, because his whole dream was of a world united in glad acceptance of the challenge of Islam, the challenge to man and men to make themselves sharers with God in the creation of a perfect and perfectly self-realizing Universe.

Brighter shall shine men's clay
Than angels' light, one day;
Earth through our Destiny
Turn to a starry sky.

The fancies in our head
That upon storms were fed
One day shall soar, and clear
The whirlpool of the sphere.

Why askest thou of me?
Consider Man, and see

How, Mind-developed still,
Sublime this subject will

Come fashioned forth, sublime,
This common thought, in time,
And with its beauty's rapture
Even God's heart shall capture.
                         (From *Persian Psalms*.)

Thou, who hast made with the Invisible
Thy covenant, and burst forth like a flood
From the shore's bondage, as a sapling rise
Out of this garden's soil; attach thy heart
To the Unseen, yet ever with the seen
Wage conflict, since this being visible
Interprets that unviewed, and prelude is
To the o'ermastery of hidden powers.
All otherness is only to subdue,
Its breast a target for the well-winged shaft;
God's fiat *Be*! made other manifest
So that thy arrows might be sharp to pierce
The steely anvil. Truly it requires
A tightly knotted cord, to whet and prove
The wit of the resolver. Art thou a bud?
Interpret in thyself the flowery mead;
Art thou a dewdrop? Dominate the sun!
If thou art equal to the bold emprise,
Melt thou this sun-lion with one torrid breath!
Whoever hath subdued the things perceived
Can of one atom reconstruct a world,
And he whose shaft would pierce the angel's breast
First fastens Adam to his saddle-bow;
He first resolves the knot phenomena
And, mastering Being, proves his lofty powers.
Mountain and wilderness, river and plain,
All land and sea—these are the scholar's slate
On which the man of vision learns to read.
O thou who slumberest, by dull opiates drugged,
And namest mean this world material,
Rise up, and open thy besotted eyes!
Call thou not mean thy world by Law compelled;
Its purpose is to enlarge the Muslim's soul,
To challenge his potentialities;

The body it assaults with fortune's sword
That thou mayest see if there be blood within;
Dash thou thy breast against its jagged rock
Until it pierce thy flesh, and prove thy bone.
God counts this world the portion of good men,
Commits its splendour to believers' eyes;
It is a road the caravan must pass,
A touchstone the believer's gold to assay;
Seize thou this world, that it may not seize thee
And in its pitcher swallow thee like wine.
The stallion of thy thought is parrot-swift,
Striding the whole wide heavens in a bound;
Urged ever onwards by the needs of life,
Raised up to rove the skies, though earthbound still;
That, having won the mastery of the powers
Of this world-order, thou mayest consummate
The perfecting of thy ingenious crafts.
Man is the deputy of God on earth,
And o'er the elements his rule is fixed;
On earth thy narrowness receiveth breadth,
Thy toil takes on fair shape. Ride thou the wind;
Put bridle on that swift-paced dromedary.
Dabble thy fingers in the mountain's blood;
Draw up the lustrous waters of the pearl
From ocean's bottom; in this single field
A hundred worlds are hidden, countless suns
Veiled in these dancing motes. This glittering ray
Shall bring to vision the invisible,
Disclose uncomprehended mysteries.
Take splendour from the world-inflaming sun,
The arch-illuming levin from the storm;
All stars and planets dwelling in the sky,
Those lords to whom the ancient peoples prayed,
All those, my master, wait upon thy word
And are obedient servants to thy will.
In prudence plan the quest, to make it sure,
Then master every spirit, all the world.

(From *The Mysteries of Selflessness.*)

While Iqbal was proclaiming his message of challenge and inspiration to all the Muslim peoples, using by preference (though he also wrote much fine and stirring poetry in his native Urdu) the Persian to emphasize the universality of his proclamation, brother poets in

other colonized lands were expressing in Arabic the same passion
for freedom and self-determination. An unknown bard in Morocco
gave the Riff warriors in revolt against their foreign rulers brave
rhymes to sing as they rode behind Abdul Krim.

> Mid the flying dust,
> Neath the darkened sky,
> Where the bright swords thrust
> And Death rides nigh:
> Let the soft winds stream
> With our loyal cheer
> Unto Abdul Krim,
> Valorous Emir.
> Our Riff is a lair,
> And its lions we;
> We defend our Riff!
>
> Triumph of the free,
> That be our delight;
> Right proud are we
> Of our Moorish knight.
> When he bids to war,
> What befalls the foe?
> Cringing slaves they are
> To the sharp sword's blow.
> Our Riff is a lair,
> And its lions we;
> We defend our Riff!
>
> Too long they enslave,
> And abase our pride;
> Arise, ye brave,
> To the reckoning-tide!
> Let them taste the flail
> Of our lance and sword,
> While loud we hail
> Our heroic Lord!
> Our Riff is a lair,
> And its lions we;
> We defend our Riff!

In Tunisia the young Abu 'l-Qāsim al-Shābī, a poet of great promise cut off in his prime, was sounding a stern warning to the
'Protectors' who had robbed his country of its independence.

Imperious despot, insolent in strife,
Lover of ruin, enemy of life!
You mock the anguish of an impotent land
Whose people's blood has stained your tyrant hand,
And desecrate the magic of this earth,
Sowing your thorns, to bring despair to birth.

Patience! Let not the Spring delude you now,
The morning light, the skies' unclouded brow;
Fear gathers in the broad horizon's murk
Where winds are rising, and deep thunders lurk;
When the weak weeps, receive him not with scorn—
Who soweth thorns, shall not his flesh be torn?

Wait! Where you thought to reap the lives of men,
The flowers of hope, never to bloom again,
Where you have soaked the furrows' heart with blood,
Drenched them with tears, until they overflowed,
A gale of flame shall suddenly consume,
A bloody torrent sweep you to your doom!

In Egypt a multitude of poets were arising to fill the void left by
Ḥāfiẓ Ibrāhīm and Shauqī. Some, like Aḥmad Zakī Abū Shādī,
evoked the memory of long-past glory of their country.

Ramses sits on his high throne, and on either hand
Slaves attending; richly-jewelled his courtiers stand.
Liquid floweth the music; the lute's low, vibrant notes
Softly answer the silver singing of silver throats;
Still and lovely as chiselled marble, the maidens sing
Fair as ever an artist dreamed, to delight a king.
Row on row the mighty chiefs with offerings rare
Lifted up in the pride of power superbly stare;
Costly-broidered the great fans upraised on high
Swing sweeping the rathe breeze and refreshingly;
Brightly flash in the vast chamber the carvings gay
Outgleaming the spring's mantle of rich array.
Precious offerings these, precious and proud they are,
Hither brought for the king's pleasure from near and far;
But the king, the most mighty, with high disdain
Stares askance, and the gifts speak him fair in vain,
Naught he accounts of all their worth and their eloquence,
Nay, though wondrous fine they be reckoned long ages hence. . . .

Others, like the popular Maḥmūd Abu 'l-Wafā, continued the old tradition of courtly verse, as he in his *Coronation Ode* composed for the handsome youth who proved to be the last to sit on the throne of Egypt.

> If Crowns are the high ornament of Kings,
> Kings are the true adornment of their lands:
> And if the Crown heeds no man's counsellings
> But him the People trusts and understands;
>
> And if the Crown will never succour seek
> Of any man, except his hands be clean;
> And if the Crown be pure of spirit, meek
> In majesty, compassionate, serene;
>
> And if the Crown be merciful of heart,
> Noble in bounty, greatly generous;
> And if the Crown to learning true impart
> Due honour, and exalt high genius;
>
> And if the Crown the People's good decree,
> Oppressing none by his imperious hand;
> Then is the Crown arrayed in Majesty,
> The People glorious, and sublime the Land.

A favourite theme of Egyptian poets was not unnaturally the river Nile and the well-loved countryside, with its millennial memories, giving a sweet if sentimental music as in the verses of ʿAlī Maḥmūd Taha.

> When the river sports with the trees' shade
>   and the clouds flirt with the moon,
> And songbirds pant their throbbing breath
>   betwixt the dew and the bloom;
> When the ringdove mourneth her sad love
>   and of cruel fate doth croon,
> And the breeze brushes the stream's brow
>   and kisses the sail-spread boom;
>
> When nightbound earth to the wondering eye
>   a myriad charms displays,
> In the deep gloom stands a willow-tree
>   unknown to the gathered shade;
> And there with vagabond heart I sit
>   and stare with downcast gaze,
> Or lift my sight to the far sky
>   and the stars' slow cavalcade.

I watch your face 'neath the palm's fronds
   and hear your voice by the stream,
Till my sadness wearies the gloom's self,
   and sorrow protests of my pain,
And creation marvels at my distress,
   and in pity the dawn stars gleam;
Then I rise and go, for the time comes
   when we shall meet again.

Much poetry was written during this period far removed indeed from the tumult of contemporary politics, recalling the soft cadences of the old Moorish lute. 'Abd al-Wahhāb 'Azzām, successively Professor of Persian and Ambassador to Pakistan, wrote occasional verses of classical distinction.

Flower by the river
   Freshly blowing,
Beauty all a-quiver,
   Proudly glowing;

O'er its petals playing
   Breeze unbidden,
Loveliness displaying
   Secrets hidden.

In the water gazing,
   Self-reflected,
Till, the wind erasing,
   Turns, rejected.

Fate upon the flower
   Doom fulfilleth,.
Petals' silent shower
   Dying spilleth.

Where is youth, once gleaming
   Gay with gladness,
Beautiful, and dreaming
   All of madness?

What is youth? A blossom
   Swift decaying,
On the water's bosom
   Image-playing.

But a very different kind of vision inspired the desperate youth of Egypt growing up in a society believed to be corrupt, in which the prizes went not to merit but to privilege, and the disillusioned patriot felt himself to be a stranger in his own country. In the late 1940's 'Abd al-Qādir al-Qaṭṭ, then a student in London, wrote the following poem.

On a road whose waymarks are the bones of starving men and slain,
Never earth embracing heaven in the vastness of the plain,
Void and hollow, sight despairing ever to achieve its goal,
Here beneath the load of life I stagger onward, sick of soul,
    Weary of a youth that yields me naught but pain.

Through the press of high ambition hope-distraught I hurry on,
Questing ever friendship, in a world where friendship there is none,
Desolate of heart, yet in my heart desires and hankerings,
Soul athirst, and in my ears the babble of the fountain sings
    Far behind the veil, beyond the vast unknown.

On I hurry through the desert of the world, without a friend
Save a sore bewildered spirit, and a heart that will not mend;
Through the wilderness I struggle, while upon my sight are borne
Lightning-flashes bright with hopes, like phantoms of a rising
                                   morn
    When the long night's mist and murk are nigh to end.

Long ago I knew the lightning's menace, though so flattering fair,
And I saw the rains imprisoned in the dark, enfolded air;
Yet whene'er a pleasant slumber sought my eyelids to beguile,
Parched and thirsting my ambitions urged me forward all the
                                   while,
    And the mirage still preserved me from despair.

Rocks I clamber, not resolving; but a wanderer am I
And the wanderer must onward, though the pass be hard and high;
Now no more I ask, 'What purpose? Whither does my journey
                                   wind?'
Wherefore ask? The desert's heart uncomprehending is, and blind,
    Heeding not my questions, making no reply.

On my way how many gardens, gardens tranquil and serene,
And the trees bent low with fruits full ripe and various, I have
                                   seen!
O'er the stage of motley colours struts the shade majestical,
And between wide banks the river broadly runs, embracing all,
    Figured blossoms, groves entwining, thickets green.

Ah, how oft have I beholding yearned towards those orchards fair,
And I left the road, supposing that the way I sought was there;
To the grass my feet would stumble, and I cried, 'The task is o'er,'
And I raised my hands to heaven, my Creator to adore
   With repentance and with praises and with prayer.

But behold! within the garden soldiers arrogant arrayed,
Recking naught for my devotions, and the holy prayers I prayed;
And among them one who shouted, 'Drive the aggressor from
                              our mead;
Dares a stranger covet our beloved kingdom in his greed?
   Soldiers! Shake aloft the spear, and bare the blade!'

Fluttered then my hands to earthward, that were lifted to their
                              Lord,
Vanished was the vision, broken, silenced the adoring word.
'Nay,' I cried, 'this war, my people, was for other men prepared;
I am one of you; so long and weary through the waste I fared;
   Will you put your brother wolflike to the sword?

'Desert nights have I companioned, nights of horror and of dread,
Days of torrid heat, the pebbles throbbing in their stony bed;
All its woe the waste bestowed, but all its beauty hid from me—
Blessed freshness of the sunrise, and the sunset's wizardry,
   These it gave not, but the parching sand instead.

'O my friends! How fresh your garden, and your shade is long and
                              cool;
Surely there is homing for me in your pastures bountiful;
Suffer me to get me healing for my wounds, and then depart—
Little time will I abide here, for a weariness of heart
   Urges me toward yon slopes delectable.'

'O my friends! Why, thou intruder, we were never friends to thee;
Get thee gone into thy desert; there thy couch is, broad and free.
We are sprung from loins of glory; we belong not to thy dust;
But if hardship presses on thee, learn to overcome thy lust—
   Leave the world to them whose right is luxury!'

And a dumb and stagnant silence settled o'er the meadow there,
Hushed the brook its gentle babble, ceased the fluttering rose
                              to stir;
Darker grew the gathered shadow, till it seemed to frown on me,
And the wind to my bewildered fancy whispered sullenly:
   'Thou deservest not our friendship, wanderer!'

And I cried, 'O weary feet, back to your pilgrimage again!
Panting throat, my fancy's promise must console thee for thy pain;
Suffer patiently this cruel thirst, that silences my song—
Surely in my virgin garden on the morrow, cool and long,
    Waters cool and liquid honey thou shalt drain.

'Far beyond these barren deserts, where the distant hills ascend
Waits inviolate my garden, and its boughs to harvest bend;
Never man beheld my garden, none has breathed its fragrant scent,
And my heart with hope o'erfloweth, after so long banishment
    I shall come there, and shall rest there, in the end.'

In Syria, liberated from centuries of Turkish rule in 1918 only to pass
under an even more alien administration, Khair al-Dīn al-Ziriklī
despaired of the cherished dream of the Arab renascence.

I weep for a land fashioned to beauty fair
    Beyond compare;
I weep for a heritage of glory and fame,
    A hard, far aim.

I weep for spirits too indolent to urge men
    To battle again;
I weep for the splendour of empire and the boast
    Turned all to a ghost.

For neighbouring Lebanon suffering a like fate, the Christian poet
Mikhā'īl Nu'aima, emigrant to the United States who returned
home, wrote a bitter elegy.

Comrade, the warrior in the west
Returning boasts what he achieved,
And hallows the heroic best
Whereof his country is bereaved.
Praise not the victors, nor revile
Rejoicing the defeated foe;
Kneel silently with me awhile
And let your heart be bowed in woe
And bleed,
As we lament our dead.

Comrade, the soldier from the wars
Comes to his fatherland again
To find him healing for his scars,

And friends to ease him of his pain.
Look not to find, if you shall come
Homeward, old comrades waiting here;
Hunger has left us none at home
To welcome us with loving cheer
Beside
The ghosts of those who died.

Comrade, the farmer to his field
Returns, to plough and sow once more,
After long exile to rebuild
The cottage shattered by the war.
Our hearth is wrecked by misery,
Our water-wheels are choked with sand,
The malice of our enemy
Has left no seedling in our land,
No thing
Save our dead, mouldering.

Comrade, this had not come to pass
Except we wished it so to be;
Ruin is over all, because
Ourselves willed this catastrophe.
Then shed no tears, my comrade; save
Your tale of sorrow none will hear
But follow me, and dig a grave
With pick and shovel, and inter
With me
Our dead, where none may see.

Comrade, what men are we? No land
Is ours, no neighbours, kindred none,
And let us sleep, or let us stand,
Shame is our covering alone.
Whether we dead or living be,
The world is noisome with our stench;
Come, bring a spade, and follow me,
And let us dig another trench
To lay
Our living in the clay.

The Lebanese poet Fauzī Maʻlūf, long settled in South America but keeping the flame of Arab inspiration burning so far from home, pictured the human predicament altogether as symbolized in total slavery.

I am a slave:
The slave of life and death;
From the cradle of life to the grave
Perforce my path wandereth.

Slave to whatever wrong
The laws of man contain,
Laws penned by the strong
The weak to constrain.

The strong have dipped their pen
In the blood of the weak; the sighs
Of wronged, downtrodden men
Mount up to the skies.

Slave I to destiny;
Its spare tidings of cheer
And bodings of ill to be
Choke my heart with fear.

Slave to the age I live in
Of civilization; blind
To the precious core within,
We delight in the rind.

Slave to the wealth I won
By labour to be my share;
Which having, lo! I groan
'Neath the yoke I wear.

Slave to my name;
I have spent me, body and soul,
Greedy to gain it fame
Imperishable.

Slave to my love;
In my heart I cherished it well,
Till the flames thereof
Have damned my heart to hell.

Behold, I bleed
In the grip of a slavery
Blind; delusions lead
Blindly me.

But more robust voices were also to be heard competing with, and in the end overcoming, the thin chorus of disillusion and despair. Khalīl Miṭrān, recalling the early glory of Islam, saw in mortal danger itself a renewal of hope.

O noble company of Arabs! Ye
My pride and boast, o'er every company,
Long have I chid your carelessness and sloth,
Yet not as one that might despair, or loathe,
But candidly, as if to wake a friend
Unconscious of vast perils that impend.
Long nights of intercession, and of pleas,
Your slumber kept me wakeful with unease,
Till I would cry, 'Had ever nation kept
Its bed such centuries as ye have slept?
Do ye not know, 'tis loss for those that drowse
Till noon, the spoils to them who early rouse?
Already ye outsleep, in countryside
As in built town, all men that ever died!
Ye are a folk whose chronicles abound
With noble deeds, since valour was renowned,
Yea, from when Qahtan found a hero's grave
Even to Shaiban's Qais, and Antar brave,
To that Quraishite orphan, who was lord
Of wisdom marvellous and mighty sword,
Vessel of God's revealing, battling down
Kisra, and spoiling Caesar of his crown;
And then that hero of the Arab host,
His wisdom mightiest, his experience most,
And next the incomparable ruler, he
Who spread the bounds in peerless equity;
And Affan's glorious son, who as he read
The scriptures, o'er the script his blood was shed;
And Ali, his bright sword to battle bared,
His voice from pulpit rapturously heard;
Those flashing stars innumerable that be,
Great generals, and dauntless soldiery;
Wise governors, that with accomplished skill
Revolved the world's affairs upon their will;
Scholars profound, who shed true learning's light
On human hearts, to guide mankind aright.'

All this I whispered in my people's ear,
Softly persuasive, or cried loud and clear,
And all the while reverted with the grief
Of one who would, but cannot, bring relief,
Unslumbering, yet through the nighttime drear
My faith and hope still gave my spirit cheer,

Like the Pole Star immovable, a light
That lit my thoughts, and shone upon my sight.
In vain I chid; until the terror struck,
A ghost of malice, dusty locks that shook
Upon the wind, in armour helmeted
And terribly arrayed, with treacherous tread,
Able to soar in air, to march, to ride,
To see in murk, to traverse oceans wide.
'Now is the hour of peril come,' I said,
'That shall awake them! O my soul, be glad!
Danger's the thing to stir a frozen soul,
A people's screwed-up virtue to unroll!'

When Khalīl Mardam Bey, late President of the Arabic Academy of
Damascus, composed a national anthem for Syria it was as an Arab
believing in the heroic cause of Arab Unity that he evoked the
memory of Haroun Alraschid.

Defenders of the Fatherland, all hail!
Your noble spirits cannot cringe or fail;
The Arab homeland is a hallowed shrine,
None may assail this sanctuary divine.

The coasts of Syria are as stars on high,
Vieing in splendour with the uplifted sky;
Not heaven's self is more sublimely grand
Than where our forebears glorified our land.

Our flag, dear symbol of our unity,
Quickens our hopes, and bids our hearts beat free;
Dear as our sight, and all as sable hued,
Stained with the crimson of our martyrs' blood.

Proud are our souls; our past is valorous;
Our heroes' spirits yet watch over us;
Walid was ours, Rashid our sovereign—
Shall we not build, shall we not rule again?

In neighbouring Iraq, Ma'rūf al-Ruṣāfī was also shaming his countrymen and stirring their memories of glory long ago, when Baghdad
was the capital of the world.

How long, how long wilt thou proclaim thy lay?
Thou canst not strike the slumberers awake;

Not though with art consummate thou shalt play
  Will aught avail the music thou dost make
To guide a people gone so far astray.

And thou awakest them, they slumber still,
  If thou arousest them, they sounder sleep;
Then praised be God, Who fashioned by His will
  Mankind like stones, that they may ever keep
Like stones their beds, and drowse unto their fill.

Though long I spake, till I could scarce express
  Chidings that sharper than a swordthrust were,
They never stirred; my words were profitless
  To move a folk that slept like children there,
Rocked in the cradle of their foolishness.

Begone, begone, Baghdad! Depart from me;
  No wise am I of thee, not mine art thou;
Yet, though I suffered oft and much of thee,
  Baghdad, it pains me to behold thee now
Upon the brink of great catastrophe.

Misfortune past misfortune fell upon
  Thy life so sweet, and turned it all to rue;
Canst thou no more produce a noble son?
  Nay, thou art barren of the free, the true,
Whose sons of old were heroes, every one.

The witnesses of Ignorance, behold!
  Humble thee to her shrine in worship mean;
Wilt thou not spurn her in rebellion bold
  Remembering the glory that has been,
The empire of Rashid, the Age of Gold?

Thy sway supreme no foeman dared defy,
  Thy clouds of fortune rained abundantly,
The palace of thy splendour soared on high,
  True learning had its resting-place in thee,
The crescent of thy greatness filled the sky.

                    (From *Modern Arabic Poetry*.)

So the whole world of Islam, in the first half of the twentieth
century, was loud with the voices of poets reviving the legend of an
empire long since broken and buried, a civilization which had been
the preceptor of Europe in the arts and sciences but was now reduced
to vassalage under Europe. In these opening years of the second

half of the twentieth century we have witnessed a sudden and dramatic change in the fortunes of the Muslim peoples, with the attainment of independence and sovereign nationhood by many lands that had not known the luxury of self-determination for centuries. It is no part of our programme in this book to comment on the uses which the peoples of those lands are making of their newly won freedom to rule themselves. Let it suffice that their poets still have songs to sing, and that they are not all songs of triumph and happiness in national liberation.

One great country of the world of Islam never lost its independence in the age of western imperialism. The poets of Persia, though they did not lack for themes of rebellion—against foreign exploitation of the nation's natural resources, against tyrannical rulers and ruthless landlords at home—were not called upon to become the standard-bearers in a campaign of national liberation. Neither were the Persians, being of the Shi'ite persuasion, likely to react so readily as their Sunni brothers to the battle-cry of Islamic Unity. Being a land of song, where every man is or aspires to be a poet, Persia in the first half of the twentieth century nevertheless by no means lacked for bards, composing charmingly as ever, whether in the old traditional styles or in the new fashions introduced from the West. We bring this volume to a close with a small selection of poems composed in our time by the successors of Omar and Rūmī, of Sa'dī and Ḥāfiẓ.

Īraj, who died in 1925, wrote his own epitaph in verses which would not have disgraced the greatest of the classical poets.

> Know ye, fair folk who dwell on earth
> Or shall hereafter come to birth,
> That here, with dust upon his eyes,
> Iraj, the sweet-tongued minstrel, lies.
> In this true lover's tomb interred
> A world of love is sepulchred.
> Each ringlet fair, each lovely face
> In death, as living, I embrace:
> I am the selfsame man ye knew,
> That passed his every hour with you.
> What if I quit this world's abode?
> I wait to join you on the road;
> And though this soil my refuge be,
> I watch for you unceasingly.
> Then sit a moment here, I pray,
> And let your footsteps on me stray;

My heart, attentive to your voice,
Within this earth's heart will rejoice.

The ideal of the united Muslim family has been long treasured in
Persia. Īraj gave voice to sincere filial love in a famous poem
dedicated to his mother.

They say, when first my mother bore me
    She taught me how to rest
    My lips against her breast;
Wakeful at night, and leaning o'er me
    Cradled in slumber deep,
    She taught me how to sleep.

She kissed my mouth to happy laughter,
    And in that magic hour
    She taught my rose to flower.
One letter, and two letters after,
    She taught me week by week
    Until my tongue could speak.

She took my hand in hers, and leading
    Me on, with loving talk
    She taught me how to walk.
While I have life, be this my pleading:
    Since she my being bore,
    I'll love her evermore.

The great poetess, Parvīn, who died tragically young in 1941,
expressed the old concept (now going out of fashion) of the partner-
ship of man and wife.

Know'st thou what task the man's may be
And what the wife's, philosopher?
The one a ship is, sailing free;
The other is the mariner.

Then let the captain but be wise,
And let his ship be firm, not frail,
What need they fear, though billows rise
And storm and whirlpool them assail?

For in the evil day of stress
When tossed on fate's tempestuous sea,
Their purpose being singleness,
Both will avert calamity.

> Ever the daughter of today
> Becomes the mother of the morn;
> 'Tis hers, to set on greatness' way
> The sons that of her flesh are born.

The 'King of Poets' Bahār, who in a long life which ended in 1951 played the varied parts of democratic revolutionary, university professor and learned scholar of philology, wrote many peoms in the classical style. His verses on the miracle of spring recall the best of Farrukhī or Anvarī.

> Recall how with frozen fingers December's clouds outspread
> Over the fields and uplands a mantle of ice and snow;
> Over the buried roses, over a world of lead
> Vengeful as any hangman stalked the exultant crow.
> But lo, the abiding wonder! Spirit, that never dies,
> Surges anew and vital through the upstanding trees.
> See, those spear-armed horsemen, the spreading tulips, rise
> Over the plains triumphant, hills, yea, and mountains seize.
> Behold, the eager lily leaps to delight the eye,
> Spurning the bent narcissus crouched in his self-regard.
> Deep in the springing corn-shoots the gleaming violets lie;
> Bright with a myriad jewels the wheat-swept fields are starred.
> Under the nodding willow the poppy lies in blood—
> Sudden the blow that smote her, drenched her in crimson flood.
> And now, mid the green profusion of wheat, in mingled hue
> Note how the lily argent with lily azure glows;
> So, when the sky is stippled with scattered rainclouds through,
> Here and here betwixt them the vault of heaven shows.

A more surrealistic landscape of night is painted by Khānlarī, scholar, publisher and Minister of Education.

> Night came to plunder, and with open fist
> Seized all that stirred within the hollow vale:
> Long since the river was his captive—list,
> And you might hear the river's plaintive wail.

> The garden's treasure, purple, crimson, white,
> All vanished into night's far-plundering hand;
> The walnut bough lifted its foot in fright
> High o'er the apple bough, and upwards spanned.

Like a black smoke its swirling skirt night drew,
Hastening from the lowland to the hill;
The forest's hands and feet were lost to view,
The concourse of the trees was hushed and still.

'Night! night!' the screech-owl's warning echo leapt,
And a leaf shivered on a willow limb;
Along the earth a wandering straggler crept
Until the thick mint-bushes swallowed him.

Night drew a long, warm sigh, to sleep at last
Reposeful after strife and stress, content:
A poplar and some ancient willows fast
Fled o'er the hillock's brow, incontinent.

A charming night-piece, reminiscent of the classical theme of Shīrīn caught bathing by her princely lover, comes from the pen of the distinguished archaeologist Tavallalī.

At the mid-hour of twilight, in the time
When from the west the broken moon doth climb
Pale in the sky, silent and proud and white
Mary stands in the black of night.

Waits till the moonbeams, lifting their gleam above
The mountain's battlements, from night's face remove
The shroud of darkness, waits till their lustrous flow
Bathes her limbs in a silver glow.

Now sleeps the garden; the thieving hands of the breeze
Each happy blossom's perfume shamelessly seize;
Tranquil the night is sleeping; but Mary's eyes
Watch the night in the moon-washed skies.

Little by little behind the willow's boughs
The moonbeams thievishly steal, and through the drowse
Of the black night, as Mary seeks them, astir,
Eagerly gaze they, seeking her.

Darkness gathers her skirts, and headlong flees
From the moon's radiance unto the distant trees;
Sweet, sweet is night; the moonlight dewy and deep
Floods the spirit and lulls asleep.

Amidst the garden's happy and whispering hush
Quivers the silken moon in the brook; a thrush
Burst into song this instant, and from the bough
Carols: 'Mary is bathing now.'

The ancient didactic tradition of Persia is by no means lost in these modern times, and as example we quote these verses by Yāsimī in which the legend of Socrates, beloved of the medievalists, is once more revived in a twentieth-century context.

> Socrates, the philosopher wise,
> Built him a house of a modest size.
> Forthwith about him on every side
> People shouted, and people cried;
> Each of them had a fault to tell
> Of the house he had builded up so well.
> This one said: 'It will never do;
> It's small and poky, and all askew.'
> Another murmured; 'Oh, tut-tut!
> So mean and miserable a hut
> Scarce beseems, if you want my view,
> A man so considerable as you.'
> 'Well, dear me!' a third broke out,
> 'A hovel like that? Without a doubt
> The great professor we all revere
> Can never consent to living here!'
> Everyone that his friend was named
> All with a single voice exclaimed:
> 'You can hardly call this a residence
> Appropriate to your eminence!
> It is so wretched and so small,
> One cannot move in it at all;
> It is so narrow and so tight
> One cannot budge to left or right.'
> As the philosopher heard them cry
> He laughed aloud, and made reply:
> 'Friends, you do wrong to criticize;
> I cannot call your counsel wise.
> Though my small cabin is little worth,
> It's everything I require on earth;
> All I pray is, that it may be
> Filled with friends who are true to me.'

The perennial Persian philosophy of doubt and cheerful pessimism is well propounded again in a poem by the gentle Ra'dī, Permanent Delegate to UNESCO.

> The world's a hostelry;
> Wine-worshippers are we

Drunk with the rapture fine
Of a fantasmal wine.
About our eyes we bind
A veil, to make us blind,
And for a little sup
At life's revolving cup.
We wash its golden lip
With tears, the while we sip,
And, weeping, ease our drowth,
At life's seductive mouth.
Nor opens the heart's eye
Until the day we die;
The veil, withdrawn, reveals
What secrets it conceals,
And at the end 'tis proved
This gilded cup we loved—
Since first creation's day
No wine within it lay,
But all it held, it seems,
Was fantasy, and dreams,
A little hope, some pain,
Parting, to meet again;—
And even these, to cast
Aside perforce, at last.
Brave hostelry, and O
Brave wine-bibbers of woe!

What of the future? What songs will the singers of Islam invent to resurrect the vanished past, and to inspire the present yet to be? Let us end this fugitive survey of fourteen centuries of history with the same question as that asked by Gulchīn, a Persian doctor practising in London, at the conclusion of an elegy written on a cheerless autumn evening in 1940, when German bombs were falling on English homes and a Persian medical student made ready to tend the wounded and dying.

The night-bound wind in loud lament doth cry:
'Let flower and leaf and grass in ruin lie!'
    And, as the night-arising bird makes moan,
Beneath the weeping stars in heaven's height,
Smitten by autumn's hand, in pallid flight
    Over the grasses leaf and flower are strewn.

There, o'er the delicate folds of every leaf
Life fights with Death in battle fiercely brief,
    The ancient tale of Welcome and Farewell;
Laughter, and tears, and soul-consuming sighs,
All yesterday's delightful histories,
    Remembrance of a vanished past to tell.

Bring now to mind those birds of hope in flight
Before the scarlet petals and the white,
    Silver, and violet, gold, and azure clear;
Moved by spring's breath they danced about this place
Like lovers kissing in a warm embrace
    Before the moonlit waters of the mere.

Bring now to mind how youth with joy was rife,
When to the heartbeat of delirious life
    Desires celestial did the soul entice;
Then hopes were pure and lofty to pursue,
And Heaven was a mother fond and true,
    And Time was an eternal Paradise.

O'er mountain sheer the snows in rivers flowed,
Quicksilver streams tumbling their lucent load;
    The herdsman piped amid his pasturing kine;
And maidens took their pitchers to the spring,
And o'er the turquoise hills meandering
    The scarlet tulip bore his flask of wine.

In happy sport, while yet the morn was pale,
Upon green branch the drunken nightingale
    Chanted his passion to the scarlet rose;
The dew clairvoyant, rarely provident,
Aware his life must be too shortly spent
    Upon the petal fresh trembled and froze.

So light and gay the nimble butterfly
About his favourite blossom hovered nigh;
    The busy swallows on the garden wall
Fashioned their nest of love and liberty,
Home for the morrow's family to be,
    Fashioned their nest in happy festival.

Alas! tonight the nest doth empty lie,
No swallow, blossom none, nor butterfly.
    Over the broken pinions of the leaf

The wind of autumn sighs in lonely flight,
And all that distant dream of long delight
   Is gone into the maw of death and grief.

Ah, leaves that flutter heedlessly away,
Last memories of sweet spring and summer gay,
   Tomorrow, when the sun's returning eye
Peeps twixt the mountains and the sky above,
Within this flowerless garden, bare of love,
   What on these branches shall it then descry?

BIBLIOGRAPHY

This book has been based partly on published work of the author, in part on unpublished work. Readers may find it convenient to have a list of the author's previous books. The following list excludes editions of oriental texts, except when these have been accompanied by a translation; it also excludes articles published in learned journals, certain of which have been here reprinted. Items marked with an asterisk have been in particular drawn upon in compiling this volume, and the publishers of the books concerned are thanked for permission to quote.

Majnun Layla of Shauqī. Luzac, 1933.

Mawáqif and Mukháṭabát of al-Niffarī. Luzac, 1935.

The Doctrine of the Sufis. C.U.P., 1935.

Catalogue of the Arabic MSS. in the India Office Library. Vol. 2, part 2. O.U.P., 1936.

Catalogue of the Persian Books in the India Office Library. India Office, 1937.

The Book of Truthfulness of al-Kharrāz. O.U.P., 1937.

Poems of a Persian Sufi. Heffer, 1937.

The Library of the India Office. India Office, 1938.

Specimens of Arabic and Persian paleography. India Office, 1939.

The Song of Lovers of 'Irāqī. O.U.P., 1939.

The Muslim Attitude to the War. H.M.S.O., 1940.

British Contributions to Persian studies. Longmans, 1942.

British Orientalists. Collins, 1943.

An Introduction to the History of Sufism. Longmans, 1943.

Modern Persian Reader. C.U.P., 1944.

Kings and Beggars of Sa'dī. Luzac, 1945.

Asiatic Jones. Longmans, 1946.

Fifty Poems of Ḥāfiẓ. C.U.P., 1947.

The Tulip of Sinai of Iqbāl. Royal India Society, 1947.

The Cambridge School of Arabic. C.U.P., 1948.

Immortal Rose. Luzac, 1948.

Persian Psalms of Iqbāl. Luzac, 1948.

The Rubā'iyāt of Jalāl al-Dīn Rūmī. Emery Walker, 1949.

The Rubā'īyāt of Omar Khayyám. Emery Walker, 1949.

Modern Arabic Poetry. Taylor's Foreign Press, 1950.

Sufism. Allen & Unwin, 1950.

The Spiritual Physick of Rhazes. Murray, 1950.

Sakhawiana. Emery Walker, 1951.

Avicenna on Theology. Murray, 1951.

A Second Supplementary Handlist of Muhammadan MSS. C.U.P., 1952.

*The Mystical Poems of Ibn al-Fāriḍ. Emery Walker, 1952.

The Poem of the Way. Emery Walker, 1952.

*Omar Khayyám; a New Version. Murray, 1952.

The Holy Koran; an Introduction. Allen & Unwin, 1953.

The Legacy of Persia (editor). O.U.P., 1953.

*The Ring of the Dove of Ibn Ḥazm. Luzac, 1953.

*Moorish Poetry. C.U.P., 1953.

Scheherezade. Allen & Unwin, 1953.

*The Mysteries of Selflessness of Iqbāl. Murray, 1953.

*Persian Poems. Dent, 1954.

The Chester Beatty Library; A Handlist of the Arabic Manuscripts. 7 vols. Hodges & Figgis, 1955–64.

*The Koran Interpreted. 2 vols. Allen & Unwin, 1955–56.

Salaman and Absal of Jāmī. C.U.P., 1956.

*Revelation and Reason in Islam. Allen & Unwin, 1957.

*The Seven Odes. Allen & Unwin, 1957.

*Classical Persian Literature. Allen & Unwin, 1958.

The Chester Beatty Library; A Catalogue of the Persian Manuscripts (editor and part author). 3 vols. Hodges & Figgis, 1959–62.

The Romance of the Rubáiyát. Allen & Unwin, 1959.

A Maltese Anthology. O.U.P., 1960.

Oriental Essays. Allen & Unwin, 1960.

Shiraz. University of Oklahoma Press, 1960.

Discourses of Rumi. Murray, 1961.

Dun Karm, Poet of Malta. C.U.P., 1961.

*Tales from the Masnavi. Allen & Unwin, 1962.

*More Tales from the Masnavi. Allen & Unwin, 1963.

Humāy-nāma. Luzac, 1963.

INDEX